Solomon Academy

S A T* Math

by Yeon Rhee

D1312351

20 Topic-Specific Practice Sets with Key Summaries

Review of Essential Theorems and Properties for the SAT Math Test

8 Full-Length Practice Tests

Detailed Solutions for All Questions

www.solomonacademy.net

Legal Notice

Acknowledgements

I wish to acknowledge my deepest appreciation to my wife, Sookyung, who has continuously given me wholehearted support, encouragement, and love. Without you, I could not have completed this book.

Thank you to my sons, Joshua and Jason, who have given me big smiles and inspiration. I love you all.

Thank you to my wonderful editor, Daniel Kwon, who has given me great advice and invaluable help.

About This Book

This book is catered towards mastering the quantitative reasoning sections of the SAT. The book contains 20 topic-specific summaries and 10 practice problems relative to each section. Along with the topic-specific practice sets, there are 8 full-length practice tests with detailed solutions and explanations. It is recommended that you take Test 1 as a diagnostic test to understand your current level of expertise and in which area you need improvement. Afterwards, review the key summaries and essential theorems of the SAT. After completing the practice sets, use the seven remaining practice tests to help improve your score and exhibit real test-taking conditions. There is no greater substitute than to study and practice.

Be sure to time yourself during each math section with the appropriate time limits. After completing any practice sets or test, immediately use the answer key and detailed solutions to check your answers. Review all answers. Take the time to carefully read the explanations of problems you got incorrect. If you find yourself continually missing the same type of questions, look back at the topic summaries and review the theorems and examples. Afterwards, it is necessary to fill out the scoring worksheet. Do not manipulate your score for simple errors; mark it incorrect. Set a goal of improvement for each practice test.

About Author

Yeon Rhee obtained a Masters of Arts Degree in Statistics at Columbia University, NY. He served as the Mathematical Statistician at the Bureau of Labor Statistics, DC. He is the Head Academic Director at Solomon Academy due to his devotion to the community coupled with his passion for teaching. His mission is to help students of all confidence level excel in academia to build a strong foundation in character, knowledge, and wisdom.

About Scholastic Aptitude Test

In today's society, a college degree is a perquisite to a job; likewise, a competitive SAT score is a perquisite to a university. Graduating from higher education universities allow people to have a sound foundation in a well-rounded academic career. Success in general education courses coupled with a major of student's choosing is often the formula employers seek in finding dedicated, matured individuals who have developed characteristics such as perseverance and integrity. SAT scores are not only important in deciding which college is a right-fit, but also provides scholarship opportunities and a measurement of academic strengths.

The SAT is a standardized admissions test for most college applicants in the United States of America. The test is developed and administered by the College Board, a non-profit organization, which is comprised of more than 5,900 colleges and universities. The SAT is one of many criteria that college admission boards use to consider an applicant; along with grade point average (GPA), intensity of rigorous course work, involvement in the community, extra-curricular activities, personal statement, and letters of recommendation.

The SAT scores are an opportunity for students to show their basic understanding and ability to apply knowledge in math, reading, and writing obtained in academia. The test measures literacy and writing skills along with quantitative sections. College admissions boards are interested in critical thinking, logic-based reasoning, problem-solving abilities, and communication skills.

This particular book is designed to help you master the quantitative reasoning sections. The breakdown of the math portion of the exam is as follows: two 25-minute sections and one 20-minute section. In the 70 minutes, there are 54 total mathematical questions: 44 multiple choice questions and 10 student response (Grid-ins) questions. The math sections cover a variety of topics: operations, algebra, geometry, percents and ratios, functions, and sequences are some examples. This book undergoes a summary of the key concepts and theorems needed to successfully face the SAT Math section.

Before the Test

Student Check-list

Necessities	Check
Appropriate Photo ID: Driver's License (with Photo), Government Issued Identification Card, School Identification Card, Valid Passport, Student ID form that has been prepared by your school on school stationery and includes a recognizable photograph and school seal overlapping the photo.	
Admissions Ticket	
Several No. 2 Pencils and Erasers	
Calculator with new batteries There are several different types of calculators that are permitted for the exam. Four function calculators, scientific calculators, and graphing calculators are permitted. Online-resources show specifically which calculators are allowed. Bring a calculator that is comfortable and familiar to use. You are not allowed to share calculators.	
Watch	
Snack	
Map instructions to the test-taking center written on the Admissions Ticket. Multiple alarms are set to prevent mishaps. Leaving time is set (calculate for any uncertainties such as traffic and delays).	

Before taking the test, be prepared to avoid any last-minute mishaps. It is of upmost importance for students to be relaxed prior to the start of the test. Make sure to prepare all necessary documentations and supplies the day before. Forgetting photo identification or calculators and alarm malfunction are amongst many mistakes the morning of the examination. Note: Be on time.

Study

The most helpful advice to master any portion of the SAT is to study. There is no greater substitution in achieving a better score than to study: old notes, supplementary exam books, and practice tests. This book encompasses the aforementioned strategy in a unique manner to allow you to obtain the best possible math score. Read the book, rip pages out, and actually use the book until it is worn out. Whether that means highlighting new information found in the topic summaries, test-taking strategies, or writing in your own notes in the margin, find your own innovative style of studying and use this book to the best of your advantage. This is your book just like how the exam on test day is your exam. You probably aren't used to writing in your textbooks and have become accustomed to turning in clean test with the answers written precisely; however, you are allowed to write in this book and on the exam. Learn to take notes, draw figures, and make necessary annotations. We say necessary because underlining an entire question isn't going to help you. Furthermore, no one is going to be looking in your exam to see all the different annotations you made. This book is specifically design with topic summaries, practice sets, and practice tests.

Be Prepared

One of the biggest problems students face is the ability to keep their normal pace on test day. You may have slept late or rushed out to beat traffic. There are countless variables that can go wrong on a test day which will only add to the level of stress and anxiety; therefore, prepare in advance for any uncertainties. Be on time to the test taking center. In the case that something does come up, remember, be adaptable to chaos and don't let it hinder you during the examination. Prepare all the required documentations including appropriate photo ID and admissions ticket the day before the exam. Do not underestimate a good night's rest and a small breakfast the morning of the exam.

Think Positive

The faster you understand the importance of this exam, the more likely you'll take each section with more enthusiasm. In all sections of the test, you need to think positive, analyze the questions, and check your work granted time is not a factor. Whether your parents get under your skin the morning of or you have a bad night sleep, remember that a positive mood will help you stay concentrated for a longer period of time. Not only do you have to be positive, but you have to approach every area of subject with enthusiasm. Force yourself to love math, critical-reading, and writing to find yourself with retention and heightened focus even if it is just artificial interest.

Endurance

It is of crucial importance that you learn to pace yourself on all sections of the test. This is achieved by taking multiple practice tests to understand your own ability and pace at which you answer multiple-choice questions and grid-in answers. At home, try to take the practice sections in shorter periods than the actual test; if the test takes 25 minutes to complete, set a timer and try to finish the test in 22 minutes. Take into consideration the time spent bubbling in answer choices and checking work.

As the test progresses into the later sections, you will become mentally fatigued in addition to the general stress or anxiety that comes with taking the test. Breathe. If you take the time to understand the test and prepare ahead of time, you will score better. Take all three sections of the practice test in one sitting and then review the answers. Do not take practice tests one section at a time. Practice mental endurance by replicating the test-taking environment. A quick tip is to have a watch which will allow you to constantly monitor how long you spend on each question during the exam. It is highly recommended that you bubble in the answer sheet once you have answered all questions unless you are running out of time. That said, however, you should write in Grid-In answers as you go. Note: Make sure you have a watch to time yourself correctly and know when you need to bubble in answers.

Slow Down-Read Questions Carefully

In your academic schools, you are not penalized for incorrect answers. The style of the SAT is much different than the familiar exam. Rushing through simple problems, not reading directions carefully, and spending too much time on questions designed to trick you can and will bring down your score.

Rushing through simple problems is the quickest way to bring down your score. If you do not read what the question is asking in specific, you risk the chance of losing points. All of the questions are weighted equally. Students who waste 4-6 minutes on an extremely hard question realize that they ran out of time to answer two or three questions due to the time limit.

Note: Point deductions are only for multiple choice questions. You are not penalized for incorrect answers on the student grid-in answers. Therefore, you should always put down an answer for student grid-in (free-response) questions.

Circle the questions that are hard and come back to it after you have completed the entire section. You may find that coming back to a question may be the extra push you needed in developing an innovative way of solving that problem. You must have the mental stamina and endurance to correctly pace yourself.

Contents

www.solomonacademy.net

PRACTICE SET 1

Simplifying Numerical Expressions

To simplify numerical expressions, use the **order of operations** (PEMDAS)

- P : Parenthesis
- E : Exponent
- M : Multiplication
- D : Division
- A : Addition
- S : Subtraction

The order of operations suggests to first perform any calculations inside parentheses. Afterwards, evaluate any exponents. Next, perform all multiplications and divisions working from left to right. Finally, do additions and subtractions from left to right.

Example: Simplify $12(3-4)^2 \div 4 - 2$

$$
\begin{aligned}
12(3-4)^2 \div 4 - 2 &= 12(-1)^2 \div 4 - 2 &&\text{Simplify inside the parenthesis} \\
&= 12(-1)^2 \div 4 - 2 &&\text{Evaluate the exponent} \\
&= 12 \div 4 - 2 &&\text{Do multiplication and division from left to right} \\
&= 3 - 2 &&\text{Do Subtraction} \\
&= 1
\end{aligned}
$$

EXERCISES

1. $1 + 2 + 3 - 4 + 5 + 6 + 7 - 8 =$

   (A) 4   (B) 6   (C) 8
   (D) 10   (E) 12

2. $6 \times 3 - 12 \div 2 =$

   (A) 12   (B) 9   (C) 6   (D) 3   (E) 1

3. Which of the following value is equal to $\frac{1}{2} \times 4 \times \frac{1}{3} \times 2 \times \frac{1}{4} \times 3$?

   (A) 1   (B) 2   (C) 3   (D) 4   (E) 5

4. Which of the following value is equal to the expression below?

   $$2(1+2)^2 + (2-6)$$

   (A) 5   (B) 10   (C) 14
   (D) 24   (E) 32

5. Which of the following value is equal to the expression $(-1)^2 + (-1)^3 + (-1)^4$?

   (A) 1   (B) 2   (C) 3   (D) 4   (E) 5

6. $\dfrac{10(3)^2 - 5 \times 4}{5(3 + 4)} =$

(A) 1   (B) 2   (C) 3   (D) 4   (E) 5

7. Which of the following value is equal to the expression below?

$$4\left(\sqrt{16} + \sqrt{25}\right) - 10^2 \div 4$$

(A) 5   (B) 7   (C) 9

(D) 11   (E) 13

8. What is the value of $\dfrac{3}{5}(3^2 + 4^2 + 5^2)$?

(A) 30   (B) 40   (C) 50

(D) 60   (E) 70

9. $10(2 + 3 - 4)^2 - 9(2 + 3 - 4)^2 =$

(A) 0   (B) 1   (C) 2   (D) 3   (E) 4

10. $5|-2| - |4 - 2 \times 6| =$

(A) 0   (B) 2   (C) 4   (D) 6   (E) 8

ANSWERS AND SOLUTIONS

1. (E)

Since the expression has only additions and subtractions, simplify the expression from the left to right.

$$1 + 2 + 3 - 4 + 5 + 6 + 7 - 8 = 12$$

2. (A)

Do multiplication and division first. Then, add and subtract.

$$6 \times 3 - 12 \div 2 = 18 - 6$$
$$= 12$$

3. (A)

Since the expression has only multiplications, rearrange the integers and fractions to simplify the expression easily.

$$\frac{1}{2} \times 4 \times \frac{1}{3} \times 2 \times \frac{1}{4} \times 3 = \left(2 \times \frac{1}{2}\right) \times \left(3 \times \frac{1}{3}\right) \times \left(4 \times \frac{1}{4}\right)$$
$$= 1 \times 1 \times 1$$
$$= 1$$

4. (C)

Use the order of operations (PEMDAS).

$$2(1 + 2)^2 + (2 - 6) = 2(3)^2 - 4$$
$$= 2 \times 9 - 4$$
$$= 14$$

5. (A)

$(-1)^2 = 1$, $(-1)^3 = -1$, and $(-1)^4 = 1$. Therefore, $(-1)^2 + (-1)^3 + (-1)^4 = 1$

6. (B)

Use the order of operations (PEMDAS).

$$\frac{10(3)^2 - 5 \times 4}{5(3+4)} = \frac{10(9) - (5 \times 4)}{5(7)}$$
$$= \frac{90 - 20}{35}$$
$$= 2$$

7. (D)

Since $\sqrt{16} = 4$ and $\sqrt{25} = 5$,

$$4(\sqrt{16} + \sqrt{25}) - 10^2 \div 4 = 4(4+5) - (10^2 \div 4)$$
$$= 36 - 25$$
$$= 11$$

8. (A)

Simplify the expression inside the parenthesis: $(3^2 + 4^2 + 5^2) = 50$. Therefore,

$$\frac{3}{5}(3^2 + 4^2 + 5^2) = \frac{3}{5} \times 50$$
$$= 30$$

9. (B)

Since the expression inside the parenthesis is $(2+3-4)^2 = 1$,

$$10(2+3-4)^2 - 9(2+3-4)^2 = 10(1) - 9(1)$$
$$= 1$$

10. (B)

Since $|-2| = 2$ and $|4 - (2 \times 6)| = |-8| = 8$,

$$5|-2| - |4 - 2 \times 6| = 5(2) - 8$$
$$= 2$$

PRACTICE SET 2

Simplifying and Evaluating Algebraic Expressions

Like terms are terms that have same variables and same exponents; only the coefficients may be different but can be the same. Knowing like terms is essential when you simplify algebraic expressions. For instance,

- $2x$ and $3x$: (Like terms)

- $2x$ and $3x^2$: (Not like terms since the two expressions have different exponents)

- 2 and 3 : (Like terms)

Use the **distributive property** to expand an algebraic expression that has a parenthesis.

$$x(y + z) = x \times y + x \times z$$

To simplify an algebraic expression, expand the expression using the distributive property. Then group the like terms and simplify them. For instance,

$$2(-x + 2) + 3x + 5 = -2x + 4 + 3x + 5 \qquad \text{Use distributive property to expand}$$
$$= (-2x + 3x) + (4 + 5) \qquad \text{Group the like terms and simplify}$$
$$= x + 9$$

To evaluate an algebraic expression, substitute the numerical value into the variable. When substituting a negative numerical value, make sure to use a **parenthesis** to avoid a mistake.

Example 1:   Simplify the expression $3(x^2 - 2x + 3) - 2(x^2 - x + 2)$

$$3(x^2 - 2x + 3) - 2(x^2 - x + 2) = 3x^2 - 6x + 9 - 2x^2 + 2x - 4$$
$$= (3x^2 - 2x^2) + (-6x + 2x) + (9 - 4)$$
$$= x^2 - 4x + 5$$

Example 2:   Evaluate the expression $-2x^2 + 3x$ when $x = -3$

$$-2x^2 + 3x = -2(-3)^2 + 3(-3)$$
$$= -2(9) - 9$$
$$= -27$$

Distribution or replication of any part of this page is prohibited.

EXERCISES

1. Which of the following expression equals $-(2-x)+2$?

   (A) x (B) $x-2$ (C) $x-4$
   (D) $2x$ (E) $3x$

2. Evaluate $(x-4)(x-1)$ when $x=3$

   (A) -2 (B) -1 (C) 0
   (D) 1 (E) 2

3. Simplify $3x-4y+5y-2x$

   (A) $5x+9$ (B) $-x-y$ (C) $-x+y$
   (D) $x+y$ (E) $x-y$

4. If the length of a square is $2x-3$, what is the perimeter of the square?

   (A) $4x-6$ (B) $8x-12$ (C) x^2-2x
   (D) x^2-9 (E) $4x^2+9$

5. Evaluate $x^2-yz+x+yz$ when $x=3$, $y=-2$, and $z=-3$.

   (A) 8 (B) 10 (C) 12
   (D) 14 (E) 16

6. Which of the following expression is equal to the sum of $4x+y$ and $2x+3y$ subtracted from $9x+5y$?

   (A) $x+3y$ (B) $3x+y$ (C) $3x-y$
   (D) $6x+4y$ (E) $5x+4y$

7. If $x=30$, evaluate the expression below.

   $$\frac{2x-10}{3}+\frac{3x-20}{3}+\frac{4x+30}{3}$$

   (A) 30 (B) 45 (C) 60
   (D) 75 (E) 90

8. What is the average of $9x+5$ and $5x+7$?

   (A) $6x+7$ (B) $7x+6$ (C) $7x+12$
   (D) $14x+6$ (E) $14x+12$

9. Evaluate $(\sqrt{x}-\sqrt{y})^2$ if $x=9$ and $y=25$

   (A) 256 (B) 64 (C) 16
   (D) 4 (E) 1

10. If Joshua is y years old now and his brother Jason is 7 years younger, what is Jason's age in 10 years from now?

   (A) $y-7$ (B) $y-3$ (C) $y+3$
   (D) $3y+3$ (E) $3y+7$

ANSWERS AND SOLUTIONS

1. (A)

   Use the distributive property to expand the expression inside the parenthesis.

   $$-(2-x)+2 = x-2+2$$
   $$= x$$

   Therefore, the expression $-(2-x)+2$ equals to x.

2. (A)

In order to evaluate the expression, it is not necessary to expand the expression $(x-4)(x-1)$. Just substitute 3 for x in the expression.

$$
\begin{aligned}
(x-4)(x-1) &= (3-4)(3-1) \qquad \text{Substitute 3 for } x \\
&= (-1)(2) \\
&= -2
\end{aligned}
$$

Therefore, the value of $(x-4)(x-1)$ when $x=3$ is -2.

3. (D)

Group the like terms and simplify them.

$$
\begin{aligned}
3x - 4y + 5y - 2x &= (3x - 2x) + (-4y + 5y) \\
&= x + y
\end{aligned}
$$

4. (B)

The length of the square is $2x - 3$. The perimeter of the square is four times the length of the square. Therefore,

$$
\text{Perimeter of square} = 4(2x - 3) = 8x - 12
$$

5. (C)

Before substituting 3 for x, -2 for y, and -3 for z in the expression, look at the expression carefully. You will notice that $-yz$ and yz are like terms that cancel each other out. Thus, the expression simplifies to $x^2 + x$. So, substitute 3 for x in $x^2 + x$.

$$
\begin{aligned}
x^2 - yz + x + yz &= x^2 + x + (yz - yz) \\
&= x^2 + x \qquad \text{Substitute 3 for } x \\
&= (3)^2 + 3 \\
&= 12
\end{aligned}
$$

Therefore, the value of $x^2 - yz + x + yz$ when $x = 3$, $y = -2$, and $z = -3$ is 12.

6. (B)

The sum of $4x + y$ and $2x + 3y$ equals to $6x + 4y$, which is subtracted from $9x + 5y$.

$$
\begin{aligned}
9x + 5y - (4x + y + 2x + 3y) &= 9x + 5y - (4x + 2x + y + 3y) \\
&= 9x + 5y - (6x + 4y) \\
&= 9x + 5y - 6x - 4y \\
&= (9x - 6x) + (5y - 4y) \\
&= 3x + y
\end{aligned}
$$

Therefore, the expression equals to the sum of $4x + y$ and $2x + 3y$ which is subtracted from $9x + 5y$ is $3x + y$.

7. (E)

Before substituting 30 for x, simplify the expression by adding the three fractions with the same denominators.

$$\frac{2x-10}{3} + \frac{3x-20}{3} + \frac{4x+30}{3} = \frac{2x-10+3x-20+4x+30}{3}$$

$$= \frac{2x+3x+4x-10-20+30}{3}$$

$$= \frac{9x}{3}$$

$$= 3x$$

Thus, the expression simplifies to $3x$. Therefore, the value of the expression is $3x = 3(30) = 90$.

8. (B)

To evaluate an average of two expressions, divide the sum of the two expressions by two.

$$\text{Average} = \frac{\text{Sum of two expressions}}{2}$$

$$= \frac{9x+5+5x+7}{2}$$

$$= \frac{14x+12}{2}$$

$$= 7x+6$$

Therefore, the average of $9x+5$ and $5x+7$ is $7x+6$.

9. (D)

Since $\sqrt{9} = 3$ and $\sqrt{25} = 5$, $\sqrt{9} - \sqrt{25} = -2$. Therefore,

$$(\sqrt{x} - \sqrt{y})^2 = (\sqrt{9} - \sqrt{25})^2 \qquad \text{Substitute 9 for } x \text{ and 25 for } y$$

$$= (3-5)^2$$

$$= (-2)^2$$

$$= 4$$

10. (C)

Jason is 7 years younger than his brother, Joshua, who is y years old now. So, Jason's current age is $y-7$ years old. Therefore, 10 years from now, Jason's age will be $y-7+10 = y+3$ years old.

PRACTICE SET 3

Properties of Exponents

In the expression 2^4, 2 is the base, 4 is the exponent, and 2^4 is the power. Exponents represent how many times the base is multiplied by. $2^4 = 2 \times 2 \times 2 \times 2$. The table below shows a summary of the properties of exponents .

Properties of Exponents	Example
1. $a^m \cdot a^n = a^{m+n}$	1. $2^4 \cdot 2^6 = 2^{10}$
2. $\frac{a^m}{a^n} = a^{m-n}$	2. $\frac{2^{10}}{2^3} = 2^{10-3} = 2^7$
3. $(a^m)^n = a^{mn} = (a^n)^m$	3. $(2^3)^4 = 2^{12} = (2^4)^3$
4. $a^0 = 1$	4. $(-2)^0 = 1, (3)^0 = 1, (100)^0 = 1$
5. $a^{-1} = \frac{1}{a}$	5. $2^{-1} = \frac{1}{2}$
6. $a^{\frac{1}{n}} = \sqrt[n]{a}$	6. $2^{\frac{1}{2}} = \sqrt{2}, \quad x^{\frac{1}{3}} = \sqrt[3]{x}$
7. $a^{\frac{m}{n}} = (a^m)^{\frac{1}{n}} = \sqrt[n]{a^m}$	7. $2^{\frac{3}{2}} = \sqrt[2]{2^3}, \quad x^{\frac{3}{4}} = \sqrt[4]{x^3}$
8. $a^{-\frac{m}{n}} = (a^{\frac{m}{n}})^{-1} = \frac{1}{\sqrt[n]{a^m}}$	8. $2^{-\frac{3}{4}} = (2^{\frac{3}{4}})^{-1} = \frac{1}{\sqrt[4]{2^3}}$
9. $(ab)^n = a^n b^n$	9. $(2 \cdot 3)^6 = 2^6 \cdot 3^6, \quad (2x)^2 = 2^2 x^2$
10. $\left(\frac{a}{b}\right)^n = \frac{a^n}{b^n}$	10. $\left(\frac{2}{x}\right)^3 = \frac{2^3}{x^3}$
11. $\frac{b^{-n}}{a^{-m}} = \frac{a^m}{b^n}$	11. $\frac{y^{-3}}{x^{-2}} = \frac{x^2}{y^3}$

To solve an exponential equation, make sure that expressions on both sides have the same base. If the expressions have the same base, then exponents on both sides are the same.

$$a^x = a^y \implies x = y \qquad \text{Example: } 2^x = 2^3 \implies x = 3$$

Example 1:   Simplify $\left(\frac{1}{8}\right)^{\frac{2}{3}}\left(\frac{1}{8}\right)^{-\frac{2}{3}}$

Since the two expressions have the same base, $\frac{1}{8}$, you can combine both expressions using the first exponent property shown on the table above.

$$\left(\frac{1}{8}\right)^{\frac{2}{3}}\left(\frac{1}{8}\right)^{-\frac{2}{3}} = \left(\frac{1}{8}\right)^{\frac{2}{3}-\frac{2}{3}} = \left(\frac{1}{8}\right)^0 = 1$$

Example 2:   Solve $3^{x+1} = 27$

$$3^{x+1} = 3^3$$ Since both expressions have the same base

$$x + 1 = 3$$

$$x = 2$$

EXERCISES

1. Simplify $\dfrac{x^3 \cdot x^4}{x^2}$

   (A) x^6 (B) x^5 (C) x^4

   (D) x^3 (E) x^2

2. $\sqrt[3]{2} \times \sqrt[3]{4} =$

   (A) 8   (B) 6   (C) 4   (D) 2   (E) 1

3. If $\dfrac{x}{y} = 3$, what is the value of $\dfrac{y^3}{x^3}$?

   (A) $\dfrac{1}{27}$ (B) $\dfrac{1}{18}$ (C) $\dfrac{1}{9}$

   (D) 9   (E) 27

4. If $x^2 = 2$ and $y^3 = 3$, what is the value of $(xy)^6$?

   (A) 6   (B) 8   (C) 48

   (D) 54   (E) 72

5. If $4^{3x+1} = 256$, what is the value of x ?

   (A) 0   (B) 1   (C) 2   (D) 3   (E) 4

6. If two positive integers, x and y, satisfy the following equation $24 \times 18 = 2^x 3^y$, what is the sum of the values of x and y ?

   (A) 3   (B) 4   (C) 7   (D) 12   (E) 81

7. If $25^{x+1} = 125^{2-x}$, what is the value of x ?

   (A) 3   (B) 2   (C) $\dfrac{3}{4}$ (D) $\dfrac{4}{5}$ (E) $\dfrac{5}{4}$

8. If $x^{-\frac{1}{2}} = 4$ and $y^{-2} = \dfrac{1}{16}$, what is the value of xy ?

   (A) 8   (B) 4   (C) $\dfrac{1}{4}$ (D) $\dfrac{1}{8}$ (E) $\dfrac{1}{32}$

9. If $10^x = a$, which of the following expression equals $1000a^2$?

   (A) 10^{x+1} (B) 10^{x+2} (C) 10^{x+3}

   (D) 10^{2x+1} (E) 10^{2x+3}

10. If $(4a^y)^x = 64a^{12}$, what is the value of $x+y$?

    (A) 7   (B) 6   (C) 5   (D) 4   (E) 3

ANSWERS AND SOLUTIONS

1. (B)

   Since the expressions have the same base, x, use the properties of exponents. Therefore,

   $$\frac{x^3 \cdot x^4}{x^2} = x^{3+4-2} = x^5$$

2. (D)

Instead of evaluating $\sqrt[3]{2}$ and $\sqrt[3]{4}$ separately, use the properties of exponents.

$$\sqrt[3]{2} \times \sqrt[3]{4} = 2^{\frac{1}{3}} 4^{\frac{1}{3}} = (2 \times 4)^{\frac{1}{3}}$$
$$= (8)^{\frac{1}{3}} = (2^3)^{\frac{1}{3}}$$
$$= 2$$

3. (A)

Since $\frac{x}{y} = 3$, $\frac{y}{x} = \frac{1}{3}$. Thus,

$$\frac{y^3}{x^3} = \left(\frac{y}{x}\right)^3 = \left(\frac{1}{3}\right)^3 = \frac{1}{27}$$

Therefore, the value of $\frac{y^3}{x^3}$ is $\frac{1}{27}$.

4. (E)

First, expand $(xy)^6$ by using the properties of exponents. Afterwards, substitute 2 for x^2 and 3 for y^3 in the expression.

$$(xy)^6 = x^6 y^6$$
$$= (x^2)^3 (y^3)^2 \qquad \text{Substitute 2 for } x^2 \text{ and 3 for } y^3$$
$$= 8(9)$$
$$= 72$$

Therefore, the value of $(xy)^6$ is 72.

5. (B)

To solve an exponential equation, both expressions must have the same base. Change 256 to 4^4 and then solve the equation.

$$4^{3x+1} = 256$$
$$4^{3x+1} = 4^4 \qquad \text{Since both sides have the same base}$$
$$3x + 1 = 4$$
$$x = 1$$

Therefore, the value of x is 1.

6. (C)

Find the prime factorization of 24 and 18 separately: $24 = 2^3 \times 3$, and $18 = 2 \times 3^2$.

$$24 \times 18 = 2^x 3^y$$
$$2^3 \times 3 \times 2 \times 3^2 = 2^x 3^y$$
$$2^4 \times 3^3 = 2^x 3^y$$

Thus, $x = 4$ and $y = 3$. Therefore, the sum of the values of $x + y$ is $4 + 3 = 7$.

7. (D)

The expressions on the left and right have different bases of 25 and 125, respectively. Change both bases to $25 = 5^2$ and $125 = 5^3$ and solve the equation.

$$25^{x+1} = 125^{2-x}$$
$$(5^2)^{x+1} = (5^3)^{2-x}$$
$$5^{2x+2} = 5^{6-3x} \qquad \text{Since both sides have the same base}$$
$$2x + 2 = 6 - 3x$$
$$5x = 4$$
$$x = \frac{4}{5}$$

Therefore, the value of x is $\frac{4}{5}$.

8. (C)

Raise both sides of $x^{-\frac{1}{2}} = 4$ to the power of -2 to find the value of x. Additionally, raise both sides of $y^{-2} = \frac{1}{16}$ to the power of $-\frac{1}{2}$ to find the value of y.

$$x^{-\frac{1}{2}} = 4 \qquad\qquad\qquad y^{-2} = \frac{1}{16}$$
$$(x^{-\frac{1}{2}})^{-2} = (4)^{-2} \qquad\qquad (y^{-2})^{-\frac{1}{2}} = (4^{-2})^{-\frac{1}{2}}$$
$$x = \frac{1}{16} \qquad\qquad\qquad y = 4$$

Thus, $x = \frac{1}{16}$ and $y = 4$. Therefore, $xy = \frac{1}{16}(4) = \frac{1}{4}$.

9. (E)

$$1000a^2 = 10^3 a^2 \qquad \text{Substitute } a \text{ for } 10^x$$
$$= 10^3 (10^x)^2 \qquad \text{Use the properties of exponents}$$
$$= 10^3 \cdot 10^{2x}$$
$$= 10^{2x+3}$$

Therefore, $1000a^2$ equals to 10^{2x+3}.

10. (A)

Expand the expression $(4a^y)^x$ on the left side by using the properties of exponents. Additionally, change 64 to 4^3 in the expression on the right side.

$$(4a^y)^x = 64a^{12}$$
$$4^x a^{xy} = 4^3 a^{12}$$

Since the expressions on the left and right side have the same bases, 4 and a, compare exponents on the left and right side. Thus, $x = 3$ and $xy = 12$. This means that the value of y is 4. Therefore, $x + y = 7$.

PRACTICE SET 4

Solving Equations and Word Problems

Solving an equation is finding the value of the variable that makes the equation true. In order to solve an equation, use the rule called SADMEP with inverse operations (SADMEP is the reverse order of the order of operations, PEMDAS). Inverse operations are the operations that cancel each other. Addition and subtraction, and multiplication and division are good examples.

SADMEP suggests to first cancel subtraction or addition. Then, cancel division or multiplication next by applying corresponding inverse operation. Below is an example that shows you how to solve $2x - 1 = 5$, which involves subtraction and multiplication.

$$
\begin{aligned}
&\qquad\qquad\qquad\qquad\qquad\qquad\quad \checkmark \qquad\quad \checkmark \\
2x - 1 &= 5 \qquad\qquad\qquad S\ A\ D\ M\ E\ P \\
+1 &= +1 \qquad\qquad\qquad \text{Addition to cancel substraction} \\
2x &= 6 \qquad\qquad\qquad\ \text{Division to cancel multiplication} \\
x &= 3
\end{aligned}
$$

Solving word problems involve translating verbal phrases into mathematical equations. The table below summarizes the guidelines.

Verbal Phrase	Exression
A number	x
Is	$=$
Of	$\times$
Percent	0.01 or $\frac{1}{100}$
The sum of x and y	$x + y$
Three more than twice a number	$2x + 3$
The difference of x and y	$x - y$
3 is subtracted from a number	$x - 3$
4 less than a number	$x - 4$
A number decreased by 5	$x - 5$
6 less a number	$6 - x$
The product of x and y	xy
6 times a number	$6x$
The quotient of x and y	$\frac{x}{y}$
A number divided by 9	$\frac{x}{9}$

    www.solomonacademy.net

Example: 5 more than the quotient of x and 3 is 14. What is the number?

$$\frac{x}{3} + 5 = 14$$

$\checkmark \checkmark$

$S\ A\ D\ M\ E\ P$

$$-5 = -5$$

Subtraction to cancel addition

$$\frac{x}{3} = 9$$

Multiplication to cancel division

$$x = 27$$

EXERCISES

1. If $5x - 3 = 7$, what is the value of $2x$?

(A) 0   (B) 1   (C) 2   (D) 3   (E) 4

2. If $3(x - 2) = 2(x - 2)$, then $x =$

(A) 2   (B) 3   (C) 4   (D) 6   (E) 8

3. If $5x - (x + 6) = 18$, what is the value of $x + 6$?

(A) 4   (B) 8   (C) 12
(D) 16   (E) 20

4. If $x^2 - x - 2 = x^2 - 2x - 3$, then $x =$

(A) -3 (B) -2 (C) -1
(D) 1   (E) 3

5. If $2x$ subtracted from 6 equals 9 less than x, what is the value of x ?

(A) 6   (B) 5   (C) 4   (D) 3   (E) 2

6. If $2(x + y) = 6$, what is the value of $3x + 3y$?

(A) 5   (B) 7   (C) 8   (D) 9   (E) 12

7. If $4xy - 6 = 2x + 3y$ and $y = 2$, then what is the value of x ?

(A) 2   (B) 3   (C) 4   (D) 5   (E) 6

8. If two thirds of the sum of $6x$ and 9 equals $2x$ less 8, what is the value of x ?

(A) -8 (B) -7 (C) -5
(D) 3   (E) 7

9. If $x = \frac{2y}{a}$, which of the following expression equals $6a$?

(A) $\dfrac{3x}{y}$ (B) $\dfrac{6x}{y}$ (C) $\dfrac{6y}{x}$
(D) $\dfrac{12x}{y}$ (E) $\dfrac{12y}{x}$

10. Joshua has $300 in his savings account. If he saves $200 per week, in how many weeks will he have saved a total amount of $2100 in his savings account?

(A) 5   (B) 6   (C) 7   (D) 8   (E) 9

ANSWERS AND SOLUTIONS

1. (E)

$$5x - 3 = 7$$
$$+3 = +3$$
$$5x = 10$$
$$x = 2$$

✓ ✓
$S\ A\ D\ M\ E\ P$
Addition to cancel substraction
Division to cancel multiplication

Therefore, the value of $2x$ is $2(2) = 4$.

2. (A)

Expand the expressions inside the parenthesis on the left and right side by using the distributive property.

$$3(x - 2) = 2(x - 2)$$
$$3x - 6 = 2x - 4$$
$$3x - 2x = -4 + 6$$
$$x = 2$$

Use the distributive property

3. (C)

Simplify the expression on the left side and solve the equation.

$$5x - (x + 6) = 18$$
$$5x - x - 6 = 18$$
$$4x = 24$$
$$x = 6$$

Therefore, $x + 6 = 12$.

4. (C)

Cancel out x^2 on each side and solve for x.

$$x^2 - x - 2 = x^2 - 2x - 3$$
$$-x - 2 = -2x - 3$$
$$2x - x = -3 + 2$$
$$x = -1$$

Subtract x^2 from each side

5. (B)

$2x$ subtracted from 6 can be expressed as $6 - 2x$. 9 less than x can be expressed as $x - 9$.

$$6 - 2x = x - 9$$
$$-3x = -15$$
$$x = 5$$

6. (D)

You can not solve for the value of x and y separately since you only have one equation with two variables. Instead, multiply the equation by $\frac{3}{2}$ and find the value of $3x + 3y$.

$$\frac{3}{2} \times 2(x + y) = \frac{3}{2} \times 6 \qquad \text{Multiply both sides by } \frac{3}{2}$$
$$3(x + y) = 9$$
$$3x + 3y = 9$$

7. (A)

Substituting 2 for y simplifies the equation to $8x - 6 = 2x + 6$.

$$4xy - 6 = 2x + 3y \qquad \text{Substitute 2 for } y$$
$$8x - 6 = 2x + 6$$
$$6x = 12$$
$$x = 2$$

8. (B)

Two thirds of the sum of $6x$ and 9 can be expressed as $\frac{2}{3}(6x + 9)$ and $2x$ less 8 can be expressed as $2x - 8$.

$$\frac{2}{3}(6x + 9) = 2x - 8 \qquad \text{Use the distributive property}$$
$$4x + 6 = 2x - 8$$
$$2x = -14$$
$$x = -7$$

9. (E)

From the equation $x = \frac{2y}{a}$, write a in terms of y and x. Afterwards, evaluate $6a$.

$$x = \frac{2y}{a} \qquad \text{Multiply both sides by } a$$
$$ax = 2y \qquad \text{Divide both sides by } x$$
$$a = \frac{2y}{x} \qquad \text{Multiply both sides by 6}$$
$$6a = \frac{12y}{x}$$

10. (D)

Define x as the number of weeks Joshua needs to save the total amount of \$2100. Since Joshua will save \$200 per week, the amounts that Joshua will save in x weeks will be $200x$. Thus,

$$200x + 300 = 2100$$
$$200x = 1800$$
$$x = 9$$

Therefore, Joshua needs 9 weeks to save the total amount of \$2100.

PRACTICE SET 5

Solving Absolute Value Equations and Radical Equations

SAT Math problems involve solving simple equations to more complicated types such as absolute value equations and radical equations.

Solving absolute value equations

The definition of the absolute value of -2, $|-2|$, is the distance between -2 and 0 on the number line. Since distance is a positive quantity, $|-2| = 2$. The definition of an absolute value can be applied to an expression or an equation.

$$|x - 2| \Longrightarrow \text{Distance between a number and 2 on the number line}$$
$$|2 - x| \Longrightarrow \text{Distance between a number and 2 on the number line}$$

Note that both $|x - 2|$ and $|2 - x|$ are equivalent.

$$|x - 2| = 3 \Longrightarrow \text{Find two numbers exactly right 3 units or left 3 units}$$
$$\text{away from 2 on the number line. The two numbers are 5 or } -1.$$
$$|x - 2| = 3 \Longrightarrow \text{Answer:} \quad x = 5 \text{ or } x = -1$$

Below is an example that shows how to solve $|x - 2| = 2$ algebraically.

$$|x - 2| = 3$$
$$x - 2 = \pm 3$$

$x - 2 = 3$	or	$x - 2 = -3$
$x = 5$	or	$x = -1$

Solving radical equations

An equation that contains a radical ($\sqrt{x}$) is called a radical equation. Often, solving a radical equation involves in squaring binomial. Below shows the binomial expansion formulas.

$$(x + y)^2 = x^2 + 2xy + y^2 \qquad \text{Common mistake: } (x + y)^2 \neq x^2 + y^2$$
$$(x - y)^2 = x^2 - 2xy + y^2 \qquad \text{Common mistake: } (x - y)^2 \neq x^2 - y^2$$

To solve a radical equation, square both sides of the equation to eliminate the square root. Then, solve for the variable. Once you get the solution of the equation, you need to substitute the solution in the original equation to check the solution. If the solution doesn't make the equation true, it is called an extraneous solution and is not a solution. Below shows how to solve a radical equation.

$$\sqrt{x + 6} = 5 \qquad \text{Square both sides}$$
$$x + 6 = 25 \qquad \text{Subtract 6 from each side}$$
$$x = 19 \qquad \checkmark \text{ (Solution)}$$

Example 1:   Solve $|2x + 4| = 6$.

$$|2x + 4| = 6$$
$$2x + 4 = \pm 6$$

$2x + 4 = 6$	or	$2x + 4 = -6$
$2x = 2$	or	$2x = -10$
$x = 1$	or	$x = -5$

Example 2:   Solve $x - 1 = \sqrt{x + 5}$.

$x - 1 = \sqrt{x + 5}$	Square both sides
$(x - 1)^2 = x + 5$	Use the binomial expansion formula
$x^2 - 2x + 1 = x + 5$	Subtract $x + 5$ from each side
$x^2 - 3x - 4 = 0$	Factor the quadratic expression
$(x + 1)(x - 4) = 0$	Use zero product property: If $ab = 0$, then $a = 0$ or $b = 0$.
$x = -1$ or $x = 4$	

Substitute -1 and 4 for x in the original equation to check the solutions.

$$(-1) - 1 = \sqrt{-1 + 5} \qquad\qquad (4) - 1 = \sqrt{4 + 5}$$
$$-2 \neq 2 \quad \text{(Not a solution)} \qquad\qquad 3 = 3 \quad \checkmark \text{(Solution)}$$

EXERCISES

1. Evaluate $|x^2 - 4x|$ if $x = 3$

   (A) -3 (B) -1 (C) 0
   (D) 1   (E) 3

2. If $\sqrt{3x} = \sqrt{4 - x}$, $x =$

   (A) -1 (B) 0   (C) 1
   (D) 2   (E) 3

3. If $|5 - 2x| = 9$, what is the solution?

   (A) -2 or 7   (B) -7 (C) -2
   (D) -7 or 2   (E) 3

4. Which of the following equation has the same solutions to $|x - 1| = 4$?

   (A) $|x + 1| = 4$ (B) $|1 - x| = 4$
   (C) $|x - 4| = 1$ (D) $|1 - x| = -4$
   (E) $|x - 4| = -1$

5. Which of the following expression is equal to $|x|$?

   (A) x (B) $\pm x$ (C) $-x$
   (D) 0   (E) 1

6. Which of the following value equals the sum of the solutions to $|3x - 6| = 9$?

   (A) 6   (B) 5   (C) 4
   (D) -5 (E) -4

www.solomonacademy.net

Distribution or replication of any part of this page is prohibited.

7. What is the solution to $\sqrt{1 - 4x} + 1 = 4$?

    (A) 2   (B) 1   (C) 0

    (D) -1 (E) -2

8. Which of the following equation has the solutions 2 and 8 ?

    (A) $|x| = 5$ (B) $|x - 2| = 8$

    (C) $|x - 8| = 2$ (D) $|x - 5| = 3$

    (E) $|x - 3| = 5$

9. Which of the following values are the solutions to $x - 3 = \sqrt{3x - 5}$?

    (A) 9   (B) 6   (C) 2 or 7

    (D) 2   (E) 7

10. If 4 is the solution to $|x - a| = 6$, which of the following values are all possible values for a ?

    (A) -2 or 10   (B) 2 or -10

    (C) -1 or 6   (D) 1 or -6

    (E) -3 or 8

ANSWERS AND SOLUTIONS

1. (E)

Substitute 3 for x in the expression and evaluate the absolute value.

$$\begin{aligned}
|x^2 - 4x| &= |(3)^2 - 4(3)| \\
&= |9 - 12| = |-3| \\
&= 3
\end{aligned}$$

2. (C)

Square both sides and solve for x.

$$\begin{aligned}
\sqrt{3x} &= \sqrt{4 - x} \\
3x &= 4 - x \\
4x &= 4 \\
x &= 1
\end{aligned}$$

3. (A)

$$\begin{aligned}
|5 - 2x| &= 9 \\
5 - 2x &= \pm 9
\end{aligned}$$

$5 - 2x = 9$	or	$5 - 2x = -9$
$-2x = 4$	or	$-2x = -14$
$x = -2$	or	$x = 7$

4. (B)

Both $|x - 1|$ and $|1 - x|$ represent the distance between a number and 1. Thus, $|x - 1| = |1 - x|$. Therefore, $|x - 1| = 4$ and $|1 - x| = 4$ are equivalent and have the same solutions.

5. (B)

If $x > 0$, then $|x| = x$. However, if $x < 0$, then $|x| = -x$. Therefore, $|x| = \pm x$.

6. (C)

$$|3x - 6| = 9$$
$$3x - 6 = \pm 9$$

$3x - 6 = 9$	or	$3x - 6 = -9$
$3x = 15$	or	$3x = -3$
$x = 5$	or	$x = -1$

Since the solutions to $|3x - 6| = 9$ are 5 and -1, the sum of the solutions is $5 + (-1) = 4$.

7. (E)

$$\sqrt{1 - 4x} + 1 = 4 \qquad \text{Subtract 1 from each side}$$
$$\sqrt{1 - 4x} = 3 \qquad \text{Square both sides}$$
$$1 - 4x = 9 \qquad \text{Solve for } x$$
$$-4x = 8$$
$$x = -2$$

Substitute -2 for x in the original equation to check the solution. Since $\sqrt{1 - 4(-2)} + 1 = 4$ is true, $x = -2$ is the solution.

8. (D)

Substituting 2 and 8 in each answer choice takes time. Instead, first find the average of 2 and 8, which is 5. Since 2 and 8 are left 3 units and right 3 units from 5, respectively, set up an absolute value equation such as $|x - 5| = 3$.

9. (E)

$$x - 3 = \sqrt{3x - 5} \qquad \text{Square each side}$$
$$(x - 3)^2 = 3x - 5 \qquad \text{Use the binomial expansion formula}$$
$$x^2 - 6x + 9 = 3x - 5 \qquad \text{Subtract } 3x \text{ and add 5 to each side}$$
$$x^2 - 9x + 14 = 0 \qquad \text{Factor the quadratic expression}$$
$$(x - 2)(x - 7) = 0 \qquad \text{Use zero product property: If } ab = 0, \text{ then } a = 0 \text{ or } b = 0.$$
$$x = 2 \qquad \text{or} \qquad x = 7$$

Substitute 2 and 7 in the original equation to check the solutions.

$(2) - 3 = \sqrt{3(2) - 5}$	$(7) - 3 = \sqrt{3(7) - 5}$
$-1 \neq 1 \qquad \text{(Not a solution)}$	$4 = 4 \qquad \checkmark \text{ (Solution)}$

Therefore, only solution to $x - 3 = \sqrt{3x - 5}$ is 7.

10. (A)

Since 4 is a solution to $|x - a| = 6$, substitute 4 for x in the equation and solve for a.

$$|x - a| = 6 \qquad \text{Substitute 4 for } x$$
$$|4 - a| = 6 \qquad \text{Since } |4 - a| = |a - 4|$$
$$|a - 4| = 6$$
$$a - 4 = \pm 6$$

$$a - 4 = 6 \qquad \text{or} \qquad a - 4 = -6$$
$$a = 10 \qquad \text{or} \qquad a = -2$$

Therefore, all possible values for a are -2 and 10.

PRACTICE SET 6

Solving Inequalities and Compound Inequalities

Solving Inequalities

Solving an inequality is exactly the same as solving an equation. To solve an inequality, use SADMEP (Reverse order of the PEMDAS). In most cases, the inequality symbol remains unchanged. However, there are only two cases in which the inequality symbol must be reversed. The first case is when you multiply or divide each side by a negative number. The second case is when you take a reciprocal of each side. For instance,

Case 1

$2 < 3$

$-2 > -3$

Case 2

$2 < 3$

$\dfrac{1}{2} > \dfrac{1}{3}$

Solving Compound Inequalities

There are two types of compound inequalities: **And** compound inequality and **Or** compound inequality.

And Compound Inequality: $-5 \le 2x - 1 \le 7$

Or Compound Inequality: $x - 4 < -3 \quad \text{or} \quad 2x + 1 > 7$

Below shows how to solve each type of compound inequality.

$$-5 \le 2x - 1 \le 7 \qquad \text{And compound inequality}$$
$$+1 \le \quad\;\; +1 \le +1 \qquad \text{Add 1 to each side}$$
$$-4 \le 2x \le 8 \qquad \text{Divide each side by 2}$$
$$-2 \le x \le 4$$

Thus, x is greater than or equal to -2 <u>and</u> less than or equal to 4

$$x - 4 < -3 \quad \text{or} \quad 2x + 1 > 7 \qquad \text{Or compound inequality}$$
$$x < 1 \quad \text{or} \quad x > 3$$

Thus, x is less than 1 <u>or</u> greater than 3

Example: Solve $-3x + 2 > x + 10$

$$-3x + 2 > x + 10 \qquad \text{Subtract } x \text{ from each side}$$
$$-4x + 2 > 10 \qquad \text{Subtract 2 from each side}$$
$$-4x > 8 \qquad \text{Divide each side by } -4$$
$$x < -2 \qquad \text{Reverse the inequality symbol}$$

EXERCISES

1. Solve the inequality $2x + 1 < 5$

   (A) $x < 2$ (B) $x < -2$ (C) $x > 2$
   (D) $x > -2$ (E) $x < -3$

2. Solve the inequality $-2 \le 3x + 1 \le 10$

   (A) $-3 \le x \le 3$ (B) $-1 \le x \le 1$
   (C) $0 \le x \le 2$ (D) $-3 \le x \le 1$
   (E) $-1 \le x \le 3$

3. Solve the inequality $-4x - 8 > 12$

   (A) $x > -5$ (B) $x < -5$ (C) $x > 5$
   (D) $x < 5$ (E) $x < 1$

4. What is the solution to the following inequality $3x + 1 < -5$ or $2x - 1 > 7$?

   (A) $x < -2$ or $x > 4$
   (B) $x < -2$ or $x > -4$
   (C) $x < 2$ or $x > 4$
   (D) $-2 < x < 4$
   (E) $2 < x < 4$

5. Solve $3(2x - 4) < 2(x + 4)$

   (A) $x < 3$ (B) $x > 4$ (C) $x < 5$
   (D) $x > 6$ (E) $x < 7$

6. How many positive integer values of x satisfy $-2(x - 8) > x - 2$?

   (A) 1   (B) 2   (C) 3
   (D) 4   (E) 5

7. If the solution to $4 - 2x > x + 16$ is $x < a$, what is the value of a ?

   (A) 6   (B) 4   (C) 2
   (D) -4 (E) -6

8. Solve $-10 \le -3x - 4 < 5$

   (A) $-3 \le x < 2$ (B) $-3 < x \le 2$
   (C) $-2 \le x < 3$ (D) $-2 < x \le 3$
   (E) $2 \le x < -3$

9. If 4 less than a number is less than 4 and greater than -3, find the number.

   (A) $0 < x < 7$ (B) $1 < x < 7$
   (C) $1 < x < 8$ (D) $0 < x < 8$
   (E) $2 < x < 9$

10. If 3 more than twice a number is at most 11 and at least 5, find the number.

   (A) $2 < x < 8$ (B) $2 \le x \le 8$
   (C) $1 \le x < 4$ (D) $1 < x \le 4$
   (E) $1 \le x \le 4$

ANSWERS AND SOLUTIONS

1. (A)

$$2x + 1 < 5 \quad \text{Subtract 1 from each side}$$
$$2x < 4 \quad \text{Divide each side by 2}$$
$$x < 2$$

2. (E)

$$-2 \leq 3x + 1 \leq 10 \qquad \text{Subtract 1 from each side}$$
$$-3 \leq 3x \leq 9 \qquad \text{Divide each side by 3}$$
$$-1 \leq x \leq 3$$

3. (B)

$$-4x - 8 > 12 \qquad \text{Add 8 to each side}$$
$$-4x > 20 \qquad \text{Divide each side by } -4$$
$$x < -5 \qquad \text{Reverse the inequality symbol}$$

4. (A)

$$3x + 1 < -5 \qquad \text{or} \qquad 2x - 1 > 7$$
$$3x < -6 \qquad \text{or} \qquad 2x > 8$$
$$x < -2 \qquad \text{or} \qquad x > 4$$

5. (C)

$$3(2x - 4) < 2(x + 4) \qquad \text{Expand each side using the distributive property}$$
$$6x - 12 < 2x + 8 \qquad \text{Subtract } 2x \text{ from each side}$$
$$4x - 12 < 8 \qquad \text{Add 12 to each side}$$
$$4x < 20 \qquad \text{Divide each side by 4}$$
$$x < 5$$

6. (E)

$$-2(x - 8) > x - 2 \qquad \text{Expand left side using the distributive property}$$
$$-2x + 16 > x - 2 \qquad \text{Subtract } x \text{ from each side}$$
$$-3x + 16 > -2 \qquad \text{Subtract 16 from each side}$$
$$-3x > -18 \qquad \text{Divide each side by } -3 \text{ and reverse the inequality symbol}$$
$$x < 6$$

The positive integer values of x for which $x < 6$ are 1, 2, 3, 4, and 5. Therefore, there are 5 positive integer values of x that satisfy the original inequality.

7. (D)

$$4 - 2x > x + 16 \qquad \text{Subtract } x \text{ from each side}$$
$$4 - 3x > 16 \qquad \text{Subtract 4 from each side}$$
$$-3x > 12 \qquad \text{Divide each side by } -3 \text{ and reverse the inequality symbol}$$
$$x < -4$$

Therefore, the value of a is -4.

8. (B)

$$-10 \leq -3x - 4 < 5 \qquad \text{Add 4 to each side}$$
$$-6 \leq -3x < 9 \qquad \text{Divide each side by } -3 \text{ and reverse the inequality symbols}$$
$$2 \geq x > -3 \qquad \text{Rearrange the inequality}$$
$$-3 < x \leq 2$$

9. (C)

Translate the verbal phrases into an **And compound** inequality. Let x be the number. Then, 4 less than a number can be expressed as $x - 4$.

$$-3 < x - 4 < 4 \qquad \text{Add 4 to each side}$$
$$1 < x < 8$$

10. (E)

At most means $\leq$ and **at least** means $\geq$. Let x be the number. Then, 3 more than a twice a number can be expressed as $2x + 3$.

$$5 \leq 2x + 3 \leq 11 \qquad \text{Subtract 3 from each side}$$
$$2 \leq 2x \leq 8 \qquad \text{Divide each side by 2}$$
$$1 \leq x \leq 4$$

PRACTICE SET 7

Solving Absolute Value Inequalities

Solving absolute value inequalities involve two compound inequalities: And compound inequality and Or compound inequality. Absolute value with **less than inequality** symbol creates an **And** compound inequality. However, absolute value with **greater than inequality** symbol creates an **Or** compound inequality. A phrase **Less-And Great-Or** will help you memorize the following rules. For instance,

$$|x - 2| < 3 \quad \text{(Less)} \quad \implies \quad -3 < x - 2 < 3 \quad \text{(And)}$$
$$|x - 2| > 3 \quad \text{(Great)} \quad \implies \quad x - 2 < -3 \quad \text{or} \quad x - 2 > 3 \quad \text{(Or)}$$

$|x - 2|$ represents the distance between a number and 2. Thus, the meanings of the absolute value inequalities are as follows.

$|x - 2| < 3 \quad \implies \quad$ Find all the numbers **within** right 3 units and left 3 units from 2

$|x - 2| > 3 \quad \implies \quad$ Find all the numbers **more than** right 3 units or left 3 units from 2

Example 1:   Solve $|x - 2| < 3$

$$|x + 2| < 3 \quad \implies \quad -3 < x + 2 < 3$$
$$-5 < x < 1$$

Example 2:   Solve $|2x - 4| > 6$

$$|2x - 4| > 6 \quad \implies \quad 2x - 4 < -6 \quad \text{or} \quad 2x - 4 > 6$$
$$2x < -2 \quad \text{or} \quad 2x > 10$$
$$x < -1 \quad \text{or} \quad x > 5$$

EXERCISES

1. Solve the inequality $|x + 3| > 7$

   (A) $\ -4 < x < 10$

   (B) $\ -10 < x < 4$

   (C) $\ x < -3 \ $ or $ \ x > 7$

   (D) $\ x < -10 \ $ or $ \ x > 4$

   (E) $\ x < -4 \ $ or $ \ x > 10$

2. Solve the inequality $|2x + 1| < 5$

   (A) $\ -3 < x < 2$

   (B) $\ -2 < x < 3$

   (C) $\ x < -3 \ $ or $ \ x > 2$

   (D) $\ x < -2 \ $ or $ \ x > 3$

   (E) $\ x < -1 \ $ or $ \ x > 5$

3. Solve the inequality $|x + 3| - 2 \leq 5$

   (A) $-6 \leq x \leq 4$
   (B) $-4 \leq x \leq 6$
   (C) $-10 \leq x \leq 4$
   (D) $x \leq -4$ or $x \geq 6$
   (E) $x \leq -10$ or $x \geq 4$

4. Solve the inequality $2|x - 2| \geq 6$

   (A) $x \leq -5$ or $x \geq 1$
   (B) $x \leq -1$ or $x \geq 5$
   (C) $x \leq -2$ or $x \geq 6$
   (D) $-1 \leq x \leq 5$
   (E) $-2 \leq x \leq 6$

5. Which of the following inequality has the solution $2 < x < 6$?

   (A) $|x - 2| > 4$ (B) $|x - 2| < 4$
   (C) $|x - 4| > 2$ (D) $|x - 4| < 2$
   (E) $|x - 6| < 2$

6. Which of the following inequality has the solution $x < -1$ or $x > 5$?

   (A) $|x - 3| > 2$ (B) $|x - 3| < 2$
   (C) $|x - 2| > 3$ (D) $|x - 2| < 3$
   (E) $|x + 1| > 5$

7. What is the smallest integer value of x that satisfies $|2x - 4| < 6$?

   (A) -1 (B) 0 (C) 1
   (D) 2 (E) 3

8. How many positive integer values of x satisfy $|3x - 2| \leq 7$?

   (A) 3 (B) 4 (C) 5
   (D) 6 (E) 7

9. Which of the following inequality has the solution such as a set of all real numbers more than 5 units from 1 ?

   (A) $|x - 2| > 3$ (B) $|x - 5| < 1$
   (C) $|x - 5| > 1$ (D) $|x - 1| < 5$
   (E) $|x - 1| > 5$

10. To ride a roller coaster at an amusement park, a child must be between 42 inches and 54 inches tall exclusive. Which of the following inequality represents the height requirement for a child?

    (A) $|x - 42| > 54$ (B) $|x - 42| < 12$
    (C) $|x - 42| > 12$ (D) $|x - 48| > 6$
    (E) $|x - 48| < 6$

ANSWERS AND SOLUTIONS

1. (D)

   Use the phrase **Less-And Great-Or**. Solving an absolute value inequality with greater than inequality symbol creates Or compound inequality.

   $$|x + 3| > 7 \implies \begin{array}{l} x + 3 < -7 \quad \text{or} \quad x + 3 > 7 \\ x < -10 \quad \text{or} \quad x > 4 \end{array}$$

2. (A)

Use the phrase **Less-And Great-Or**. Solving an absolute value inequality with less than inequality symbol creates And compound inequality.

$$|2x + 1| < 5 \implies -5 < 2x + 1 < 5 \qquad \text{Subtract 1 from each side}$$
$$-6 < 2x < 4 \qquad \text{Divide each side by 2}$$
$$-3 < x < 2$$

3. (C)

Add 2 to each side and solve the inequality by using the phrase **Less-And Great-Or**.

$$|x + 3| - 2 < 5 \implies |x + 3| < 7 \implies -7 < x + 3 < 7$$
$$-10 < x < 4$$

4. (B)

Divide each side by 2 and solve the inequality.

$$2|x - 2| \geq 6 \implies |x - 2| \geq 3 \implies x - 2 \leq -3 \text{ or } x - 2 \geq 3$$
$$x \leq -1 \text{ or } x \geq 5$$

5. (D)

Instead of solving each inequality in the answer choices, let's set up an absolute value inequality from the solution $2 < x < 6$. The mean of 2 and 6 is $\frac{2+6}{2} = 4$. 2 is far left from the mean, and 6 is far right from mean. Both 2 and 6 are 2 units from the mean. Since we try to find all the numbers within 2 units from the mean, the inequality can be expressed as $|x - \text{Mean}| < \text{Distance}$. Therefore, $|x - 4| < 2$ is the answer.

6. (C)

Set up an absolute value inequality from the solution $x < -1$ or $x > 5$. The mean of -1 and 5 is 2. -1 is left 3 units from the mean and 5 is right 3 units from the mean. Since we try to find all the numbers more than 3 units from the mean, the inequality can be expressed as $|x - \text{Mean}| > \text{Distance}$. Therefore, $|x - 2| > 3$ is the answer.

7. (B)

Solve the absolute value inequality. Then, find the smallest integer from the solution.

$$|2x - 4| < 6 \implies -6 < 2x - 4 < 6 \qquad \text{Add 4 to each side}$$
$$-2 < 2x < 10 \qquad \text{Divide each side by 2}$$
$$-1 < x < 5$$

Thus, the integer values of x for which $-1 < x < 5$ are 0, 1, 2, 3, and 4. Therefore, the smallest integer value of x is 0.

8. (A)

Solve the absolute value inequality. Then, find out how many positive integers belong to the solution.

$$|3x - 2| \leq 7 \qquad \implies \qquad \begin{aligned} -7 &\leq 3x - 2 \leq 7 \\ -5 &\leq 3x \leq 9 \\ -\frac{5}{3} &\leq x \leq 3 \end{aligned}$$

The positive integer values of x for which $-\frac{5}{3} \leq x \leq 3$ are 1, 2, and 3. Therefore, there are 3 positive integer values of x that satisfy the inequality.

9. (E)

The distance from 1 to a number can be expressed as $|x - 1|$ and **more than 5 units** can expressed as > 5. Therefore, a set of all numbers more than 5 units from 1 can be expressed as $|x - 1| > 5$.

10. (E)

Let x be the height of a child. Since a child must be between 42 inches and 54 inches tall exclusive, $42 < x < 54$. Use $|x - \text{Mean}| < \text{Distance}$. The mean of 42 and 54 is 48. The height of a child should be within 6 from the mean. Therefore, the absolute value inequality can be expressed as $|x - 48| < 6$.

PRACTICE SET 8

Fractions, Ratios, Rates, and Proportions

A **fraction** represents a part of a whole. In the fraction $\frac{4}{5}$, the numerator 4 means that the fraction represents 4 equal parts, and the denominator 5 means that 5 parts make up a whole.

A **ratio** is a fraction that compares two quantities measured in the same units. The ratio of a to b can be written as $a : b$ or $\frac{a}{b}$. If the ratio of a number of apples to that of oranges in a store is $3 : 4$ or $\frac{3}{4}$, it means that there are 3 apples to every 4 oranges in the store.

A **rate** is a ratio that compares two quantities measured in different units. A rate is usually expressed as a unit rate. A unit rate is a rate per one unit of a given quantity. The rate of a per b can be written as $\frac{a}{b}$. If a car travels 100 miles in 2 hours, the car travels at a rate of 50 miles per hour.

A **proportion** is an equation that states that two ratios are equal. A proportion can be written as

$$a : b = c : d \qquad \text{or} \qquad \frac{a}{b} = \frac{c}{d}$$

The proportion above reads a is to b as c is to d. To solve the value of a variable in a proportion, use the cross product property and then solve for the variable. For instance,

$$\frac{x}{2} = \frac{6}{3} \qquad \text{Cross product property}$$
$$3x = 2 \times 6$$
$$x = 4$$

Example: Simplify $\frac{x}{2} + \frac{x}{3}$

$$\frac{x}{2} + \frac{x}{3} = \frac{3x}{6} + \frac{2x}{6} \qquad \text{Common denominator is 6}$$
$$= \frac{5x}{6}$$

EXERCISES

1. Simplify $\frac{2x - 3y}{y}$

   (A) $\dfrac{2x}{y} - 3$ (B) $\dfrac{2x}{y} + 2$ (C) $\dfrac{2}{xy} - 3$

   (D) $\dfrac{2}{xy} + 2$ (E) $2x - 2y$

2. Two-thirds of students in a class are girls. If one-half of the girls wear glasses, what fractional part of students are girls who wear glasses?

   (A) $\dfrac{1}{8}$ (B) $\dfrac{1}{6}$ (C) $\dfrac{1}{5}$

   (D) $\dfrac{1}{4}$ (E) $\dfrac{1}{3}$

3. If the ratio of a to b is $2 : 3$ and the ratio of c to b is $3 : 4$, which of the following is equal to the ratio of a to c ?

(A) $\dfrac{1}{2}$ (B) $\dfrac{2}{3}$ (C) $\dfrac{3}{4}$

(D) $\dfrac{8}{9}$ (E) $\dfrac{9}{10}$

4. If a student can type 120 words in 3 minutes, at this rate, how many words can she type in 5 minutes?

(A) 240   (B) 200   (C) 180

(D) 160   (E) 120

5. A 45-inch string is cut into two pieces. If the ratio of the longer piece to the shorter piece is $3 : 2$, what is the length of the shorter piece?

(A) 9   (B) 12   (C) 18

(D) 27   (E) 36

6. If $2x - 3y = 0$, what is $\dfrac{x}{y}$?

(A) $\dfrac{3}{2}$ (B) $\dfrac{2}{3}$ (C) $\dfrac{5}{3}$

(D) $\dfrac{3}{5}$ (E) $\dfrac{5}{2}$

7. $\dfrac{x}{2} + \dfrac{x}{3} + \dfrac{x}{4} = 26$, $x =$

(A) 12   (B) 16   (C) 18

(D) 20   (E) 24

8. If a car travels at a rate of 48 miles per hour, how many miles does it travel in 40 minutes?

(A) 28   (B) 32   (C) 36

(D) 40   (E) 42

9. 10 people who build at the same rate can frame a house in 6 days. What fractional part of a house can 4 people frame a house in 3 days?

(A) $\dfrac{1}{2}$ (B) $\dfrac{1}{3}$ (C) $\dfrac{1}{4}$

(D) $\dfrac{1}{5}$ (E) $\dfrac{1}{6}$

10. If Joshua can wash x cars in y hours, how many cars does he wash in z hours?

(A) $\dfrac{xy}{z}$ (B) $\dfrac{yz}{x}$ (C) $\dfrac{xz}{y}$

(D) $\dfrac{x}{yz}$ (E) $\dfrac{z}{xy}$

ANSWERS AND SOLUTIONS

1. (A)

$$\frac{2x - 3y}{y} = \frac{2x}{y} - \frac{3y}{y}$$
$$= \frac{2x}{y} - 3$$

2. (E)

Let x be the total number of students in the class. Two-thirds of the students are girls. Thus, the number of girls can be expressed as $\frac{2}{3}x$. Since one-half of the girls wear glasses, the number of girls who wear glasses can be expressed as $\frac{1}{2}(\frac{2}{3}x)$ or $\frac{1}{3}x$. Therefore, one-third of the students are girls who wear glasses.

3. (D)

Since $\frac{a}{b} = \frac{2}{3}$ and $\frac{c}{b} = \frac{3}{4}$, the ratio $\frac{a}{c}$ can be calculated using the two given ratios.

$$
\begin{aligned}
\frac{a}{c} &= \frac{a}{b} \times \frac{b}{c} \qquad \left(\text{Since } \frac{c}{b} = \frac{3}{4} \implies \frac{b}{c} = \frac{4}{3}\right) \\
&= \frac{2}{3} \times \frac{4}{3} \\
&= \frac{8}{9}
\end{aligned}
$$

4. (B)

If a student can type 120 words in 3 minutes, she can type $120 \div 3 = 40$ words in 1 minute. Therefore, she can type $40 \times 5 = 200$ words in 5 minutes.

5. (C)

The ratio of the longer piece to the shorter piece is $3 : 2$. Instead of using 3 for the longer piece and 2 for the shorter piece directly, multiply the ratio $3 : 2$ by x so that a new ratio is $3x : 2x$. Now, $3x$ represents the length of the longer piece and $2x$ represents the length of the shorter piece. If you add the longer and shorter pieces together, the sum of these lengths is equal to the length of the original string, 45 inches. Thus,

$$
\begin{aligned}
3x + 2x &= 45 \\
5x &= 45 \\
x &= 9
\end{aligned}
$$

Therefore, the length of the shorter piece is $2x = 2(9) = 18$ inches.

6. (A)

$$
\begin{aligned}
2x - 3y &= 0 && \text{Add } 3y \text{ to each side} \\
2x &= 3y && \text{Divide each side by 2} \\
x &= \frac{3}{2}y && \text{Divide each side by } y \\
\frac{x}{y} &= \frac{3}{2}
\end{aligned}
$$

7. (E)

The least common multiple of 2, 3, and 4 is 12. Multiply each side by 12 to eliminate fractions.

$$
\begin{aligned}
12 \times \left(\frac{x}{2} + \frac{x}{3} + \frac{x}{4}\right) &= 26 \times 12 && \text{Use the distributive property} \\
6x + 4x + 3x &= 26(12) \\
13x &= 26(12) \\
x &= \frac{26(12)}{13} \\
x &= 24
\end{aligned}
$$

Therefore, the value of x is 24.

8. (B)

48 miles per hour means that the car travels 48 miles in one hour. There are 60 minutes in one hour. Set up a proportion in terms of miles and minutes.

$$48_{\text{miles}} : 60_{\text{minutes}} = x_{\text{miles}} : 40_{\text{minutes}}$$

$$\frac{48}{60} = \frac{x}{40} \qquad \text{Use cross product property}$$

$$60x = 48 \times 40$$

$$x = 32$$

Therefore, the car travels 32 miles in 40 minutes.

9. (D)

Let's define work as the number of people times the number of days. The work required to frame a house is $10_{\text{people}} \times 6_{\text{days}} = 60_{\text{people} \times \text{days}}$. If 4 people frame in 3 days, the work they finish is $4_{\text{people}} \times 3_{\text{days}} = 12_{\text{people} \times \text{days}}$. Thus,

$$\text{A fractional part of a house} = \frac{12_{\text{people} \times \text{days}}}{60_{\text{people} \times \text{days}}}$$

$$= \frac{1}{5}$$

Therefore, 4 people can frame $\frac{1}{5}$ of the house in 3 days.

10. (C)

Let's set up a proportion and solve for w.

$$x_{\text{cars}} : y_{\text{hours}} = w_{\text{cars}} : z_{\text{hours}}$$

$$\frac{x}{y} = \frac{w}{z} \qquad \text{Use cross product property}$$

$$yw = xz$$

$$w = \frac{xz}{y}$$

Therefore, Joshua can wash $\frac{xz}{y}$ cars in z hours.

www.solomonacademy.net

PRACTICE SET 9

Linear Equations

The **slope**, m, of a line is a number that describes the steepness of the line. The larger the absolute value of the slope, $|m|$, the steeper the line is (closer to y-axis). If a line passes through the points (x_1, y_1) and (x_2, y_2), the slope m is defined as

$$m = \frac{\text{Rise}}{\text{Run}} = \frac{y_2 - y_1}{x_2 - x_1}$$

If the points (x_1, y_1) and (x_2, y_2) are given, the following formulas are useful in solving SAT math problems.

Midpoint Formula: $\left(\dfrac{x_1 + x_2}{2}, \dfrac{y_1 + y_2}{2} \right)$

Distance Formula: $D = \sqrt{(x_2 - x_1)^2 + (y_2 - y_1)^2}$

An equation of a line can be written in three different forms.

1. **Slope-intercept form:** $y = mx + b$,   where m is slope and b is y-intercept.

2. **Point-slope form:**   If the slope of a line is m and the line passes through the point (x_1, y_1),

$$y - y_1 = m(x - x_1)$$

3. **Standard form:** $Ax + By = C$,   where A, B, and C are integers.

Below classifies the lines by slope.

- Lines that rise from left to right have positive slope.

- Lines that fall from left to right have negative slope.

- Horizontal lines have zero slope (example: $y = 2$).

- Vertical lines have undefined slope (example: $x = 2$).

- Parallel lines have the same slope.

- Perpendicular lines have negative reciprocal slopes (product of the slopes equals -1).

The x-intercept of a line is a point where the line crosses x-axis. **The y-intercept** of a line is a point where the line crosses y-axis.

To find the x-intercept of a line $\Longrightarrow$ Substitute 0 for y and solve for x

To find the y-intercept of a line $\Longrightarrow$ Substitute 0 for x and solve for y

Example: If the slope of a line is 3 and the y-intercept is -4, write an equation of the line.

In slope-intercept form, $y = mx + b$, m represents the slope and b represents the y-intercept. Thus, $m = 2$ and $b = -4$. Therefore, the equation of the line is $y = 2x - 4$.

EXERCISES

1. If a line passes through the points $(-2, 3)$ and $(1, 9)$, what is the slope of the line?

    (A) -3 (B) -2 (C) -1
    (D) $\dfrac{1}{3}$ (E) 2

2. What are the x and y coordinates of the midpoint between $(6, 5)$ and $(-2, 1)$?

    (A) $(4, 3)$ (B) $(2, 4)$ (C) $(4, 2)$
    (D) $(3, 2)$ (E) $(2, 3)$

3. What is the distance between $(-1, -3)$ and $(4, 9)$?

    (A) 13 (B) 12 (C) 10
    (D) 8 (E) 5

4. Which of the following line has a slope of zero?

    (A) $y = 2x - 3$ (B) $y = -2x + 3$
    (C) $y = -2$ (D) $x = -2$
    (E) $x + y = 0$

5. If a point $(1, a)$ lies on the line $y = -3x + 4$, what is the value of a ?

    (A) -1 (B) 0 (C) 1
    (D) 2 (E) 3

6. If the equation of the line is $2x + 3y = 6$, what is the x-intercept of the line?

    (A) -6 (B) -3 (C) 2
    (D) 3 (E) 6

7. Which of the following line is parallel to $y = 4x + 1$?

    (A) $y = 4x + 2$ (B) $y = -4x + 2$
    (C) $y = \dfrac{1}{4}x + 2$ (D) $y = -\dfrac{1}{4}x + 2$
    (E) $y = -\dfrac{1}{4}x - 2$

8. What is the equation of the line that is parallel to $y = \frac{1}{2}x + 3$ and passes $(4, 7)$?

    (A) $y = \dfrac{1}{2}x - 5$ (B) $y = \dfrac{1}{2}x + 5$
    (C) $y = -\dfrac{1}{2}x + 5$ (D) $y = -\dfrac{1}{2}x - 3$
    (E) $y = -2x + 5$

9. Which of the following line is perpendicular to $y = \frac{1}{3}x - 2$?

    (A) $-x + 3y = 6$ (B) $-x - 3y = 6$
    (C) $-2x + y = 4$ (D) $3x - y = 4$
    (E) $3x + y = 4$

10. What is the equation of the perpendicular bisector of a line segment connected by $(1, 5)$ and $(5, 3)$?

    (A) $y = 2x + 2$ (B) $y = 2x - 2$
    (C) $y = \dfrac{1}{2}x + 2$ (D) $y = \dfrac{1}{2}x - 2$
    (E) $y = -\dfrac{1}{2}x + 2$

ANSWERS AND SOLUTIONS

1. (E)

$$\text{Slope} = \frac{y_2 - y_1}{x_2 - x_1} = \frac{9 - 3}{1 - (-2)} = \frac{6}{3} = 2$$

2. (E)

$$\text{Midpoint} = \left(\frac{x_1 + x_2}{2}, \frac{y_1 + y_2}{2} \right) = \left(\frac{6 + (-2)}{2}, \frac{5 + 1}{2} \right) = (2, 3)$$

3. (A)

$$\begin{aligned}
\text{Distance} &= \sqrt{(x_2 - x_1)^2 + (y_2 - y_1)^2} \\
&= \sqrt{(4 - (-1))^2 + (9 - (-3))^2} \\
&= \sqrt{5^2 + 12^2} \\
&= 13
\end{aligned}$$

Therefore, the distance between $(-1, -3)$ and $(4, 9)$ is 13.

4. (C)

Horizontal lines have a slope of zero. Any horizontal lines can be written as $y = k$, where k=constant. Therefore, $y = -2$ is the answer.

5. (C)

Since point, $(1, a)$, is on the line, $(1, a)$ is the solution to the equation $y = -3x + 4$. Substitute 1 for x and a for y in the equation and solve for a.

$$\begin{aligned}
y &= -3x + 4 \qquad \text{Substitute 1 for } x \text{ and } a \text{ for } y \\
a &= -3(1) + 4 \\
a &= 1
\end{aligned}$$

Therefore, the value of a is 1.

6. (D)

To find the x-intercept of the line $2x + 3y = 6$, substitute 0 for y in the equation and solve for x.

$$\begin{aligned}
2x + 3y &= 6 \qquad \text{Substitute 0 for } y \\
2x + 3(0) &= 6 \\
x &= 3
\end{aligned}$$

Therefore, the x-intercept of the line is 3.

7. (A)

Two lines are parallel if they have the same slope. Thus, the slope of the parallel line must be 4. Since the only equation of the line that has the slope of 4 is $y = 4x + 2$ in answer choices, (A) is the correct answer.

8. (B)

Two parallel lines have the same slope. Thus, the slope of the parallel line is $\frac{1}{2}$. Start with the slope-intercept form, $y = mx + b = \frac{1}{2}x + b$. Since the point $(4, 7)$ is on the line, $(4, 7)$ is a solution to the equation $y = \frac{1}{2}x + b$. Substitute 4 for x and 7 for y in the equation and then solve for b.

$$y = \frac{1}{2}x + b \qquad \text{Substitute 4 for } x \text{ and 7 for } y$$
$$7 = \frac{1}{2}(4) + b \qquad \text{Solve for } b$$
$$b = 5$$

Therefore, the equation of the parallel line that passes through $(4, 7)$ is $y = \frac{1}{2}x + 5$.

9. (E)

The slope of the perpendicular line to $y = \frac{1}{3}x - 2$ is -3. Each equation in the answer choices is written in standard form. Rewrite each equation of the line in slope-intercept form and choose the equation of the line that has the slope of -3.

$$
\begin{array}{lll}
\text{(A)} & -x + 3y = 6 & \implies & y = \frac{1}{3}x + 2 \\
\text{(B)} & -x - 3y = 6 & \implies & y = -\frac{1}{3}x - 2 \\
\text{(C)} & -2x + y = 4 & \implies & y = 2x + 4 \\
\text{(D)} & 3x - y = 4 & \implies & y = 3x - 4 \\
\text{(E)} & 3x + y = 4 & \implies & y = -3x + 4
\end{array}
$$

Therefore, (E) is the correct answer.

10. (B)

The slope of the line segment connected by $(1, 5)$ and $(5, 3)$ is

$$\text{Slope} = \frac{3 - 5}{5 - 1} = -\frac{1}{2}$$

The midpoint between $(1, 5)$ and $(5, 3)$ is

$$\text{Midpoint} = \left(\frac{1 + 5}{2}, \frac{5 + 3}{2} \right) = (3, 4)$$

The slope of the perpendicular bisector is negative reciprocal of $-\frac{1}{2}$, or 2. The equation of the perpendicular bisector in slope-intercept form is $y = 2x + b$. Since the perpendicular bisector passes through the midpoint of the line segment, $(3, 4)$ is the solution to the equation $y = 2x + b$.

$$y = 2x + b \qquad \text{Substitute 3 for } x \text{ and 4 for } y$$
$$4 = 2(3) + b$$
$$b = -2$$

Therefore, the equation of the perpendicular bisector is $y = 2x - 2$.

PRACTICE SET 10

Solving Systems of Linear Equations

A system means more than one. A linear equation represents a line. Thus, a **system of linear equations** represent more than one line. Below is an example of a system of linear equations.

$$2x - y = 5$$
$$3x + y = 10$$

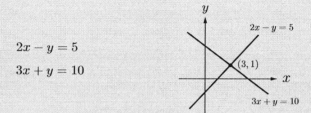

A solution to a system of linear equations is an ordered pair (x, y) that satisfies each equation in the system. In other words, a solution to a system of linear equation is an intersection point that lies on both lines. In the figure above, $(3, 1)$ is an ordered pair that satisfies each equation,

$$2x - y = 5 \implies 2(3) - 1 = 5$$
$$3x + y = 10 \implies 3(3) + 1 = 10$$

and is the intersection point of both lines.

Solving a system of linear equations means finding the x and y coordinates of the intersection point of the lines. There are two methods to solve a system of linear equations: **substitution** and **linear combinations**.

1. Substitution method
In the example above, write y in terms of x in the first equation. $2x - y = 5 \implies y = 2x - 5$. Substitute $2x - 5$ for y in the second equation.

$$3x + y = 10 \implies 3x + (2x - 5) = 10$$
$$5x - 5 = 10$$
$$x = 3 \implies y = 2x - 5 = 2(3) - 5 = 1$$

The solution to the system using the substitute method is $(3, 1)$.

2. Linear combinations method
In the example above, the coefficient of the y variable in each equation is opposite. Thus, adding the two equations eliminates the y variables. Then, solve for x.

$$2x - y = 15$$
$$\underline{3x + y = 10} \qquad \text{Add two equations}$$
$$5x = 15$$
$$x = 3$$

47

Substitute 3 for x in the first equation and solve for y.

$$2x - y = 5 \quad \Longrightarrow \quad 2(3) - y = 5 \quad \Longrightarrow \quad y = 1$$

The solution to the system using the linear combinations method is $(3, 1)$.

Example: Solve the system of linear equations below.

$$y = x - 4$$
$$2x + y = 2$$

Solve the system of equations using the substitution method.

$$2x + y = 2 \qquad \text{Substitute } y = x - 4 \text{ for } y$$
$$2x + (x - 4) = 2$$
$$3x - 4 = 2$$
$$x = 2 \quad \Longrightarrow \quad y = x - 4 = (2) - 4 = -2$$

Therefore, the solution to the system is $(2, -2)$.

EXERCISES

1. If $3x + 2y = 5$ and $5x - 2y = 3$, what is the value of $x + 3$?

   (A) 1   (B) 2   (C) 3

   (D) 4   (E) 5

2. If $-x + 3y = 16$ and $y = 2x - 3$, what is the value of y ?

   (A) 3   (B) 4   (C) 5

   (D) 6   (E) 7

3. If $x - y = 6$ and $2x + 4y = 9$, what is the value of $2x + 2y$?

   (A) 8   (B) 10   (C) 12

   (D) 15   (E) 18

4. If $-2x + 2y = 12$ and $\frac{x}{2} = \frac{y}{6}$, what is the value of x ?

   (A) 2   (B) 3   (C) 4

   (D) 5   (E) 6

$$3x - y = m$$
$$-2x + 5y = n$$

5. If $x = 3$ and $y = 2$ are solutions to the system of equations above, what is the value of $m + n$?

   (A) 11   (B) 9   (C) 7

   (D) 5   (E) 3

6. If the two lines, $y = 2x$ and $y = 6 - x$ intersect, what are the x and y coordinates of the intersection point?

   (A) $(4, 8)$ (B) $(4, 2)$ (C) $(3, 6)$

   (D) $(3, 2)$ (E) $(2, 4)$

7. If $x - y = 1$ and $x + y = 7$, what is the value of $3x - 2y$?

   (A) 6   (B) 5   (C) 4

   (D) 3   (E) 2

8. If $3x - 4y = -1$ and $-4x + 3y = 6$, what is the solution to the system of equations?

   (A) $(-3, -2)$ (B) $(-2, -3)$

   (C) $(3, -2)$ (D) $(3, 2)$

   (E) $(2, 3)$

9. Joshua and Jason saved $1000 together. Joshua saved $100 more than twice the amount that Jason saved. How much did Jason save?

   (A) $400   (B) $350   (C) $300

   (D) $250   (E) $200

10. A store sells desks and chairs. A store makes a profit of $15 per desk and $8 per chair. If the store sold a total of 23 desks and chairs and made the total profit of $240, how many chairs did the store sell?

   (A) 5   (B) 8   (C) 10

   (D) 12   (E) 15

ANSWERS AND SOLUTIONS

1. (D)

   Use the linear combinations method.

   $$3x + 2y = 5$$
   $$5x - 2y = 3 \qquad \text{Add two equations}$$
   $$\overline{}$$
   $$8x \quad\;\; = 8$$
   $$x = 1$$

   Therefore, $x + 3 = 4$.

2. (E)

   Use the substitution method.

   $$-x + 3y = 16 \qquad \text{Substitute } 2x - 3 \text{ for } y$$
   $$-x + 3(2x - 3) = 16$$
   $$5x - 9 = 16 \quad \implies \quad x = 5$$

   Therefore, $y = 2x - 3 = 2(5) - 3 = 7$.

3. (B)

   Add the two equations and divide the result by $\frac{2}{3}$ to find the value of $2x + 2y$.

   $$x - y = 6$$
   $$2x + 4y = 9 \qquad \text{Add two equations}$$
   $$\overline{}$$
   $$3x + 3y = 15 \qquad \text{Multiply each side by } \frac{2}{3}$$
   $$2x + 2y = 10$$

   Therefore, the value of $2x + 2y = 10$.

4. (B)

Multiply each side of the equation $\frac{x}{2} = \frac{y}{6}$ by 6 to obtain $y = 3x$. Then, use the substitution method.

$$-2x + 2y = 12 \qquad \text{Substitute } 3x \text{ for } y$$
$$-2x + 2(3x) = 12$$
$$4x = 12$$
$$x = 3$$

Therefore, the value of x is 3.

5. (A)

Substitute 3 for x and 2 for y in the first equation to solve for m.

$$3x - y = m \qquad \text{Substitute 3 for } x \text{ and 2 for } y$$
$$3(3) - 2 = m \qquad \text{Solve for } m$$
$$m = 7$$

Then, substitute 3 for x and 2 for y in the second equation to solve for n.

$$-2x + 5y = n \qquad \text{Substitute 3 for } x \text{ and 2 for } y$$
$$-2(3) + 5(2) = n \qquad \text{Solve for } n$$
$$n = 4$$

Thus, $n = 4$. Therefore, the value of $m + n = 11$.

6. (E)

In order to find the intersection point that lies on both lines $y = 2x$ and $y = 6 - x$, use the substitution method.

$$y = 6 - x \qquad \text{Substitute } 2x \text{ for } y$$
$$2x = 6 - x$$
$$3x = 6$$
$$x = 2$$

Thus, $x = 2$ and $y = 2x = 2(2) = 4$. Therefore, the x and y coordinates of the intersection point is $(2, 4)$.

7. (A)

Use the linear combinations method.

$$x - y = 1$$
$$\underline{x + y = 7} \qquad \text{Add two equations}$$
$$2x \quad = 8$$
$$x = 4$$

    www.solomonacademy.net

Since $x = 4$, substitute 4 for x in the first equation to solve for y.

$$x - y = 1 \qquad \text{Substitute 4 for } x$$
$$4 - y = 1 \qquad \text{Solve for } y$$
$$y = 3$$

Thus, $x = 4$ and $y = 3$. Therefore, the value of $3x - 2y = 3(4) - 2(3) = 6$.

8. (A)

Use the linear combinations method. Since the coefficients of x in the first and second equation are 3 and -4, find the least common multiple (LCM) of 3 and 4, which is 12. Thus, multiply the first equation by 4, and multiply the second equation by 3 to obtain the same coefficient of x, 12.

$$3x - 4y = -1 \quad \xrightarrow{\text{Multiply by 4}} \quad 12x - 16y = -4$$
$$-4x + 3y = 6 \quad \xrightarrow{\text{Multiply by 3}} \quad -12x + 9y = 18$$

Add two equations to eliminate x variables.

$$
\begin{aligned}
12x - 16y &= -4 \\
\underline{-12x + 9y} &= \underline{18} \qquad \text{Add two equations} \\
-7y &= 14 \\
y &= -2
\end{aligned}
$$

Substitute -2 for y in the first equation and solve for x.

$$3x - 4y = -1 \qquad \text{Substitute } -2 \text{ for } y$$
$$3x - 4(-2) = -1$$
$$3x = -9$$
$$x = -3$$

Thus, $x = -3$ and $y = -2$. Therefore, the solution to the system of equations is $(-3, -2)$.

9. (C)

Let x be the amount that Jason saved. Since Joshua saved \$100 more than twice the amount that Jason saved, $2x + 100$ represents the amount that Joshua saved. Joshua and Jason saved \$1000 together. Thus, the sum of x and $2x + 100$ equals 1000.

$$x + 2x + 100 = 1000$$
$$3x + 100 = 1000$$
$$3x = 900$$
$$x = 300$$

Therefore, the amount that Jason saved, x, is \$300.

10. (E)

Let's define x as the number of desks that the store sold and y as the number of chairs that the store sold. Set a system of equations using the x and y variables. First, set up the first equation in terms of a total number of desks and chairs that the store sold. The store sold a total of 23 desks and chairs: $x + y = 23$. Second, set up the second equation in terms of $240 profit that the store made after selling x numbers of desks and y numbers of chairs: $15x + 8y = 240$. Next, multiply each side of the first equation by -15.

$$x + y = 23 \quad \xrightarrow{\text{Multiply by } -15} \quad -15x - 15y = -345$$
$$15x + 8y = 240$$

Use the linear combinations method.

$$-15x - 15y = -345$$
$$\underline{15x + 8y = 240} \qquad \text{Add two equations}$$
$$-7y = -105$$
$$y = 15$$

Therefore, the number of chairs that the store sold, y, is 15.

PRACTICE SET 11

Quadratic Functions and Quadratic Equations

Quadratic functions

A quadratic function is a polynomial function of degree 2 and can be expressed in three forms.

Standard form:	$y = ax^2 + bx + c$	
Vertex form:	$y = a(x - h)^2 + k,$	Vertex (h, k)
Factored form:	$y = a(x - p)(x - q),$	where p and q are x-intercepts.

The graph of a quadratic function is a parabola. Depending on the value of the **leading coefficient**, $a\,(a \neq 0)$, the graph of a quadratic function either opens up or opens down.

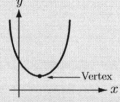

Figure 1: If $a > 0$, opens up

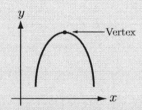

Figure 2: If $a < 0$, opens down

The vertex is a minimum point when the parabola opens up as shown in figure 1 and a maximum point when the parabola opens down as shown in figure 2. Below summarizes how to find the x-coordinate of the vertex from each form.

$$\text{Standard form: } y = ax^2 + bx + c \implies x = -\frac{b}{2a}$$

$$\text{Vertex form: } y = a(x - h)^2 + k \implies x = h$$

$$\text{Factored form: } y = a(x - p)(x - q) \implies x = \frac{p + q}{2}$$

To evaluate the y-coordinate of the vertex, substitute the value of the x-coordinate in each form.

The x-intercept and y-intercept of quadratic functions

- To solve for the x-intercept: substitute 0 for y. Then, quadratic functions becomes quadratic equations as shown below.

$$\text{Standard form: } y = ax^2 + bx + c \implies ax^2 + bx + c = 0$$

$$\text{Vertex form: } y = a(x - h)^2 + k \implies a(x - h)^2 + k = 0$$

$$\text{Factored form: } y = a(x - p)(x - q) \implies a(x - p)(x - q) = 0$$

- To solve for the y-intercept: substitute 0 for x and evaluate the y-intercept.

Solving quadratic equations

Solving a quadratic equation is finding the x-intercepts of the quadratic function. There are two methods to solve a quadratic equation: **Factoring** and **Quadratic formula**.

Factoring

Factoring is an important tool that is required for solving a quadratic equation. Factoring is opposite of expanding. Factoring a quadratic expression is to write the expression as a product of two linear terms. Below is an example.

$$(x-2)(x-3) \xrightarrow{\text{Expanding}} x^2 - 5x + 6$$
$$x^2 - 5x + 6 \xrightarrow{\text{Factoring}} (x-2)(x-3)$$

If a quadratic equation can be expressed as $x^2+(p+q)x+pq = 0$, it can be factored as $(x+p)(x+q) = 0$. For instance,

$$x^2 - 5x + 6 = 0 \implies x^2 + (-2+-3)x + (-2)(-3) = 0 \implies (x-2)(x-3) = 0$$

Once a quadratic equation is written in a factored form, use the **zero product property** to solve the equation.

$$\text{Zero product property:} \qquad \text{If } ab = 0, \text{ then } a = 0 \text{ or } b = 0$$

Thus, the solutions to $(x-2)(x-3) = 0$ is

$$(x-2)(x-3) = 0 \implies (x-2) = 0 \text{ or } (x-3) = 0 \implies x = 2 \text{ or } x = 3$$

The Quadratic Formula

The quadratic formula is a general formula for solving quadratic equations. The solutions to the quadratic equation $ax^2 + bx + c = 0$ are as follows:

$$x = \frac{-b \pm \sqrt{b^2 - 4ac}}{2a}$$

Example 1:   Find the vertex of $y = x^2 - 2x + 3$

$$x\text{-coordinate of the vertex:} \qquad x = -\frac{b}{2a} = -\frac{-2}{2(1)} = 1$$

Substitute 1 for x in $y = x^2 - 2x + 3$ to find the y-coordinate of the vertex.

$$y = x^2 - 2x + 3 = (1)^2 - 2(1) + 3 = 2$$

Therefore, the vertex of $y = x^2 - 2x + 3$ is $(1, 2)$.

Example 2:   Solve the quadratic equation $x^2 - 2x - 8 = 0$

Factor the quadratic equation $x^2 - 2x - 8 = 0$

$$x^2 - 2x - 8 = 0 \implies x^2 + (-4+2)x + (-4)(2) = 0 \implies (x-4)(x+2) = 0$$

Use the zero product property to solve the quadratic equation.

$$(x-4)(x+2) = 0 \implies (x-4) = 0 \text{ or } (x+2) = 0 \implies x = 4 \text{ or } x = -2$$

EXERCISES

1. What is the y-intercept of the quadratic function $y = x^2 - 4x + 3$?

    (A) -4 (B) -3 (C) -1
    (D) 2 (E) 3

2. Which of the following ordered pair equals the vertex of $y = (x+1)^2 - 3$?

    (A) $(1, -3)$ (B) $(-1, -3)$
    (C) $(-1, 3)$ (D) $(3, -1)$
    (E) $(-3, -1)$

3. What are the x-intercepts of the quadratic function $y = x^2 - 11x + 30$?

    (A) -5 or 6 (B) 5 or 6
    (C) 5 or -6 (D) -5 or -6
    (E) 3 or 10

4. What is the x-coordinate of the vertex if $y = 2(x-3)(x-7)$?

    (A) 5 (B) 4 (C) 3
    (D) -4 (E) -5

5. What is the maximum value of the quadratic function $y = -2(x-1)^2 + 5$?

    (A) 5 (B) 3 (C) 1
    (D) -1 (E) -5

6. If $x^2 + x + 1 = 0$, what is the value of $2x^2 + 2x + 6$?

    (A) 1 (B) 2 (C) 3
    (D) 4 (E) 5

7. If 3 is the solution to $y = x^2 - x - a$, what is the value of the other solution?

    (A) -2 (B) -1 (C) 0
    (D) 1 (E) 2

8. If a point $(3, -2)$ is on the quadratic function $y = a(x-2)(x-4)$, what is the value of a ?

    (A) -2 (B) 1 (C) 2
    (D) 4 (E) 6

9. If $y = x^2 + mx + n$ has two x-intercepts, 4 and -3, what is $m + n$?

    (A) -15 (B) -13 (C) 1
    (D) 7 (E) 15

10. If the area of a square with side length of $x - 1$ equals the perimeter of an equilateral triangle with side length of $x + 5$, what is the area of the square?

    (A) 4 (B) 9 (C) 16
    (D) 25 (E) 36

ANSWERS AND SOLUTIONS

1. (E)

   To find the y-intercept, substitute 0 for x in $y = x^2 - 4x + 3$.

   $$y = x^2 - 4x + 3$$
   $$= (0)^2 - 4(0) + 3$$
   $$= 3$$

   Therefore, the y-intercept of $y = x^2 - 4x + 3$ is 3.

2. (B)

   The quadratic function $y = (x + 1)^2 - 3$ is expressed in the vertex form.

   $$y = (x + 1)^2 - 3 \implies y = (x - (-1))^2 - 3$$

   Therefore, the vertex is $(-1, -3)$.

3. (B)

   To find the x-intercept, substitute 0 for y and solve the quadratic equation.

   $$\begin{aligned} x^2 - 11x + 30 &= 0 & &\text{Factor } x^2 - 11x + 30 \\ (x - 5)(x - 6) &= 0 & &\text{Use the zero product property} \\ x = 5 \ \ \text{or} \ \ x &= 6 \end{aligned}$$

   Therefore, the x-intercepts of the quadratic function $y = x^2 - 11x + 30$ are 5 or 6.

4. (A)

   The quadratic function is expressed in factored form. The x-coordinate of the vertex is the mean of the x-intercepts of the quadratic function. Since the x-intercepts are 3 and 7, the x-coordinate of the vertex is $x = \frac{3+7}{2} = 5$.

5. (A)

   The vertex of the quadratic function is $(1, 5)$. It is a maximum point because the quadratic function opens down $(a < 0)$. The maximum value of the quadratic function is same as y coordinate of the vertex. Therefore, the maximum value of the quadratic function is 5.

6. (D)

   Instead of solving the quadratic equation $x^2 + x + 1 = 0$ by using the quadratic formula, you can evaluate $2x^2 + 2x + 6$ directly. First, subtract 1 from each side of $x^2 + x + 1 = 0$ to obtain $x^2 + x = -1$.

   $$\begin{aligned} 2x^2 + 2x + 6 &= 2(x^2 + x) + 6 & &\text{Substitute } x^2 + x = -1 \\ &= 2(-1) + 6 \\ &= 4 \end{aligned}$$

   Therefore, the value of $2x^2 + 2x + 6$ is 4.

7. (A)

Since 3, or an ordered pair $(3, 0)$, is the solution to the quadratic equation, substitute 3 for x and 0 for y in the equation and solve for a.

$$x^2 - x - a = y \qquad \text{Substitute 3 for } x \text{ and 0 for } y$$
$$(3)^2 - (3) - a = 0$$
$$a = 6$$

$x^2 - x - a = 0$ becomes $x^2 - x - 6 = 0$. Use the factoring method to solve other solution.

$$x^2 - x - 6 = 0 \qquad \text{Use the factoring method}$$
$$(x + 2)(x - 3) = 0 \qquad \text{Use the zero product property}$$
$$x = -2 \quad \text{or} \quad x = 3$$

Therefore, other solution to the quadratic equation is -2.

8. (C)

The point $(3, -2)$ is on the quadratic function. This means that when you substitute 3 for x and -2 for y in the equation, the equation holds true.

$$y = a(x - 2)(x - 4) \qquad \text{Substitute 3 for } x \text{ and } -2 \text{ for } y$$
$$-2 = a(3 - 2)(3 - 4) \qquad \text{Solve for } a$$
$$a = 2$$

9. (B)

Write each x-intercept as a factor. $4 \implies (x - 4)$, and $-3 \implies (x - (-3))$. Then, write the quadratic function in the factored form and expand it.

$$y = (x - 4)(x + 3)$$
$$y = x^2 + 3x - 4x - 12$$
$$y = x^2 - x - 12$$

Compare $y = x^2 - x - 12$ to $y = x^2 + mx + n$. Thus, $m = -1$ and $n = -12$. Therefore, the value of $m + n = -13$.

10. (E)

The area of the square with side length of $x - 1$ is $(x - 1)^2$. The perimeter of the equilateral triangle with side length of $x + 5$ is $3(x + 5)$. Set the area and the perimeter equal to each other and solve for x. Choose the positive value of x since the length of the square is positive.

$$(x - 1)^2 = 3(x + 5)$$
$$x^2 - 2x + 1 = 3x + 15$$
$$x^2 - 5x - 14 = 0$$
$$(x + 2)(x - 7) = 0$$
$$x = -2 \quad \text{or} \quad x = 7$$

Thus, $x = 7$. Therefore, the area of the square is $(x - 1)^2 = (7 - 1)^2 = 36$.

PRACTICE SET 12

Direct Variation and Inverse Variation

Direct Variation

If y varies directly with x or y is proportional to x, then x and y have a relationship called **direct variation**. This means that as the x value gets larger, the y value gets larger. Additionally, as the x value gets smaller, the y value gets smaller. A direct variation is expressed as

$$y = kx \qquad \text{or} \qquad \frac{y}{x} = k$$

where k is the constant of variation. In most cases, you need to solve the constant of variation, k, from the given information.

Inverse Variation

If y varies inversely with x or y is inversely proportional to x, then x and y have a relationship called **inverse variation**. This means that as the x value gets larger, the y value gets smaller. Furthermore, as the x value gets smaller, the y value gets larger. An inverse variation is expressed as

$$y = \frac{k}{x} \qquad \text{or} \qquad xy = k$$

where k is the constant of variation.

Example: The variables x and y vary directly. If $x = 2$ when $y = 6$, find the value of x when $y = -3$.

Start with the equation $y = kx$. First, find the value of k using the given information.

$$y = kx \qquad\qquad \text{Substitute 2 for } x \text{ and 6 for } y$$
$$6 = 2k \qquad\qquad \text{Solve for } k$$
$$k = 3$$

Thus, the direct variation is $y = 3x$. To find the value of x when $y = -3$, substitute -3 for y in the equation $y = 3x$.

$$y = 3x \qquad\qquad \text{Substitute } -3 \text{ for } y$$
$$-3 = 3x \qquad\qquad \text{Solve for } x$$
$$x = -1$$

Therefore, the value of x when $y = -3$ is -1.

EXERCISES

1. The variables x and y varies directly. When $x = 4$, $y = 16$. Which of the following equation relates x and y ?

   (A) $x = \dfrac{4}{y}$ (B) $x = 4y$

   (C) $y = 4x$ (D) $y = \dfrac{4}{x}$

   (E) $y = \dfrac{x}{4}$

2. The variables x and y varies inversely. When $x = 4$, $y = 2$. Which of the following equation relates x and y ?

   (A) $x = 4y$ (B) $x = 8y$

   (C) $x = \dfrac{y}{8}$ (D) $y = \dfrac{8}{x}$

   (E) $y = \dfrac{x}{8}$

3. y is proportional to x. When $x = 4$, $y = 2$. What is x when $y = 4$?

   (A) 8   (B) 6   (C) 4
   (D) 2   (E) 1

4. x varies inversely with y. When $x = 3$, $y = 4$. What is y when $x = 2$?

   (A) 1   (B) 2   (C) 3
   (D) 4   (E) 6

5. Which of the following equation does not represent a direct variation?

   (A) $y = 2x$ (B) $y = \dfrac{x}{2}$

   (C) $\dfrac{y}{x} = 3$ (D) $y = 4x + 1$

   (E) $\dfrac{x}{y} = 5$

6. Which of the following equation does not represent an inverse variation?

   (A) $y = \dfrac{2}{x}$ (B) $y = \dfrac{x}{3}$

   (C) $xy = 2$ (D) $x = \dfrac{3}{y}$

   (E) $y = \dfrac{1}{2x}$

7. The variables x and y vary directly. When $y = 6$, $x = 4$. What is y when $x = -2$?

   (A) 3   (B) 1   (C) 0
   (D) -1 (E) -3

8. x is inversely proportional to y. When $x = \frac{3}{4}$, $y = \frac{8}{3}$. What is the value of x when $y = \frac{1}{4}$?

   (A) -12 (B) -8 (C) -4
   (D) 8   (E) 12

9. A study shows that the weight(in pounds) and the height(in inches) of students vary directly. When the height of a student is 5 feet, the weight of the student is 120 pounds. What is the weight of a student if the height of the student is 6 feet?

   (A) 128   (B) 132   (C) 136
   (D) 140   (E) 144

10. A high school plans a field trip to the museum. The cost per student varies inversely with a total number of students going on the field trip. When fifty students are going on the field trip, the cost per student is \$4. What is the cost per student when forty students are going on the trip to the museum?

    (A) 3   (B) 4   (C) 5
    (D) 8   (E) 10

ANSWERS AND SOLUTIONS

1. (C)

The variables x and y vary directly. Let's start with $y = kx$, where k is the constant of variation. To find the value of k, use the given information: $y = 16$ when $x = 4$. Thus, substitute 4 for x and 16 for y in the equation and find the value of k.

$$y = kx \qquad \qquad \text{Substitute 4 for } x \text{ and 16 for } y$$
$$16 = 4k \qquad \qquad \text{Solve for } k$$
$$k = 4$$

Therefore, the equation that relates x and y is $y = 4x$.

2. (D)

The variables x and y vary inversely. Let's start with $y = \frac{k}{x}$, where k is the constant of variation. To find the value of k, use the given information: $y = 2$ when $x = 4$. Thus, substitute 4 for x and 2 for y in the equation and find the value of k.

$$y = \frac{k}{x} \qquad \qquad \text{Substitute 4 for } x \text{ and 2 for } y$$
$$2 = \frac{k}{4} \qquad \qquad \text{Solve for } k$$
$$k = 8$$

Therefore, the equation that relates x and y is $y = \frac{8}{x}$.

3. (A)

y is proportional to x is the same as y varies directly with x. So, start with $y = kx$. When $x = 4$, $y = 2$. To find the value of k, substitute 4 for x and 2 for y.

$$y = kx \qquad \qquad \text{Substitute 4 for } x \text{ and 2 for } y$$
$$2 = 4k \qquad \qquad \text{Solve for } k$$
$$k = \frac{1}{2}$$

Thus, the equation that relates x and y is $y = \frac{1}{2}x$. In order to find the value of x when $y = 4$, substitute 4 for y and solve for x.

$$y = \frac{1}{2}x \qquad \qquad \text{Substitute 4 for } y$$
$$4 = \frac{1}{2}x \qquad \qquad \text{Solve for } x$$
$$x = 8$$

Therefore, the value of x when $y = 4$ is 8.

4. (E)

Since x varies inversely with y, start with $y = \frac{k}{x}$. Substitute 4 for y and 3 for x to find the value of k.

$$y = \frac{k}{x} \qquad\qquad \text{Substitute 4 for } y \text{ and 3 for } x$$

$$4 = \frac{k}{3} \qquad\qquad \text{Solve for } k$$

$$k = 12$$

Thus, the equation that relates x and y is $y = \frac{12}{x}$. Substitute 2 for x to find the value of y.

$$y = \frac{12}{x} \qquad\qquad \text{Substitute 2 for } x$$

$$y = \frac{12}{2} \qquad\qquad \text{Solve for } y$$

$$y = 6$$

Therefore, the value of y when $x = 2$ is 6.

5. (D)

The direct variation can be expressed as $y = kx$ or $\frac{y}{x} = k$, where k is the constant of variation.

(A) $y = 2x$ \qquad\qquad Direct variation

(B) $y = \frac{x}{2} \implies y = \frac{1}{2}x$ \qquad Direct variation

(C) $\frac{y}{x} = 3$ \qquad\qquad Direct variation

(D) $y = 4x + 1$ \qquad\qquad Not a direct variation

(E) $\frac{x}{y} = 5 \implies \frac{y}{x} = \frac{1}{5}$ \qquad Direct variation

Therefore, (D) is the correct answer.

6. (B)

The inverse variation can be expressed as $y = \frac{k}{x}$ or $xy = k$, where k is the constant of variation.

(A) $y = \frac{2}{x}$ \qquad\qquad Inverse variation

(B) $y = \frac{x}{3} \implies y = \frac{1}{3}x$ \qquad Direct variation

(C) $xy = 2$ \qquad\qquad Inverse variation

(D) $x = \frac{3}{y} \implies xy = 3$ \qquad Inverse variation

(E) $y = \frac{1}{2x} \implies xy = \frac{1}{2}$ \qquad Inverse variation

Therefore (B) is the correct answer.

7. (E)

The variables x and y vary directly. Let's start with $y = kx$.

$$y = kx \qquad \text{Substitute 4 for } x \text{ and 6 for } y$$
$$6 = 4k \qquad \text{Solve for } k$$
$$k = \frac{3}{2}$$

Thus, the equation that relates x and y is $y = \frac{3}{2}x$. To find the value of y, substitute -2 for x.

$$y = \frac{3}{2}x \quad \Longrightarrow \quad y = \frac{3}{2}(-2) = -3$$

Therefore, the value of y when $x = -2$ is -3.

8. (D)

The variable x is inversely proportional to y. Let's start with $xy = k$. Substitute $\frac{3}{4}$ for x and $\frac{8}{3}$ for y to find the value of k.

$$xy = k \qquad \text{Substitute } \frac{3}{4} \text{ for } x \text{ and } \frac{8}{3} \text{ for } y$$
$$\left(\frac{3}{4}\right)\left(\frac{8}{3}\right) = k \qquad \text{Solve for } k$$
$$k = 2$$

Thus, the equation that relates x and y is $xy = 2$. To find the value of x, substitute $\frac{1}{4}$ for y.

$$xy = 2 \qquad \text{Substitute } \frac{1}{4} \text{ for } y$$
$$\frac{1}{4}x = 2 \qquad \text{Solve for } x$$
$$x = 8$$

Therefore, the value of x when $y = \frac{1}{4}$ is 8.

9. (E)

Define W as the weight of the student in pounds and H as the height of the student in inches. The variables W and H vary directly. So, let's start with $W = kH$. Substitute 120 for W and 60 for H(5 feet is 60 inches).

$$W = kH \qquad \text{Substitute 120 for } W \text{ and 60 for } H$$
$$120 = 60k \qquad \text{Solve for } k$$
$$k = 2$$

Thus, the equation that relates W and H is $W = 2H$. In order to find the value of W, substitute 72 (6 feet is 72 inches) for H.

$$W = 2H = 2(72) = 144$$

Therefore, the weight of a student whose height is 6 feet is 144 pounds.

10. (C)

Let C be the cost per student and N be the total number of students going on the field trip. The variables C and N vary inversely. So, let's start with $C = \frac{k}{N}$. Substitute 4 for C and 50 for N.

$$C = \frac{k}{N} \qquad \text{Substitute 4 for } C \text{ and 50 for } N$$

$$4 = \frac{k}{50} \qquad \text{Solve for } k$$

$$k = 200$$

Thus, the equation that relates C and N is $C = \frac{200}{N}$. Then, substitute 40 for N to find the value of C.

$$C = \frac{200}{N} \qquad \text{Substitute 40 for } N$$

$$C = \frac{200}{40} \qquad \text{Solve for } C$$

$$C = 5$$

Therefore, when the forty students are going on the trip to museum, the cost per student is $5.

PRACTICE SET 13

Classifying Angles

An angle is formed by two rays and is measured in degrees (°). The angle A is expressed as $\angle A$ and the measure of the angle A is expressed as $m\angle A$.

Two angles, A and B, that have the same measure are called **congruent angles**. They are expressed as $\angle A \cong \angle B$.

Angles are classified by their measures.

- Acute angle is less than 90°.

- Right angle is 90°.

- Obtuse angle is greater than 90°.

- Straight angle is 180°.

- Vertical angles are formed by intersecting two lines. Vertical angles are congruent. In the figure below, $\angle 1$ and $\angle 3$, and $\angle 2$ and $\angle 4$ are vertical angles.

- Complementary angles are two angles whose sum of their measures is 90°. In the figure below, $\angle 5$ and $\angle 6$ are complementary angles.

- Supplementary angles are two angles whose sum of their measures is 180°. In the figure below, $\angle 7$ and $\angle 8$ are supplementary angles.

Vertical angles

Complementary angles

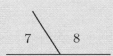

Supplementary angles

Example: Two angles are complementary. If one angle measures $x + 10$ and the other angle measures $2x + 5$, what is the value of x ?

Two angles are complementary angles if the sum of their measures is 90°.

$$x + 10 + 2x + 5 = 90$$
$$3x + 15 = 90$$
$$3x = 75$$
$$x = 25$$

When two parallel lines are cut by a third line called the transversal, the following angles are formed.

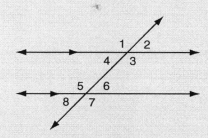

- Corresponding angles are congruent: $\angle 1 \cong \angle 5$, $\angle 4 \cong \angle 8$, $\angle 2 \cong \angle 6$, and $\angle 3 \cong \angle 7$.

- Alternate interior angles are congruent: $\angle 4 \cong \angle 6$, and $\angle 3 \cong \angle 5$.

- Alternate exterior angles are congruent: $\angle 1 \cong \angle 7$, and $\angle 2 \cong \angle 8$.

- Consecutive angles are supplementary: $\angle 4$ and $\angle 5$, and $\angle 3$ and $\angle 6$ are supplementary. In other words, $m\angle 4 + m\angle 5 = 180°$, and $m\angle 3 + m\angle 6 = 180°$.

EXERCISES

1. In the figure below, two lines intersect to form two pairs of vertical angles. What is the value of x ?

$3x + 10$

$2x + 40$

   (A) 30   (B) 50   (C) 70
   (D) 90   (E) 110

2. Two angles are supplementary. If one angle measures x and the other angle measures $x + 30$, what is the value of x ?

   (A) 60   (B) 65   (C) 70
   (D) 75   (E) 80

3. Two angles are complementary. If the measure of one angle is twice the measure of the other angle, what is the measure of the larger angle?

   (A) 20   (B) 30   (C) 40
   (D) 50   (E) 60

4. Two angles are supplementary. If the ratio of the measure of the smaller angle to that of the larger angle is 5 : 7, what is the measure of the smaller angle?

   (A) 60   (B) 65   (C) 70
   (D) 75   (E) 80

5. Two angles are complementary angles. What is the mean of the complementary angles?

   (A) 30   (B) 45   (C) 60
   (D) 75   (E) 90

Distribution or replication of any part of this page is prohibited.

6. If the two lines are parallel in the figure below, what is the value of $x + y$?

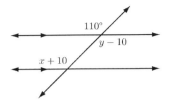

(A) 220   (B) 200   (C) 180
(D) 160   (E) 140

7. $\angle A$ and $\angle B$ are complementary angles. $\angle B$ and $\angle C$ are complementary angles. If $m\angle A = 40$, what is the $m\angle C$?

(A) 30   (B) 35   (C) 40
(D) 45   (E) 50

8. A straight angle is divided into three smaller angles. If the measures of three smaller angles are consecutive even integers, what is the measure of the largest angle?

(A) 58   (B) 59   (C) 60
(D) 61   (E) 62

9. If the two lines are parallel in the figure below, what is the value of x ?

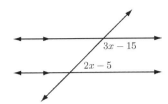

(A) 40   (B) 45   (C) 50
(D) 55   (E) 60

10. Angles A and B are supplementary angles. Angles B and C are complementary angles. If the measure of angle B is 10 less than three times the measure of angle C, what is the sum of the measures of angle A and C ?

(A) 150   (B) 140   (C) 130
(D) 120   (E) 110

ANSWERS AND SOLUTIONS

1. (A)

Vertical angles are congruent. Thus, set $3x + 10$ and $2x + 40$ equal to each other and solve for x.

$$3x + 10 = 2x + 40$$
$$x = 30$$

Therefore, the value of x is 30.

2. (D)

Since the two angles are supplementary, the sum of their measures is $180°$.

$$x + x + 30 = 180$$
$$2x + 30 = 180$$
$$x = 75$$

Therefore, the value of x is 75.

3. (E)

Define x as the measure of the smaller angle. Then, $2x$ is the measure of the larger angle. Since the two angles are complementary, the sum of their measures is $90°$.

$$x + 2x = 90$$
$$3x = 90$$
$$x = 30$$

Therefore, the measure of the larger angle is $2x = 2(30) = 60°$.

4. (D)

The ratio of the measures of the two angles is $5 : 7$. So, let $5x$ be the measure of the smaller angle and $7x$ be the measure of the larger angle. Since the two angles are supplementary, the sum of their measures is $180°$.

$$5x + 7x = 180$$
$$12x = 180$$
$$x = 15$$

Therefore, the measure of the smaller angle is $5x = 5(15) = 75°$.

5. (B)

The definition of the mean is the sum of the two numbers divided by 2. Since the two angles are complementary, the sum of their measures is $90°$. Therefore, the mean of two complementary angles is $\frac{90}{2} = 45°$.

6. (A)

The angles $110°$ and $y - 10$ are vertical angles and congruent. Thus,

$$y - 10 = 110$$
$$y = 120$$

Additionally, angles $110°$ and $x + 10$ are corresponding angles and congruent. Thus,

$$x + 10 = 110$$
$$x = 100$$

Thus, $x = 100$ and $y = 120$. Therefore, the value of $x + y = 220$.

7. (C)

The angles A and B are complementary. Thus, the sum of their measures is $90°$. Since the measure of angle A is $40°$, the measure of angle B is $50°$. Additionally, since angles B and C are complementary and the measure of angle B is $50°$, the measure of angle C is $40°$. Furthermore, the measure of angle C can be obtained according to the congruent complements theorem.

$$m\angle A + m\angle B = 90°$$
$$m\angle C + m\angle B = 90°$$
$$\therefore \quad m\angle A = m\angle C = 40°$$

8. (E)

Let x be the measure of the middle angle. Since the measures of the three angles are consecutive even integer, $x + 2$ is the measure of the largest angle and $x - 2$ is the measure of the smallest angle. Because the three angles are formed from the straight angle, the sum of their measures is $180°$.

$$x - 2 + x + x + 2 = 180$$
$$3x = 180$$
$$x = 60$$

Therefore, the measure of the largest angle is $x + 2 = 60 + 2 = 62°$.

9. (A)

Since angles $3x - 15$ and $2x - 5$ are consecutive angles, they are supplementary angles whose sum of their measures is $180°$.

$$3x - 15 + 2x - 5 = 180$$
$$5x - 20 = 180$$
$$x = 40$$

Therefore, the value of x is 40.

10. (B)

Angles B and C are complementary angles whose sum of their measures is $90°$. Let x be the measure of angle C. Then, $3x - 10$ is the measure of angle B.

$$3x - 10 + x = 90$$
$$4x - 10 = 90$$
$$x = 25$$

Thus, the measure of angle C is $25°$ and the measure of angle B is $3x - 10 = 3(25) - 10 = 65°$. Since angle A and B are supplementary, the measure of angle A is $180 - 65 = 115°$. Therefore, the sum of the measures of angle A and C is $115 + 25 = 140°$.

PRACTICE SET 14

Types and Theorems of Triangles

A triangle is a figure formed by three segments joining three points called **vertices**. A triangle ABC is expressed as $\triangle ABC$. A triangle can be classified according to its sides or its angles.

Classification by Sides

- Equilateral triangle: All sides are equal in length. The measure of each angle is $60°$.

- Isosceles triangle: Two sides are equal in length. If two sides of a triangle are congruent, then the angles (**base angles**) opposite them are congruent as shown in the figure below.

- Scalene triangle: All sides are unequal in length.

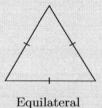 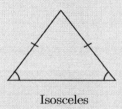 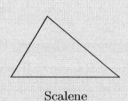

  Equilateral   Isosceles   Scalene

Classification by Angles

- Acute triangle: All interior angles measure less than $90°$.

- Right triangle: One of the interior angles measures $90°$.

- Obtuse triangle: One of the interior angles measures more than $90°$.

  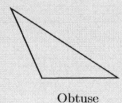

  Acute   Right   Obtuse

Area of a Triangle

- The area of a triangle is $A = \frac{1}{2}bh$, where b is base and h is height.

- The area of an equilateral triangle with side length of s is $A = \frac{\sqrt{3}}{4}s^2$.

- The areas of two triangles are equal if the bases and heights of the two triangles are the same.

Theorems of triangles

- **Triangle sum theorem**: The sum of the measures of interior angles of a triangle is $180°$.

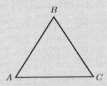

$$m\angle A + m\angle B + m\angle C = 180°$$

- **Exterior angle theorem**: The measure of an exterior angle of a triangle is equal to the sum of the measures of the two non-adjacent interior angles.

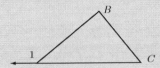

$$m\angle 1 = m\angle B + m\angle C$$

- **Triangle inequality theorem**: The length of a side of a triangle is always less than the sum of the lengths of the other two sides, but always greater than the difference of the lengths of the other two sides. For instance, let a, b, and c be the lengths of the three sides of a triangle, where $a < b < c$. Then, the triangle inequality satisfies the following.

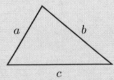

$$c - b < a < c + b$$
$$c - a < b < c + a$$
$$b - a < c < b + a$$

- **Midsegment theorem**: The segment connecting the midpoints of two sides of a triangle is called midsegment. It is parallel to the third side and is half as long.

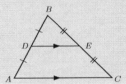

$$\overline{DE} \parallel \overline{AC}$$
$$DE = \tfrac{1}{2}AC$$

- **Law of Sines**: The largest angle is opposite the longest side and the smallest angle is opposite the shortest side. For instance, let a and b be the sides opposite the angles A and B, respectively. The law of sines satisfies the following.

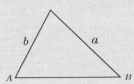

$$\text{If } m\angle B < m\angle A \implies b < a$$
$$\text{If } b < a \implies m\angle B < m\angle A$$

www.solomonacademy.net

Example: If the measures of the angles of a triangle are $x+5$, $2x+10$, and $3x+15$, what is the measure of the largest angle?

The sum of the measures of interior angles of a triangle is $180°$. Thus,

$$x + 5 + 2x + 10 + 3x + 15 = 180$$
$$6x + 30 = 180$$
$$x = 25$$

Therefore, the measure of the largest angle is $3x + 15 = 3(25) + 15 = 90°$.

EXERCISES

1. What is the area of the equilateral triangle with side length of 6 ?

   (A) $6\sqrt{3}$ (B) $9\sqrt{3}$ (C) $12\sqrt{3}$
   (D) $15\sqrt{3}$ (E) $18\sqrt{3}$

2. In the figure below, what is the measure of $\angle x$?

   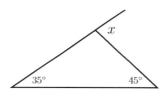

   (A) 60   (B) 65   (C) 70
   (D) 75   (E) 80

3. If the equal sides of an isosceles triangle are $3x+3$ and $2x+7$, what is the length of the equal sides of the isosceles triangle?

   (A) 18   (B) 15   (C) 12
   (D) 10   (E) 8

4. In an isosceles triangle, the ratio of the measure of the base angle to that of the vertex angle is 2 : 1, what is the measure of the vertex angle?

   (A) 18   (B) 24   (C) 36
   (D) 48   (E) 72

5. If the x and y coordinates of three vertices of a triangle are $(4,0)$, $(9,0)$ and $(2,4)$, what is the area of the triangle?

   (A) 30   (B) 20   (C) 15
   (D) 10   (E) 5

6. In the triangle below, $AC = BC$. What is $m\angle BCD$?

   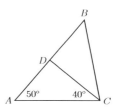

   (A) 40   (B) 45   (C) 50
   (D) 55   (E) 60

7. In the triangle below, D and E are midpoints of the sides of the triangle. If $A(-4, 2)$ and $C(2, 10)$, what is DE ?

   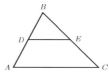

   (A) 5   (B) 6   (C) 8
   (D) 9   (E) 10

     www.solomonacademy.net

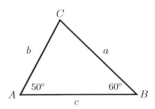

8. In triangle ABC above, a, b and c are the lengths of the sides opposite the angles A, B and C, respectively. Which of the following inequality is true?

(A) $c < a < b$ (B) $c < b < a$

(C) $a < c < b$ (D) $a < b < c$

(E) $b < c < a$

9. If the lengths of the sides of a triangle are 4, 5 and x, how many integer values of x are possible?

(A) 5   (B) 6   (C) 7

(D) 8   (E) 9

10. In triangle ABC, the points D, E and F are the midpoints of the each side of the triangle. If the perimeter of the triangle ABC is 30, what is the perimeter of the triangle DEF ?

(A) 30   (B) 25   (C) 20

(D) 18   (E) 15

ANSWERS AND SOLUTIONS

1. (B)

The area of the equilateral triangle with side length of s is $\frac{\sqrt{3}}{4}s^2$.

$$\text{Area of equilateral triangle} = \frac{\sqrt{3}}{4}(6)^2$$
$$= 9\sqrt{3}$$

Therefore, the area of the equilateral triangle with side length of 6 is $9\sqrt{3}$.

2. (E)

$\angle x$ is the exterior angle of the triangle. Since the measure of the exterior angle is equal to the sum of the measures of the two non-adjacent interior angles, $m\angle x = 35° + 45° = 80°$. Therefore, the measure of $\angle x$ is $80°$.

3. (B)

Since $3x + 3$ and $2x + 7$ are the equal sides of the isosceles triangle, set $3x + 3$ and $2x + 7$ equal to each other and solve for x.

$$3x + 3 = 2x + 7$$
$$3x - 2x = 7 - 3$$
$$x = 4$$

Therefore, the length of the equal sides of the isosceles triangle is $3x + 3 = 3(4) + 3 = 15$.

4. (C)

Since the ratio of the measure of the base angle to that of the vertex angle is $2 : 1$, let x be the measure of the vertex angle and $2x$ be the measure of the each base angle in the isosceles triangle. Since the sum of the measures of interior angles of triangle BDC is $180°$,

$$x + 2x + 2x = 180$$
$$5x = 180$$
$$x = 36$$

Therefore, the measure of the vertex angle is $36°$.

5. (D)

In the figure below, the two points $(4, 0)$ and $(9, 0)$ are on the x axis.

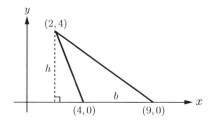

Thus, the base of the triangle is $b = 9 - 4 = 5$. Since the point $(2, 4)$ is 4 units above the x axis, the height of the triangle is $h = 4$. Therefore, the area of the triangle is $A = \frac{1}{2}bh = \frac{1}{2}(5)(4) = 10$.

6. (A)

Since $AC = BC$, triangle ACB is an isosceles triangle. $\angle B$ and $\angle A$ are base angles of the isosceles triangle and are congruent. Thus, $m\angle B = m\angle A = 50°$. Additionally, $\angle BDC$ is an exterior angle of the triangle ADC. Thus, $m\angle BDC = m\angle DAC + m\angle DCA = 90°$. Since the sum of the measures of interior angles of triangle BDC is $180°$,

$$m\angle BCD + m\angle BDC + m\angle B = 180° \qquad \text{Substitute } m\angle BDC = 90° \text{ and } m\angle B = 50°$$
$$m\angle BCD + 90° + 50° = 180°$$
$$m\angle BCD = 40°$$

7. (A)

The distance between $A(-4, 2)$ and $C(2, 10)$ is

$$AC = \sqrt{(2 - (-4))^2 + (10 - 2)^2} = \sqrt{6^2 + 8^2} = 10$$

$\overline{DE}$ is the midsegment of the triangle. It is parallel to $\overline{AC}$ and half as long. Therefore, $DE = \frac{1}{2}AC = \frac{1}{2}(10) = 5$.

8. (D)

Since the sum of the measures of interior angles of $\triangle ABC$ is $180°$, $m\angle ACB = 70°$. Thus, $\angle C$ is the largest angle and $\angle A$ is the smallest angle. According to the law of sines which states that the largest angle is opposite the longest side and the smallest angle is opposite the shortest side, c is the longest side and a is the shortest side. Therefore, $a < b < c$ is true.

9. (C)

Use the triangle inequality theorem: the length of a side of a triangle is always less than the sum of the lengths of the other two sides, but always greater than the difference of the lengths of the other two sides. Since the lengths of the sides of the triangle are 4, 5, and x,

$$5 - 4 < x < 5 + 4$$
$$1 < x < 9$$

The possible integer values of x for which $1 < x < 9$ are $x = 2, 3, \cdots, 8$. Therefore, there are 7 integer values for x.

10. (E)

In the triangle below, the perimeter of triangle ABC is $AC + AB + BC = 30$.

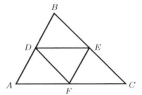

Since $\overline{DE}$, $\overline{FE}$, and $\overline{DF}$ are the midsegments of the triangle, $DE = \frac{1}{2}AC$, $FE = \frac{1}{2}AB$, and $DF = \frac{1}{2}BC$. Thus, The perimeter, P, of the triangle DEF is half the perimeter of the triangle ABC as shown below.

$$
\begin{aligned}
P &= DE + FE + DF \\
&= \frac{1}{2}AC + \frac{1}{2}AB + \frac{1}{2}BC \\
&= \frac{1}{2}(AC + AB + BC) \qquad \text{Since } AC + AB + BC = 30 \\
&= \frac{1}{2}(30) \\
&= 15
\end{aligned}
$$

Therefore, the perimeter of triangle DEF is 15.

PRACTICE SET 15

Pythagorean Theorem and Special Right Triangles

In the right triangle, shown at the right, the longest side opposite the right angle is called the **hypotenuse** and the other two sides are called **legs** of the triangle. There is a special relationship between the length of the hypotenuse and the lengths of the legs. It is known as the Pythagorean theorem.

Pythagorean Theorem
In the right triangle above, the square of the length of the hypotenuse is equal to the sum of the squares of the lengths of the legs.

$$c^2 = a^2 + b^2$$

The Pythagorean theorem is very useful because it helps you find the length of the third side of a right triangle when the lengths of two sides of the right triangle are known.

Pythagorean Triples
A Pythagorean triple consists of three positive integers, $a - b - c$. It represents integer lengths of the sides of a right triangle such that $c^2 = a^2 + b^2$. The most well-known Pythagorean triple is $3 - 4 - 5$. Below is a list of the Pythagorean triples that are required for solving math problems.

$$3 - 4 - 5 \qquad\qquad 5 - 12 - 13 \qquad\qquad 7 - 24 - 25 \qquad\qquad 8 - 15 - 17$$

Any multiple of a Pythagorean triple is also a Pythagorean triple. For instance, $6 - 8 - 10$ is a Pythagorean triple because it is a multiple of $3 - 4 - 5$. In other words, $(3 - 4 - 5) \times 2 = 6 - 8 - 10$.

45°-45°-90° Special Right Triangles

In a 45°-45°-90° right triangle, the sides of the triangle are in the ratio $1 : 1 : \sqrt{2}$, respectively. In other words, the length of the hypotenuse is $\sqrt{2}$ times the length of each leg.

$$\text{Hypotenuse} = \text{Leg} \times \sqrt{2} \quad \Longleftrightarrow \quad \text{Leg} = \frac{\text{Hypotenuse}}{\sqrt{2}}$$

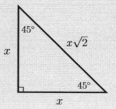

30°-60°-90° Special Right Triangles

In a 30°-60°-90° triangle, the sides of the triangle are in the ratio $1 : \sqrt{3} : 2$, respectively. In other words, the length of the hypotenuse is twice the length of the shorter leg, and the length of the longer leg is $\sqrt{3}$ times the length of the shorter leg.

$$\text{Hypotenuse} = \text{Shorter leg} \times 2$$

$$\text{Longer leg} = \text{Shorter leg} \times \sqrt{3}$$

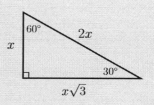

Example: In an isosceles right triangle, the length of each leg is 5. What is the length of the hypotenuse of the right triangle?

The length of the hypotenuse is $\sqrt{2}$ times the length of the each leg. Therefore, the length of the hypotenuse is $5\sqrt{2}$.

EXERCISES

1. In a right triangle, the length of the hypotenuse is 13 and the length of one leg is 5. What is the length of the other leg?

   (A) 4   (B) 6   (C) 8
   (D) 10   (E) 12

2. If the area of a square is 100, what is the length of the diagonal?

   (A) $5\sqrt{2}$ (B) $10\sqrt{2}$ (C) $10\sqrt{3}$
   (D) 20   (E) $20\sqrt{2}$

3. In an equilateral triangle with side length of 4, what is the height of the triangle?

   (A) $2\sqrt{3}$ (B) 3   (C) $3\sqrt{2}$
   (D) 4   (E) $4\sqrt{3}$

4. Two trains leave a station at the same time. One train is traveling North at a rate of 30 mph and the other train is traveling East at a rate of 40 mph. After 5 hours, how far apart are they in miles?

   (A) 200   (B) 225   (C) 250
   (D) 300   (E) 350

5. In a right triangle ABC, $m\angle C = 90°$, and $m\angle B = 60°$. If the length of the hypotenuse is 12, what is the area of the triangle?

   (A) $9\sqrt{3}$ (B) $12\sqrt{2}$ (C) $12\sqrt{3}$
   (D) $18\sqrt{2}$ (E) $18\sqrt{3}$

6. In triangle ABC below, $AB = 13$ and $AC = 14$. If $AD = 5$, what is BC ?

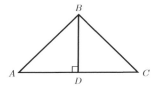

   (A) 12   (B) 13   (C) 14
   (D) 15   (E) 16

7. In an isosceles right triangle ABC, B is the right angle. If $AC = 20$, what is the perimeter of the triangle?

   (A) 20   (B) 40
   (C) $20 + 20\sqrt{2}$ (D) $20 + 30\sqrt{2}$
   (E) $40 + 20\sqrt{2}$

8. In the figure below, $AB = 1$, $BC = 2$, and $CD = 2$. What is AD ?

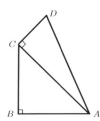

   (A) $\sqrt{29}$ (B) 4   (C) $\sqrt{13}$
   (D) 3   (E) 2

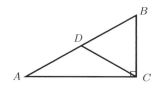

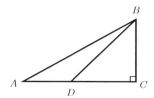

Note: Figure not drawn to scale.

9. In the triangle above, $m\angle A = 30°$ and $AD = CD$. If $AB = 20$, what is the length of $\overline{CD}$?

(A) 6   (B) 7   (C) 8

(D) 9   (E) 10

10. In the triangle above, $m\angle A = 30°$ and $m\angle BDC = 45°$. If $BC = 10$, what is the length of $\overline{AD}$?

(A) $10\sqrt{3}$ (B) $10\sqrt{3} - 10$

(C) $10\sqrt{3} + 10$ (D) $20\sqrt{3}$

(E) $20 - 10\sqrt{3}$

ANSWERS AND SOLUTIONS

1. (E)

Since the triangle is a right triangle, use the Pythagorean theorem: $c^2 = a^2 + b^2$, where c is the hypotenuse, and a and b are the legs of the triangle. The length of the hypotenuse is 13 and the length of one leg is 5. Thus, $c = 13$ and $a = 5$.

$$c^2 = a^2 + b^2$$ Substitute 13 for c and 5 for a

$$13^2 = 5^2 + b^2$$ Subtract 25 from each side

$$b^2 = 144$$ Solve for b

$$b = 12$$ Since $b > 0$

Therefore, the length of the other leg is $b = 12$. It is worth noting that the length of the other leg can be easily obtained by using the Pythagorean triple: $5 - 12 - 13$.

2. (B)

In the figure below, the area of the square is 100 which means that the length of the side of the square is 10. The square consists of two 45°-45°-90° triangles whose sides are in the ratio $1 : 1 : \sqrt{2}$.

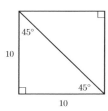

The diagonal of the square is the hypotenuse of the two triangles. The length of the hypotenuse is $\sqrt{2}$ times the length of each leg. Therefore, the length of the diagonal of the square is $10\sqrt{2}$.

3. (A)

In the figure below, the equilateral triangle consists of two 30°-60°-90° triangle whose sides are in the ratio $1 : \sqrt{3} : 2$.

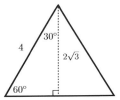

The height of the equilateral triangle is the longer leg of the 30°-60°-90° triangle and is opposite the angle 60°. Thus, the length of the height is half the length of the hypotenuse times $\sqrt{3}$. Therefore, the height of the equilateral triangle is $\frac{1}{2}(4)\sqrt{3} = 2\sqrt{3}$.

4. (C)

After 5 hours, the train heading North travels $5 \times 30 = 150$ miles and the other train heading East travels $5 \times 40 = 200$ miles. Use the Pythagorean triple to find out how far they are apart. $(3 - 4 - 5) \times 50 = 150 - 200 - 250$. Therefore, the two trains are 250 miles apart in 5 hours.

5. (E)

In the figure below, $\overline{BC}$ is the shorter leg and its length is half the length of the hypotenuse. Thus, $BC = 6$. $\overline{AC}$ is the longer leg and its length is $\sqrt{3}$ times the length of the shorter leg. Thus, $AC = 6\sqrt{3}$.

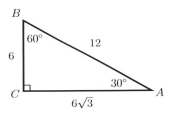

Therefore, the area of the triangle is $A = \frac{1}{2}bh = \frac{1}{2}(6\sqrt{3})(6) = 18\sqrt{3}$.

6. (D)

In the figure below, $AC = 14$ and $AD = 5$. Thus, $DC = 14 - 5 = 9$.

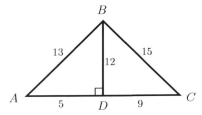

In right triangle ABD, AB, and AD are known. Use the Pythagorean triple $5 - 12 - 13$ to find BD. Thus, $BD = 12$. In right triangle CBD, CD, and BD are known. Use a multiple of the Pythagorean triple $3 - 4 - 5$ to find BC: $(3 - 4 - 5) \times 3 = 9 - 12 - 15$. Therefore, $BC = 15$.

7. (C)

An isosceles right triangle is a 45°-45°-90° right triangle whose sides are in the ratio $1 : 1 : \sqrt{2}$. AC is the length of the hypotenuse of the isosceles right triangle and $AC = 20$. The length of each leg is $\frac{\text{hypotenuse}}{\sqrt{2}} = \frac{20}{\sqrt{2}} = 10\sqrt{2}$. Therefore, the perimeter of the isosceles right triangle is

$$\text{Perimeter of isosceles right triangle} = 20 + 10\sqrt{2} + 10\sqrt{2}$$
$$= 20 + 20\sqrt{2}$$

8. (D)

In the figure below, find AC using the Pythagorean theorem.

$$AC^2 = AB^2 + BC^2 = 1^2 + 2^2$$
$$AC^2 = 5 \quad \Longrightarrow \quad AC = \sqrt{5}$$

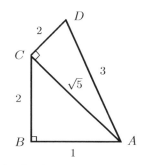

Since AC and CD are known, use the Pythagorean theorem again to find AD.

$$AD^2 = AC^2 + CD^2 = (\sqrt{5})^2 + 2^2$$
$$AD^2 = 9 \quad \Longrightarrow \quad AD = 3$$

9. (E)

In the figure below, triangle ADC is an isosceles triangle. Thus, $m\angle A = m\angle DCA = 30°$.

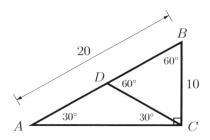

$\angle BDC$ is an exterior angle of the triangle ADC so that $m\angle BDC = m\angle A + m\angle DCA = 60°$. In the right triangle ABC, $m\angle A = 30°$ and $m\angle B = 60°$. Thus, the triangle DBC is an equilateral triangle. More over, $\overline{BC}$ is the shorter leg of the 30°-60°-90° right triangle ABC and its length is half the length of the hypotenuse. Thus, $BC = 10$. Since $\overline{CD} \cong \overline{BC}$, the length of $\overline{CD}$ is 10.

www.solomonacademy.net

10. (B)

In the figure below, $m\angle BDC = m\angle DBC = 45°$ so that triangle DBC is an isosceles right triangle. Since $\overline{BC}$ and $\overline{DC}$ are legs of the isosceles right triangle, $BC = DC = 10$.

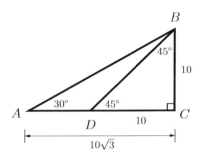

In the right triangle ABC, $m\angle A = 30°$ and $m\angle ABC = 60°$. Thus, triangle ABC is a 30°-60°-90° right triangle. Since $\overline{AC}$ is the longer leg and $\overline{BC}$ is the shorter leg of triangle ABC, the length of $\overline{AC}$ is $\sqrt{3}$ times the length of the $\overline{BC}$. Thus, $AC = 10\sqrt{3}$. Since the length of $\overline{AD}$ equals the length of $\overline{AC}$ minus the length of $\overline{DC}$,

$$AD = AC - DC$$
$$= 10\sqrt{3} - 10$$

Therefore, the length of $\overline{AD}$ is $10\sqrt{3} - 10$.

PRACTICE SET 16

Properties and Areas of Quadrilaterals

A **quadrilateral** is a four-sided closed figure. It has four straight sides and four vertices. The sum of the measures of interior angles is 360°.

There are special types of quadrilaterals: parallelogram, rectangle, rhombus, square, and trapezoid. Some quadrilaterals can be other types of the quadrilaterals. For instance, a square can be a rectangle as well as a parallelogram. Below shows the properties and areas of the special types of the quadrilaterals.

Parallelogram

- Opposite sides are parallel. $\overline{AB} \parallel \overline{DC}$, $\overline{BC} \parallel \overline{AD}$

- Opposite sides are congruent. $\overline{AB} \cong \overline{DC}$, $\overline{BC} \cong \overline{AD}$

- Opposite angles are congruent. $\angle A \cong \angle C$, $\angle B \cong \angle D$

- Consecutive angles are supplementary.
  $m\angle A + m\angle D = 180°$, $m\angle A + m\angle B = 180°$

- Diagonals bisect each other. $\overline{AE} \cong \overline{CE}$, $\overline{BE} \cong \overline{DE}$

- Area $= bh$, where b is the base and h is the height.

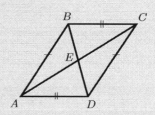

Rhombus

- A parallelogram with four congruent sides. Thus, a rhombus has all the properties of a parallelogram.

- Diagonals are perpendicular to each other.

- Diagonals bisect a pair of opposite angles.
  $\angle 1 \cong \angle 5$, $\angle 8 \cong \angle 4$, $\angle 2 \cong \angle 6$, $\angle 3 \cong \angle 7$

- Area $= \frac{1}{2}d_1 d_2$, where d_1 and d_2 are the lengths of the diagonals.

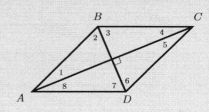

Rectangle

- A parallelogram with four right angles. Thus, a rectangle has all the properties of a parallelogram.

- Diagonals are equal in length.

- Area $= lw$, where l is the length and w is the width.

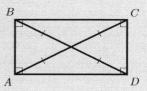

Square

- A square is a rhombus and a rectangle. Thus, a square has all the properties of a rhombus and a rectangle.

- Diagonals are equal in length.

- Area $= S^2$, where S is the length of the side. Or, Area $= \frac{1}{2}d^2$, where d is the length of the diagonal.

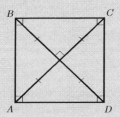

Trapezoid

- A quadrilateral with exactly one pair of parallel sides. $\overline{BC} \parallel \overline{AD}$

- Area $= \frac{1}{2}(b_1 + b_2)h$, where b_1 is the length of the top side, b_2 is the length of the bottom side, and h is the height.

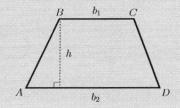

Isosceles Trapezoid

- A trapezoid with congruent nonparallel sides (Legs).

- The base angles are congruent.

- Diagonals are congruent.

- Area $= \frac{1}{2}(b_1 + b_2)h$, where b_1 is the length of the top side, b_2 is the length of the bottom side, and h is the height.

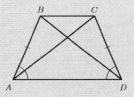

Example: If the measures of the interior angles of a quadrilateral are $40°$, $x + 30$, $2x$, and $3x - 10$, what is the value of x ?

The sum of the measures of the interior angles of a quadrilateral is $360°$. Thus,

$$40 + x + 30 + 2x + 3x - 10 = 360$$
$$6x + 60 = 360$$
$$6x = 300$$
$$x = 50$$

Therefore, the value of x is $50°$.

EXERCISES

1. If the length of the diagonal of the square is 10, what is the area of the square?

   (A) 150   (B) 100   (C) 75
   (D) 50   (E) 25

2. If the lengths of two sides of the rhombus are $x + 15$ and $3x - 7$, what is the length of each side of the rhombus?

   (A) 11   (B) 18   (C) 26
   (D) 33   (E) 36

3. In the parallelogram below, the measures of the two interior angles are given. What is the value of x ?

   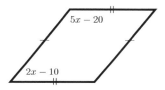

   (A) 20   (B) 30   (C) 40
   (D) 50   (E) 60

4. The lengths of the top side and the bottom side of the trapezoid are 5 and 15, respectively. If the area of the trapezoid is 100, what is the height of the trapezoid?

   (A) 4   (B) 6   (C) 8
   (D) 10   (E) 12

5. In the parallelogram $ABCD$, the diagonals AC and BD are equal in length. What is the measure of the angle A ?

   (A) 30   (B) 45   (C) 60
   (D) 75   (E) 90

6. The length of a square is increased by 4 and the width of a square is decreased by 2 so that the square becomes a rectangle. If the area of the rectangle is the same as the area of the square, what is the length of the square?

   (A) 4   (B) 5   (C) 6
   (D) 7   (E) 8

7. If the lengths of the diagonals of the rhombus are 24 and 10, what is the perimeter of the rhombus?

   (A) 136   (B) 72   (C) 52
   (D) 36   (E) 13

8. In the square $ABCD$, the x and y coordinates of vertices, A and C are $(-2, -3)$ and $(3, 3)$, respectively. What is the slope of $\overline{BD}$?

   (A) $\dfrac{6}{5}$ (B) $-\dfrac{6}{5}$ (C) $-\dfrac{5}{6}$
   (D) $\dfrac{5}{6}$ (E) $\dfrac{3}{4}$

9. If a smaller square is inscribed in a larger square, what is the ratio of the area of the smaller square to that of the larger square?

   (A) $4 : 1$ (B) $2 : 1$ (C) $1 : 4$
   (D) $1 : 3$ (E) $1 : 2$

10. In the isosceles trapezoid $ABCD$, $AB = 5$, $BC = 10$ and $AD = 16$, what is the height of the isosceles trapezoid?

    (A) 3   (B) 4   (C) 5
    (D) 6   (E) 7

ANSWERS AND SOLUTIONS

1. **(D)**

   The diagonals of a square are equal in length. Since the square is a rhombus and the length of the diagonal of the square is 10, use the area of rhombus formula: Area $= \frac{1}{2}d^2$, where d is the length of the diagonal of a square.

   $$\text{Area of rhombus} = \frac{1}{2}d^2 = \frac{1}{2}(10)^2 = 50$$

   Therefore, the area of the square is 50.

2. **(C)**

   A rhombus has four congruent sides. Thus, $3x - 7$ and $x + 15$ are the same.

   $$3x - 7 = x + 15$$
   $$2x = 22$$
   $$x = 11$$

   Therefore, the length of each side of the rhombus is $x + 15 = 11 + 15 = 26$.

3. **(B)**

   The angles $5x - 20$ and $2x - 10$ are consecutive angles and are supplementary. Thus, the sum of their measures is $180°$.

   $$5x - 20 + 2x - 10 = 180$$
   $$7x - 30 = 180$$
   $$x = 30$$

   Therefore, the value of x is 30.

4. **(D)**

   Use the area of trapezoid formula: $A = \frac{1}{2}(b_1 + b_2)h$, where b_1 is the length of the top side, b_2 is the length of the bottom side, and h is the height. Substitute 5 for b_1, 15 for b_2, and 100 for A to find the height of the trapezoid.

   $$A = \frac{1}{2}(b_1 + b_2)h$$
   $$100 = \frac{1}{2}(5 + 15)h$$
   $$h = 10$$

   Therefore, the height of the trapezoid is 10.

5. **(E)**

   If the diagonals of the parallelogram are equal in length, the parallelogram is either a rectangle or a square. Since a rectangle and square has four right angles, the measure of angle A is $90°$.

6. (A)

Let x be the side length of the square. Since the length of the square is increased by 4 and the width of the square is decreased by 2, $x + 4$ is the length of the rectangle and $x - 2$ is the width of the rectangle. Thus, the area of the square is x^2 and the area of the rectangle is $(x + 4)(x - 2)$. Since the area of the square is the same as the area of the rectangle, set x^2 and $(x + 4)(x - 2)$ equal to each other and solve for x.

$$
\begin{aligned}
(x + 4)(x - 2) &= x^2 \qquad &&\text{Expand } (x + 4)(x - 2) \\
x^2 - 2x + 4x - 8 &= x^2 \qquad &&\text{Cancel out } x^2 \\
2x - 8 &= 0 \qquad &&\text{Solve for } x \\
x &= 4
\end{aligned}
$$

Therefore, the length of the square is 4.

7. (C)

In the rhombus below, the lengths of the diagonals are 24 and 12. Since the diagonals bisect each other and they are perpendicular, $AC = \frac{1}{2}(24) = 12$, $BC = \frac{1}{2}(10) = 5$, and $\triangle ABC$ is a right triangle.

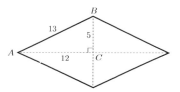

In order to find the length of the side of the rhombus which is the hypotenuse of $\triangle ABC$, use the Pythagorean theorem: $AB^2 = 5^2 + 12^2$ or use the Pythagorean triple $5 - 12 - 13$. Thus, the length of the side of the rhombus, AB, is 13. Therefore, the perimeter of the rhombus is $13 \times 4 = 52$.

8. (C)

In the square below, the x and y coordinates of vertices A and C are $(-2, -3)$ and $(3, 3)$, respectively. Find the slope of $\overline{AC}$ by using the slope formula: Slope $= \frac{y_2 - y_1}{x_2 - x_1}$. Thus,

$$
\text{Slope of } \overline{AC} = \frac{3 - (-3)}{3 - (-2)} = \frac{6}{5}
$$

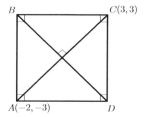

Since the diagonals of the square, $\overline{AC}$ and $\overline{BD}$, are perpendicular to each other, the slope of $\overline{BD}$ is the negative reciprocal of the slope of $\overline{AC}$ or $-\frac{5}{6}$. Therefore, the slope of $\overline{BD}$ is $-\frac{5}{6}$.

9. (E)

In the figure below, the smaller square is inscribed in the larger square. The area of the smaller square is shaded.

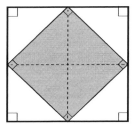

The two diagonals of the smaller square are drawn with the dotted lines. So, it's easy to see the area of shaded region equals the area of the unshaded region. Since the area of the larger square equals the sum of the areas of shaded and unshaded regions, the area of the larger square is twice the area of the shaded region which represents the area of the smaller square. Therefore, the ratio of the area of the smaller square to that of the larger square is 1 : 2.

10. (B)

In the isosceles trapezoid below, the heights are drawn from $\overline{BC}$ to $\overline{AD}$ so that $FE = 10$.

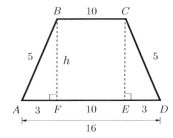

Since $\triangle ABF \cong \triangle DCE$, $AF = DE = 3$. Triangle ABF is a right triangle. In order to find the height of the isosceles trapezoid, BF, use the Pythagorean theorem: $5^2 = 3^2 + BF^2$, or use the Pythagorean triple $3 - 4 - 5$. Thus, $BF = 4$. Therefore, the height of the isosceles trapezoid is 4.

PRACTICE SET 17

Similar Polygons

Two polygons are **similar** if their corresponding angles are congruent and the ratios of their corresponding sides are equal. The symbol $\sim$ is used to indicate that two polygons are similar.

In the figures shown at right, $\triangle ABC \sim \triangle DEF$. Therefore,

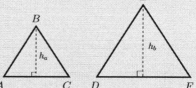

$$\angle A \cong \angle D, \angle B \cong \angle E, \angle C \cong \angle F$$

$$\frac{AB}{DE} = \frac{BC}{EF} = \frac{AC}{DF}$$

Theorems

- If two polygons are similar, the ratio of any pair of corresponding segments (heights or medians) is equal to the ratio of any pair of corresponding sides. If $\triangle ABC \sim \triangle DEF$ shown above, the ratio of heights is equal to

$$\frac{h_a}{h_b} = \frac{AB}{DE} = \frac{BC}{EF} = \frac{AC}{DF}$$

- If two polygons are similar, the ratio of their perimeters is equal to the ratio of any pair of corresponding sides. If $\triangle ABC \sim \triangle DEF$, the ratio of perimeters is equal to

$$\frac{\text{Perimeter of } \triangle ABC}{\text{Perimeter of } \triangle DEF} = \frac{AB}{DE} = \frac{BC}{EF} = \frac{AC}{DF}$$

- If two polygons are similar, the ratio of their areas is equal to the square of the ratio of any pair of corresponding sides. If $\triangle ABC \sim \triangle DEF$, the ratio of areas is equal to

$$\frac{\text{Area of } \triangle ABC}{\text{Area of } \triangle DEF} = \left(\frac{AB}{DE}\right)^2 = \left(\frac{BC}{EF}\right)^2 = \left(\frac{AC}{DF}\right)^2$$

Example: If there are two equilateral triangles with side lengths of 2 and 3 respectively, what is the ratio of the perimeter of the smaller equilateral triangle to that of the larger equilateral triangle?

Although you may find the perimeter of each equilateral triangle and the ratio of the perimeters, use the theorem such that if the two polygons are similar, the ratio of their perimeters is equal to the ratio of any pair of corresponding sides. Since two equilateral triangles are similar and have side lengths of 2 and 3, the ratio of the perimeter of the smaller equilateral triangle to that of the larger equilateral triangle is $2 : 3$.

EXERCISES

1. In the figure below, the two rectangles are similar. What is the value of x ?

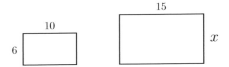

   (A) 4   (B) 5   (C) 6
   (D) 8   (E) 9

2. $\triangle ABC \sim \triangle DEF$. The lengths of the sides of $\triangle ABC$ are 2, 3, and 4. If the length of the shortest side of $\triangle DEF$ is 6, what is the length of the longest side of $\triangle DEF$?

   (A) 6   (B) 9   (C) 12
   (D) 15   (E) 18

3. In the figure below, $\triangle ABC \sim \triangle DEF$. What is the value of x ?

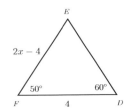
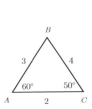

   (A) 4   (B) 5   (C) 6
   (D) 8   (E) 12

4. Triangles ABC and DEF are equilateral triangles. If the ratio of the height of triangle ABC to that of triangle DEF is 2 : 3, what is the ratio of the area of triangle ABC to that of triangle DEF ?

   (A) 2 : 3   (B) 3 : 2   (C) 2 : 5
   (D) 9 : 4   (E) 4 : 9

5. The ratio of the side lengths of the two squares is 1 : 2. If the sum of their areas is 150, what is the area of the larger square?

   (A) 130   (B) 120   (C) 110
   (D) 100   (E) 90

6. In the figure below, $\triangle ABC \sim \triangle DEF$. What is the measure of the angle E ?

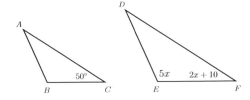

   (A) 130   (B) 120   (C) 110
   (D) 100   (E) 90

7. If the length and width of a rectangle are increased by 30% each, how much bigger is the area of the larger rectangle than the area of the smaller rectangle?

   (A) 30%   (B) 45%   (C) 60%
   (D) 69%   (E) 90%

8. In the figure below, $AB \parallel DE$. If $AC = 3$ and $EC = 6$, what is the ratio of the perimeter of $\triangle EDC$ to that of $\triangle ABC$?

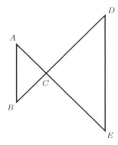

   (A) 4 : 1   (B) 3 : 1   (C) 2 : 1
   (D) 1 : 2   (E) 1 : 4

9. In the figure below, $AB = 10$ and $BD = 2$. If $DE = 6$, then what is AC?

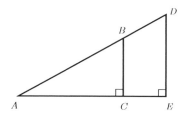

(A) $5\sqrt{3}$ (B) $6\sqrt{2}$ (C) 10

(D) $8\sqrt{2}$ (E) $10\sqrt{3}$

10. In the figure below, $AD = 8$ and $DB = 2$. What is the length of $\overline{CD}$?

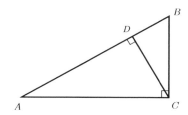

(A) 3   (B) 4   (C) 5

(D) 6   (E) 7

ANSWERS AND SOLUTIONS

1. (E)

   Since the rectangles are similar, the ratio of their corresponding sides are equal. Let's set up a proportion to find the value of x.

   $$\frac{10}{15} = \frac{6}{x} \qquad \text{Cross Multiply}$$
   $$10x = 90$$
   $$x = 9$$

   Therefore, the value of x is 9.

2. (C)

   The lengths of the shortest side of $\triangle ABC$ and $\triangle DEF$ are 2 and 6, respectively. Thus, the ratio of lengths of the shortest side is 1:3. In other words, the lengths of the sides of $\triangle DEF$ are three times longer than the lengths of sides of $\triangle ABC$. Thus, the lengths of the sides of $\triangle DEF$ are $(2, 3, 4) \times 3 = (6, 9, 12)$. Therefore, the length of the longest side of $\triangle DEF$ is 12.

3. (C)

   In the figure below, $\triangle ABC \sim \triangle DEF$ such that $\overline{BC}$ corresponds to $\overline{EF}$.

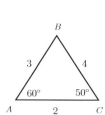

     www.solomonacademy.net

Let's set a proportion up and solve for x.

$$\frac{4}{2x-4} = \frac{AC}{DF}$$

$AC = 2$ and $DF = 4$

$$\frac{4}{2x-4} = \frac{1}{2}$$

Cross Multiply

$$2x - 4 = 8$$

$$x = 6$$

Therefore, the value of x is 6.

4. (E)

The equilateral triangles ABC and DEF are similar. Thus, the ratio of their areas is equal to the square of the ratio of any pair of corresponding sides, which are the heights of the triangles in this case. Thus,

$$\frac{\text{Area of } \triangle ABC}{\text{Area of } \triangle DEF} = \left(\frac{\text{Height of } \triangle ABC}{\text{Height of } \triangle DEF}\right)^2 = \left(\frac{2}{3}\right)^2 = \frac{4}{9}$$

Therefore, the ratio of the area of triangle ABC to that of triangle DEF is $4 : 9$.

5. (B)

The two squares are similar. Since the ratio of the side lengths of the squares is $1 : 2$, the ratio of the areas of the squares is $1 : 4$. Let x be the area of the smaller square and $4x$ be the area of the larger square. The sum of the areas of the two squares is $5x = 150$. Thus, $x = 30$. Therefore, the area of the larger square is $4x = 4(30) = 120$.

6. (D)

$\triangle ABC \sim \triangle DEF$ so that $m\angle C = m\angle F$. Thus, $2x + 10 = 50 \implies x = 20$. Therefore, the measure of the angle E is $5x = 5(20) = 100$.

7. (D)

Let x and y be the length and width of the rectangle, respectively. The area of the rectangle is xy. Since the length and the width of the rectangle is increased by 30%, the length and the width of the larger rectangle can be expressed as $1.3x$ and $1.3y$, respectively. Thus, the area of the larger rectangle is $1.3x \times 1.3y = 1.69xy$. Therefore, the area of the larger rectangle, $1.69xy$, is 69% bigger than the area of the smaller rectangle, xy.

8. (C)

Since $AB \parallel DE$, $\angle A$ and $\angle E$ are alternate interior angles so that $\angle A \cong \angle E$. For the same reason, $\angle B \cong \angle D$. Additionally, $\angle C$ is the vertex angle of both $\triangle ABC$ and $\triangle EDC$. Thus, $\triangle ABC \sim \triangle EDC$. Since $AC = 3$ and $EC = 6$,

$$\frac{\text{Perimeter of } \triangle EDC}{\text{Perimeter of } \triangle ABC} = \frac{EC}{AC} = \frac{6}{3} = \frac{2}{1}$$

Therefore, the ratio of the perimeter of $\triangle EDC$ to that of $\triangle ABC$ is $2 : 1$.

9. (A)

$\overline{BC} \perp \overline{AE}$ and $\overline{DE} \perp \overline{AE}$ which means that $\overline{BC} \parallel \overline{DE}$. $\angle A$ is the common angle for both triangles $\triangle ABC$ and $\triangle ADE$. Since $\overline{BC} \parallel \overline{DE}$, $\angle ABC$ and $\angle ADE$ are corresponding angles so that $\angle ABC \cong \angle ADE$. Thus, $\triangle ABC \sim \triangle ADE$. Because the ratio of corresponding sides are equal in similar triangles, $AB : AD = 10 : 12 = 5 : 6$ and $BC : DE = 5 : 6$. Since $DE = 6$, $BC = 5$. $\triangle ABC$ is a right triangle where $AB = 10$ and $BC = 5$. Use the Pythagorean theorem to solve for AC. Since AC represents the length of the side of the triangle, choose the positive value for AC.

$$AC^2 + 5^2 = 10^2$$
$$AC^2 = 75$$
$$AC = 5\sqrt{3} \qquad \text{Since } AC > 0$$

10. (B)

Let p and q be the complementary angles such that $m\angle p + m\angle q = 90°$. Assigning p and q to the angles in the figure below makes it easier to see which two triangles are similar. In the right triangle ADC, $\angle A$ and $\angle ACD$ are complementary angles. Let's assign p to $\angle A$, and q to $\angle ACD$ as shown in the figure below.

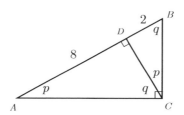

In the right triangle ABC, $\angle A$ and $\angle B$ are complementary angles. Since p is already assigned to $\angle A$, assign q to $\angle B$. Additionally, in the right triangle BCD, $\angle B$ and $\angle BCD$ are complementary angles. Thus, assign p to $\angle BCD$ since q is already assigned to $\angle B$.

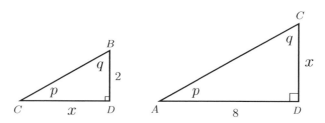

Using the complementary angles p and q, $\triangle CBD \sim \triangle ACD$. Let x be the length of $\overline{CD}$ and set up a proportion.

$$\frac{x}{2} = \frac{8}{x}$$
$$x^2 = 16$$
$$x = 4 \qquad x > 0$$

Therefore, the length of $\overline{CD}$ is 4.

     www.solomonacademy.net

PRACTICE SET 18

Properties and Theorems of Circles

Circles

A **circle** is a set of all points that are equidistant from a fixed point called the **center** of the circle. The distance from the center to a point on the circle is the **radius** of the circle. If the radius of a circle, r, is given, the circumference, C, and the area, A, are as follows:

$$C = 2\pi r, \qquad A = \pi r^2$$

A **chord** is a line segment whose endpoints are on the circle. A **diameter** is a chord that passes through the center of the circle. A diameter is the longest chord and is twice the length of the radius.
In figure 1, O is the center, $\overline{OC}$ is the radius, and $\overline{AB}$ is a chord and a diameter.

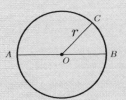

Figure 1

The diameter or the radius of the circle is a perpendicular bisector of a chord. In figure 2, the radius $\overline{OC}$ is a perpendicular bisector of chord $\overline{AB}$. $\overline{OC}$ divides $\overline{AB}$ into two equal smaller segments and $\overline{OC} \perp \overline{AB}$.

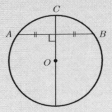

Figure 2

Tangent lines to a circle

A **tangent line** is a line that is drawn from outside of the circle and touches the circle at exactly one point. The point at which a tangent line touches the circle is the **point of tangency**.

A tangent line is **perpendicular** to the radius drawn to the point of tangency. In figure 3, A is the point of tangency and l is the tangent line to the circle. $\overline{OA} \perp l$.

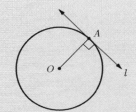

Figure 3

Central angles and Inscribed angles

A **central angle** is an angle whose vertex is on the center of the circle and whose sides are the radii. An **inscribed angle** is an angle whose vertex is on the circle and whose sides are the chords of the circle. In figure 4, $\angle AOB$ is the central angle and $\angle ACB$ is the inscribed angle.

If the central angle and the inscribed angle contains the same part of the circumference of the circle, the measure of the inscribed angle is half the measure of the central angle. In figure 4,

$$m\angle ACB = \frac{1}{2}m\angle AOB$$

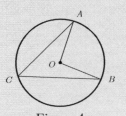

Figure 4

Inscribed Triangles

A triangle inscribed in a semicircle is a right triangle. The hypotenuse of a right triangle inscribed in a semicircle is the diameter of the semicircle. In figure 5, the central angle is 180° and $\angle C$ is the inscribed angle. Since the measure of the inscribed angle is half the measure of the central angle,

$$m\angle C = \frac{1}{2} \text{ central angle} = \frac{1}{2}(180°) = 90°$$

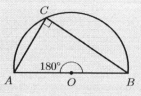

Figure 5

Inscribed Circles and Circumscribed Circles

An **inscribed circle** is a circle that lies in a polygon and touches all sides of the polygon. In figure 6, a circle is inscribed in the square.

$$\text{Radius of inscribed circle} = \frac{1}{2} \times \text{Length of square}$$

A **circumscribed circle** is a circle that passes through all the vertices of the polygon. In general, a circle is circumscribed about a polygon means exactly the same as a polygon is inscribed in the circle.

In figure 7, a square is inscribed in the circle. The diagonal of the square is the diameter of the circle. Triangle ABC is a 45°-45°-90° special right triangle. There are relationships between the length of the square and the radius of the circumscribed circle.

$$\text{Length of square} = \text{Radius} \times \sqrt{2}$$

$$\text{Radius} = \text{Length of square} \times \frac{\sqrt{2}}{2}$$

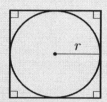

Figure 6

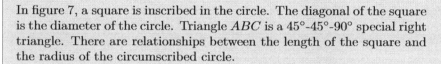

Figure 7

Arc length and Area of a sector

An arc is a part of the circumference of a circle. A part can be expressed as the ratio of the central angle to 360°. An arc is shown in figure 8.

$$\text{Arc length} = 2\pi r \times \frac{\theta}{360°}, \quad \text{where } \theta \text{ is the central angle}$$

A sector is a part of the area of a circle. A part can be expressed as the ratio of the central angle to 360°. A sector is shown in figure 8.

$$\text{Area of a sector} = \pi r^2 \times \frac{\theta}{360°}, \quad \text{where } \theta \text{ is the central angle}$$

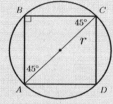

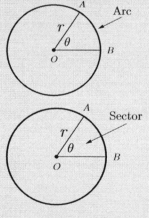

Figure 8

Example: If the radius of a circle is 6 and the measure of the central angle is 120°, what is the arc length of the circle?

$$\text{Arc length} = 2\pi r \times \frac{120°}{360°}$$
$$= 2\pi(6) \times \frac{1}{3}$$
$$= 4\pi$$

EXERCISES

1. In the figure below, if $m\angle AOB = 70°$, what is $m\angle ABO$?

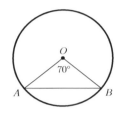

   (A) 50°   (B) 55°   (C) 60°

   (D) 65°   (E) 70°

2. The x and y coordinates of the center of a circle is $(1, 2)$. If a point is on the circle and has the x and y coordinates $(7, 10)$, what is the radius of the circle?

   (A) 6   (B) 8   (C) 10

   (D) 12   (E) 14

3. If a circle is inscribed in a square with side length of 10, what is the circumference of the circle?

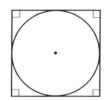

   (A) 2π (B) 4π (C) 6π

   (D) 8π (E) 10π

4. There are two concentric circles with radii 2 and 3, respectively. What is the area of the region that lies outside the smaller circle and inside the larger circle?

   (A) π (B) 2π (C) 3π

   (D) 4π (E) 5π

5. In the figure below, what is the area of the shaded region if the radius of the circle is 6 ?

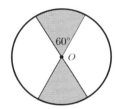

   (A) 14π (B) 12π (C) 10π

   (D) 8π (E) 6π

6. In the figure below, the radius of the circle is 5 and $AB = 5\sqrt{3}$. What is OB ?

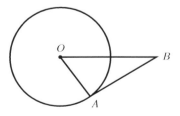

   (A) 4   (B) 6   (C) 8

   (D) 10   (E) 12

7. In the figure below, a square with side length of 6 is inscribed in the circle. What is the area of the circle?

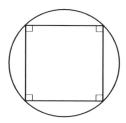

(A) 12π (B) 15π (C) 18π

(D) 21π (E) 24π

8. In the figure below, $\triangle ABC$ is inscribed in the semicircle. If $m\angle BAC = 60°$ and the radius of the circle is 10, what is AB ?

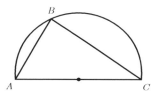

(A) 8   (B) 10   (C) $10\sqrt{2}$

(D) $10\sqrt{3}$ (E) 15

9. In the figure below, $AB = 8$ and $OC = 8$. What is the area of $\triangle ABO$?

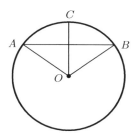

(A) $16\sqrt{3}$ (B) $16\sqrt{2}$ (C) $12\sqrt{3}$

(D) $12\sqrt{2}$ (E) 12

10. In the figure below, the radius of the circle is 12. If $m\angle A = 60°$, what is the perimeter of the shaded region?

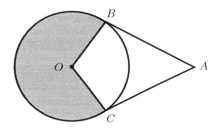

(A) 16π (B) 24π

(C) $16\pi + 24$ (D) $24\pi + 24$

(E) $32\pi + 24$

ANSWERS AND SOLUTIONS

1. (B)

$\overline{OA}$ and $\overline{OB}$ are the radii of the circle so that $OA = OB$. Thus, $\triangle AOB$ is an isosceles triangle. Since the sum of the measures of interior angles of a triangle is $180°$ and the base angles of an isosceles triangle are congruent, $m\angle BAO = m\angle ABO = \frac{180-70}{2} = 55°$.

2. (C)

The distance between the center of the circle, $(1, 2)$, and the point on the circle, $(7, 10)$, is the same as the radius. In order to find the radius, use the distance formula.

$$\text{Radius} = \sqrt{(x_2 - x_1)^2 + (y_2 - y_1)^2} = \sqrt{(7 - 1)^2 + (10 - 2)^2} = \sqrt{100} = 10$$

Therefore, the radius of the circle is 10.

3. (E)

The radius of the circle is half the length of the square. Thus, the radius is 5. Therefore, the circumference of the circle is $2\pi r = 2\pi(5) = 10\pi$.

4. (E)

Concentric circles share the same center. In the figure below, the area of the region that lies outside the smaller circle and inside the larger circle is shaded.

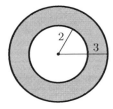

To get the area of the shaded region, subtract the area of the smaller circle from the area of the larger circle. Therefore, the area of the shaded region is $\pi(3)^2 - \pi(2)^2 = 5\pi$.

5. (B)

In the figure below, the shaded region consists of two sectors that have the same central angles, 60°.

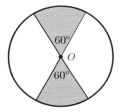

The area of each sector is $\pi(6)^2 \times \frac{60°}{360°} = 6\pi$. Therefore, the area of the shaded region is $2 \times 6\pi = 12\pi$.

6. (D)

In the figure below, $\overline{OA}$ is the radius of the circle and $\overline{AB}$ is tangent to the circle at A. The tangent line is perpendicular to the radius drawn to the point of tangency, A. Thus, $\triangle OAB$ is the right triangle.

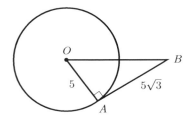

Use the Pythagorean Theorem to find OB.

$$OB^2 = 5^2 + (5\sqrt{3})^2 = 100$$
$$OB = 10 \qquad (OB > 0)$$

7. (C)

In the figure below, the diagonal of the square is the diameter of the circle.

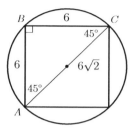

$\triangle ABC$ is a 45°-45°-90° special right triangle whose sides are in the ratio $1 : 1 : \sqrt{2}$. Since $AB = BC = 6$, $AC = 6\sqrt{2}$. Thus, the diameter and the radius of the circle are $6\sqrt{2}$ and $3\sqrt{2}$, respectively. Therefore, the area of the circumscribed circle is $\pi r^2 = \pi(3\sqrt{2})^2 = 18\pi$.

8. (B)

In the figure below, $\triangle ABC$ is inscribed in the circle so that it is a right triangle. $\overline{AC}$ is the hypotenuse of $\triangle ABC$ and its length is twice the radius of the circle. Thus, $AC = 20$.

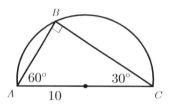

$\angle A$ and $\angle C$ are complementary angles. Since $m\angle BAC = 60°$, $m\angle BCA = 30°$. Thus, $\triangle ABC$ is a 30°-60°-90° special right triangle whose sides are in the ratio $1 : \sqrt{3} : 2$. $\overline{AB}$ is the shorter leg of triangle ABC so that its length is half the length of the hypotenuse. Therefore, $AB = \frac{1}{2}AC = \frac{1}{2}(20) = 10$.

9. (A)

In the figure below, $\overline{OC}$ is the radius of the circle so that it is a perpendicular bisector of the chord, $\overline{AB}$.

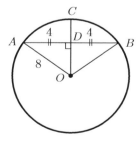

Thus, $m\angle ODA = 90°$ and $AD = BD = 4$. Since $\triangle AOD$ is a right triangle, use the Pythagorean theorem, $8^2 = OD^2 + 4^2$ to find OD. Thus, $OD = 4\sqrt{3}$. Therefore, the area of the $\triangle ABO$ is $\frac{1}{2}bh = \frac{1}{2}(AB)(OD) = \frac{1}{2}(8)(4\sqrt{3}) = 16\sqrt{3}$.

10. (C)

In the figure below, $\overline{AB}$ and $\overline{AC}$ are the tangent lines to the circle at B and C, respectively so that $\overline{AB} \perp \overline{OB}$ and $\overline{AC} \perp \overline{OC}$. Thus, $m\angle B = 90°$ and $m\angle C = 90°$. Since the sum of the measures of interior angles of a quadrilateral $ABOC$ is $360°$, $m\angle BOC = 120°$.

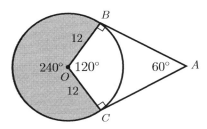

The measure of the central angle of the arc is $360° - m\angle BOC = 360° - 120° = 240°$. Thus,

$$\text{Arc length} = 2\pi r \times \frac{\text{Central angle}}{360°}$$
$$= 2\pi(12) \times \frac{240°}{360°}$$
$$= 24\pi \times \frac{2}{3}$$
$$= 16\pi$$

The perimeter of the shaded region equals the sum of the arc length and the radii, OB and OC. Therefore, the perimeter of the shaded region is $16\pi + 12 + 12 = 16\pi + 24$.

PRACTICE SET 19

Patterns and Data Analysis

Patterns

A **pattern** is a set of numbers or objects that are closely related by a specific rule. Understanding a pattern is very important because it helps you predict what will happen next in the set of numbers or objects.

For instance, the figure above shows a pattern which consists of a circle, a triangle, and a square in that order. If the pattern is repeated continuously, how do you predict which one of the three figures is the 36th figure? Since 36 is a multiple of 3 and every third figure is a square, the 36th figure is a square.

Arithmetic sequence and Geometric sequence
There are two most common number patterns: arithmetic sequence and geometric sequence.
A **sequence or progression** is an ordered list of numbers.

- In an arithmetic sequence, add or subtract the same number(common difference) to one term to get the next term.

- In geometric sequence, multiply or divide one term by the same number(common ratio) to get the next term.

- In both sequences, the first term, the second term, and n^{th} term are expressed as a_1, a_2, and a_n respectively.

Type	Definition	Example	n^{th} term
Arithmetic sequence	The common difference between any consecutive terms is constant.	$1, 3, 5, 7, \ldots$	$a_n = a_1 + (n-1)d$ where d is the common difference.
Geometric sequence	The common ratio between any consecutive terms is constant	$2, 4, 8, 16, \ldots$	$a_n = a_1 \times r^{n-1}$ where r is the common ratio.

    www.solomonacademy.net

Data Analysis

Mean, or **Average**, is the sum of all elements in a set divided by the number of elements in the set. For instance, if there are 3, 7, and 11 in a set, the mean $= \frac{3+7+11}{3} = 7$.

Median is the middle number when a set of numbers is arranged from least to greatest.

- If there is a n (odd number) number of numbers in a set, the median is the middle number which is $\left(\frac{n+1}{2}\right)^{\text{th}}$ number in the set. For instance, if there are 3, 2, 5, 7, and 10 in a set, arrange the numbers in the set from least to greatest: 2, 3, 5, 7, and 10. Since there are 5 numbers in the set, the median is the $\frac{5+1}{2} = 3^{\text{rd}}$ number in the set. Thus, the median is 5.

- If there is a n (even number) number of numbers in a set, the median is the average of the two middle numbers which are the $\left(\frac{n}{2}\right)^{\text{th}}$ and $\left(\frac{n}{2}+1\right)^{\text{th}}$ numbers. For instance, if there are 1, 4, 6, 8, 9, and 11 in a set, the median is the average of 3rd number and 4th number in the set. Thus, the median is $\frac{6+8}{2} = 7$.

Mode is a number that appears most frequently in a set. It is possible to have more than one mode or no mode in a set.

Range is the difference between the greatest number and the least number in a set.

Example: There are 2, 4, 8, 10, and x in a set. If the range of the set is 13, what is the value of x ?

The range is the difference between the greatest number and the least number. The least number in the set is 2. If 10 is the greatest number in the set, the range would be 8. Thus, x must be the greatest number. Therefore, the value of x is 15.

EXERCISES

1. If the pattern below is repeated continuously, what is the 48th letter in the pattern?

$$B, \quad C, \quad D, \quad E, \quad A, \quad B, \quad C, \ldots$$

  (A) A (B) B (C) C
  (D) D (E) E

2. In the sequence below, the nth term is defined as $a_n = n^2 + 1$. What is the 7th term in the sequence?

$$2, \ 5, \ 10, \ 17, \ \ldots$$

  (A) 50   (B) 42   (C) 35
  (D) 26   (E) 20

3. In a set of 5, 1, 10, x, and 16, where $10 < x < 16$, which of the following is the median of the set?

(A) 1   (B) 5   (C) 10
(D) x (E) 16

4. Jason scored 91, 95, and 94 in the first three tests. What score does he get on the 4th test so that his overall average for the four tests is 94 ?

(A) 96   (B) 97   (C) 98
(D) 99   (E) 100

5. If the volume of a balloon is doubled every three minutes, in how many minutes is the volume of the balloon eight times larger than the initial volume of the balloon?

(A) 6   (B) 8   (C) 9
(D) 12   (E) 16

6. In the arithmetic sequence $3, 7, 11, 15, \ldots$ what is the value of the 17th term?

(A) 76   (B) 67   (C) 56
(D) 45   (E) 37

7. There are 1, 3, 4, 7, and 10 in a set. If 3 is added to each number in the set, what is the positive difference of the new mean and the new median of the set?

(A) 1   (B) 2   (C) 3
(D) 4   (E) 5

8. In a set of five positive integers, the mode is 4, the median is 5, and the mean is 6. What is the greatest of these integers?

(A) 7   (B) 8   (C) 9
(D) 10   (E) 11

9. A car travels at 60 miles per hour for 2 hours on a trip and travels at 40 miles per hour for three hours on the returning trip. What is the average speed of the entire trip?

(A) 55   (B) 50   (C) 48
(D) 45   (E) 42

10. In the arithmetic sequence, the 3rd term is 17 and the 10th term is 73. What is the 15th term?

(A) 95   (B) 97   (C) 103
(D) 108   (E) 113

ANSWERS AND SOLUTIONS

1. (D)

The pattern consists of B, C, D, E and A. It is repeated continuously. Since every 5th letter is A, the 45th letter is also A. Thus, the 46th letter is B, the 47th letter is C, and the 48th letter is D.

2. (A)

To find the 7th term in the sequence, substitute 7 for n in $a_n = n^2 + 1$.

$$a_n = n^2 + 1 \qquad \text{Substitute 7 for } n$$
$$a_7 = (7)^2 + 1 = 50$$

Therefore, the 7th term in the sequence is 50.

3. (C)

Arrange the numbers in the set from least to greatest: 1, 5, 10, x, 16. The median is the middle number of the set. Therefore, the median is 10.

4. (A)

The average of four tests is 94. This means that Jason should get a total score of $94 \times 4 = 376$ for the four tests. The sum of scores of the first three tests is $91 + 95 + 94 = 280$. Therefore, the score of the fourth test is $376 - 280 = 96$.

5. (C)

Let's define V_0 as the initial volume of the balloon. The volume of the balloon is doubled every 3 minutes:

$$\text{In 3 minutes} = 2V_0$$
$$\text{In 6 minutes} = 2(2V_0) = 4V_0$$
$$\text{In 9 minutes} = 2(4V_0) = 8V_0$$

Therefore, in 9 minutes, the volume of the balloon is eight times larger than the initial volume of the balloon.

6. (B)

In an arithmetic sequence, the first term, $a_1 = 3$ and the common difference, $d = 7 - 3 = 4$. Use the nth term formula to find the 17th term.

$$a_n = a_1 + (n-1)d \qquad \text{Substitute 17 for } n, \text{3 for } a_1, \text{and 4 for } d$$
$$a_{17} = 3 + (17-1)4 = 67$$

Therefore, the value of the 17th term is 67.

7. (A)

The mean of the set is $\frac{1+3+4+7+10}{5} = 5$. The median of the set is the middle number, 4. If 3 is added to each number in the set, the new mean is $5 + 3 = 8$, and the new median is $4 + 3 = 7$. Therefore, the positive difference of the new mean the new median is $8 - 7 = 1$.

8. (E)

Since the mean of the five positive integers is 6, the sum of the five positive integers is $5 \times 6 = 30$. Define x as the second greatest integer and y as the greatest integer in the set. Let's consider three cases shown below. In case 1, the median is 4 because there are three 4's. This doesn't satisfy the given information such that the median is 5. Thus, case 1 is false.

Case 1: $4 + 4 + 4 + x + y = 30$ mode=4, median=4: It doesn't work
Case 2: $4 + 4 + 5 + 5 + y = 30$ mode=4 and 5, median=5: It doesn't work
Case 3: $4 + 4 + 5 + x + y = 30$ mode=4, median=5: It works

In case 2, there are two 4's and two 5's in which the mode are both 4 and 5. This doesn't satisfy the given information such that the mode is 4. Thus, case 2 is false. Finally, in case 3, there are two 4's and one 5. If x is greater than 5, the mode is 4 and median is 5 which satisfy the given information. x must be smallest positive integer greater than 5 so that y will have the greatest possible value. Thus, $x = 6$ and $y = 11$. Therefore, the greatest of these integers is 11.

9. (C)

On the trip, the car travels $60 \times 2 = 120$ miles. On the returning trip, the car travels $40 \times 3 = 120$ miles. Thus,

$$\text{The average speed} = \frac{\text{Total distance}}{\text{Total number of hours}}$$

$$= \frac{120 \text{ miles} + 120 \text{ miles}}{2 \text{ hours} + 3 \text{ hours}}$$

$$= \frac{240 \text{ miles}}{5 \text{ hours}}$$

$$= 48 \text{ miles per hour}$$

Therefore, the average speed of the entire trip is 48 miles per hour.

10. (E)

Write the 10th term and 3rd term of the arithmetic sequence in terms of a_1 and d using the nth term formula: $a_n = a_1 + (n-1)d$.

$$a_{10} = a_1 + 9d = 73$$
$$a_3 = a_1 + 2d = 17$$

Use the linear combinations method to solve for d and a_1.

$$a_1 + 9d = 73$$
$$\underline{a_1 + 2d = 17} \qquad \text{Subtract two equations}$$
$$7d = 56 \qquad \text{Divide both sides by 7}$$
$$d = 8$$

Substitute $d = 8$ in $a_3 = a_1 + 2d = 17$ and solve for a_1. Thus, $a_1 = 1$. Therefore, the 15th term of the arithmetic sequence is $a_{15} = a_1 + 14d = 1 + 14(8) = 113$.

PRACTICE SET 20

Counting and Probability

Counting

Counting integers

How many positive integers are there between 42 and 97 inclusive? Are there 54, 55, or 56 integers? Even in this simple counting problem, many students are not sure what the right answer is. A rule for counting integers is as follows:

$$\text{The number of integers} = \text{Greatest integer} - \text{Least integer} + 1$$

According to this rule, the number of integers between 42 and 97 inclusive is $97 - 42 + 1 = 56$ integers.

Counting points on a line

There is a line whose length is 200 feet. If points are placed every 2 feet staring from one end, how many points are on the line?

The pattern above suggests that a rule for counting the number of points on a line is as follows:

$$\text{Total number of points on a line} = \frac{\text{Length of a line}}{\text{Distance between each point}} + 1$$

For instance, if a line is 6 feet long, there are $\frac{6}{2} + 1 = 4$ points on the line as shown above. Therefore, if a line is 200 feet long, there are $\frac{200}{2} + 1 = 101$ points on the line.

Counting points on a circle

There is a circle whose circumference is 200 feet. If points are placed every 2 feet on the circumference of the circle, how many points are on the circle?

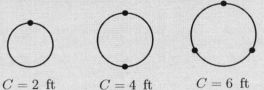

$C = 2$ ft $C = 4$ ft $C = 6$ ft

The pattern above suggests that a rule for counting the total number of points on a circle is as follows:

$$\text{Total number of points on a circle} = \frac{\text{Circumference of a circle}}{\text{Distance between each point}}$$

According to this rule, if the circumference of a circle is 200 feet, there are $\frac{200}{2} = 100$ points on the circle.

The fundamental counting principle

If one event can occur in m ways and another event can occur in n ways, then the number of ways both events can occur is $m \times n$. For instance, Jason has three shirts and four pairs of jeans. He can dress up in $3 \times 4 = 12$ different ways.

Venn Diagram

A venn diagram is very useful in counting. It helps you count numbers correctly.

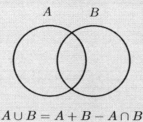

$$A \cup B = A + B - A \cap B$$

In the figure above, $A \cup B$ represents the combined area of two circles A and B. $A \cap B$ represents the common area where the two circles overlap. The venn diagram suggests that the combined area $(A \cup B)$ equals the sum of areas of circles $(A + B)$ minus the common area $(A \cap B)$.

In counting, each circle A and B represents a set of numbers. $n(A)$ and $n(B)$ represent the number of elements in set A and B, respectively. For instance, $A = \{2, 4, 6, 8, 10\}$ and $n(A) = 5$. Thus, the total number of elements that belong to either set A or set B, $n(A \cup B)$, can be counted as follows:

$$n(A \cup B) = n(A) + n(B) - n(A \cap B)$$

Let's find out how many positive integers less than or equal to 20 are divisible by 2 or 3. Define A as the set of numbers divisible by 2 and B as the set of numbers divisible by 3.

$$A = \{2, 4, 6, \cdots, 18, 20\}, \qquad n(A) = 10$$
$$B = \{3, 6, 9, 12, 15, 18\}, \qquad n(B) = 6$$
$$A \cap B = \{6, 12, 18\}, \qquad n(A \cap B) = 3$$

Notice that $A \cap B = \{6, 12, 18\}$ are multiples of 2 and multiples of 3. They are counted twice so they must be excluded in counting. Thus,

$$n(A \cup B) = n(A) + n(B) - n(A \cap B)$$
$$= 10 + 6 - 3$$
$$= 13$$

Therefore, the total number of positive integers less than or equal to 20 that are divisible by 2 or 3 is 13.

www.solomonacademy.net

Probability

The definition of probability of an event, E, is as follows:

$$\text{Probability(E)} = \frac{\text{The number of outcomes event } E \text{ can happen}}{\text{The total number of possible outcomes}}$$

Probability is a measure of how likely an event will happen. Probability can be expressed as a fraction, a decimal, and a percent, and is measured on scale from 0 to 1. Probability can not be less than 0 nor greater than 1.

- Probability equals 0 means an event will never happen.

- Probability equals 1 means an event will always happen.

- Higher the probability, higher chance an event will happen.

For instance, what is the probability of selecting a prime number at random from 1 to 5? In this problem, the event E is selecting a prime number from three possible prime numbers: 2, 3, and 5. The total possible outcomes are numbers from 1 to 5. Thus, the probability of selecting a prime number is $P(E) = \frac{\{2,3,5\}}{\{1,2,3,4,5\}} = \frac{3}{5}$.

Geometric probability

Geometric probability involves the length or area of the geometric figures. The definition of the geometric probability is as follows:

$$\text{Geometric probability} = \frac{\text{Area of desired region}}{\text{Total area}}$$

In the figure below, a circle is inscribed in the square with side length of 10. Assuming that a dart always lands inside the square, what is the probability that a dart lands on a region that lies outside the circle and inside the square?

The area of the square is $10^2 = 100$, and the area of the circle is $\pi(5)^2 = 25\pi$. Thus, the area of desired region is $100 - 25\pi$.

$$\begin{aligned}
\text{Geometric probability} &= \frac{\text{Area of desired region}}{\text{Total area}} \\
&= \frac{100 - 25\pi}{100} \\
&= \frac{25(4 - \pi)}{100} \\
&= \frac{4 - \pi}{4}
\end{aligned}$$

Example: You toss a coin four times. How many different outcomes are possible?

Event 1, event 2, event 3, and event 4 are tossing a first coin, second coin, third coin, and fourth coin, respectively. For each event, there are two possible outcomes: head or tail. According to the fundamental counting principle, there are $2 \times 2 \times 2 \times 2 = 16$ possible outcomes for the four events.

EXERCISES

1. There are three red, two yellow, and five blue cards. What is the probability that a blue card is selected at random?

    (A) $\dfrac{3}{5}$ (B) $\dfrac{1}{2}$ (C) $\dfrac{2}{5}$

    (D) $\dfrac{3}{10}$ (E) $\dfrac{1}{5}$

2. How many positive integers are there between 19 and 101 exclusive?

    (A) 78   (B) 79   (C) 80
    (D) 81   (E) 82

3. There are four types of breads, five types of meats, and three types of cheese. Assuming you have to select one of each category, how many different sandwiches can you make?

    (A) 60   (B) 50   (C) 40
    (D) 30   (E) 12

4. Toss a coin twice. What is the probability that you have one head and one tail?

    (A) $\dfrac{1}{4}$ (B) $\dfrac{1}{2}$ (C) $\dfrac{3}{4}$

    (D) $\dfrac{4}{5}$ (E) 1

5. On a road that is 200 feet long, trees are placed every 4 feet starting from one end. How many tree are on the road?

    (A) 49   (B) 50   (C) 51
    (D) 52   (E) 53

6. There are two concentric circles whose radii are 2 and 3, respectively. Assuming a dart never land on the outside the larger circle, what is the probability that a dart lands on the shaded region?

    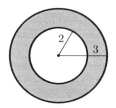

    (A) $\dfrac{1}{3}$ (B) $\dfrac{1}{2}$ (C) $\dfrac{2}{3}$

    (D) $\dfrac{3}{4}$ (E) $\dfrac{5}{9}$

7. There is a square-shaped plot of land whose side length is 50 feet. If posts are placed every 5 feet on the perimeter of the land, how many posts are on the land?

    (A) 39   (B) 40   (C) 41
    (D) 42   (E) 43

8. How many three digit numbers are there whose digits in the hundreds place and ones place are the same? (Assume that a nonzero digit is in the hundreds place.)

    (A) 80   (B) 81   (C) 90
    (D) 100   (E) 121

9. There are 36 marbles in a bag. They are either blue, red, or green marbles. The number of green marbles is twice the number of blue marbles. The number of the red marbles is 8 more than the number of blue marbles. What is the probability that a red marble is selected at random in a bag?

(A) $\dfrac{1}{3}$ (B) $\dfrac{13}{36}$ (C) $\dfrac{7}{18}$

(D) $\dfrac{5}{12}$ (E) $\dfrac{4}{9}$

10. If a number is selected at random from 1 to 30 inclusive, what is the probability that the selected integer is divisible by 2 or 3 ?

(A) $\dfrac{8}{15}$ (B) $\dfrac{9}{15}$ (C) $\dfrac{2}{3}$

(D) $\dfrac{11}{15}$ (E) $\dfrac{4}{5}$

ANSWERS AND SOLUTIONS

1. (B)

There are 10 cards. Out of these cards, there are 5 blue cards. Therefore, the probability of selecting a blue card is $\frac{5}{10} = \frac{1}{2}$.

2. (D)

The two numbers, 19 and 101, are excluded. Therefore, the number of integers from 20 and 100 is $100 - 20 + 1 = 81$.

3. (A)

Event 1, event 2, and event 3 are selecting one out of 4 types of breads, one out of 5 types of meats, and one out of 3 types of cheese, respectively. According to the fundamental counting principle, you can make $4 \times 5 \times 3 = 60$ different sandwiches.

4. (B)

Event 1 is tossing a first coin and event 2 is tossing a second coin. According to the fundamental counting principle, there are $2 \times 2 = 4$ outcomes. The four outcomes are HH, HT, TH, and TT. Out of these outcomes, there are two outcomes that have one head and one tail: HT and TH. Therefore, the probability that you have one head and one tail is $\frac{2}{4} = \frac{1}{2}$.

5. (C)

This problem is exactly the same as counting points on the line. The road is 200 feet long and trees are placed every 4 feet.

$$\text{Total number of trees on the road} = \frac{\text{Length of the road}}{\text{Distance between each tree}} + 1$$

$$= \frac{200}{4} + 1$$

$$= 51$$

Therefore, there are 51 trees on the road.

6. (E)

The area of the larger circle is $\pi(3)^2 = 9\pi$. The area of the shaded region is $\pi(3)^2 - \pi(2)^2 = 5\pi$.

$$\text{Geometric probability} = \frac{\text{Area of the shaded region}}{\text{Area of larger circle}} = \frac{5\pi}{9\pi} = \frac{5}{9}$$

Therefore, the probability that a dart lands on the shaded region is $\frac{5}{9}$.

7. (B)

This problem is exactly the same as counting points on the circle. The perimeter of the square-shaped plot of land is $50 \times 4 = 200$ feet. The posts are placed every 5 feet.

$$\text{Total number of posts on the land} = \frac{\text{Perimeter of the land}}{\text{Distance between each post}}$$

$$= \frac{200}{5}$$

$$= 40$$

Therefore, there are 40 posts on the land.

8. (C)

Event 1 is selecting a digit in the hundreds place and ones place. There are 9 possible outcomes: 1 through 9. Event 2 is a selecting a digit in the tens place. There are 10 possible outcomes: 0 through 9. Therefore, according to the fundamental counting principle, there are $9 \times 10 = 90$ three digit numbers whose digits in hundreds place and the ones place are the same.

9. (D)

Let x be the number of blue marbles. Then, the number of green marbles is $2x$, and the number of red marble is $x + 8$. Since there are 36 marbles, set up an equation and solve for x.

$$x + x + 8 + 2x = 36$$

$$4x + 8 = 36$$

$$4x = 28$$

$$x = 7$$

Thus, the number of the red marble is $x + 8 = 15$. Therefore, the probability that a red marble is selected at random is $\frac{15}{36} = \frac{5}{12}$.

10. (C)

Let's define A as the set of integers that are divisible by 2, B as the set of integers that are divisible by 3, and $A \cap B$ as the set of integers that are divisible by 2 and 3, respectively.

$$A = \{2, 4, 6, \cdots, 28, 30\}, \qquad n(A) = 15$$
$$B = \{3, 6, 9, \cdots, 27, 30\}, \qquad n(B) = 10$$
$$A \cap B = \{6, 12, 18, 24, 30\}, \qquad n(A \cap B) = 5$$

Thus, the number of integers less than or equal to 30 that are divisible by 2 or 3, $n(A \cup B)$, is

$$n(A \cup B) = n(A) + n(B) - n(A \cap B)$$
$$= 15 + 10 - 5$$
$$= 20$$

Out of the integers from 1 to 30 inclusive, there are 20 integers that are divisible by 2 or 3. Therefore, the probability that a selected integer is divisible by 2 or 3 is $\frac{20}{30} = \frac{2}{3}$.

SECTION 1
Time — 25 minutes
20 Questions

Directions: Solve each problem in this section and enter your answer by marking the circle on the answer sheet. You may use all the space provided for your work.

Notes

1. You may use a calculator during this test.

2. All numbers used in this test are real numbers.

3. Unless noted, the domain and the range of a function used in this test are sets of real numbers.

4. Figures in this test provide useful information in solving problems. They are drawn as accurately as possible. Otherwise, figures not drawn to scale will be labeled as such. Figures lie in a plane.

Information

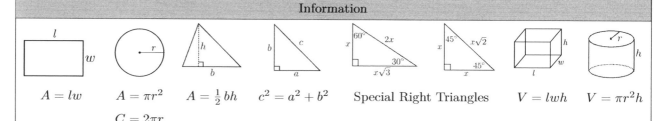

$A = lw$ $A = \pi r^2$ $A = \frac{1}{2}bh$ $c^2 = a^2 + b^2$ Special Right Triangles $V = lwh$ $V = \pi r^2 h$

$C = 2\pi r$

The degree measure of arc in a circle is 360.

The sum of the measures of the interior angles of a triangle is 180.

---

1. If A is a set of all multiples of 2 and B is a set of all multiples of 3, how many positive integer less than 15 belong to both A and B ?

   (A)   0

   (B)   1

   (C)   2

   (D)   3

   (E)   4

2. x, y, and z are integers such that $0 < x < y < z$. Which of the following must be greatest?

   (A) $z - x$

   (B) $z - y$

   (C) $x + y$

   (D) $y + z$

   (E) $x + z$

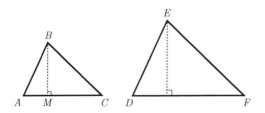

Note: Figure not drawn to scale.

3. $\triangle ABC$ and $\triangle DEF$ are similar triangles. If $AC = 10$, $BM = 5$, and $DF = 20$, what is the area of $\triangle DEF$?

(A) 100

(B) 125

(C) 150

(D) 175

(E) 200

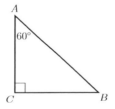

Note: Figure not drawn to scale.

4. If $AB = 10$, what is the perimeter of $\triangle ABC$?

(A) $10\sqrt{3}$

(B) $15 + 5\sqrt{3}$

(C) $20\sqrt{3}$

(D) 30

(E) $30\sqrt{3}$

5. Four less than three times a number equals five more than twelve times the number. What is the number?

(A) -2

(B) -1

(C) 0

(D) 1

(E) $\frac{1}{5}$

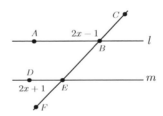

6. In the figure above, $l \parallel m$. If the measure of $\angle ABC$ is $2x - 1$ and the measure of $\angle DEF$ is $2x + 1$, what is the value of x ?

(A) 35

(B) 45

(C) 50

(D) 60

(E) 75

7. If $\dfrac{16}{x} = \dfrac{2}{y}$, what is the value of $\dfrac{y}{x}$?

    (A) $\frac{1}{8}$

    (B) $\frac{1}{4}$

    (C) $\frac{1}{2}$

    (D)   8

    (E)   32

8. Joshua has taken four tests in math class. The four test scores are 87, 88, 92, and 89. In order for him to get an A in the class, he needs to get an average of at least 90 on the 5 tests. Which of the following score, s, must he receive to get an A ? (Let s be the score on his 5th test.)

    (A) $s < 94$

    (B) $s \geq 94$

    (C) $s \leq 90$

    (D) $s > 90$

    (E) $s \geq 90$

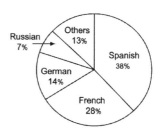

9. The pie chart above shows the distribution of foreign languages for a group of high school students. If the number of students who take French is 560, what is the number of students who take Spanish?

    (A)   580

    (B)   600

    (C)   680

    (D)   760

    (E)   840

10. Students walked into the Auditorium with rows of two. Jennifer noticed that her row is the 29th row from the front and the 21st row from the back. How many students went to the Auditorium?

    (A)   49

    (B)   50

    (C)   98

    (D)   100

    (E)   102

11. Of the 43 students in a group, each student plays Tennis, Soccer, both or neither. 25 students play Tennis, 28 students play soccer and 5 students play neither. If 15 students play both Tennis and Soccer, what is the sum of the number of students who play only Tennis or only Soccer?

   (A)   16

   (B)   23

   (C)   33

   (D)   38

   (E)   43

12. Which of the followings are properties of parallelograms?

   I. Opposite angles are congruent.

   II. Diagonals are perpendicular to each other.

   III. Diagonals bisect each other.

   IV. Consecutive angles are supplementary.

   (A)   I & II

   (B)   II & III

   (C)   II &IV

   (D)   I & III & IV

   (E)   II & III & IV

13. Four people who work at the same rate painted half of a house in 6 days. How many additional people are needed to paint the remaining part of the house in 2 days?

   (A)   2

   (B)   4

   (C)   5

   (D)   6

   (E)   8

Note: Figure not drawn to scale.

14. In the figure above, a hexagonal nut has a circle with a radius of 3 at the center. The side length of the hexagonal shape is 6. If the hexagonal shape can be divided into six equilateral triangles, what is the area of shaded region of the hexagonal nut?

   (A) $36 - 6\pi$

   (B) $48 - 9\pi$

   (C) $54\sqrt{2} - 9\pi$

   (D) $54\sqrt{3} - 9\pi$

   (E) $72 - 6\pi$

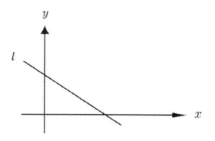

15. In the figure above, a line l crosses the x-axis at 6 and crosses the y-axis at 3. If the line l is reflected over x-axis, which of the following must be the equation of the new line?

    (A) $y = \frac{1}{2}x - 3$

    (B) $y = -\frac{1}{2}x - 3$

    (C) $y = \frac{1}{2}x + 3$

    (D) $y = -\frac{1}{2}x + 3$

    (E) $y = 2x - 3$

$$xy = 1$$
$$x + \frac{1}{y} = 5$$

16. What is the value of $y + \frac{1}{x}$?

    (A) $\frac{1}{5}$

    (B) $\frac{2}{5}$

    (C) $\frac{4}{5}$

    (D) $\frac{5}{4}$

    (E)   2

17. When Jason was heading to his office between 7 am and 8 am in the morning, he noticed that the hour hand and the minute hand of a clock formed 90°. When he returned home between 5 pm and 6 pm, he noticed that the hour hand and the minute hand of the clock formed 90° again. Which of the following is closest to the greatest number of hours that he was away from home?

    (A)   8 hours and 20 minutes

    (B)   9 hours

    (C)   9 hours and 40 minutes

    (D)   10 hours and 20 minutes

    (E)   11 hours

---

18. When the positive integer k is divided by 6, the remainder is 2. When the positive integer n is divided by 6, the remainder is 1. Which of the following has a remainder of 0 when divided by 6?

    (A) $kn + 2$

    (B) $kn + 3$

    (C) $kn + 4$

    (D) $kn + 5$

    (E) kn

19. Which of the following has the solution set such that all real numbers are within 3 units away from 2?

    (A) $|x| > 5$

    (B) $|x - 2| > 3$

    (C) $|x - 2| < 3$

    (D) $|x - 3| > 2$

    (E) $|x - 3| < 2$

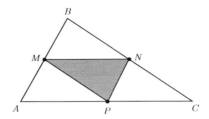

20. In the figure above, triangle ABC is on the xy coordinate plane. The coordinates of the three vertices of triangle ABC are as follows: $A(3, 1)$, $B(7, 9)$, and $C(15, 1)$. If the points M, N, and P are the midpoints of segments $\overline{AB}$, $\overline{BC}$, and $\overline{AC}$, respectively, what is the area of the shaded region?

    (A)   10

    (B)   12

    (C)   24

    (D)   35

    (E)   36

STOP

SECTION 2
Time — 25 minutes
18 Questions

Directions: This section contains two types of questions: Multiple-Choice questions and Free-Response questions. For question 1-8, solve each problem in this section and enter your answer by marking the circle on the answer sheet. You may use all the space provided for your work.

Notes

1. You may use a calculator during this test.

2. All numbers used in this test are real numbers.

3. Unless noted, the domain and the range of a function used in this test are sets of real numbers.

4. Figures in this test provide useful information in solving problems. They are drawn as accurately as possible. Otherwise, figures not drawn to scale will be labeled as such. Figures lie in a plane.

Information

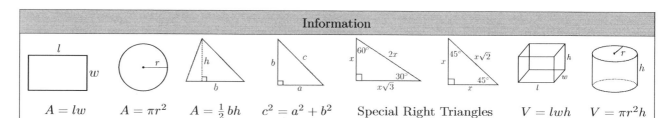

$$A = lw \qquad A = \pi r^2 \qquad A = \tfrac{1}{2}bh \qquad c^2 = a^2 + b^2 \qquad \text{Special Right Triangles} \qquad V = lwh \qquad V = \pi r^2 h$$

$$C = 2\pi r$$

The degree measure of arc in a circle is 360.

The sum of the measures of the interior angles of a triangle is 180.

1. If $b = -3$, $a = 1$, $c = -2$, what is the value of $b^2 - 4ac$?

    (A)   18

    (B)   17

    (C)   1

    (D)   −1

    (E)   −3

2. A circle has a diameter of 4. What is the ratio of its circumference to its area?

    (A)   1 : 6

    (B)   1 : 4

    (C)   1 : 3

    (D)   1 : 2

    (E)   1 : 1

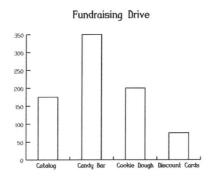

Fundraising Drive

3. The graph shows the amount of money collected by four different fundraising products for a school band. Of the total amount of money collected, what percent did cookie dough collect?

(A) 25

(B) 30

(C) 35

(D) 40

(E) 45

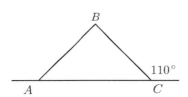

4. The degree measure of $\angle A$ is $\frac{5}{6}$ of the degree measure of $\angle B$. What is the degree measure of $\angle B$?

(A) 50

(B) 55

(C) 60

(D) 70

(E) 90

5. You are selling two types of tickets for a high school play: student tickets and adult tickets. After selling 385 tickets, you realized that the number of student tickets sold is four more than twice as many as the number of adult tickets sold. What is the number of student tickets sold?

(A) 120

(B) 127

(C) 258

(D) 265

(E) 285

6. You have a savings account. The amount A you have deposited into your account after t years can be modeled by a linear equation, $A = mt + b$. You have deposited \$1250 into your savings account after two years and deposited \$3000 after 9 years. How much money do you put into your savings account every year?

(A) 175

(B) 200

(C) 225

(D) 250

(E) 500

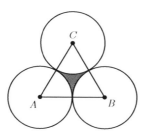

7. In the figure above, three congruent circles are tangent to each other. The radius of each circle is 6. What is the area of the shaded region between the three circles?

(A) 6π

(B) 18π

(C) $9\sqrt{3} - 6\pi$

(D) $18\sqrt{3} - 18\pi$

(E) $36\sqrt{3} - 18\pi$

8. An airplane is flying back and forth from city A to city B. The two cities are d miles apart. If the plane is flying with the wind, it takes 2 hours to travel from city A to city B. However, if the plane is flying against the wind, it takes 3 hours to travel from city B to city A. Assuming that the speed of the airplane and the wind remain the same throughout the trip, which of the following must be the speed of the wind in terms of d ?

(A) $\frac{5d}{12}$

(B) $\frac{d}{2}$

(C) $\frac{d}{5}$

(D) $\frac{d}{6}$

(E) $\frac{d}{12}$

Direction: For each of the 10 remaining Free-Response questions, solve the problem and enter your answer by marking the circle in the special grid as shown in the examples below.

Answer: $\frac{3}{7}$ Answer: 6.75   Answer: 124

Either position is correct.

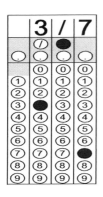   

- Fill in one circle in each column.

- Each circle must be filled in correctly. Otherwise, you will not receive any credit.

- Convert all mixed numbers such as $1\frac{1}{2}$ to either 1.5 or $\frac{3}{2}$.

- For decimal answers that are longer than the number of grids provided, you must round or truncate the decimal. However, you must fill in all of the grids provided to ensure your answer is accurate as possible. For example, $0.666\ldots$ must be marked as .666 or .667.

- Answers are always positive.

- Write in the answer at the top of the grid to avoid mistakes when marking the circles.

- On problems that have more than one answer, fill in only one correct answer.

9. $\sqrt{3-x} = 9$. What is the value of $|x-3|$?

10. In a high school football game, the blue team must move 20 yards forward to score a touchdown in the final four plays. The blue team moved 7 yards forward, 4 yards backward, and 5 yards forward for the first three plays. How many yards must the blue team move forward to win?

11. The circumference of a circular garden is 300 feet. If a post is placed every three feet around the circumference of the garden, how many posts are there?

12. Five different points, A, B, E, C, and D lie on the same line in that order. The two points B and C trisect the segment $\overline{AD}$ whose length is 36. Point E is the midpoint of the segment $\overline{BC}$. What is the length of the segment $\overline{DE}$?

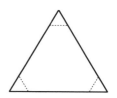

Note: Figure not drawn to scale.

13. In the figure above, each corner of an equilateral triangle, with side length of 25, is cut into a smaller equilateral triangle with side length of 3. What is the perimeter of the remaining figure?

14. In an arithmetic sequence, the value of the fourth term is 17 and that of the fifteenth term is 61. What is the value of the second term?

15. If $x = -2$ is a solution of $ax^2 + bx + 11 = 0$, what is the value of $6b - 12a$?

17. A set consists of six different positive integers: 14, 8, 4, x, 87, and 23. 4 is the smallest and 87 is the largest integer in the set. What is the largest integer value of x so that the median of the six different integers is greatest?

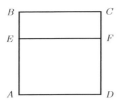

16. In the figure above, rectangle $ABCD$ is divided into two smaller rectangles. If the ratio of the area of rectangle $BCFE$ to that of rectangle $AEFD$ is 3 to 7, what is the ratio of BE to AE ? (Write the answer in either integer or simplest fraction.)

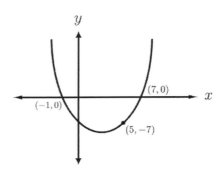

18. The graph of a function, $f(x) = a(x+1)(x-7)$ is shown above. If the function passes through $(-1, 0)$, $(7, 0)$, and $(5, -7)$, what is the value of a ?

STOP

SECTION 3
Time – 20 minutes
16 Questions

Notes

1. You may use a calculator during this test.

2. All numbers used in this test are real numbers.

3. Unless noted, the domain and the range of a function used in this test are sets of real numbers.

4. Figures in this test provide useful information in solving problems. They are drawn as accurately as possible. Otherwise, figures not drawn to scale will be labeled as such. Figures lie in a plane.

Information

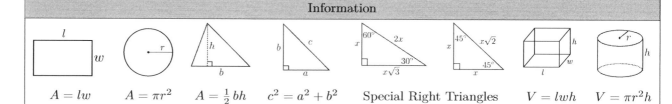

$$A = lw \qquad A = \pi r^2 \qquad A = \tfrac{1}{2}bh \qquad c^2 = a^2 + b^2 \qquad \text{Special Right Triangles} \qquad V = lwh \qquad V = \pi r^2 h$$

$$C = 2\pi r$$

The degree measure of arc in a circle is 360.

The sum of the measures of the interior angles of a triangle is 180.

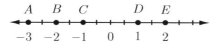

1. In the figure above, five points A, B, C, D, and E lie on a number line. Which of the following point has a value equal to $C(A - B)$?

(A) A

(B) B

(C) C

(D) D

(E) E

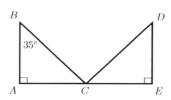

2. C is the midpoint of $\overline{AE}$. If $BC = DC$, which of the following is the degree measure of angle CDE ?

(A) 65

(B) 55

(C) 45

(D) 35

(E) 25

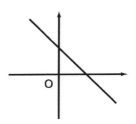

3. The graph above shows a linear equation, $f(x) = mx + b$. Which of the following is the greatest in value?

   (A) $f(-5)$

   (B) $f(-3)$

   (C) $f(0)$

   (D) $f(3)$

   (E) $f(5)$

4. The coordinates of the three vertices of a right triangle are $(0,0)$, $(5,0)$, and $(5,12)$. What is the value of the length of the longest side of the triangle?

   (A) 13

   (B) 12

   (C) 11

   (D) 10

   (E) 9

5. A track team coach records the lap time after a student finishes his run. The student runs three times and his three lap times are 1 minutes and 50 seconds, 2 minutes and 5 seconds, and 2 minutes and 20 seconds. What is the average (arithmetic mean) lap time for the three runs?

   (A) 1 minutes and 50 seconds

   (B) 1 minutes and 55 seconds

   (C) 2 minutes

   (D) 2 minutes and 5 seconds

   (E) 2 minutes and 10 seconds

6. Which of the following systems of linear equations has a solution of $(2, -3)$?

   (A) $2x + y = 1$
         $3x + y = 9$

   (B) $2x + y = 1$
         $3x - y = 9$

   (C) $2x - y = 1$
         $3x + y = 9$

   (D) $2x - y = 1$
         $3x - y = 9$

   (E) $2x - y = 1$
         $3x + y = -9$

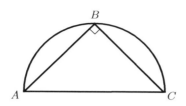

Note: Figure not drawn to scale.

7. In the figure above, an isosceles right triangle ABC is inscribed in a semicircle with a radius of 8. Which of the following must be the area of triangle ABC ?

(A) 16

(B) $32\sqrt{2}$

(C) 64

(D) $64\sqrt{2}$

(E) 128

$$F = \frac{9}{5}C + 32$$

8. The equation above is used to convert degrees Celsius C to degrees Fahrenheit F. Which of the following must be the equation that convert degrees Fahrenheit F to degree Celsius C ?

(A) $C = \frac{5}{9}(F + 32)$

(B) $C = \frac{5}{9}(F - 32)$

(C) $C = \frac{5}{9}F + 32$

(D) $C = \frac{5}{9}F - 32$

(E) $C = \frac{5F - 32}{9}$

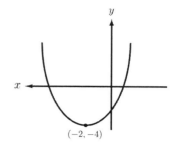

9. In the graph above, the minimum value of a parabola is located at $(-2, -4)$. If the graph is shifted right 4 units and then up 2 units so that the new graph never passes through the origin, what is the total number of x-intercept(s) and y-intercept(s)?

(A) 0

(B) 1

(C) 2

(D) 3

(E) 4

$$\frac{x - 2}{x} = \frac{2}{x + 3}$$

10. Which of the following must be the solution to the proportion above?

(A) 2 only

(B) -3 only

(C) -2 and 3

(D) 2 and -3

(E) -2 and -3

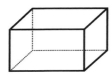

11. In the rectangular box above, the length of the box is three times the width of the box. The height of the box is $\frac{2}{3}$ of the length of the box. If the volume of the box is 162, what is the surface area of the rectangular box?

    (A) 198

    (B) 171

    (C) 144

    (D) 121

    (E) 99

12. The product of a and the sum of b and c is divided by the quotient of a and c. Which of the following must be the result?

    (A) b

    (B) $bc + 2c$

    (C) $bc + c^2$

    (D) $\dfrac{c}{b+c}$

    (E) $\dfrac{b+c}{c}$

$$\frac{2^x \cdot 4^y}{8^z} = 64$$

13. Which of the following must be true about the equation above?

    (A) $\dfrac{xy}{z} = 64$

    (B) $x + y - z = 64$

    (C) $x + 2y - 3z = 6$

    (D) $x + y - 3z = 6$

    (E) $x + 2y + 3z = 64$

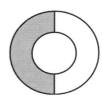

14. In the figure above, a target consists of two concentric circles with radii of 1 and 2, respectively. Assuming a dart only lands either on or inside the target, what is the probability that the dart lands on the shaded area?

    (A) $\dfrac{1}{4}$

    (B) $\dfrac{3}{8}$

    (C) $\dfrac{1}{2}$

    (D) $\dfrac{5}{8}$

    (E) $\dfrac{2}{3}$

15. The arithmetic mean of $y - 1, 2y - 2,$ and $3y - 4$ is x. The arithmetic mean of $x, 2x - 3,$ and $3x - 5$ is y. Which of the following must be the value of $x + y$?

(A) 1

(B) 2

(C) 3

(D) 4

(E) 5

$$P(x) = -\frac{1}{8}x^2 + 21x + 110$$

16. The profit that a factory makes after producing x numbers of items could be modeled by the function, $P(x)$ above. If the factory only makes items in groups of 10, which of the following must be the number of items that the factory should produce to get the maximum profit?

(A) 80

(B) 90

(C) 100

(D) 110

(E) 120

STOP

SAT Math Scoring Worksheet

Directions: In order to calculate your score correctly, fill out the blank spaces from A through K on the table below. After calculating your raw score, round the raw score to the nearest whole number. The scaled score can be determined using the *"SAT Math Test Score Conversion Table"* on the next page.

SAT Math Score			
A. Section 1 Number Correct		**F.** Section 1 Number Incorrect	
B. Section 2 Questions 1-8 Number Correct		**G.** Section 2 Questions 1-8 Number Incorrect	
C. Section 2 Questions 9-18 Number Correct			
D. Section 3 Number Correct		**H.** Section 3 Number Incorrect	
E. Total Correct A+B+C+D		**I.** Total Incorrect (F+G+H)÷4	
J. Total Unrounded Raw Score **E − I**		**K. Total Rounded Raw Score** **Round to nearest whole number**	

SAT Math Scaled Score:

SAT Math Test Score Conversion Table			
Raw Score	**Scaled Score**	**Raw Score**	**Scaled Score**
54	800	24	480
53	780	23	470
52	760	22	460
51	740	21	450
50	720	20	440
49	710	19	430
48	700	18	430
47	690	17	420
46	680	16	420
45	670	15	410
44	660	14	400
43	650	13	400
42	640	12	390
41	640	11	380
40	630	10	380
39	620	9	370
38	610	8	360
37	600	7	350
36	590	6	340
35	580	5	330
34	570	4	320
33	560	3	310
32	560	2	300
31	550	1	280
30	540	0	270
29	530	−1	250
28	520	−2	230
27	510	−3	210
26	500	−4 and below	200
25	490		

SECTION 1

Time — 25 minutes
20 Questions

Directions: Solve each problem in this section and enter your answer by marking the circle on the answer sheet. You may use all the space provided for your work.

Notes	1. You may use a calculator during this test.
	2. All numbers used in this test are real numbers.
	3. Unless noted, the domain and the range of a function used in this test are sets of real numbers.
	4. Figures in this test provide useful information in solving problems. They are drawn as accurately as possible. Otherwise, figures not drawn to scale will be labeled as such. Figures lie in a plane.

Information

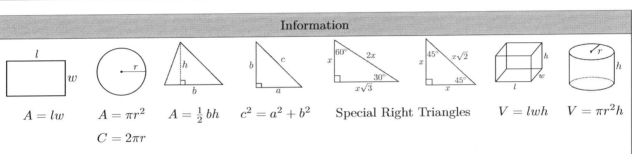

$A = lw$ $A = \pi r^2$ $A = \frac{1}{2}bh$ $c^2 = a^2 + b^2$ Special Right Triangles $V = lwh$ $V = \pi r^2 h$

$C = 2\pi r$

The degree measure of arc in a circle is 360.

The sum of the measures of the interior angles of a triangle is 180.

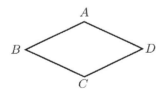

1. The quadrilateral shown above is a rhombus. If $AD = 2x - 1$ and $CD = x + 1$, what is the the value of x ?

(A) 2

(B) 3

(C) 4

(D) 5

(E) 6

2. Sue bought 2 oranges at \$1.19 each and 2 mangoes at \$1.89 each at the store yesterday. The store goes on sales today. The new price of each orange and mango are \$0.99 and \$1.59, respectively. How much would Sue have saved if she bought the same number of fruits at the store today?

(A) \$0.50

(B) \$0.60

(C) \$0.80

(D) \$0.90

(E) \$1.00

3. Which of the following expression is equal to x multiplied by the sum of $2x$ and $3x$?

(A) $6x^3$

(B) $5x^3$

(C) $6x$

(D) $6x^2$

(E) $5x^2$

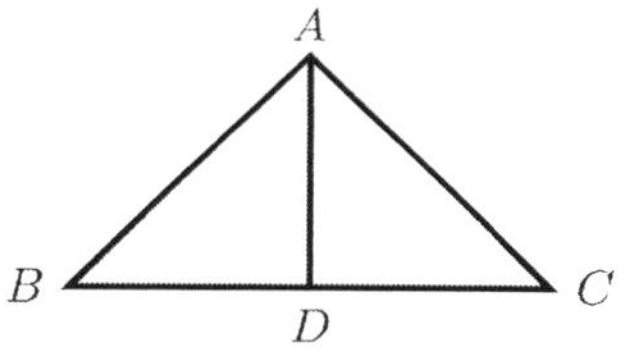

Note: Figure not drawn to scale.

4. In the triangle above, $\overline{AD} \perp \overline{BC}$. If $AB = \sqrt{2}$ and $AD = BD = CD$, what is the area of $\triangle BAC$?

(A) 1

(B) $\sqrt{2}$

(C) 2

(D) $2\sqrt{2}$

(E) 4

5. Which of the following fraction is the largest in value?

(A) $\dfrac{x}{3}$ divided by $\dfrac{x}{5}$

(B) $\dfrac{x}{3}$ divided by $\dfrac{x}{4}$

(C) $\dfrac{x}{4}$ divided by $\dfrac{x}{5}$

(D) $\dfrac{x}{4}$ divided by $\dfrac{x}{6}$

(E) $\dfrac{x}{5}$ divided by $\dfrac{x}{7}$

6. The average of the three numbers, 1, 2, and $x + 3$ is k. What is the value of x in terms of k ?

(A) $k - 6$

(B) $k - 4$

(C) $3k - 8$

(D) $3k - 6$

(E) $3k - 4$

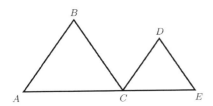

7. In the figure above, $\overline{AB} \parallel \overline{CD}$ and $\overline{BC} \parallel \overline{DE}$. The three points, A, C, and E lie on the same line. If $m\angle BAC = 70°$ and $m\angle ABC = 40°$, what is the measure of $\angle BCD$?

(A) 20

(B) 30

(C) 40

(D) 50

(E) 60

8. If 100 is divided by 3, the quotient is q and the remainder is r. Which of the following expression is equal to 100?

(A) $3r + q$

(B) $3q + r$

(C) $qr + 3$

(D) $r(q + 3)$

(E) $q(3 + r)$

$$0 \le x^2 \le 9$$

9. The set, S, consists of integers that satisfy the inequality above. How many elements does set S have?

(A) 3

(B) 4

(C) 5

(D) 6

(E) 7

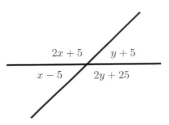

10. Two lines intersect and form two pairs of vertical angles. What is the value of $x + y$?

(A) 80

(B) 90

(C) 100

(D) 110

(E) 120

Bicycling	♡ ♡
Running	♡ ♡ ♡ ♡ ♡ ♡
Rowing	♡ ♡ ♡ ♡
Swimming	♡ ♡ ♡

♡ = 1400 Calories

11. Mr. Rhee is going to a gym to lose weight. The table above summarizes the types of cardiovascular exercises he had done in March. Assuming 3500 calories is equal to 1 pound of body fat, how many pounds of body fat did Mr. Rhee lose in March?

(A) 6

(B) 7

(C) 8

(D) 9

(E) 10

12. Which of the following expression is equal to $\dfrac{x(y+z)}{yz}$?

(A) $\dfrac{x}{y} + \dfrac{z}{y}$

(B) $\dfrac{x}{y} + \dfrac{y}{z}$

(C) $\dfrac{x}{z} + \dfrac{x}{y}$

(D) $\dfrac{x}{z} + \dfrac{y}{x}$

(E) $\dfrac{z}{x} + \dfrac{x}{y}$

13. In a circular track whose circumference is 400 m, Joshua and Jason are running in opposite directions from a starting position. Joshua is running 5 m/s and Jason is running 3 m/s. By the time Joshua and Jason meet each other for the first time, how many meters did Joshua run?

(A) 300

(B) 250

(C) 200

(D) 150

(E) 100

$$f(x) = -2(x-7)^2 + 16$$

14. In the equation above, the parabola, $f(x)$, has a maximum value at $x = 7$. At what value of x does $f(x+10)$ have the maximum value?

(A) -3

(B) 6

(C) 10

(D) 17

(E) 26

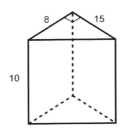

Note: Figure not drawn to scale.

15. In the right triangular prism above, the top face and the bottom face are identical right triangles. What is the surface area of the triangular prism including the top and bottom faces?

(A) 680

(B) 520

(C) 420

(D) 360

(E) 240

$$\sqrt{x^2 + x} > \sqrt{419}$$

16. If $x > 0$, what is the least positive integer value of x that satisfies the inequality shown above?

(A) 23

(B) 22

(C) 21

(D) 20

(E) 19

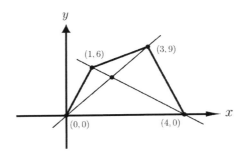

17. In the figure above, each of the two lines passes through the two vertices of the quadrilateral and intersects inside the quadrilateral. What is the x and y coordinate of the intersection point?

(A) $\left(\frac{8}{5}, \frac{24}{5}\right)$

(B) $\left(\frac{24}{5}, \frac{8}{5}\right)$

(C) $\left(\frac{9}{5}, \frac{27}{5}\right)$

(D) $(2, 5)$

(E) $\left(2, \frac{28}{5}\right)$

18. On the number line above, a total of nine tick marks will be placed from $\sqrt{0.81}$ to $\sqrt{6.25}$ inclusive. If all the tick marks are evenly spaced, what is the length between any consecutive tick marks?

(A) 0.16

(B) 0.18

(C) 0.20

(D) 0.22

(E) 0.24

1	x	y	4
		6	9
	11	10	
13			16

19. In the table above, positive integers from 1 to 16 are arranged such that the sum of the numbers in any horizontal, vertical, or main diagonal line is always the same number. If $y > x$, which of the following is the value of x in the table?

   (A)   14

   (B)   12

   (C)   8

   (D)   3

   (E)   2

$$x^{-\frac{1}{2}} = m^{\frac{1}{3}}$$
$$y^3 = n^2$$

20. Which of the following expression is equal to the product of x and y ?

   (A) $\left(mn \right)^{\frac{2}{3}}$

   (B) $\left(mn \right)^{\frac{3}{2}}$

   (C) $\left(\dfrac{n}{m} \right)^{\frac{2}{3}}$

   (D) $\left(\dfrac{m}{n} \right)^{\frac{3}{2}}$

   (E) $\left(\dfrac{n}{m} \right)^{\frac{3}{2}}$

STOP

SECTION 2
Time — 25 minutes
18 Questions

Directions: This section contains two types of questions: Multiple-Choice questions and Free-Response questions. For question 1-8, solve each problem in this section and enter your answer by marking the circle on the answer sheet. You may use all the space provided for your work.

Notes

1. You may use a calculator during this test.

2. All numbers used in this test are real numbers.

3. Unless noted, the domain and the range of a function used in this test are sets of real numbers.

4. Figures in this test provide useful information in solving problems. They are drawn as accurately as possible. Otherwise, figures not drawn to scale will be labeled as such. Figures lie in a plane.

| Information |

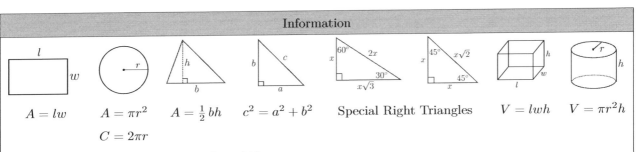

$A = lw$ $A = \pi r^2$ $A = \frac{1}{2}bh$ $c^2 = a^2 + b^2$ Special Right Triangles $V = lwh$ $V = \pi r^2 h$

$C = 2\pi r$

The degree measure of arc in a circle is 360.

The sum of the measures of the interior angles of a triangle is 180.

1. The post office charges \$1.45 for the first ounce and \$0.69 for each additional ounce of a package. If the weight of the package is 10 ounces, which of the following expression represents the total cost, in dollars, of the package?

    (A) $1.45 + 0.69$

    (B) $0.69 + 1.45(9)$

    (C) $0.69 + 1.45(10)$

    (D) $1.45 + 0.69(9)$

    (E) $1.45 + 0.69(10)$

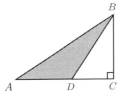

Note: Figure not drawn to scale.

2. In the figure above, $AD = 4$, $DC = 2$, and the area of $\triangle ABC = 21$. What is the area of the shaded region?

    (A)   13

    (B)   14

    (C)   15

    (D)   16

    (E)   17

x	$f(x)$
-2	8
-1	2
0	0
1	2
2	8

3. The table above shows the x and y coordinate of points on the graph of a function. Which of the following function passes through all the points?

   (A) $y = 2x + 12$

   (B) $y = 2x$

   (C) $y = 2x^2$

   (D) $y = 2x^2 - 8$

   (E) $y = -2x^2$

4. Which of the following number has a remainder of 3 if the number is divided by the sum of its digits?

   (A) 25

   (B) 32

   (C) 41

   (D) 47

   (E) 49

5. If $x^2 = 2$, what is the value of $\left(x + \dfrac{1}{x}\right)^2$?

   (A) $\dfrac{5}{2}$

   (B) $\dfrac{7}{2}$

   (C) $\dfrac{9}{2}$

   (D) $\dfrac{11}{2}$

   (E) $\dfrac{13}{2}$

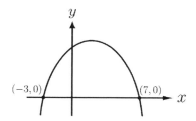

6. The graph above shows the graph of a quadratic function. Which of the following is the equation of the axis of symmetry, a line that passes through the vertex and divides the graph into two perfect halves, of the quadratic function?

   (A) $x = 2$

   (B) $y = 2$

   (C) $x = 4$

   (D) $y = 4$

   (E) $x = 10$

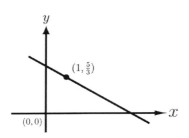

7. In the graph above, the slope of the line is $-\dfrac{1}{3}$. What is the area of the triangular region bounded by the line, x-axis, and y-axis?

   (A) 4

   (B) 6

   (C) 8

   (D) 10

   (E) 12

8. Car A is 80 miles west of a train station. Car B is 35 miles south of the same train station. At noon, car B begins traveling 55 mph due north of the station. Two hours later, car A begins traveling 50 mph due east of the station. At 5 pm, how far apart are these two cars?

   (A) 250

   (B) 300

   (C) 350

   (D) 450

   (E) 500

Direction: For each of the 10 remaining Free-Response questions, solve the problem and enter your answer by marking the circle in the special grid as shown in the examples below.

Answer: $\frac{3}{7}$ Answer: 6.75   Answer: 124

Either position is correct.

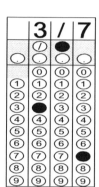
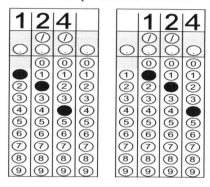

- Fill in one circle in each column.

- Each circle must be filled in correctly. Otherwise, you will not receive any credit.

- Convert all mixed numbers such as $1\frac{1}{2}$ to either 1.5 or $\frac{3}{2}$.

- For decimal answers that are longer than the number of grids provided, you must round or truncate the decimal. However, you must fill in all of the grids provided to ensure your answer is accurate as possible. For example, $0.666\ldots$ must be marked as .666 or .667.

- Answers are always positive.

- Write in the answer at the top of the grid to avoid mistakes when marking the circles.

- On problems that have more than one answer, fill in only one correct answer.

9. $|x - 5| = 4$. What is one of the possible solutions?

10. Three points A, B, and C lie on the same number line, not necessarily in that order. Point A and point B are 50 units apart and point C and point A are 17 units apart. What is the maximum distance that point C and point B are apart?

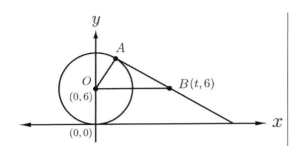

Note: Figure not drawn to scale.

11. In the figure above, a line that passes through point B is tangent to a circle at point A. The center of the circle, O, is along the y axis. If $AB = 8$, what is the value of t ?

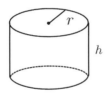

12. In the cylinder above, the height, h, is 5. The sum of the area of the top and bottom faces is 32π and the surface area excluding the top and bottom faces is $a\pi$. What is the value of a ?

13. If $\sqrt{6x - 8} = 2\sqrt{x}$, what is the value of x ?

14. How many positive integers less than 100 are divisible by 4 or 5?

15. If $x = -6$ is a solution to $x^2 + bx - 30 = 0$, what is the other solution?

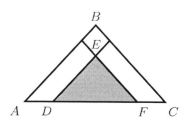

17. In the figure above, $\overline{AB} \parallel \overline{DE}$ and $\overline{BC} \parallel \overline{EF}$. If the ratio of DF to AC is 2 to 3, what is the ratio of the area of the shaded region to that of the unshaded region?

16. If $8^{2x} = 2^{x+3}$, what is the value of x ?

18. Two standard dice are rolled. What is the probability that the product of the two numbers shown on top of the two dice is even?

STOP

www.solomonacademy.net

SECTION 3
Time – 20 minutes
16 Questions

Directions: Solve each problem in this section and enter your answer by marking the circle on the answer sheet. You may use all the space provided for your work.

Notes

1. You may use a calculator during this test.

2. All numbers used in this test are real numbers.

3. Unless noted, the domain and the range of a function used in this test are sets of real numbers.

4. Figures in this test provide useful information in solving problems. They are drawn as accurately as possible. Otherwise, figures not drawn to scale will be labeled as such. Figures lie in a plane.

Information

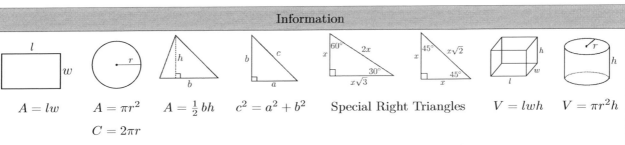

$A = lw$ $A = \pi r^2$ $A = \frac{1}{2}bh$ $c^2 = a^2 + b^2$ Special Right Triangles $V = lwh$ $V = \pi r^2 h$

$C = 2\pi r$

The degree measure of arc in a circle is 360.

The sum of the measures of the interior angles of a triangle is 180.

---

1. x is three times y and y is one less than twice of z. If $z = 3$, what is the value of x ?

(A) -15

(B) -10

(C) 9

(D) 15

(E) 21

x	1	2	3	4	5
y	7	11	15	19	

2. If the pattern shown on the table above continues, what is the value of y when $x = 5$?

(A) 19

(B) 20

(C) 21

(D) 22

(E) 23

3. Joshua and Alex ordered a pizza and ate half of it. One hour later, they ate $\frac{2}{3}$ of the remaining part of the pizza. What fractional part of the pizza have Joshua and Alex eaten?

(A) $\frac{1}{6}$

(B) $\frac{1}{3}$

(C) $\frac{1}{2}$

(D) $\frac{2}{3}$

(E) $\frac{5}{6}$

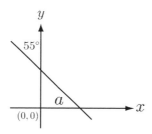

4. In the graph above, a line passes through the x and y axis. What is the measure of $\angle a$?

(A) 25

(B) 35

(C) 45

(D) 55

(E) 65

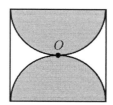

5. In the figure above, Point O is the center of the square with side length of 8. Two semicircles are tangent to each other inside the square. What is the area of the shaded region?

(A) 18π

(B) 16π

(C) 14π

(D) 12π

(E) 10π

6. The sum of x and y is 12. If $y = 2x - 3$, what is the value of y ?

(A) 7

(B) 6

(C) 5

(D) 4

(E) 3

143

7. Jason deposited $133 into his savings account. He withdrew $16 from his savings account to pay for a calculator. He wants to buy as many books as possible with the remaining money in his account. What is the maximum number of books he can buy if each book costs $15?

(A) 5

(B) 6

(C) 7

(D) 8

(E) 9

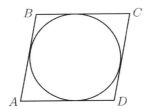

Note: Figure not drawn to scale.

8. In the figure above, a circle is inscribed in parallelogram $ABCD$. The diameter of the circle is the height of the parallelogram. If $AD = 5$ and the radius of the circle is 3, what is the area of parallelogram $ABCD$?

(A) 15

(B) 25

(C) 30

(D) 35

(E) 45

9. There are three books on a bookshelf: two math books and a history book. If you arrange these three books, how many different arrangements are possible?

(A) 27

(B) 9

(C) 6

(D) 3

(E) 1

10. What is the arithmetic mean of the first eight nonnegative even integers?

(A) 5

(B) 6

(C) 7

(D) 8

(E) 9

$$-4 \leq -2x + 2 \leq 6$$

11. Which of the following is the solution to the inequality above?

    (A) $3 \leq x \leq -2$

    (B) $-2 \leq x \leq 3$

    (C) $-5 \leq x \leq 0$

    (D) $0 \leq x \leq -5$

    (E) $-4 \leq x \leq 1$

12. All of the numbers have the same number of factors except which of the following?

    (A)   4

    (B)   9

    (C)   25

    (D)   49

    (E)   51

13. Point A and point B are located on the xy coordinate plane. A line that passes through the two points, A and B, has a slope of $\frac{3}{2}$. Point A and point B are reflected about the y-axis so that they become A' and B'. What is the slope of a new line that passes through point A' and point B' ?

    (A) $\dfrac{2}{3}$

    (B) $\dfrac{3}{2}$

    (C) $\dfrac{1}{2}$

    (D) $-\dfrac{2}{3}$

    (E) $-\dfrac{3}{2}$

14. If a car factory produces x cars in y months, how many cars does the car factory produce in z years?

    (A) $\dfrac{xz}{y}$

    (B) $\dfrac{xy}{z}$

    (C) $\dfrac{12yz}{x}$

    (D) $\dfrac{12xz}{y}$

    (E) $\dfrac{12xy}{z}$

15. An indoor swimming pool opens at 9 am and children start swimming. Staff at the swimming pool strictly follow a safety rule such that children must take a 10 minute break every 45 minutes. According to the safety rule, children take the first break time starting at 9:45 am until 9:55 am. If the swimming pool closes at 6 pm, at what time would last break time begin?

(A) 5:00 pm

(B) 5:05 pm

(C) 5:10 pm

(D) 5:15 pm

(E) 5:20 pm

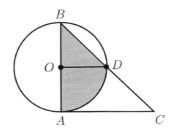

Note: Figure not drawn to scale.

16. In the figure above, the measure of $\angle ABC$ is 45° and $\overline{OD} \parallel \overline{AC}$. If the circumference of the circle is 8π, what is the area of the shaded region?

(A) 4π

(B) $4\pi + 8$

(C) 8π

(D) $8\pi + 8$

(E) $16\pi + 16$

STOP

SAT Math Scoring Worksheet

Directions: In order to calculate your score correctly, fill out the blank spaces from A through K on the table below. After calculating your raw score, round the raw score to the nearest whole number. The scaled score can be determined using the *"SAT Math Test Score Conversion Table"* on the next page.

SAT Math Score			
A. Section 1 Number Correct		**F.** Section 1 Number Incorrect	
B. Section 2 Questions 1-8 Number Correct		**G.** Section 2 Questions 1-8 Number Incorrect	
C. Section 2 Questions 9-18 Number Correct			
D. Section 3 Number Correct		**H.** Section 3 Number Incorrect	
E. Total Correct A+B+C+D		**I.** Total Incorrect (F+G+H)÷4	
J. Total Unrounded Raw Score **E − I**		**K. Total Rounded Raw Score** Round to nearest whole number	

SAT Math Scaled Score: [   ]

SAT Math Test Score Conversion Table			
Raw Score	**Scaled Score**	**Raw Score**	**Scaled Score**
54	800	24	480
53	780	23	470
52	760	22	460
51	740	21	450
50	720	20	440
49	710	19	430
48	700	18	430
47	690	17	420
46	680	16	420
45	670	15	410
44	660	14	400
43	650	13	400
42	640	12	390
41	640	11	380
40	630	10	380
39	620	9	370
38	610	8	360
37	600	7	350
36	590	6	340
35	580	5	330
34	570	4	320
33	560	3	310
32	560	2	300
31	550	1	280
30	540	0	270
29	530	−1	250
28	520	−2	230
27	510	−3	210
26	500	−4 and below	200
25	490		

SECTION 1
Time — 25 minutes
20 Questions

Directions: Solve each problem in this section and enter your answer by marking the circle on the answer sheet. You may use all the space provided for your work.

Notes

1. You may use a calculator during this test.

2. All numbers used in this test are real numbers.

3. Unless noted, the domain and the range of a function used in this test are sets of real numbers.

4. Figures in this test provide useful information in solving problems. They are drawn as accurately as possible. Otherwise, figures not drawn to scale will be labeled as such. Figures lie in a plane.

Information

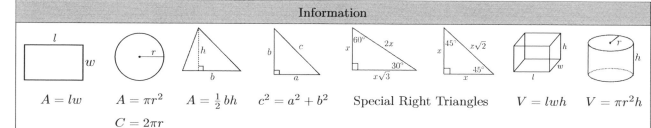

$$A = lw \qquad A = \pi r^2 \qquad A = \tfrac{1}{2}bh \qquad c^2 = a^2 + b^2 \qquad \text{Special Right Triangles} \qquad V = lwh \qquad V = \pi r^2 h$$

$$C = 2\pi r$$

The degree measure of arc in a circle is 360.

The sum of the measures of the interior angles of a triangle is 180.

1. Sue is packing for a trip to Europe. She has two suitcases that weigh 43 pounds each and three backpacks that weigh 12 pounds each. What is the total weight of her luggage in pounds?

   (A)   55

   (B)   79

   (C)   98

   (D)   110

   (E)   122

2. If car A is traveling 60 miles per hour, what is the total distance that car A would travel in three hours?

   (A)   200 miles

   (B)   180 miles

   (C)   120 miles

   (D)   60 miles

   (E)   20 miles

www.solomonacademy.net

3. If the area of each face of a cube is 9, what is the volume of the cube?

(A) 9

(B) 18

(C) 27

(D) 36

(E) 54

4. A tulip grows $\frac{1}{2}$ of an inch for a week. At this rate, how many weeks will it take the tulip to grow 1 foot?

(A) 12 weeks

(B) 16 weeks

(C) 20 weeks

(D) 24 weeks

(E) 28 weeks

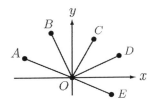

5. In the graphs above, which of the following segment has the largest value of slope?

(A) $\overline{OC}$

(B) $\overline{OD}$

(C) $\overline{OE}$

(D) $\overline{OA}$

(E) $\overline{OB}$

6. The Pythagorean theorem states that in a right triangle, the square of the length of the hypotenuse is equal to the sum of the squares of the lengths of the legs. Which of the following is a set of three positive integers that satisfies the Pythagorean theorem?

(A) $1, 1, \sqrt{2}$

(B) $6, 8, 9$

(C) $5, 12, 15$

(D) $7, 23, 25$

(E) $8, 15, 17$

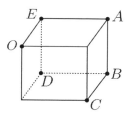

7. In the rectangular box shown above, the length, width, and height of the box are unknown. Which of the following segment is the longest?

(A) $\overline{OA}$

(B) $\overline{OB}$

(C) $\overline{OC}$

(D) $\overline{OD}$

(E) $\overline{OE}$

8. Which of the following linear equation never intersect the line $3y - 2x = 3$?

(A) $y = \dfrac{3}{2}x + 6$

(B) $y = -\dfrac{3}{2}x + 6$

(C) $-2x - 3y = 6$

(D) $-2x + 3y = 6$

(E) $2x + 3y = 6$

9. If $a = 2^x$ and $b = 3^x$, what is 6^x in terms of a and b ?

(A) $a + b$

(B) $a - b$

(C) $a^2 - b^2$

(D) ab

(E) $\dfrac{b}{a}$

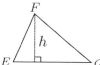
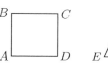

Note: Figure not drawn to scale.

10. In the figure above, square $ABCD$ and triangle EFG have the same areas. If $AB = 2\sqrt{2}$ and $EG = 4\sqrt{2}$, what is the height of triangle EFG ?

(A) $6\sqrt{2}$

(B) $5\sqrt{2}$

(C) $4\sqrt{2}$

(D) $3\sqrt{2}$

(E) $2\sqrt{2}$

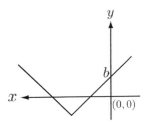

11. The graph of $y = 2|x + 3| - 1$ shown above crosses the y-axis at b. What is the y-coordinate of b ?

(A) 6

(B) 5

(C) 4

(D) 3

(E) 2

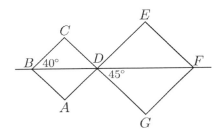

Note: Figure not drawn to scale.

12. In the figure above, two quadrilaterals $ABCD$ and $DEFG$ are parallelograms. What is the measure of $\angle EFG$?

(A) 75

(B) 80

(C) 85

(D) 90

(E) 105

x	1	2	4	5	10
y	10	5	2.5	2	1

13. The table above shows five points on the graph of a function. Which of the following function best represents the table above?

(A) $y = 10x$

(B) $y = 10x^2$

(C) $y = |x + 10|$

(D) $y = \dfrac{10}{x}$

(E) $y = \dfrac{x}{10}$

$$9, 27, 81, 243, \cdots$$

14. In the geometric sequence above, the first term is 9, the second term is 27, and so on and so forth. What is the ratio of the 19th term to the 17th term?

(A) $\dfrac{1}{9}$

(B) $\dfrac{1}{3}$

(C) 3

(D) 6

(E) 9

$$x^2 - 6x + a = (x + b)^2$$

15. The equation above shows that the expression on the left side is equal to the expression on the right side. What is the value of $a + b$?

    (A) -12

    (B) -6

    (C)   6

    (D)   9

    (E)   12

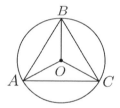

Note: Figure not drawn to scale.

16. In the figure above, the radius of the circle is 10. If the measure of $\angle OAC$ is $30°$, what is the height of $\triangle ABC$?

    (A)   10

    (B) $10\sqrt{3}$

    (C)   15

    (D) $15\sqrt{3}$

    (E)   20

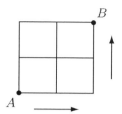

17. As shown in the grid above, Joshua is walking to point B from point A . He is only allowed to walk either right or up, neither left nor down. How many distinct 4-unit paths are there from point A to point B ?

    (A)   3

    (B)   4

    (C)   5

    (D)   6

    (E)   7

$$x^2 - y^2 = 27$$
$$x - y = 3$$

18. From the equations above, what is the value of $x^2 + y^2$?

    (A)   18

    (B)   27

    (C)   36

    (D)   45

    (E)   51

19. For all numbers a and b, a linear function, $f(x)$, satisfies $f(a) > f(b)$ if $a < b$. Which of the following statement must be true about the graph of the linear function $f(x)$ on the xy-coordinate plane?

    (A)   A line with undefined slope.

    (B)   A line with zero slope.

    (C)   A line with positive slope.

    (D)   A line with negative slope.

    (E)   A line that passes through the origin.

20. Joshua is riding his bicycle to visit Alex's house. He averages x miles per hour on the way to Alex's house and averages y miles per hour on the way home. What is the average speed of the entire trip in terms of x and y ?

    (A) $\dfrac{xy}{2}$

    (B) $\dfrac{x+y}{2}$

    (C) $\dfrac{2}{x+y}$

    (D) $\dfrac{2xy}{x+y}$

    (E) $\dfrac{x+y}{xy}$

STOP

www.solomonacademy.net

SECTION 2
Time — 25 minutes
18 Questions

Directions: This section contains two types of questions: Multiple-Choice questions and Free-Response questions. For question 1-8, solve each problem in this section and enter your answer by marking the circle on the answer sheet. You may use all the space provided for your work.

Notes
1. You may use a calculator during this test.
2. All numbers used in this test are real numbers.
3. Unless noted, the domain and the range of a function used in this test are sets of real numbers.
4. Figures in this test provide useful information in solving problems. They are drawn as accurately as possible. Otherwise, figures not drawn to scale will be labeled as such. Figures lie in a plane.

Information

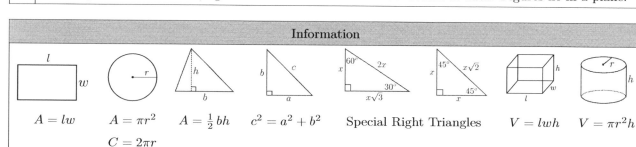

$A = lw$ $A = \pi r^2$ $A = \frac{1}{2}bh$ $c^2 = a^2 + b^2$ Special Right Triangles $V = lwh$ $V = \pi r^2 h$

$C = 2\pi r$

The degree measure of arc in a circle is 360.

The sum of the measures of the interior angles of a triangle is 180.

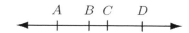

Note: Figure not drawn to scale.

1. If $AD = 15$ and $BC = 14$, what is the value of $AB + CD$?

   (A) 5

   (B) 4

   (C) 3

   (D) 2

   (E) 1

2. The perimeter of an equilateral triangle is the same as the perimeter of a square with side length of 6. What is the length of the side of the equilateral triangle?

   (A) 5

   (B) 6

   (C) 7

   (D) 8

   (E) 9

3. Point $A(-2, -3)$ and point $B(4, 5)$ are located on the xy-coordinate plane. Where is the midpoint between point A and point B located?

   (A) $(-1, 2)$

   (B) $(0, 0)$

   (C) $(1, 1)$

   (D) $(3, 4)$

   (E) $(6, 8)$

4. A clock is malfunctioning. The minute hand of the clock only moves and indicates correct time every 12 minutes. For instance, the clock indicates 12 pm between 12 pm to 12:11 pm and indicates correct time at 12:12 pm. How many times does the clock indicate correct time between 12:10 pm and 5:35 pm?

   (A) 23 times

   (B) 24 times

   (C) 25 times

   (D) 26 times

   (E) 27 times

5. $f(x)$ is a function such that $f(x) = \sqrt{x + k}$, where k is a constant. If $f(-2) = 1$, what is the value of $f(1)$?

   (A) 5

   (B) 4

   (C) 3

   (D) 2

   (E) 1

   I. The solutions to $x^2 = 81$ are 9 or -9.

   II. The values of $\sqrt{4}$ are 2 or -2.

   III. The value of $\dfrac{1}{0}$ is undefined.

   IV. If $x < 0$, $|x| = x$.

6. Which of the following statements above are true?

   (A) I only

   (B) I & III

   (C) I & IV

   (D) II & III

   (E) I & III & IV

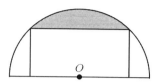

7. In the figure above, a rectangle is inscribed in the semicircle with center O. The length of the rectangle is twice the width of the rectangle. If the radius of the semicircle is 6, what is the perimeter of the shaded region above?

   (A) 3π

   (B) $3\pi + 6$

   (C) $3\pi + 6\sqrt{2}$

   (D) $3\pi + 12$

   (E) $6\pi + 6\sqrt{2}$

8. Mr. Rhee, Sue, Joshua, and Jason are taking a family photo on a long sofa. What is the probability that Mr. Rhee and Sue sit next to each other?

   (A) $\dfrac{1}{6}$

   (B) $\dfrac{1}{5}$

   (C) $\dfrac{1}{4}$

   (D) $\dfrac{1}{3}$

   (E) $\dfrac{1}{2}$

Direction: For each of the 10 remaining Free-Response questions, solve the problem and enter your answer by marking the circle in the special grid as shown in the examples below.

Answer: $\frac{3}{7}$ Answer: 6.75   Answer: 124

Either position is correct.

   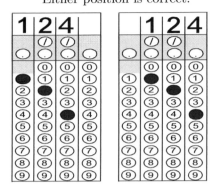

- Fill in one circle in each column.

- Each circle must be filled in correctly. Otherwise, you will not receive any credit.

- Convert all mixed numbers such as $1\frac{1}{2}$ to either 1.5 or $\frac{3}{2}$.

- For decimal answers that are longer than the number of grids provided, you must round or truncate the decimal. However, you must fill in all of the grids provided to ensure your answer is accurate as possible. For example, $0.666\ldots$ must be marked as .666 or .667.

- Answers are always positive.

- Write in the answer at the top of the grid to avoid mistakes when marking the circles.

- On problems that have more than one answer, fill in only one correct answer.

9. How many positive integers less than twelve are prime numbers?

10. If $x = y - 15$, what is the value of $y - x$?

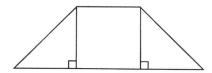

Note: Figure not drawn to scale.

11. In the figure above, the trapezoid consists of two isosceles right triangles and a square. If the length of the hypotenuse of the right triangle is $5\sqrt{2}$, what is the area of the trapezoid?

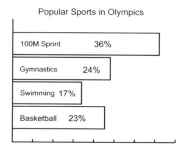

12. A survey asks people in the US which sport they are going to watch in the upcoming Olympics. The chart above shows the results of the survey. If the US population is 300 million, how many more people, in million, are going to watch the most popular sport compared to the least popular sport in the chart?

13. Mr. Rhee is 5 ft 9 inches tall. His son, Joshua, is $\frac{2}{3}$ of Mr. Rhee's height. What is the difference of their heights in inches?

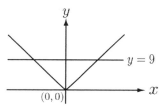

Note: Figure not drawn to scale.

14. In the graph above, the function $y = |x|$ intersects $y = 9$ at $x = a$ and $x = b$ on the xy-coordinate plane (a and b are not shown on the graph). If $a < b$, what is the value of b ?

$$\sqrt{x+y} = \sqrt{x} + \sqrt{y}$$

15. If $y > 0$, the equation above is only true when $x = ?$

16. In a store, Jason paid \$39 for one book and two DVDs. If he buys two books and one DVD, he would pay \$27. What is the average price of the book and the DVD?

17. A big water bottle on the cooler was full on Monday. Students drank one-fourth the water on Tuesday, one-third of the remaining on Wednesday, one-half of the remaining on Thursday. What fractional part of the water would be remaining in the water bottle?

$$xy + x + y + 1 = 77$$

18. If the positive integers x and y satisfy the equation above, what is one possible value of x ?

STOP

SECTION 3
Time – 20 minutes
16 Questions

Directions: Solve each problem in this section and enter your answer by marking the circle on the answer sheet. You may use all the space provided for your work.

Notes

1. You may use a calculator during this test.

2. All numbers used in this test are real numbers.

3. Unless noted, the domain and the range of a function used in this test are sets of real numbers.

4. Figures in this test provide useful information in solving problems. They are drawn as accurately as possible. Otherwise, figures not drawn to scale will be labeled as such. Figures lie in a plane.

Information

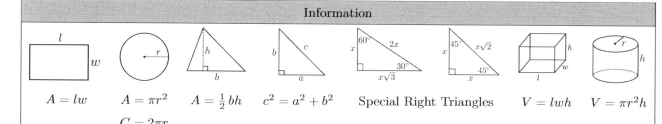

$A = lw$ $A = \pi r^2$ $A = \frac{1}{2}bh$ $c^2 = a^2 + b^2$ Special Right Triangles $V = lwh$ $V = \pi r^2 h$

$C = 2\pi r$

The degree measure of arc in a circle is 360.

The sum of the measures of the interior angles of a triangle is 180.

1. At store A, three pens cost \$2.04. However, at store B, three pens cost \$2.25. How much money, in cents, do you save per pen if you buy three pens at store A ?

   (A) 0.07

   (B) 0.21

   (C) 0

   (D) 7

   (E) 21

2. A triangle is a 30°- 60°- 90° special right triangle. If the length of the hypotenuse is 8, then what is the length of the side opposite the angle 30° ?

   (A) $2\sqrt{2}$

   (B) 4

   (C) $4\sqrt{3}$

   (D) 6

   (E) $6\sqrt{3}$

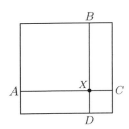

Note: Figure not drawn to scale.

3. In the figure above, point X lies inside a square with side length of 10. If $\overline{AC}$ and $\overline{BD}$ are parallel to the sides of the square, what is the value of $XA + XB + XC + XD$?

   (A)   20

   (B)   17

   (C)   15

   (D)   12

   (E)   10

4. If the square of a number is equal to the number, what is the value of the number?

   (A)   0 only

   (B)   1 only

   (C)   2 only

   (D)   0 or 1

   (E)   1 or 2

5. If $(x+2)^3 = 64$, what is the value of $\dfrac{1}{x+2}$?

   (A) $\dfrac{1}{5}$

   (B) $\dfrac{1}{4}$

   (C) $\dfrac{1}{3}$

   (D)   2

   (E)   4

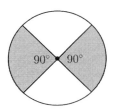

Note: Figure not drawn to scale.

6. In the figure above, the radius of the circle is 2. What is the area of the shaded region?

   (A) $\dfrac{\pi}{2}$

   (B) π

   (C) 2π

   (D) 3π

   (E) 4π

7. If the sum of five consecutive even integers is 120, what is the value of the largest integer?

   (A)   20

   (B)   22

   (C)   24

   (D)   26

   (E)   28

8. What is the sum of the units digit of the first seven positive squares?

   (A)   20

   (B)   25

   (C)   30

   (D)   35

   (E)   40

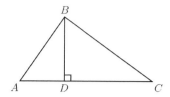

9. In the figure above, $BD = x$ and $AC = 2x - 2$. Which of the following expression best represents the area, A, of $\triangle ABC$?

   (A) $A = 3x - 2$

   (B) $A = x^2 - 2$

   (C) $A = x^2 - x$

   (D) $A = 2x^2 - 2$

   (E) $A = 2x^2 - 2x$

10. In a set of five distinct positive integers, the average of the two smallest integers is 2, the average of the three smallest integers is 3, the average of the four smallest is 4, and the average of all five integers is 5. What is the largest integer in the set?

   (A)   9

   (B)   10

   (C)   11

   (D)   12

   (E)   13

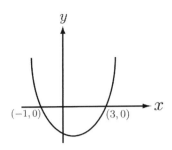

11. The graph above shows the graph of a quadratic function $y = (x - p)(x + q)$. If $|p| > |q|$, what is the value of $p + q$?

(A)   2

(B)   3

(C)   4

(D) -2

(E) -4

12. A farmer wants to build a fence around his rectangular field. In addition, he wants to divide it in half with a fence perpendicular to the longer side of the rectangular field so that it becomes two smaller squares. If the total length of the fence is 350 feet, what is the length of the shorter side of the rectangular field?

(A)   20 feet

(B)   30 feet

(C)   40 feet

(D)   50 feet

(E)   60 feet

13. Let $x \, \Phi \, n = \dfrac{20 - x}{\sqrt{n}}$. Which of the following expression has the largest value?

(A) $15 \, \Phi \, 20$

(B) $10 \, \Phi \, 20$

(C) $15 \, \Phi \, 40$

(D) $10 \, \Phi \, 40$

(E) $5 \, \Phi \, 80$

$$19, 23, 27, \cdots, 131, 135$$

14. In the sequence above, how many terms are there between 19 and 135 inclusive?

(A)   26

(B)   27

(C)   28

(D)   29

(E)   30

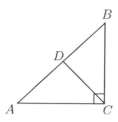

Note: Figure not drawn to scale.

15. In $\triangle ABC$ shown above, $\overline{CD}$ is drawn to $\overline{AB}$ so that $\overline{CD}\perp\overline{AB}$. If $AB = 10$ and $AC = 8$, what is the length of $\overline{CD}$?

   (A)   2

   (B)   2.4

   (C)   4

   (D)   4.8

   (E)   6

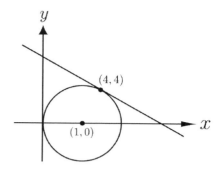

Note: Figure not drawn to scale.

16. In the figure above, the center of a circle is located at $(1, 0)$ and a line is tangent to the circle at $(4, 4)$. What is the equation of the tangent line?

   (A) $4x + 3y = 28$

   (B) $4x - 3y = 4$

   (C) $3x - 4y = -4$

   (D) $3x + 4y = 28$

   (E) $3x - 4y = -4$

STOP

SAT Math Scoring Worksheet

Directions: In order to calculate your score correctly, fill out the blank spaces from A through K on the table below. After calculating your raw score, round the raw score to the nearest whole number. The scaled score can be determined using the *"SAT Math Test Score Conversion Table"* on the next page.

SAT Math Score			
A. Section 1 Number Correct		**F.** Section 1 Number Incorrect	
B. Section 2 Questions 1-8 Number Correct		**G.** Section 2 Questions 1-8 Number Incorrect	
C. Section 2 Questions 9-18 Number Correct			
D. Section 3 Number Correct		**H.** Section 3 Number Incorrect	
E. Total Correct A+B+C+D		**I.** Total Incorrect (F+G+H)÷4	
J. Total Unrounded Raw Score E − I		**K. Total Rounded Raw Score** Round to nearest whole number	

SAT Math Scaled Score:

SAT Math Test Score Conversion Table			
Raw Score	Scaled Score	Raw Score	Scaled Score
54	800	24	480
53	780	23	470
52	760	22	460
51	740	21	450
50	720	20	440
49	710	19	430
48	700	18	430
47	690	17	420
46	680	16	420
45	670	15	410
44	660	14	400
43	650	13	400
42	640	12	390
41	640	11	380
40	630	10	380
39	620	9	370
38	610	8	360
37	600	7	350
36	590	6	340
35	580	5	330
34	570	4	320
33	560	3	310
32	560	2	300
31	550	1	280
30	540	0	270
29	530	−1	250
28	520	−2	230
27	510	−3	210
26	500	−4 and below	200
25	490		

SECTION 1
Time — 25 minutes
20 Questions

Directions: Solve each problem in this section and enter your answer by marking the circle on the answer sheet. You may use all the space provided for your work.

Notes

1. You may use a calculator during this test.

2. All numbers used in this test are real numbers.

3. Unless noted, the domain and the range of a function used in this test are sets of real numbers.

4. Figures in this test provide useful information in solving problems. They are drawn as accurately as possible. Otherwise, figures not drawn to scale will be labeled as such. Figures lie in a plane.

Information

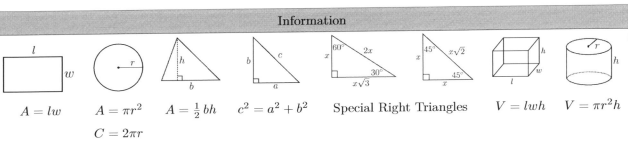

$A = lw$ $A = \pi r^2$ $A = \frac{1}{2} bh$ $c^2 = a^2 + b^2$ Special Right Triangles $V = lwh$ $V = \pi r^2 h$

$C = 2\pi r$

The degree measure of arc in a circle is 360.

The sum of the measures of the interior angles of a triangle is 180.

---

1. What is the solution to $-3x > 6$?

   (A) $x > 9$

   (B) $x > 2$

   (C) $x < -9$

   (D) $x > -2$

   (E) $x < -2$

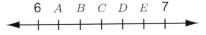

2. On the number line above, which letter is the closest to 6.6?

   (A) A

   (B) B

   (C) C

   (D) D

   (E) E

$$1, \frac{1}{2}, \frac{1}{4}, \cdots$$

3. In the sequence above, what is the value of the fifth term?

   (A) $\frac{1}{6}$

   (B) $\frac{1}{8}$

   (C) $\frac{1}{12}$

   (D) $\frac{1}{16}$

   (E) $\frac{1}{32}$

4. Joshua is running 3 feet per second. If Jason is 100 yards ahead of Joshua, how long will it take, in minutes and seconds, for Joshua to catch up to Jason?

   (A) Exactly 2 minutes

   (B) 1 minute and 40 seconds

   (C) 1 minute and 20 seconds

   (D) Exactly 1 minute

   (E) 0 minute and 40 seconds

5. In the figure above, a rectangle whose area is 16 is divided into two smaller rectangles so that the ratio of the area of the larger rectangle to that of the smaller rectangle is 3 to 1. What is the area of the smaller rectangle?

   (A) 2

   (B) 4

   (C) 6

   (D) 9

   (E) 12

6. In the figure above, a circle is inscribed in a square. If the perimeter of the square is 36, what is the diameter of the circle?

   (A) 6

   (B) 7

   (C) 8

   (D) 9

   (E) 10

7. The positive difference of x and y is 5. If $x < y$ and $y = 8$, what is the value of x ?

   (A)   4

   (B)   3

   (C)   2

   (D) -1

   (E) -3

8. If $x < 0$, what is the value of x that satisfies $(x - 1)^2 = 4$?

   (A)   3

   (B)   2

   (C) -1

   (D) -2

   (E) -3

9. Which of the following linear equation is perpendicular to each other?

   (A) $y = \dfrac{1}{2}x + 4$

            $x - 2y = 6$

   (B) $y = \dfrac{1}{2}x + 4$

            $x + 2y = 6$

   (C) $y = \dfrac{1}{3}x + 4$

            $3x - y = 6$

   (D) $y = \dfrac{1}{3}x + 4$

            $3x - y = -6$

   (E) $y = \dfrac{1}{3}x + 4$

            $3x + y = 6$

x	-2	0	3	5
y	7	3	-3	k

10. The table above shows the four points on a straight line. If the slope of the line is -2, what is the value of k ?

   (A) -3

   (B) -4

   (C) -5

   (D) -6

   (E) -7

11. In a dog park, there are thirty dogs. Eighteen dogs have short hair and twelve dogs have spots. What is the largest number of dogs that can have both short hair and spots?

(A) 12

(B) 13

(C) 14

(D) 15

(E) 16

12. Which of the following expression is equal to 2^{3-2x} ?

(A) $\dfrac{6}{2^x}$

(B) $\dfrac{6}{4^x}$

(C) $\dfrac{8}{4^x}$

(D) $6 \cdot 4^x$

(E) $8 \cdot 2^x$

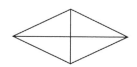

13. In the figure above, the lengths of the diagonals of the rhombus are 12 and 16. What is the perimeter of the rhombus?

(A) 20

(B) 30

(C) 40

(D) 50

(E) 60

14. The price of a pen is $4.50 in April and is increased by 100% in May. What is the price of the pen in May?

(A) $9.00

(B) $7.75

(C) $6.75

(D) $5.25

(E) $4.75

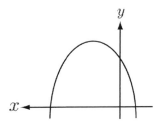

15. In the graph shown above, the x-intercepts of the quadratic function are p and q. If the quadratic function is reflected about the y-axis, what is the sum of the new x-intercepts in terms of p and q ?

    (A) $-p + q$

    (B) $-p + q$

    (C) $-p - q$

    (D) $-q + p$

    (E) $-pq$

$$A + C < B$$
$$B - D > 0$$
$$A - D < 0$$
$$D - C > D - A$$

16. In the inequalities above, A, B, C, and D represent different positive digits. Which of the following inequality must be true about A, B, C, and D ?

    (A) $A < B < C < D$

    (B) $A < C < B < D$

    (C) $C < A < B < D$

    (D) $A < C < D < B$

    (E) $C < A < D < B$

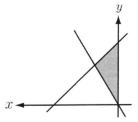

17. In the graph above, $y = x + 6$ intersects $y = -2x$. What is the area of the shaded region?

    (A)   6

    (B)   8

    (C)   10

    (D)   12

    (E)   14

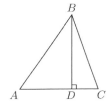

18. In the triangle above, $AB = 15$, $BC = 13$, and $AC = 14$. If CD is four less than AD, what is the area of $\triangle BCD$?

    (A)   30

    (B)   36

    (C)   42

    (D)   48

    (E)   54

19. A set, S, consists of the first five terms of an arithmetic sequence in which the third term is 19. If 4 is added to each element in set S, What is the sum of the mean and the median of the new set S ?

   (A) 38

   (B) 46

   (C) 54

   (D) 62

   (E) 70

20. The length, width, and height of a rectangular box is three, four, and five feet respectively. Each length, width, and height is divided by 3, 4, and 5 so that the rectangular box is divided into smaller cubes with sides of 1 foot. If one can of paint is needed to paint 12 square feet, how many cans of paint are needed to paint the surface area of all smaller cubes?

   (A) 5

   (B) 15

   (C) 20

   (D) 25

   (E) 30

STOP

SECTION 2
Time — 25 minutes
18 Questions

Directions: This section contains two types of questions: Multiple-Choice questions and Free-Response questions. For question 1-8, solve each problem in this section and enter your answer by marking the circle on the answer sheet. You may use all the space provided for your work.

Notes

1. You may use a calculator during this test.

2. All numbers used in this test are real numbers.

3. Unless noted, the domain and the range of a function used in this test are sets of real numbers.

4. Figures in this test provide useful information in solving problems. They are drawn as accurately as possible. Otherwise, figures not drawn to scale will be labeled as such. Figures lie in a plane.

Information

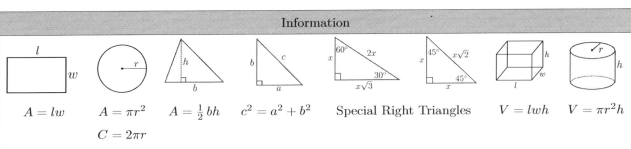

$A = lw$ $A = \pi r^2$ $A = \frac{1}{2}bh$ $c^2 = a^2 + b^2$ Special Right Triangles $V = lwh$ $V = \pi r^2 h$

$C = 2\pi r$

The degree measure of arc in a circle is 360.

The sum of the measures of the interior angles of a triangle is 180.

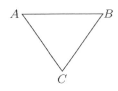

1. In $\triangle ABC$, point D and E are midpoints of segment $\overline{AC}$ and $\overline{BC}$ respectively. What is the length of $\overline{DE}$ if $AB = 10$?

   (A)   3

   (B)   4

   (C)   5

   (D)   6

   (E)   7

x	-1	1	3	5
y	-3	-3	-3	-3

2. In the table above, which of the following function contains the four ordered pairs shown on the table?

   (A) $x = 3$

   (B) $y = 3$

   (C) $y = x$

   (D) $x = -3$

   (E) $y = -3$

     www.solomonacademy.net

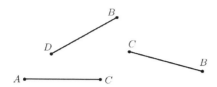

Note: Figure not drawn to scale.

3. In the figure above, $AC = 2$, $BD = 3$, and $CB = 4$. If the three segments are put together so that points A, C, B, and D are arranged on the number line in that order, what is the length of segment $\overline{AD}$?

(A)   10

(B)   9

(C)   8

(D)   7

(E)   6

4. In a triangle ABC, the measure of $\angle C$ is $90°$. If angle A and angle B are complementary and the measure of $\angle A$ is 30 less than twice the measure of $\angle B$, what is the measure of $\angle A$?

(A)   40

(B)   45

(C)   50

(D)   55

(E)   60

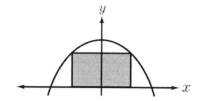

5. In the graph above, the two vertices of a rectangle are on the graph of $y = 9 - x^2$, and the other two vertices are on the x-axis at $x = -2$ and $x = 2$. What is the area of the rectangle?

(A)   10

(B)   20

(C)   30

(D)   40

(E)   50

6. Mr. Rhee is running on a treadmill. He burns three calories every twelve seconds. How many calories will he burn if he runs $\frac{2}{3}$ hour on the treadmill?

(A)   300 calories

(B)   400 calories

(C)   500 calories

(D)   600 calories

(E)   700 calories

   www.solomonacademy.net

Year	$\cdots$	9	11	13	$\cdots$
Amount	$\cdots$	$2580	$2820	$3060	$\cdots$

7. The table above shows the amount of money that Sue has in her savings account over time. If the amount of money increases at a constant rate throughout the years, how much money did Sue deposit in her savings account in the beginning?

   (A) $1250

   (B) $1500

   (C) $1750

   (D) $2000

   (E) $2250

8. Joshua arranges the numbers 1 through 10 clockwise in that order around a circle. He removes one number among the ten numbers and starts removing every third number clockwise. For instance, if he removes 1, the next number he will remove is 4, 7, and so on and so forth. If Joshua removes 4 last, which of the following number does he remove first?

   (A) 3

   (B) 5

   (C) 6

   (D) 7

   (E) 10

Direction: For each of the 10 remaining Free-Response questions, solve the problem and enter your answer by marking the circle in the special grid as shown in the examples below.

Answer: $\frac{3}{7}$ Answer: 6.75   Answer: 124

Either position is correct.

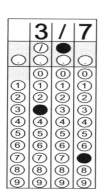
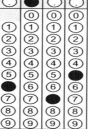
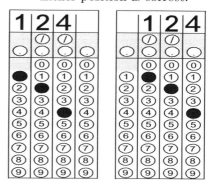

- Fill in one circle in each column.

- Each circle must be filled in correctly. Otherwise, you will not receive any credit.

- Convert all mixed numbers such as $1\frac{1}{2}$ to either 1.5 or $\frac{3}{2}$.

- For decimal answers that are longer than the number of grids provided, you must round or truncate the decimal. However, you must fill in all of the grids provided to ensure your answer is accurate as possible. For example, $0.666\ldots$ must be marked as .666 or .667.

- Answers are always positive.

- Write in the answer at the top of the grid to avoid mistakes when marking the circles.

- On problems that have more than one answer, fill in only one correct answer.

9. What is the value of $\dfrac{x-1}{3(x-2)}$ when $x = -2$?

10. If $0.01 < \dfrac{1}{k} < 0.1$ and k is an integer, what is the largest possible value of k ?

11. The length of the shorter side of a rectangle is one less than the length of the longer side of the rectangle. If the area of the rectangle is 110, what is the length of the shorter side?

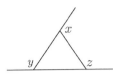

13. In the figure above, two sides of the triangle are expanded to form $\angle x$, $\angle y$, and $\angle z$. What is $m\angle x + m\angle y + m\angle z$?

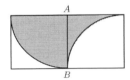

12. In the rectangle above, segment $\overline{AB}$ is drawn so that the rectangle is divided into two smaller squares. If the area of the rectangle is 98, what is the area of the shaded region?

14. A straight line crosses the x-axis at -7 and crosses the y-axis at 2. What is the slope of the line?

15. If x is a positive integer greater than 1 for which $\sqrt{x}$ and $\sqrt[3]{x}$ are both integers, what is the smallest possible value of x ?

x	$f(x)$
-2	3
-1	7
0	-5
1	-1
2	-2

16. The table above shows the function values of f at certain x values. If function p is defined by $p(x) = f(x) + g(x)$ where $g(x) = f(-2x)$ for all values of x, what is the value of $p(-1)$?

17. A ferris wheel with a diameter of 60 feet takes 35 seconds to make a rotation. If Jason rides the ferris wheel for 1 minute and 24 seconds, through what angle, in degrees, does he rotate?

18. A clock tower has a clock with a diameter of 20 feet. The tip of the minute hand moves along the circumference of the clock. When the clock indicates 4:10 pm, the tip of the minute hand of the clock is 114 feet directly above the ground. How high, in yards, is the bottom of the clock directly above the ground?

STOP

SECTION 3
Time – 20 minutes
16 Questions

Directions:	Solve each problem in this section and enter your answer by marking the circle on the answer sheet. You may use all the space provided for your work.

Notes	1. You may use a calculator during this test.
	2. All numbers used in this test are real numbers.
	3. Unless noted, the domain and the range of a function used in this test are sets of real numbers.
	4. Figures in this test provide useful information in solving problems. They are drawn as accurately as possible. Otherwise, figures not drawn to scale will be labeled as such. Figures lie in a plane.

Information

$A = lw$ $A = \pi r^2$ $A = \frac{1}{2}bh$ $c^2 = a^2 + b^2$ Special Right Triangles $V = lwh$ $V = \pi r^2 h$

$C = 2\pi r$

The degree measure of arc in a circle is 360.

The sum of the measures of the interior angles of a triangle is 180.

---

1. $x = 2y$ and $y = 3z$. If $x = 24$, what is the value of z ?

(A) 2

(B) 3

(C) 4

(D) 6

(E) 8

2. In the figure above, two circles are externally tangent to each other. The ratio of the radius of the larger circle to that of the smaller circle is 2 to 1. If the length of a segment connecting the center of each circle is 15, what is the radius of the larger circle?

(A) 5

(B) 6

(C) 7

(D) 8

(E) 10

3. One yard of wire is divided into two pieces. The length of the shorter piece is 8 inches, which is $\frac{2}{7}$ of the length of the longer piece. What is the length of the longer piece in inches?

   (A)   24 inches

   (B)   26 inches

   (C)   28 inches

   (D)   30 inches

   (E)   32 inches

4. In a geometric sequence, the fourth term is 11 and the sixth term is 99. What is the value of the fifth term?

   (A)   22

   (B)   33

   (C)   44

   (D)   55

   (E)   66

5. Two stores A and B go on sale on the same item. Stores A and B give 9% and 16% discounts respectively. If the price of the item is x and you buy the item at store B, how much money would you save in terms of x ?

   (A) $0.007x$

   (B) $0.07x$

   (C) $0.7x$

   (D) $7x$

   (E) $70x$

6. Which of the following point below satisfies the equation $y - 3 = |2 - x|$?

   (A) $(-2, 3)$

   (B) $(-1, 4)$

   (C) $(3, 2)$

   (D) $(4, 1)$

   (E) $(5, 6)$

7. If $\sqrt{2} + \sqrt{8} + \sqrt{32} = n\sqrt{2}$, what is the value of n ?

(A) 5

(B) 6

(C) 7

(D) 8

(E) 9

9. How many factors of 96 are odd?

(A) 1

(B) 2

(C) 3

(D) 4

(E) 5

Note: Figure not drawn to scale.

8. In the figure above, $AB \parallel DE$, $AB = 5$, and $DE = 10$. If the area of $\triangle ABC = 15$, what is the height of $\triangle DCE$?

(A) 4

(B) 6

(C) 8

(D) 10

(E) 12

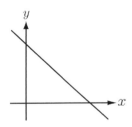

10. The graph above shows the graph of $y = 5 - x$. If $0 < x < 5$, how many points (x, y) are on the graph above have integer value of x and y ?

(A) 6

(B) 5

(C) 4

(D) 3

(E) 2

11. A ladder of 10 feet is leaning against the wall so that the bottom of the ladder is 6 feet away from the wall. If the top of the ladder starts sliding down the wall 1 foot per second, how far away is the bottom of the ladder from the wall after 2 seconds?

(A) 8 feet

(B) 7 feet

(C) 6 feet

(D) 5 feet

(E) 4 feet

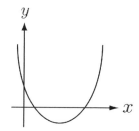

12. The graph above shows the graph of a quadratic function $y = (x-1)(x-3)$. If the graph is reflected about the x axis, what is the new x and y coordinate of the vertex?

(A) $(-2, -3)$

(B) $(-2, -1)$

(C) $(-2, 1)$

(D) $(2, -1)$

(E) $(2, 1)$

13. In the figures above, the cone and the cylinder have the same radius and the same height. If the cone is put inside the cylinder whose volume is V, what is the volume outside the cone but inside the cylinder in terms of V ?

(A) $\frac{2}{3}V$

(B) $\frac{5}{8}V$

(C) $\frac{1}{2}V$

(D) $\frac{3}{8}V$

(E) $\frac{1}{3}V$

14. There are four seats in a room and four students A, B, C, and D take each seat. A and B do not want to sit next to each other. However, C and D want to sit next to each other. A wants to sit left of C and B wants to sit closer to D than to C. Which of the following seating arrangement satisfies the four students? List the four students from the left.

(A) $B - C - D - A$

(B) $B - D - C - A$

(C) $A - C - D - B$

(D) $A - D - C - B$

(E) $A - D - B - C$

15. There are forty seven students in a class. Each student plays either tennis or baseball or both. The number of students who play baseball is three more than twice the number of students who play both sports. The number of students who play tennis is three times the number of students who play baseball. How many students in the class play only tennis?

(A)   13

(B)   18

(C)   26

(D)   34

(E)   39

16. Joshua is three times as old as his younger brother, Jason. In six years, Joshua will be twice as old as Jason. How many years from now will Jason be two-thirds as old as Joshua?

(A)   18

(B)   16

(C)   14

(D)   12

(E)   10

STOP

SAT Math Scoring Worksheet

Directions: In order to calculate your score correctly, fill out the blank spaces from A through K on the table below. After calculating your raw score, round the raw score to the nearest whole number. The scaled score can be determined using the *"SAT Math Test Score Conversion Table"* on the next page.

SAT Math Score			
A. Section 1 Number Correct		**F.** Section 1 Number Incorrect	
B. Section 2 Questions 1-8 Number Correct		**G.** Section 2 Questions 1-8 Number Incorrect	
C. Section 2 Questions 9-18 Number Correct			
D. Section 3 Number Correct		**H.** Section 3 Number Incorrect	
E. Total Correct A+B+C+D		**I.** Total Incorrect (F+G+H)÷4	
J. Total Unrounded Raw Score E − I		**K. Total Rounded Raw Score** Round to nearest whole number	

SAT Math Scaled Score:

SAT Math Test Score Conversion Table

Raw Score	Scaled Score	Raw Score	Scaled Score
54	800	24	480
53	780	23	470
52	760	22	460
51	740	21	450
50	720	20	440
49	710	19	430
48	700	18	430
47	690	17	420
46	680	16	420
45	670	15	410
44	660	14	400
43	650	13	400
42	640	12	390
41	640	11	380
40	630	10	380
39	620	9	370
38	610	8	360
37	600	7	350
36	590	6	340
35	580	5	330
34	570	4	320
33	560	3	310
32	560	2	300
31	550	1	280
30	540	0	270
29	530	−1	250
28	520	−2	230
27	510	−3	210
26	500	−4 and below	200
25	490		

SECTION 1
Time — 25 minutes
20 Questions

Directions: Solve each problem in this section and enter your answer by marking the circle on the answer sheet. You may use all the space provided for your work.

Notes
1. You may use a calculator during this test.
2. All numbers used in this test are real numbers.
3. Unless noted, the domain and the range of a function used in this test are sets of real numbers.
4. Figures in this test provide useful information in solving problems. They are drawn as accurately as possible. Otherwise, figures not drawn to scale will be labeled as such. Figures lie in a plane.

Information

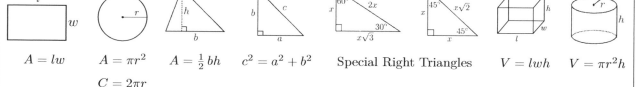

$A = lw$ $A = \pi r^2$ $A = \frac{1}{2}bh$ $c^2 = a^2 + b^2$ Special Right Triangles $V = lwh$ $V = \pi r^2 h$

$C = 2\pi r$

The degree measure of arc in a circle is 360.

The sum of the measures of the interior angles of a triangle is 180.

---

1. If the area of a square is 4, what is the perimeter of the square?

(A) 8

(B) 7

(C) 6

(D) 5

(E) 4

2. Let $\begin{vmatrix} a & b \\ c & d \end{vmatrix} = ad - bc.$ $\begin{vmatrix} 5 & 6 \\ 5 & 7 \end{vmatrix} = ?$

(A) 1

(B) 2

(C) 3

(D) 4

(E) 5

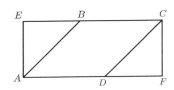

3. In the figure above, $AECF$ is a rectangle and $ABCD$ is a rhombus. If the length of $\overline{EB}$ is 6, what is length of $\overline{FD}$?

(A) 2

(B) 4

(C) 6

(D) 8

(E) 10

4. Two numbers x and y are on the number line. If the midpoint of x and y is 5, what is the value of x in terms of y ?

(A) $10 + y$

(B) $10 - y$

(C) $5 + y$

(D) $5 - y$

(E) $y - 5$

5. Joshua starts walking due south 4 feet per second. At the same time, Jason starts walking due west 3 feet per second. If they start walking from the same location, how far apart are they after 10 seconds?

(A) 70 feet

(B) 65 feet

(C) 60 feet

(D) 55 feet

(E) 50 feet

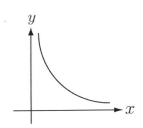

6. The graph above shows the graph of $f(x) = \dfrac{2}{x}$. At what value of x is $f(x)$ equal to 4?

(A) $\dfrac{1}{4}$

(B) $\dfrac{1}{2}$

(C) 1

(D) 2

(E) 4

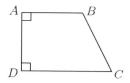

7. In the figure above, $AB = 12$, $CD = 17$ and $AD = 12$. What is the length of $\overline{BC}$?

(A) 11

(B) 12

(C) 13

(D) 14

(E) 15

8. Mr. Rhee starts running. For the first second, he is running away 7 meters from the starting position. For the next second, he is running 3 meters toward the starting position. If he continues running in this pattern, how far is Mr. Rhee away from the starting position after 11 seconds?

(A) 20 meters

(B) 21 meters

(C) 23 meters

(D) 25 meters

(E) 27 meters

9. What is the sum of the two x-intercepts of the function $f(x) = (2x - 3)(2x + 1)$?

(A) -2

(B) -1

(C) $-\dfrac{1}{2}$

(D) 1

(E) 2

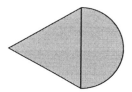

10. The figure above consists of an equilateral triangle and a semicircle. If the diameter of the semicircle is 8, what is the perimeter of the shaded area?

(A) $8 + 4\pi$

(B) $12 + 8\pi$

(C) $16 + 4\pi$

(D) $16 + 8\pi$

(E) $24 + 8\pi$

11. There are two red marbles and a certain number of green and blue marbles in a bag. If the probability of selecting a red marble is $\frac{1}{6}$, how many non-red marbles are in the bag?

(A) 10

(B) 8

(C) 6

(D) 4

(E) 2

12. Four more than twice a number is at least 12 and is at most 16. What is the range of the number?

(A) $2 < x < 4$

(B) $2 < x \leq 4$

(C) $4 < x < 6$

(D) $4 \leq x < 6$

(E) $4 \leq x \leq 6$

Time	Average Speed
9 am to 10 am	50 miles per hour
10 am to 11:30 am	60 miles per hour
11:30 am to 12:00pm	Break
12:00 pm to 4:00 pm	55 miles per hour

13. According to the chart above, what is the total distance that Mr. Rhee traveled between 9 am to 4 pm ?

(A) 200 miles

(B) 240 miles

(C) 280 miles

(D) 320 miles

(E) 360 miles

14. For all non-negative integers n, $n\Psi$ is defined as the product of all positive consecutive odd integers less than or equal to n. For instance, $7\Psi = 7 \times 5 \times 3 \times 1$. What is the value of $\dfrac{15\Psi}{12\Psi}$?

(A) 143

(B) 156

(C) 195

(D) 210

(E) 225

www.solomonacademy.net

15. A clock indicates 9:33 pm now. When the clock indicates 9:42 pm, what angle, in degrees, does the minute hand rotate?

(A)   54°

(B)   58°

(C)   62°

(D)   66°

(E)   70°

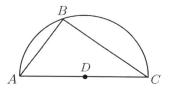

16. In the figure above, $\triangle ABC$ is inscribed in a semicircle whose center is D. The measure of $\angle A$ is twice the measure of $\angle C$. If $BC = 10\sqrt{3}$, what is $AB + AC$?

(A)   20

(B) $20 + 5\sqrt{2}$

(C) $20 + 5\sqrt{3}$

(D)   30

(E)   50

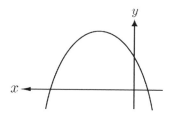

17. The graph above shows the graph of a quadratic function $y = -2(x + 1)^2 + 7$. What is the maximum value of the function?

(A) -1

(B)   5

(C)   6

(D)   7

(E)   8

18. There are twenty nine questions on a math exam worth a total of one hundred points. Each question is worth either three points or four points. How many questions on the math exam are worth four points?

(A)   12

(B)   13

(C)   14

(D)   15

(E)   16

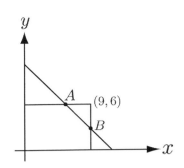

Note: Figure not drawn to scale.

19. In the figure above, two vertices of the rectangle are on the x-axis and the right upper corner of the rectangle is located at $(9,6)$. If the line $y = -\dfrac{4}{3}x + 14$ intersects the rectangle at A and B, what is the length of $\overline{AB}$?

    (A) $\sqrt{8}$

    (B) $\sqrt{13}$

    (C) $\sqrt{18}$

    (D) 4

    (E) 5

20. The digits 1 through 4 are randomly arranged to make a four-digit number. What is the probability that the four-digit number is divisible by 4?

    (A) $\dfrac{1}{6}$

    (B) $\dfrac{1}{4}$

    (C) $\dfrac{1}{3}$

    (D) $\dfrac{2}{3}$

    (E) $\dfrac{3}{4}$

STOP

SECTION 2
Time — 25 minutes
18 Questions

Directions: This section contains two types of questions: Multiple-Choice questions and Free-Response questions. For question 1-8, solve each problem in this section and enter your answer by marking the circle on the answer sheet. You may use all the space provided for your work.

Notes	
1.	You may use a calculator during this test.
2.	All numbers used in this test are real numbers.
3.	Unless noted, the domain and the range of a function used in this test are sets of real numbers.
4.	Figures in this test provide useful information in solving problems. They are drawn as accurately as possible. Otherwise, figures not drawn to scale will be labeled as such. Figures lie in a plane.

Information

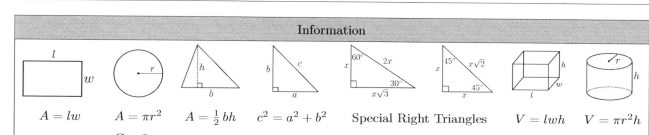

$A = lw$ $A = \pi r^2$ $A = \frac{1}{2}bh$ $c^2 = a^2 + b^2$ Special Right Triangles $V = lwh$ $V = \pi r^2 h$

$C = 2\pi r$

The degree measure of arc in a circle is 360.

The sum of the measures of the interior angles of a triangle is 180.

Red, Blue, White, Green, Yellow, $\cdots$

1. In a clothing store, all the T-shirts are arranged in the pattern shown above. What is the color of the seventeenth T-shirt?

   (A)   Red

   (B)   Blue

   (C)   White

   (D)   Green

   (E)   Yellow

2. What is the length of the diagonal of a square whose side length is 7?

   (A)   14

   (B) $7\sqrt{3}$

   (C) $7\sqrt{2}$

   (D) $5\sqrt{3}$

   (E) $5\sqrt{2}$

3. If $\sqrt{3 - x} = 3$, what is the value of x ?

    (A)   12

    (B)   3

    (C)   0

    (D)   −3

    (E)   −6

5. If $2^n = 3$, what is the value of 2^{n+2} ?

    (A)   5

    (B)   9

    (C)   12

    (D)   15

    (E)   18

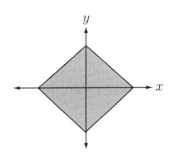

Note: Figure not drawn to scale.

4. On the graph of $|x| + |y| \le 5$ shown above, which of the following ordered pair lies outside the shaded region?

    (A) $(1, 3)$

    (B) $(0, 5)$

    (C) $(-1, 4)$

    (D) $(-2, -3)$

    (E) $(-4, -2)$

6. If you toss a coin three times, what is the probability that two heads will be shown?

    (A) $\dfrac{1}{8}$

    (B) $\dfrac{1}{4}$

    (C) $\dfrac{3}{8}$

    (D) $\dfrac{1}{2}$

    (E) $\dfrac{5}{8}$

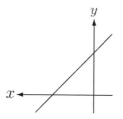

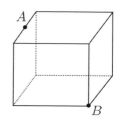

7. The graph above shows $y = 5x + 6$. If the line is shifted right 2 units and down 1 unit, what is an equation of the new line?

(A) $y = 3x + 5$

(B) $y = 3x - 5$

(C) $y = 5x + 1$

(D) $y = 5x - 5$

(E) $y = 5x - 10$

8. The cube shown above has a side length of 2. Point A is the midpoint of one side of the cube and point B is located at one vertex of the cube. If a segment is drawn from point A to point B, what is the length of $\overline{AB}$?

(A) 2

(B) 3

(C) $2\sqrt{2}$

(D) $2\sqrt{3}$

(E) $3\sqrt{2}$

Direction: For each of the 10 remaining Free-Response questions, solve the problem and enter your answer by marking the circle in the special grid as shown in the examples below.

Answer: $\frac{3}{7}$ Answer: 6.75   Answer: 124

Either position is correct.

 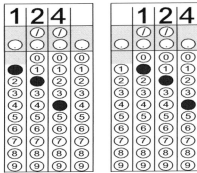

- Fill in one circle in each column.

- Each circle must be filled in correctly. Otherwise, you will not receive any credit.

- Convert all mixed numbers such as $1\frac{1}{2}$ to either 1.5 or $\frac{3}{2}$.

- For decimal answers that are longer than the number of grids provided, you must round or truncate the decimal. However, you must fill in all of the grids provided to ensure your answer is accurate as possible. For example, $0.666\ldots$ must be marked as .666 or .667.

- Answers are always positive.

- Write in the answer at the top of the grid to avoid mistakes when marking the circles.

- On problems that have more than one answer, fill in only one correct answer.

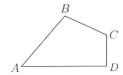

9. In quadrilateral $ABCD$ shown above, $m\angle D = 90°$. If the ratio of other three interior angles of the quadrilateral is 2:3:4, what is the measure of the largest interior angle of the quadrilateral in degrees?

10. If $x = -1$ is a solution to $x^2 - 11x - C = 0$, what is the the value of C ?

www.solomonacademy.net

$$y = 3x + 7$$
$$y = -3x + 7$$

11. When the two lines shown above intersect each other, the x and y coordinates of the intersection point is (a, b). What is the sum of a and b ?

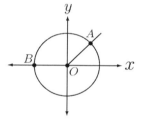

12. In the figure above, the center of circle O is located at the origin. A part of a line $y = x$ intersects the circle at point A. Point B is on the circle and on the x-axis. What is the measure of $\angle AOB$ in degrees?

13. $\triangle ABC$ is an equilateral triangle. If the height of the equilateral triangle is $12\sqrt{3}$, what is the perimeter of the equilateral triangle?

$$xz + yz - 12z = 0$$

14. If $z > 0$, what is the value of $x + y$?

15. If the average of two consecutive odd integers is 18, what is the value of the larger integer?

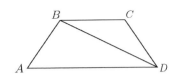

17. In the figure above, $ABCD$ is an isosceles trapezoid. If $BC = 12$, $AD = 18$, and $BD = 17$, what is the area of the isosceles trapezoid?

16. A square with side length of 4 is cut into several smaller squares with side lengths of integer values less than four. Assume that there is no wasted area. When cut, what is the smallest number of smaller squares?

18. If a sphere is inscribed in a cube, the ratio of the volume of the sphere to that of the cube is $\dfrac{\pi}{n}$. What is the value of n ?

$$\boxed{\text{STOP}}$$

SECTION 3
Time – 20 minutes
16 Questions

Directions: Solve each problem in this section and enter your answer by marking the circle on the answer sheet. You may use all the space provided for your work.

Notes

1. You may use a calculator during this test.

2. All numbers used in this test are real numbers.

3. Unless noted, the domain and the range of a function used in this test are sets of real numbers.

4. Figures in this test provide useful information in solving problems. They are drawn as accurately as possible. Otherwise, figures not drawn to scale will be labeled as such. Figures lie in a plane.

Information

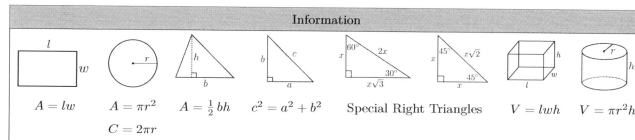

$$A = lw \qquad A = \pi r^2 \qquad A = \tfrac{1}{2}bh \qquad c^2 = a^2 + b^2 \qquad \text{Special Right Triangles} \qquad V = lwh \qquad V = \pi r^2 h$$

$$C = 2\pi r$$

The degree measure of arc in a circle is 360.

The sum of the measures of the interior angles of a triangle is 180.

---

1. $x + xy = y + 4$. If $y = 2$, what is the value of x ?

    (A)   5

    (B)   4

    (C)   3

    (D)   2

    (E)   1

2. If the two lines are parallel, what is the value of $2x$?

    (A)   40

    (B)   35

    (C)   30

    (D)   25

    (E)   20

3. Sue reads 6 pages in 10 minutes. At the same rate, how many pages will she read in 1 hour?

(A) 60

(B) 54

(C) 48

(D) 42

(E) 36

4. If the length of a square is $x + 3$, what is the area of the square in terms of x ?

(A) $x^2 + 9$

(B) $x^2 + 6x + 9$

(C) $6x + 9$

(D) $4x + 12$

(E) $2x + 6$

5. If May 5th is on Thursday, on what day of the week is May 18th?

(A) Monday

(B) Tuesday

(C) Wednesday

(D) Thursday

(E) Friday

6. The lengths of the three sides of a triangle are 4, 5 and n. What is the largest possible integer value of n ?

(A) 7

(B) 8

(C) 9

(D) 10

(E) 11

www.solomonacademy.net

7. If $|2 - x| = 5$, what is the sum of the solutions?

   (A)   1
   (B)   2
   (C)   3
   (D)   4
   (E)   5

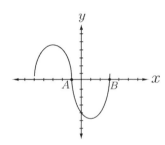

8. In the figure above, circle O is tangent to a line at point A and $\triangle OAB$ is an isosceles right triangle. If $AB = 4$, what is the area of the shaded region?

   (A) 14π
   (B) 12π
   (C) 10π
   (D) 8π
   (E) 6π

9. If $5^{y+1} = \left(\dfrac{1}{5}\right)^{2y-2}$, what is the value of y ?

   (A) $\dfrac{3}{4}$
   (B) $\dfrac{2}{3}$
   (C) $\dfrac{1}{3}$
   (D)   1
   (E)   3

10. In the xy plane, a function $f(x)$ crosses the x-axis at $A(-1, 0)$ and $B(3, 0)$. Which of the following expression has the largest value?

    (A) $f(3)$
    (B) $f(1)$
    (C) $f(0)$
    (D) $f(-1)$
    (E) $f(-2)$

Time	Departure Time
7:00 am-8:00 am	Every 10 minutes
8:00 am-9:00 am	Every 15 minutes
9:00 am-10:00 am	Every 20 minutes

11. The table above shows departure times at a train station. If the first train left the station at 7 am and the last train left at 10 am, how many trains left the station between 7 am to 10 am?

    (A) 12

    (B) 13

    (C) 14

    (D) 15

    (E) 16

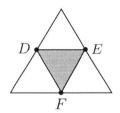

12. In the figure above, points D, E and F are the midpoints of the three sides of an equilateral triangle with area $16\sqrt{3}$. What is the area of the $\triangle DEF$?

    (A) $12\sqrt{3}$

    (B) $10\sqrt{3}$

    (C) $8\sqrt{3}$

    (D) $6\sqrt{3}$

    (E) $4\sqrt{3}$

13. Set S consists of 5 positive integers: x, y, 7, 12, and 14. If the mean and the mode of set S are 10 and 7 respectively, what is the product of x and y ?

    (A) 80

    (B) 70

    (C) 60

    (D) 50

    (E) 40

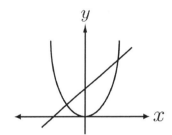

Note: Figure not drawn to scale.

14. In the graph above, a line $y = 3x + 4$ intersects a parabola $y = x^2$. What are the x coordinates of the two intersection points?

    (A) $x = -2$ or $x = 3$

    (B) $x = -2$ or $x = 4$

    (C) $x = -1$ or $x = 3$

    (D) $x = -1$ or $x = 4$

    (E) $x = -1$ or $x = 5$

15. Ten cards, each labeled with a number from 1 through 10, are in a bag. What is the smallest number of cards you need to select so that at least one prime number is guaranteed among the selected cards?

(A) 7

(B) 6

(C) 5

(D) 4

(E) 3

16. A penny, a nickel, a dime, and a quarter are in a bag. If you select two coins at random, how many different total values are possible?

(A) 5

(B) 6

(C) 7

(D) 8

(E) 9

STOP

SAT Math Scoring Worksheet

Directions: In order to calculate your score correctly, fill out the blank spaces from A through K on the table below. After calculating your raw score, round the raw score to the nearest whole number. The scaled score can be determined using the *"SAT Math Test Score Conversion Table"* on the next page.

SAT Math Score			
A. Section 1 Number Correct		**F.** Section 1 Number Incorrect	
B. Section 2 Questions 1-8 Number Correct		**G.** Section 2 Questions 1-8 Number Incorrect	
C. Section 2 Questions 9-18 Number Correct			
D. Section 3 Number Correct		**H.** Section 3 Number Incorrect	
E. Total Correct A+B+C+D		**I.** Total Incorrect (F+G+H)÷4	
J. Total Unrounded Raw Score **E − I**		**K. Total Rounded Raw Score** **Round to nearest whole number**	

SAT Math Scaled Score: [ ]

SAT Math Test Score Conversion Table			
Raw Score	**Scaled Score**	**Raw Score**	**Scaled Score**
54	800	24	480
53	780	23	470
52	760	22	460
51	740	21	450
50	720	20	440
49	710	19	430
48	700	18	430
47	690	17	420
46	680	16	420
45	670	15	410
44	660	14	400
43	650	13	400
42	640	12	390
41	640	11	380
40	630	10	380
39	620	9	370
38	610	8	360
37	600	7	350
36	590	6	340
35	580	5	330
34	570	4	320
33	560	3	310
32	560	2	300
31	550	1	280
30	540	0	270
29	530	−1	250
28	520	−2	230
27	510	−3	210
26	500	−4 and below	200
25	490		

SECTION 1
Time — 25 minutes
20 Questions

Directions: Solve each problem in this section and enter your answer by marking the circle on the answer sheet. You may use all the space provided for your work.

Notes

1. You may use a calculator during this test.

2. All numbers used in this test are real numbers.

3. Unless noted, the domain and the range of a function used in this test are sets of real numbers.

4. Figures in this test provide useful information in solving problems. They are drawn as accurately as possible. Otherwise, figures not drawn to scale will be labeled as such. Figures lie in a plane.

Information

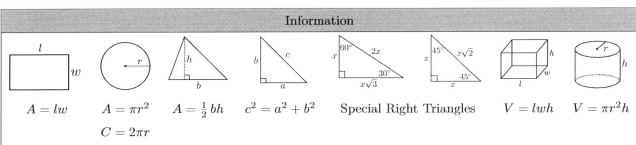

$$A = lw \qquad A = \pi r^2 \qquad A = \tfrac{1}{2}bh \qquad c^2 = a^2 + b^2 \qquad \text{Special Right Triangles} \qquad V = lwh \qquad V = \pi r^2 h$$

$$C = 2\pi r$$

The degree measure of arc in a circle is 360.

The sum of the measures of the interior angles of a triangle is 180.

1. If the length of a cube is 3, what is the volume of the cube?

   (A) 9

   (B) 12

   (C) 27

   (D) 36

   (E) 54

2. The sum of x and y is 18. The difference of y and x is 4. If $x < y$, which of the following systems of linear equations can be solved to find the value of x and y ?

   (A) $x + y = 9$
        $y - x = 4$

   (B) $x + y = 18$
        $y - x = 4$

   (C) $x + y = 18$
        $x - y = 4$

   (D) $xy = 18$
        $y - x = 4$

   (E) $xy = 18$
        $x - y = 4$

3. How many odd numbers are there between 1 and 100 inclusive?

   (A)   47

   (B)   48

   (C)   49

   (D)   50

   (E)   51

4. y varies directly with x. $y = 6$ when $x = 3$. What is the value of x when $y = 4$?

   (A)   1

   (B)   2

   (C)   4

   (D)   6

   (E)   8

5. In the right triangle above, $CB = \sqrt{2}$ and $AC = \sqrt{3}$. What is the length of $\overline{AB}$?

   (A) $\sqrt{5}$

   (B) $\sqrt{6}$

   (C)   4

   (D)   5

   (E)   6

$$B = \{9, 6, 11, 5, 12, 15\}$$

6. As shown above, set B has six positive integers. What is the median of set B ?

   (A)   11

   (B)   10

   (C)   9

   (D)   6

   (E)   5

7. If $6(p-q) = 36$, which of the following value is equal to $4p - 4q$?

   (A) 12

   (B) 16

   (C) 20

   (D) 24

   (E) 28

9. The numbers 1 through 10 inclusive are in a hat. If a number is selected at random, what is the probability that the number is neither divisible by 3 nor 4?

   (A) $\dfrac{1}{4}$

   (B) $\dfrac{1}{3}$

   (C) $\dfrac{1}{2}$

   (D) $\dfrac{2}{3}$

   (E) $\dfrac{3}{10}$

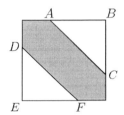

8. In the figure above, points B and E are two vertices of a square with side length of 6. If $\triangle ABC$ and $\triangle DEF$ are isosceles triangles and $AB = DE = 4$, what is the area of the shaded region?

   (A) 12

   (B) 16

   (C) 20

   (D) 24

   (E) 28

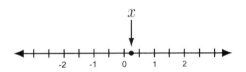

10. As shown above, x is on the number line. Which of the following expression has the largest value?

   (A) x

   (B) x^2

   (C) x^3

   (D) $\dfrac{1}{x}$

   (E) $\dfrac{1}{x^2}$

11. How many positive integer values of x satisfy $x^2 - 3x < 0$?

    (A) 1

    (B) 2

    (C) 3

    (D) 4

    (E) 5

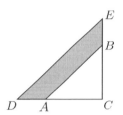

12. In the figure above, $\triangle ABC$ and $\triangle DEC$ are isosceles right triangles. If $AC = 4$ and $DC = 6$, what is the perimeter of the shaded region ABED ?

    (A) $6\sqrt{2} + 4$

    (B) $10\sqrt{2}$

    (C) $10\sqrt{2} + 4$

    (D) $16\sqrt{2}$

    (E) $24\sqrt{2} + 4$

$$x + y = 10 - z$$
$$x - y = 16 + z$$

13. In the system of equations above, what is the value of x ?

    (A) 26

    (B) 13

    (C) 11

    (D) 9

    (E) 5

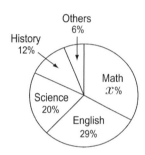

14. As shown above, Joshua made a weekly study plan on the chart that shows the distribution of his study hours over various subjects. If the total study hours is 10 hours in a week, how many hours and minutes will he spend on math?

    (A) 2 hours and 18 minutes

    (B) 2 hours and 30 minutes

    (C) 3 hours and 18 minutes

    (D) 3 hours and 30 minutes

    (E) 4 hours and 18 minutes

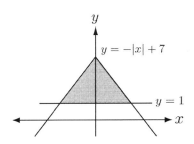

15. $y = 1$ intersects $y = -|x| + 7$ as shown in the figure above. What is the area of the shaded region?

   (A) 18

   (B) 24

   (C) 30

   (D) 36

   (E) 42

16. Sue traveled 220 miles at 55 miles per hour. How many minutes longer would the return trip take if she travels at 50 miles per hour?

   (A) 60 minutes

   (B) 48 minutes

   (C) 40 minutes

   (D) 24 minutes

   (E) 12 minutes

17. A ball is dropped from a height of 8 yards. Each time it strikes the ground, it bounces up to half of its previous height. How many times does the ball need to strike the ground before its height is less than 3 feet?

   (A) once

   (B) twice

   (C) three times

   (D) four times

   (E) five times

18. x, y, and z are positive integers. If $x = 3y$ and $x^2 + y^2 = z$, which of the following cannot be equal to z ?

   (A) 10

   (B) 36

   (C) 90

   (D) 160

   (E) 250

Move	Direction	Distance
1st	South	1 foot
2nd	West	2 feet
3rd	North	3 feet
4th	East	4 feet
5th	South	5 feet
6th	West	6 feet
7th	North	7 feet
8th	East	8 feet

19. Mr. Rhee starts walking according to the directions above. For instance, on the first move, he walks 1 foot due south from the starting position. He then walks 2 feet due west on the second move, walks 3 feet due north on the third move, and so on and so forth. When Mr. Rhee finishes the 8th move, how far is he from the starting position?

(A) $4\sqrt{2}$

(B) $5\sqrt{2}$

(C) $6\sqrt{2}$

(D) 5

(E) 10

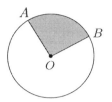

20. In the figure above, the central angle $AOB = x°$. If the area of the shaded region is three times the length of minor arc AB, what is the radius of the circle?

(A) 2

(B) 4

(C) 6

(D) 8

(E) 10

STOP

SECTION 2
Time — 25 minutes
18 Questions

> **Directions:** This section contains two types of questions: Multiple-Choice questions and Free-Response questions. For question 1-8, solve each problem in this section and enter your answer by marking the circle on the answer sheet. You may use all the space provided for your work.

Notes

1. You may use a calculator during this test.

2. All numbers used in this test are real numbers.

3. Unless noted, the domain and the range of a function used in this test are sets of real numbers.

4. Figures in this test provide useful information in solving problems. They are drawn as accurately as possible. Otherwise, figures not drawn to scale will be labeled as such. Figures lie in a plane.

Information

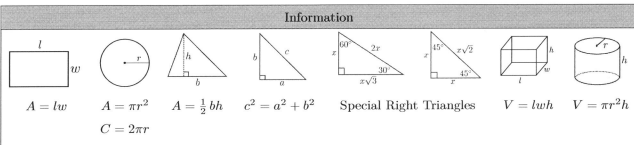

$A = lw$ $A = \pi r^2$ $A = \frac{1}{2}bh$ $c^2 = a^2 + b^2$ Special Right Triangles $V = lwh$ $V = \pi r^2 h$

$C = 2\pi r$

The degree measure of arc in a circle is 360.

The sum of the measures of the interior angles of a triangle is 180.

---

1. If $2x + 3y = 12$ and $y - 1 = 1$, what is the value of x ?

   (A) 3

   (B) 4

   (C) 5

   (D) 6

   (E) 7

2. What is the slope of a line that passes through the points $(-1, 2)$ and $(1, 8)$?

   (A) -3

   (B) -2

   (C) 1

   (D) 2

   (E) 3

3. x years ago from now, Jason was y years old. How old will he be in x years from now?

(A) $y + 3x$

(B) $y + 2x$

(C) $y + x$

(D) $y - x$

(E) $y - 2x$

x	-1	1	3	5
y	9	1	1	9

4. The table above shows four ordered pairs on the graph of $y = (x - k)^2$. What is the value of k ?

(A) -3

(B) -2

(C) 1

(D) 2

(E) 3

5. Joshua walks x feet in y seconds. How many feet will Joshua walk in z minutes?

(A) $\dfrac{xy}{z}$

(B) $\dfrac{60xy}{z}$

(C) $\dfrac{xz}{y}$

(D) $\dfrac{60xz}{y}$

(E) $\dfrac{yz}{60x}$

6. There are 12 parallelograms. Each parallelogram is either a rectangle, a rhombus, or both. If there are 7 rhombuses and 8 rectangles, how many parallelograms are squares among the 12 parallelograms?

(A) 1

(B) 2

(C) 3

(D) 4

(E) 5

www.solomonacademy.net

7. ABC represents a three-digit number greater than 200, where $A < B < C$. If B and C are multiples of A, and C is three more than B, which of the following number can be the three-digit number ABC ?

(A) 136

(B) 248

(C) 269

(D) 369

(E) 447

$$(x + y)^{\frac{1}{2}} = 4$$
$$(x - y)^{\frac{3}{2}} = 8$$

8. In the equations above, what is the value of $x^2 - y^2$?

(A) 8

(B) 12

(C) 36

(D) 48

(E) 64

Direction: For each of the 10 remaining Free-Response questions, solve the problem and enter your answer by marking the circle in the special grid as shown in the examples below.

Answer: $\frac{3}{7}$ Answer: 6.75   Answer: 124

Either position is correct.

- Fill in one circle in each column.
- Each circle must be filled in correctly. Otherwise, you will not receive any credit.
- Convert all mixed numbers such as $1\frac{1}{2}$ to either 1.5 or $\frac{3}{2}$.
- For decimal answers that are longer than the number of grids provided, you must round or truncate the decimal. However, you must fill in all of the grids provided to ensure your answer is accurate as possible. For example, $0.666\ldots$ must be marked as .666 or .667.

- Answers are always positive.
- Write in the answer at the top of the grid to avoid mistakes when marking the circles.
- On problems that have more than one answer, fill in only one correct answer.

9. If $x - 2 = -7$, what is the value of $\dfrac{8 - 4x}{4}$?

10. If the length of the diagonal of a square is 10, what is the area of the square?

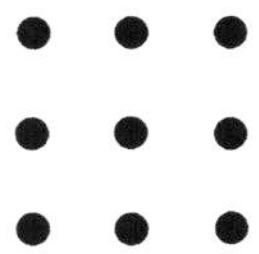

11. In the figure above, all the nine points are equally spaced. How many different lines can be drawn that connect at least two points?

12. Two numbers are selected at random without replacement from the set $\{1, 2, 3, 4\}$ to form a two-digit number. What is the probability that the two-digit number selected is a prime number?

13. If $2 \leq x \leq 5$ and $3 \leq y \leq 6$, what is the largest value of $\dfrac{xy}{x+y}$?

14. If a number, n, is divided by k, the remainder is 5. What is the remainder if $n - k$ is divided by k ?

$$4, 11, 18, 25, \cdots$$

15. In the sequence above, what is the value of the 24th term?

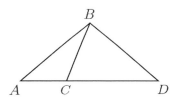

16. In the figure above, points A, C, and D are on the same line. If $AC : CD = 1 : 2$, what is the ratio of the area of $\triangle ABC$ to that of $\triangle CBD$?

17. 6 people who work at the same rate can paint a house in 4 days. What fractional part of the house can 3 people paint the house is 6 days?

18. A line $y = ax + 2$ passes through quadrants I, II, and III. If two lines $y = ax + 2$ and $y = -2x + 8$ intersect at $(t, t + 3)$, what is the value of a ?

$$\boxed{\textbf{STOP}}$$

SECTION 3
Time – 20 minutes
16 Questions

Directions: Solve each problem in this section and enter your answer by marking the circle on the answer sheet. You may use all the space provided for your work.

Notes	
	1. You may use a calculator during this test.
	2. All numbers used in this test are real numbers.
	3. Unless noted, the domain and the range of a function used in this test are sets of real numbers.
	4. Figures in this test provide useful information in solving problems. They are drawn as accurately as possible. Otherwise, figures not drawn to scale will be labeled as such. Figures lie in a plane.

Information

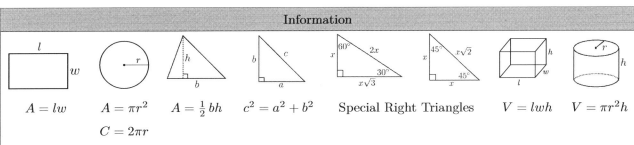

$$A = lw \qquad A = \pi r^2 \qquad A = \tfrac{1}{2}bh \qquad c^2 = a^2 + b^2 \qquad \text{Special Right Triangles} \qquad V = lwh \qquad V = \pi r^2 h$$

$$C = 2\pi r$$

The degree measure of arc in a circle is 360.

The sum of the measures of the interior angles of a triangle is 180.

1. What is the distance between point $A(0,6)$ and point $B(8,0)$?

    (A) 2

    (B) 6

    (C) 10

    (D) 14

    (E) 20

2. In triangle ABC, $m\angle C = 90°$ and $m\angle B = 60°$. If $AC = 5\sqrt{3}$, what is the length of $\overline{AB}$?

    (A) $10\sqrt{3}$

    (B) 10

    (C) $5\sqrt{3}$

    (D) $5\sqrt{2}$

    (E) 5

$$P = R - 2E$$

3. The profit of a company is determined by the equation shown above. In the equation, P represents profit, R represents revenue, and E represents expenses. What is the profit of the company when the expenses is \$1250 and the revenue is \$3250?

   (A) \$450

   (B) \$750

   (C) \$1250

   (D) \$1750

   (E) \$2000

4. 75% of a number is 20% of 30. What is the number?

   (A) 6

   (B) 8

   (C) 10

   (D) 12

   (E) 14

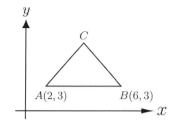

5. In the figure above, $\triangle ABC$ is an isosceles triangle such that $CA = CB$. If the area of the $\triangle ABC = 6$, what are the coordinates of point C ?

   (A) $(3, 3)$

   (B) $(3, 6)$

   (C) $(4, 3)$

   (D) $(4, 6)$

   (E) $(4, 9)$

6. A set, S, has three numbers and the average of set S is x. A set, T, has four numbers and the average of set T is y. Which of the following expression represents the average of the two sets, S and T ?

   (A) $\dfrac{x + y}{2}$

   (B) $\dfrac{x + y}{7}$

   (C) $\dfrac{xy}{2}$

   (D) $\dfrac{3x + 4y}{2}$

   (E) $\dfrac{3x + 4y}{7}$

7. $f(x) = -x^2 + 4x + 5$. If $f(k) = f(0)$, which of the following can be the value of k ?

    (A)   4

    (B)   3

    (C)   2

    (D)   1

    (E) -1

8. Let $S(x)$ be the sum of all the positive integers less than or equal to x. For example, $S(5) = 1 + 2 + 3 + 4 + 5 = 15$. What is the value of $S(20) - S(9)$?

    (A)   165

    (B)   155

    (C)   145

    (D)   135

    (E)   125

9. Joshua was born in May. May has 31 days. The statements below describe his birthday. When is Joshua's birthday?

    • even number

    • divisible by 3

    • not divisible by 9

    • has 6 factors

    (A)   May 30th

    (B)   May 24th

    (C)   May 18th

    (D)   May 12th

    (E)   May 6th

    I. A square is a rectangle.

    II. A rhombus is a parallelogram.

    III. A parallelogram is a trapezoid.

    IV. A rectangle is a rhombus.

10. Which of the following statements above are true?

    (A)   I & II

    (B)   I & III

    (C)   I & IV

    (D)   II & III

    (E)   I & II & IV

 www.solomonacademy.net

11. Two numbers are selected at random without replacement from the set $\{2, 3, 5, 7\}$ to form a fraction. What is the probability that the fraction formed is a proper fraction?

    (A) $\dfrac{1}{4}$

    (B) $\dfrac{3}{8}$

    (C) $\dfrac{1}{2}$

    (D) $\dfrac{5}{8}$

    (E) $\dfrac{3}{4}$

$$|2x + 4| < 6$$

12. Which of the following is the solution to the inequality above?

    (A) $x < 1$

    (B) $x > 1$

    (C) $1 < x < 5$

    (D) $-7 < x < 1$

    (E) $-5 < x < 1$

13. Let x be a positive integer. From digit 0 to 9, how many digits can not be the units digits of the square of x ?

    (A) 2 digits

    (B) 3 digits

    (C) 4 digits

    (D) 5 digits

    (E) 6 digits

14. In square $ABCD$, $\overline{AC}$ and $\overline{BD}$ are the diagonals of the square. What is the product of the slopes of the two diagonals $\overline{AC}$ and $\overline{BD}$?

    (A) -2

    (B) -1

    (C) $-\dfrac{1}{2}$

    (D) 1

    (E) $\dfrac{1}{2}$

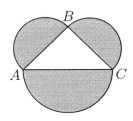

Note: Figure not drawn to scale.

15. In $\triangle ABC$ shown above, $AB = 6$, $BC = 8$, and $AC = 10$. There are three semicircles on each side of the triangle. What is the total area of the shaded regions?

    (A) 50π

    (B) 45π

    (C) 35π

    (D) 25π

    (E) 15π

16. The sum of the ages of Mr. Rhee and Joshua is 47. The sum of the ages of Joshua and Sue is 46. The sum of the ages of Sue and Mr. Rhee is 79. What is the sum of all the ages of Mr. Rhee, Joshua, and Sue?

    (A) 83

    (B) 84

    (C) 85

    (D) 86

    (E) 87

$\boxed{\textbf{STOP}}$

SAT Math Scoring Worksheet

Directions: In order to calculate your score correctly, fill out the blank spaces from A through K on the table below. After calculating your raw score, round the raw score to the nearest whole number. The scaled score can be determined using the *"SAT Math Test Score Conversion Table"* on the next page.

SAT Math Score			
A. Section 1 Number Correct		**F.** Section 1 Number Incorrect	
B. Section 2 Questions 1-8 Number Correct		**G.** Section 2 Questions 1-8 Number Incorrect	
C. Section 2 Questions 9-18 Number Correct			
D. Section 3 Number Correct		**H.** Section 3 Number Incorrect	
E. Total Correct A+B+C+D		**I.** Total Incorrect (F+G+H)÷4	
J. Total Unrounded Raw Score E − I		**K. Total Rounded Raw Score** Round to nearest whole number	

SAT Math Scaled Score:

SAT Math Test Score Conversion Table			
Raw Score	**Scaled Score**	**Raw Score**	**Scaled Score**
54	800	24	480
53	780	23	470
52	760	22	460
51	740	21	450
50	720	20	440
49	710	19	430
48	700	18	430
47	690	17	420
46	680	16	420
45	670	15	410
44	660	14	400
43	650	13	400
42	640	12	390
41	640	11	380
40	630	10	380
39	620	9	370
38	610	8	360
37	600	7	350
36	590	6	340
35	580	5	330
34	570	4	320
33	560	3	310
32	560	2	300
31	550	1	280
30	540	0	270
29	530	−1	250
28	520	−2	230
27	510	−3	210
26	500	−4 and below	200
25	490		

www.solomonacademy.net

SECTION 1
Time — 25 minutes
20 Questions

Directions: Solve each problem in this section and enter your answer by marking the circle on the answer sheet. You may use all the space provided for your work.

Notes

1. You may use a calculator during this test.

2. All numbers used in this test are real numbers.

3. Unless noted, the domain and the range of a function used in this test are sets of real numbers.

4. Figures in this test provide useful information in solving problems. They are drawn as accurately as possible. Otherwise, figures not drawn to scale will be labeled as such. Figures lie in a plane.

Information

$A = lw$ $A = \pi r^2$ $A = \frac{1}{2}bh$ $c^2 = a^2 + b^2$ Special Right Triangles $V = lwh$ $V = \pi r^2 h$

$C = 2\pi r$

The degree measure of arc in a circle is 360.

The sum of the measures of the interior angles of a triangle is 180.

---

1. How many edges does a cube have?

   (A) 6

   (B) 8

   (C) 9

   (D) 10

   (E) 12

2. If x is a positive integer and y is a negative integer, which of the following expression must be a positive integer?

   (A) $x - y$

   (B) $x + y$

   (C) xy

   (D) $\dfrac{x}{y}$

   (E) $x^2 - y^2$

$$-1, 1, -1, 1, \cdots$$

3. In the sequence above, what is the value of the 28th term?

(A) 28

(B) 14

(C) 0

(D) 1

(E) −1

x	−1	0	1
y	−2	0	−2

4. The table above shows three ordered pairs on the graph of $y = ax^2$. What is the value of a ?

(A) −2

(B) −1

(C) 1

(D) 2

(E) 3

5. A circular shaped pizza has a radius of 8. If the pizza is cut into 8 equal slices, what is the sum of the area of the 5 slices?

(A) 10π

(B) 16π

(C) 24π

(D) 32π

(E) 40π

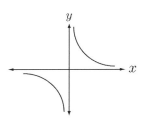

6. Which of the following function best represents the graph above?

(A) $y = \dfrac{1}{x}$

(B) $y = x$

(C) $y = x^2$

(D) $y = \sqrt{x}$

(E) $y = |x|$

7. If a number is divided by 2, 3, 4, 5, and 6, the remainders are 1, 2, 3, 1, and 5, respectively. Which of the following could be the number?

(A) 7

(B) 11

(C) 13

(D) 15

(E) 17

$$\frac{x+2}{4} + \frac{y+1}{4} + \frac{z-3}{4}$$

8. In the expression above, x, y, and z represent the measures of the interior angles of a triangle. What is the value of the expression above?

(A) 45°

(B) 60°

(C) 70°

(D) 80°

(E) 90°

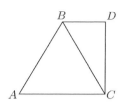

9. In the figure above, $ABDC$ is a trapezoid. If $m\angle C = 90°$ and $\triangle ABC$ is an equilateral triangle, what is the measure of $\angle ABD$?

(A) 100°

(B) 110°

(C) 120°

(D) 130°

(E) 140°

10. If $2x^2 - 5x + 2 = 0$, what is the product of the solutions?

(A) $-\dfrac{5}{2}$

(B) -1

(C) 1

(D) $\dfrac{5}{2}$

(E) 5

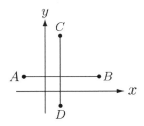

Note: Figure not drawn to scale.

11. Four points $A(-1, 2)$, $B(3, 2)$, $C(2, 3)$, and $D(2, -1)$ are on the xy coordinates plane. If M is the midpoint of $\overline{AB}$ and N is the midpoint of $\overline{CD}$, what is the distance between M and N ?

   (A)   3

   (B) $2\sqrt{2}$

   (C)   2

   (D) $\sqrt{2}$

   (E)   1

12. If $2^x = \dfrac{1}{3}$, what is the value of $\left(\dfrac{1}{4}\right)^x$?

   (A) $\dfrac{1}{9}$

   (B) $\dfrac{1}{6}$

   (C)   6

   (D)   9

   (E)   12

13. y is proportional to $x - 2$. $y = 15$ when $x = 5$. What is the value of x when $y = -10$?

   (A)   4

   (B)   3

   (C)   2

   (D)   1

   (E)   0

14. Using only the three digits, 1, 2, and 3, three-digit numbers are formed. If all the digits are used once, how many three-digit numbers formed are divisible by 3?

   (A)   7

   (B)   6

   (C)   5

   (D)   4

   (E)   3

15. Mr. Rhee traveled 120 miles at 60 miles per hour to visit his friend. On the way home, he was caught in heavy traffic so that the average speed for the entire trip was 40 miles per hour. How fast did Mr. Rhee travel on the way home in miles per hour?

    (A) 50 miles per hour

    (B) 40 miles per hour

    (C) 30 miles per hour

    (D) 20 miles per hour

    (E) 10 miles per hour

16. Jason spent half of the money in his savings account on books. A few days later, he spent two-thirds of the remaining money in his savings account on clothes. If Jason then had $100 left, how much money was in his savings account in the beginning?

    (A) $200

    (B) $400

    (C) $600

    (D) $800

    (E) $1200

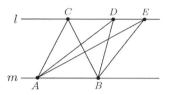

17. In the figure above, $l \parallel m$. Which of the following statements below are true?

    I. Area of $\triangle ACB$ = Area of $\triangle AEB$

    II. $AC < AD < AE$

    III. $m\angle EAB < m\angle CAB < m\angle CDA$

    (A) I only

    (B) III only

    (C) I and II only

    (D) I and III only

    (E) I and II and III only

18. What is the coordinates of the highest point on the graph of $y = -3(x+1)^2 + 2$?

    (A) $(-1, -3)$

    (B) $(-1, 2)$

    (C) $(1, -3)$

    (D) $(1, 2)$

    (E) $(3, 2)$

19. The ratio of chocolate chip cookies to oatmeal cookies in a jar is 1:2. After Joshua ate four chocolate chip cookies and half of the oatmeal cookies in the jar, the ratio of chocolate chip cookies to oatmeal cookies is 3:4. How many chocolate chip cookies are left in the jar?

(A) 10

(B) 12

(C) 14

(D) 16

(E) 18

20. In an arithmetic sequence, the sum of the first two terms is 7 and the sum of the next three terms is 33. What is the first term in the sequence?

(A) 2

(B) 3

(C) 4

(D) 5

(E) 6

STOP

SECTION 2
Time — 25 minutes
18 Questions

Directions: This section contains two types of questions: Multiple-Choice questions and Free-Response questions. For question 1-8, solve each problem in this section and enter your answer by marking the circle on the answer sheet. You may use all the space provided for your work.

Notes

1. You may use a calculator during this test.

2. All numbers used in this test are real numbers.

3. Unless noted, the domain and the range of a function used in this test are sets of real numbers.

4. Figures in this test provide useful information in solving problems. They are drawn as accurately as possible. Otherwise, figures not drawn to scale will be labeled as such. Figures lie in a plane.

Information

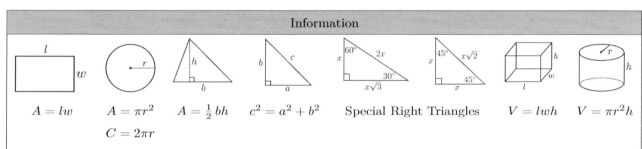

$A = lw$ $A = \pi r^2$ $A = \frac{1}{2}bh$ $c^2 = a^2 + b^2$ Special Right Triangles $V = lwh$ $V = \pi r^2 h$

$C = 2\pi r$

The degree measure of arc in a circle is 360.

The sum of the measures of the interior angles of a triangle is 180.

1. At a special sale event of a store, every two pens you purchase, you get the third pen for free of charge. If the cost of one pen is $\$k$, what is the total cost of the 15 pens at the store?

(A) $\$15k$

(B) $\$10k$

(C) $\$5k$

(D) $\$k + 10$

(E) $\$k + 5$

2. Two angles A and B are supplementary angles. If the measure of angle B is 30 more than twice the measure of angle A, what is the measure of angle B ?

(A) $40°$

(B) $50°$

(C) $120°$

(D) $130°$

(E) $140°$

3. Which of the following expression is equal to $\left(x^2\right)^3$?

   (A) $x^2 \cdot x^3$

   (B) $x^3 \cdot x^3 \cdot x^3$

   (C) $\dfrac{x^{12}}{x^2}$

   (D) $\left(x^3\right)^2$

   (E) $\left(x^{-1}\right)^7$

4. Mr. Rhee went on a diet. If his weight was 180 pounds at the beginning and he lost 30 pounds, what percent of his weight did he lose?

   (A) $16\dfrac{2}{3}\%$

   (B) $33\dfrac{1}{3}\%$

   (C) 20%

   (D) 25%

   (E) 30%

5. There are two cubes. If the ratio of the volume of the smaller cube to that of the larger cube is 8 to 27, what is the ratio of the surface area of the smaller cube to that of the larger cube?

   (A) $2:3$

   (B) $3:2$

   (C) $4:9$

   (D) $6:9$

   (E) $9:4$

6. Which of the following statement best describes the function $f(x) = \sqrt{2x+4}$?

   I. Always positive

   II. $f(0) < f(2) < f(4)$

   III. The domain of $f(x)$ is $x > -2$

   (A)   I only

   (B)   II only

   (C)   III only

   (D)   I and II

   (E)   I and II and III

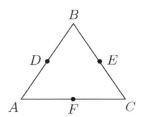

Note: Figure not drawn to scale.

7. In the triangle above, coordinates of the three vertices are $A(x, -2)$, $B(y, 6)$, and $C(z, 2)$. The midpoints of $\overline{AB}$, $\overline{BC}$, and $\overline{AC}$ are $D(1, 2)$, $E(5, 4)$, and $F(3, 0)$ respectively. What is the sum of x, y, and z ?

(A) 9

(B) 10

(C) 11

(D) 12

(E) 13

$$p \blacktriangle q = p^2 + q^2$$
$$p \blacktriangledown q = p^2 - q^2$$

8. For integers p and q, the two functions, $\blacktriangle$ and $\blacktriangledown$, are defined as shown above. If $x \blacktriangle y = 61$ and $x \blacktriangledown y = 11$, what is the smallest value of $x + y$?

(A) 11

(B) 1

(C) 0

(D) -1

(E) -11

Direction: For each of the 10 remaining Free-Response questions, solve the problem and enter your answer by marking the circle in the special grid as shown in the examples below.

Answer: $\frac{3}{7}$

Answer: 6.75

Answer: 124

Either position is correct.

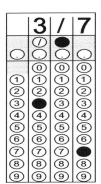
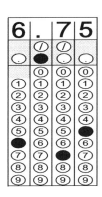
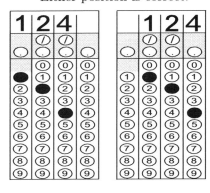

- Fill in one circle in each column.

- Each circle must be filled in correctly. Otherwise, you will not receive any credit.

- Convert all mixed numbers such as $1\frac{1}{2}$ to either 1.5 or $\frac{3}{2}$.

- For decimal answers that are longer than the number of grids provided, you must round or truncate the decimal. However, you must fill in all of the grids provided to ensure your answer is accurate as possible. For example, $0.666\ldots$ must be marked as .666 or .667.

- Answers are always positive.

- Write in the answer at the top of the grid to avoid mistakes when marking the circles.

- On problems that have more than one answer, fill in only one correct answer.

9. A number is an odd integer. If the number is multiplied by 2, how many digits from 0 to 9 will be possible for the units digit of the new number?

10. If the radius of a circle is $\dfrac{7}{\sqrt{\pi}}$, what is the area of the circle?

11. If the ratio of the interior angles of a triangle is 3:4:5, what is the degree measure of the largest angle?

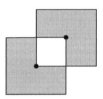

Note: Figure not drawn to scale.

12. In the figure above, two identical squares are overlapped such that one vertex of each square is at the center of the other square. If the length of the square is 8, what is the area of the shaded region?

13. If the line, $y = ax - 1$, passes through the point $(6, 3)$, what is the value of a ?

$$4, x, 36, y, 324, \cdots$$

14. In the geometric sequence above, x and y are positive integers. What is the value of $\sqrt{xy}$?

15. Joshua buys a package of four oranges for $0.75 and sells a package of three oranges for $1. If Joshua wants to make profit of $14, how many oranges does he need to sell?

16. Sue rented a car for two days. She paid the rental company a fixed daily fee plus an hourly charge for diving time. On the first day, she paid $99. On the second day, she drove the car three times as much as she did on the first day. So, she paid $179 on the second day. What is the fixed daily fee?

17. Four positive integers are added to the set $\{7, 11, 11, 15\}$ so that all the mean, median, and mode of the set are decreased by 1. What is the smallest integer in the new set?

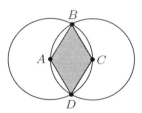

Note: Figure not drawn to scale.

18. In the figure above, the centers of the two identical circles are A and C and two circles intersect at two points B and D. If the radius of the circle is 20, the area of the shaded region $ABCD$ is $n\sqrt{3}$. What is the value of n?

SECTION 3
Time – 20 minutes
16 Questions

Directions: Solve each problem in this section and enter your answer by marking the circle on the answer sheet. You may use all the space provided for your work.

Notes

1. You may use a calculator during this test.

2. All numbers used in this test are real numbers.

3. Unless noted, the domain and the range of a function used in this test are sets of real numbers.

4. Figures in this test provide useful information in solving problems. They are drawn as accurately as possible. Otherwise, figures not drawn to scale will be labeled as such. Figures lie in a plane.

Information

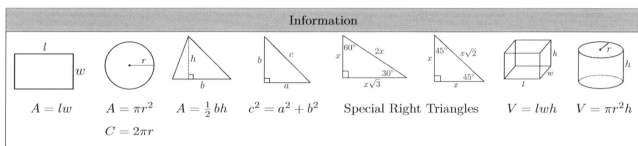

$$A = lw \qquad A = \pi r^2 \qquad A = \tfrac{1}{2}bh \qquad c^2 = a^2 + b^2 \qquad \text{Special Right Triangles} \qquad V = lwh \qquad V = \pi r^2 h$$

$$C = 2\pi r$$

The degree measure of arc in a circle is 360.

The sum of the measures of the interior angles of a triangle is 180.

1. If $4(x + 2) = 16$, what is the value of $\dfrac{x + 4}{2}$?

(A)   1

(B)   2

(C)   3

(D)   4

(E)   5

2. Three points A, B, and C are on the number line. If C is located at 1, $A - C = 2$, and $B - C = -2$, what is the distance between points A and B ?

(A)   2

(B)   3

(C)   4

(D)   5

(E)   6

Month	Regular gas price
May	$3.71
June	$3.57
July	$3.64
August	$3.61
September	$3.37
October	$3.49

3. During what time period did the price of gasoline decrease most?

   (A)   From May to June

   (B)   From June to July

   (C)   From July to August

   (D)   From August to September

   (E)   From September to October

4. If $\dfrac{4}{x+3} = \dfrac{6}{x+4}$, what is the value of x ?

   (A) -2

   (B) -1

   (C)   1

   (D)   2

   (E)   3

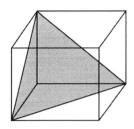

Note: Figure not drawn to scale.

5. In the figure above, three segments are drawn to form a triangle. If the length of the cube is $6\sqrt{2}$, what is the perimeter of the triangle?

   (A)   18

   (B)   24

   (C) $18\sqrt{2}$

   (D) $24\sqrt{3}$

   (E)   36

6. Students take either chess club or swimming club or both. All the students taking swimming club are juniors. Which of the following statement must be true?

   (A) Students taking both chess club and swimming club are juniors.

   (B) Students taking both chess club and swimming club are seniors.

   (C) Some students taking chess club are seniors.

   (D) All students taking chess club are juniors.

   (E) Some students taking swimming club are seniors.

7. If x is 25% less than y and z is 20% more than y, what is the ratio of z to x ?

   (A) $3:5$

   (B) $5:8$

   (C) $6:5$

   (D) $8:5$

   (E) $9:8$

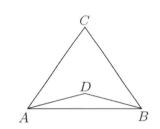

Note: Figure not drawn to scale.

8. In the figure above, two triangles ACB and ADB are isosceles triangles. If $m\angle C = 84°$ and $m\angle DAB = \dfrac{1}{3}m\angle CAB$, what is the degree measure of $\angle D$?

   (A) $84°$

   (B) $100°$

   (C) $116°$

   (D) $132°$

   (E) $148°$

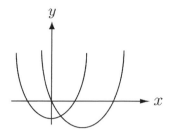

Note: Figure not drawn to scale.

9. In the figure above, two quadratic functions $y = x^2 - 4$ and $y = x^2 - 5x$ intersect. What is the x coordinate of the intersection point?

   (A) $\dfrac{2}{5}$

   (B) $\dfrac{3}{5}$

   (C) $\dfrac{4}{5}$

   (D) 1

   (E) $\dfrac{8}{5}$

10. If the product of 2000 and 5000 can be written as $1 \times 10^{n-1}$, what is the value of n ?

   (A) 9

   (B) 8

   (C) 7

   (D) 6

   (E) 5

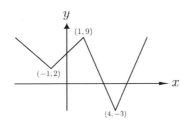

Note: Figure not drawn to scale.

11. The graph of a function $f(x)$ is shown above. If a line $y = k$, not shown above, intersects the function $f(x)$ twice, what could be the value of k ?

   (A) $k = -3$

   (B) $-3 < k < 2$

   (C) $k = 2$

   (D) $2 < k < 9$

   (E) $k = 9$

12. Jason filled a cup with equal amounts of orange juice, apple juice, and grape juice and mixed it well. He drank half of the cup and then only filled the cup with equal amounts of orange juice and apple juice. What fractional part of the cup was filled with the apple juice?

   (A) $\dfrac{5}{12}$

   (B) $\dfrac{1}{3}$

   (C) $\dfrac{1}{4}$

   (D) $\dfrac{1}{6}$

   (E) $\dfrac{1}{12}$

$$S = -1 + 2 - 3 + \cdots + 98 - 99 + 100$$

13. If the pattern shown above continues, what is the value of S ?

   (A) 10

   (B) 20

   (C) 25

   (D) 50

   (E) 100

$$2x + 3y = 26$$
$$3x - 2y = 13$$

14. In the system of linear equations above, what is the value of $x + y$?

   (A) 8

   (B) 9

   (C) 10

   (D) 11

   (E) 12

15. If $\dfrac{a}{b} = \dfrac{c}{d}$, which of the following proportion is not true?

(A) $\quad \dfrac{b}{a} = \dfrac{d}{c}$

(B) $\quad \dfrac{d}{b} = \dfrac{c}{a}$

(C) $\quad \dfrac{a}{c} = \dfrac{b}{d}$

(D) $\quad \dfrac{a+d}{b} = \dfrac{c+b}{d}$

(E) $\quad \dfrac{a+b}{b} = \dfrac{c+d}{d}$

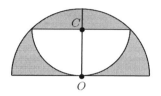

Note: Figure not drawn to scale.

16. In the figure above, O is the center of the larger semicircle and C is the center of the smaller semicircle inscribed in the larger semicircle. If the radius of the larger semicircle is 10, what is the area of the shaded region?

(A) $\quad 15\pi$

(B) $\quad 25\pi$

(C) $\quad 30\pi$

(D) $\quad 45\pi$

(E) $\quad 50\pi$

STOP

SAT Math Scoring Worksheet

Directions: In order to calculate your score correctly, fill out the blank spaces from A through K on the table below. After calculating your raw score, round the raw score to the nearest whole number. The scaled score can be determined using the *"SAT Math Test Score Conversion Table"* on the next page.

SAT Math Score			
A. Section 1 Number Correct		**F.** Section 1 Number Incorrect	
B. Section 2 Questions 1-8 Number Correct		**G.** Section 2 Questions 1-8 Number Incorrect	
C. Section 2 Questions 9-18 Number Correct			
D. Section 3 Number Correct		**H.** Section 3 Number Incorrect	
E. Total Correct A+B+C+D		**I.** Total Incorrect (F+G+H)÷4	
J. Total Unrounded Raw Score E − I		**K. Total Rounded Raw Score** Round to nearest whole number	

SAT Math Scaled Score:

SAT Math Test Score Conversion Table			
Raw Score	**Scaled Score**	**Raw Score**	**Scaled Score**
54	800	24	480
53	780	23	470
52	760	22	460
51	740	21	450
50	720	20	440
49	710	19	430
48	700	18	430
47	690	17	420
46	680	16	420
45	670	15	410
44	660	14	400
43	650	13	400
42	640	12	390
41	640	11	380
40	630	10	380
39	620	9	370
38	610	8	360
37	600	7	350
36	590	6	340
35	580	5	330
34	570	4	320
33	560	3	310
32	560	2	300
31	550	1	280
30	540	0	270
29	530	−1	250
28	520	−2	230
27	510	−3	210
26	500	−4 and below	200
25	490		

   www.solomonacademy.net

SECTION 1
Time — 25 minutes
20 Questions

Directions: Solve each problem in this section and enter your answer by marking the circle on the answer sheet. You may use all the space provided for your work.

Notes

1. You may use a calculator during this test.

2. All numbers used in this test are real numbers.

3. Unless noted, the domain and the range of a function used in this test are sets of real numbers.

4. Figures in this test provide useful information in solving problems. They are drawn as accurately as possible. Otherwise, figures not drawn to scale will be labeled as such. Figures lie in a plane.

<hr>

Information

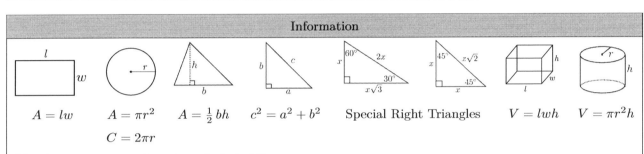

$A = lw$ $A = \pi r^2$ $A = \frac{1}{2}bh$ $c^2 = a^2 + b^2$ Special Right Triangles $V = lwh$ $V = \pi r^2 h$

$C = 2\pi r$

The degree measure of arc in a circle is 360.

The sum of the measures of the interior angles of a triangle is 180.

<hr>

1. The area of a triangle is $10\sqrt{3}$. If the height of the triangle is 5, what is the base of the triangle?

   (A) $2\sqrt{3}$

   (B) $4\sqrt{3}$

   (C) $6\sqrt{3}$

   (D) $8\sqrt{3}$

   (E) $10\sqrt{3}$

2. In the figure above, 4 congruent squares are placed side by side to form a rectangle. If the perimeter of the rectangle is 50, what is the area of two of the squares?

   (A) 10

   (B) 25

   (C) 30

   (D) 50

   (E) 100

3. The mean of three numbers is 5. If 13 is added, what is the mean of the four numbers?

   (A)   7

   (B)   8

   (C)   9

   (D)   10

   (E)   11

4. If Sue traveled 42 miles in 45 minutes, how fast, in miles per hour, did she travel?

   (A)   60 miles per hour

   (B)   56 miles per hour

   (C)   52 miles per hour

   (D)   48 miles per hour

   (E)   42 miles per hour

5. If a quadratic function $f(x) = x^2 + 3x - 4$, what is the y-intercept of $-f(x)$?

   (A)   5

   (B)   4

   (C)   1

   (D) -1

   (E) -4

E(Energy)	C(Energy Conversion)
$1 \times 10^4 \leq E < 1 \times 10^5$	4
$1 \times 10^5 \leq E < 1 \times 10^6$	5
$1 \times 10^6 \leq E < 1 \times 10^7$	6
$1 \times 10^7 \leq E < 1 \times 10^8$	7

6. In the equation $R = \dfrac{2}{3}C + 1.5$, R is the Richter scale, a number that determines the strength of earthquakes and C is an energy conversion shown on the table above. If the energy, $E = 1,000,000$, what is the value of the Richter scale, R ?

   (A)   3.5

   (B)   4.2

   (C)   4.8

   (D)   5.5

   (E)   6.2

7. On the interval $2 < x < 4$, which of the following quadratic function is decreasing?

  (A) $y = (x - 4)^2$

  (B) $y = (x - 3)^2$

  (C) $y = (x - 2)^2$

  (D) $y = (x - 1)^2$

  (E) $y = (x + 1)^2$

8. In the figure above, three lines intersect at one point to form six angles. If the degree measures of the six angles are integer values and they are not all congruent, what is the smallest possible degree measure of the largest angle?

  (A)   59

  (B)   60

  (C)   61

  (D)   177

  (E)   178

9. In order to make a two-digit number, two numbers are selected at random from digits 1 through 3 with replacement. How many two-digit numbers are possible?

  (A)   3

  (B)   6

  (C)   9

  (D)   12

  (E)   15

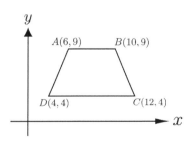

10. In the figure above, the quadrilateral $ABCD$ is a trapezoid. What is the area of the trapezoid?

  (A)   30

  (B)   40

  (C)   50

  (D)   60

  (E)   70

11. If both n and k are prime numbers, which of the following statement must be true?

(A) $n + k$ is an even number.

(B) If $n > 2$ and $k > 2$, $n + k$ is an even number.

(C) nk is an odd number.

(D) $n + k$ is a prime number.

(E) If $n < k$, $k - n$ is divisible by 3.

12. Which of the following expressions is equal to $9(9)^3$?

(A) 81^3

(B) 27^9

(C) 18^3

(D) 9^{27}

(E) 3^8

Alphabet	Assigned Value
A	1
B	2
C	3
$\vdots$	$\vdots$
Y	25
Z	26

13. Each alphabet letter has an assigned value shown on the table above. What is the sum of the assigned values of SOLOMON?

(A) 73

(B) 88

(C) 103

(D) 118

(E) 133

14. If $a + b = 1$ and $ab = -12$, what is the value of $a^2b + ab^2$?

(A) -24

(B) -12

(C) 1

(D) 12

(E) 24

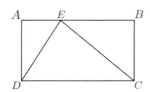

15. In the figure above, $ABCD$ is a rectangle whose area is 72 and $AD = 6$. If the ratio of three areas of $\triangle AED$, $\triangle EBC$, and $\triangle DEC$ is $1 : 2 : 3$ respectively, what is $AE : BE : DC$?

   (A) $3 : 4 : 5$

   (B) $2 : 3 : 4$

   (C) $1 : 3 : 4$

   (D) $1 : 2 : 4$

   (E) $1 : 2 : 3$

16. A number is increased by 8 and then the result is doubled. If the new result is one less than three times the original number, what is the value of the original number?

   (A)   14

   (B)   15

   (C)   16

   (D)   17

   (E)   18

17. A car's manual indicates that acceptable tire pressure for a certain model is between 28 PSI and 32 PSI, inclusive. Which of the following inequality best describes the acceptable tire pressure?

   (A) $|x - 2| \le 30$

   (B) $|x - 2| \ge 30$

   (C) $|x - 30| \le 2$

   (D) $|x - 30| \ge 2$

   (E) $|x - 32| \le 4$

18. Three points $A(x, -2)$, $B(-1, 2)$, and $C(3, 5)$ are on the same coordinates plane. If $AB = BC$, what could be the value of x ?

   (A) -4

   (B) -3

   (C) -2

   (D) -1

   (E) 0

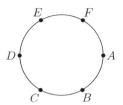

19. In the circular track whose circumference is 120 meters shown above, Joshua and Jason are running in opposite directions from the starting position, A. Joshua is running at 4 meters per second clockwise and Jason is running at 2 meters per second counterclockwise. Which of the following lettered position represents the second time Joshua and Jason meet after they begin running? (Assume that all the lettered positions are equally spaced.)

  (A) B

  (B) C

  (C) D

  (D) E

  (E) F

20. A three-digit number ABC is called an increasing number if $A < B < C$. Three numbers are selected at random from the set $\{1, 2, 3, 4\}$ without replacement to form an increasing number. What is the probability that the three-digit number formed is an increasing number?

  (A) $\dfrac{5}{6}$

  (B) $\dfrac{2}{3}$

  (C) $\dfrac{1}{2}$

  (D) $\dfrac{1}{3}$

  (E) $\dfrac{1}{6}$

STOP

www.solomonacademy.net

SECTION 2
Time — 25 minutes
18 Questions

Directions: This section contains two types of questions: Multiple-Choice questions and Free-Response questions. For question 1-8, solve each problem in this section and enter your answer by marking the circle on the answer sheet. You may use all the space provided for your work.

Notes

1. You may use a calculator during this test.

2. All numbers used in this test are real numbers.

3. Unless noted, the domain and the range of a function used in this test are sets of real numbers.

4. Figures in this test provide useful information in solving problems. They are drawn as accurately as possible. Otherwise, figures not drawn to scale will be labeled as such. Figures lie in a plane.

Information

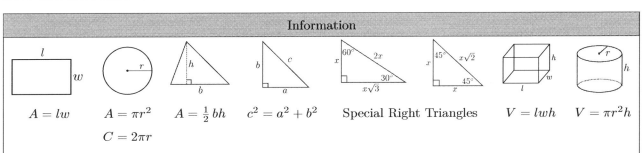

$A = lw$ $A = \pi r^2$ $A = \frac{1}{2} bh$ $c^2 = a^2 + b^2$ Special Right Triangles $V = lwh$ $V = \pi r^2 h$

$C = 2\pi r$

The degree measure of arc in a circle is 360.

The sum of the measures of the interior angles of a triangle is 180.

1. Which of the following expression must be equal to $(x - 1)(x + 2)$?

   (A) $2x + 1$

   (B) $x^2 - 2$

   (C) $x^2 + x - 2$

   (D) $x^2 - x + 2$

   (E) $x^2 - x - 2$

2. Three fifths of students in a class are boys. One third of the boys in the class wear glasses. What fractional part of the students in the class are boys who wear glasses?

   (A) $\dfrac{1}{5}$

   (B) $\dfrac{1}{4}$

   (C) $\dfrac{1}{3}$

   (D) $\dfrac{1}{2}$

   (E) $\dfrac{14}{15}$

3. The lengths of two segments $\overline{BA}$ and $\overline{CD}$ are 7 and 8 respectively. The two segments $\overline{BA}$ and $\overline{CD}$ are overlapped so that four points A, C, B, and D are arranged in that order and they become collinear points. If $BC = 6$, what is the length of $\overline{AD}$?

(A) 13

(B) 12

(C) 11

(D) 10

(E) 9

4. In the graph of $y = x^2 - 5x + 6$ which is not shown here, what is the total number of y-intercept(s) and x-intercept(s)?

(A) 1

(B) 2

(C) 3

(D) 4

(E) 5

5. There are forty students in a class. They are taking either math or chemistry or both. The number of students taking math is twice as many as the number of students taking chemistry. If there are five students taking both math and chemistry, what is the number of students taking math?

(A) 15

(B) 20

(C) 25

(D) 30

(E) 35

6. Two lines $ax + by = 5$ and $y = \dfrac{3}{4}x$ are parallel. If $b \neq 0$, what is the value of $\dfrac{a}{b}$?

(A) $\dfrac{5}{4}$

(B) $\dfrac{4}{3}$

(C) $\dfrac{3}{4}$

(D) $-\dfrac{4}{3}$

(E) $-\dfrac{3}{4}$

$$\frac{1}{\sqrt{x-2}} = \sqrt{x-2}$$

7. Which of the following must be the solutions to the equation shown above?

(A) $x = 2$ or $x = 4$

(B) $x = 1$ or $x = 3$

(C) $x = 1$ only

(D) $x = 2$ only

(E) $x = 3$ only

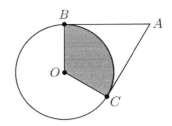

8. In the figure above, the radius of the circle is 6. Two segments drawn from point A touch the circle at two points B and C. If $m\angle A = 60°$, what is the area of the shaded region?

(A) 21π

(B) 18π

(C) 15π

(D) 12π

(E) 9π

Direction: For each of the 10 remaining Free-Response questions, solve the problem and enter your answer by marking the circle in the special grid as shown in the examples below.

Answer: $\frac{3}{7}$ Answer: 6.75   Answer: 124

Either position is correct.

  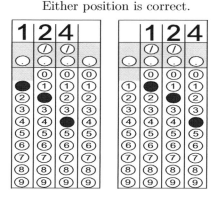

- Fill in one circle in each column.
- Each circle must be filled in correctly. Otherwise, you will not receive any credit.
- Convert all mixed numbers such as $1\frac{1}{2}$ to either 1.5 or $\frac{3}{2}$.
- For decimal answers that are longer than the number of grids provided, you must round or truncate the decimal. However, you must fill in all of the grids provided to ensure your answer is accurate as possible. For example, $0.666\ldots$ must be marked as .666 or .667.

- Answers are always positive.
- Write in the answer at the top of the grid to avoid mistakes when marking the circles.
- On problems that have more than one answer, fill in only one correct answer.

9. In the equation $x(y + z) = 24$, what is the value of y if $x = 2$ and $z = 3$?

10. There are five points on a circle. A chord is a line segment that connects two points on the circle. How many chords can be drawn?

11. In the figure above, what is the sum of the degree measures of all the marked angles?

x	2	3	4	5
y	8	27	64	k

12. If the pattern shown on the table above continues, what is the value of k ?

13. If $x > 0$, what is the solution to the equation $\sqrt{x^2 + 15} = 8$?

14. A print shop has two machines: machine A and machine B. Machine A can print 30 posters in 20 minutes and machine B can print 62 posters in 30 minutes. In the first half hour, only machine A prints posters. In the next hour, machine A and B print together. What is the total number of posters that machine A and machine B print?

15. Centreville is 16 miles due south of McLean and 12 miles due east of Brambleton on a map. How many miles are Mclean and Brambleton apart?

$$-49 \leq -3x + 2 < 11$$

16. How many positive integer values of x satisfy the inequality shown above?

17. The mean and the median of a set of five positive integers is 10 and 9 respectively. If the mode of the set is 5, what is the greatest possible range of the set of five integers?

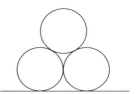

18. In the figure above, three identical circular oranges with a radius of 3 inches are arranged such that two oranges are on the ground and the third orange is on the top of the two oranges. If the top of the third orange is $a + b\sqrt{3}$ inches from the ground, what is the value of $a + b$?

SECTION 3
Time – 20 minutes
16 Questions

Directions: Solve each problem in this section and enter your answer by marking the circle on the answer sheet. You may use all the space provided for your work.

Notes

1. You may use a calculator during this test.

2. All numbers used in this test are real numbers.

3. Unless noted, the domain and the range of a function used in this test are sets of real numbers.

4. Figures in this test provide useful information in solving problems. They are drawn as accurately as possible. Otherwise, figures not drawn to scale will be labeled as such. Figures lie in a plane.

Information

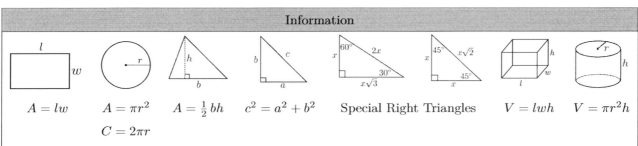

$$A = lw \qquad A = \pi r^2 \qquad A = \tfrac{1}{2}bh \qquad c^2 = a^2 + b^2 \qquad \text{Special Right Triangles} \qquad V = lwh \qquad V = \pi r^2 h$$

$$C = 2\pi r$$

The degree measure of arc in a circle is 360.

The sum of the measures of the interior angles of a triangle is 180.

---

1. If $2^3 \times 2^5 = 2^n$, what is the value of n ?

(A) 4

(B) 5

(C) 6

(D) 7

(E) 8

2. The volume of a cylinder is the base area times the height. If the base area of the cylinder is 36π and the height is 6, what is the volume of the cylinder?

(A) 216π

(B) 196π

(C) 96π

(D) 48π

(E) 6π

Per serving	Carbs	Protein	Fat
1 scrambled egg	1.3g	7g	7g
1 strip of bacon	0.1g	2.5g	10g
1 cup of hash brown	28g	2.8g	5g
1 slice of bread	23.6g	4g	2.4g

3. Joshua ate two scrambled eggs, two strips of bacon, half cup of hash brown, and two slices of bread for his breakfast. According to the table shown above, what is the total grams of protein Joshua ate in his breakfast?

   (A) 14.2 grams

   (B) 15.6 grams

   (C) 28.4 grams

   (D) 29.8 grams

   (E) 32.6 grams

4. If $2(x + 2y) = k$, what is the value of $4(2x + 4y)$ in terms of k ?

   (A) $4k + 4$

   (B) $4k$

   (C) $2k + 4$

   (D) $2k$

   (E) $k + 4$

5. What percent of 20 is 15?

   (A) $33\frac{1}{3}\%$

   (B) 50%

   (C) 75%

   (D) 87.5%

   (E) $133\frac{1}{3}\%$

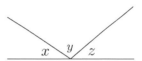

6. In the figure above, the sum of degree measures of x and y is three times the degree measure of z. what is the degree measure of z ?

   (A) $30°$

   (B) $45°$

   (C) $60°$

   (D) $75°$

   (E) $90°$

x	0	1	2
y	6	9	12

7. The table above shows the three ordered pairs on a line. What is the x-intercept of the line?

    (A) -2

    (B) -1

    (C)   0

    (D)   1

    (E)   2

$$2 \le a \le 5$$
$$3 \le b \le 6$$

8. According to the inequalities shown above, which of the following inequality must be true?

    (A) $5 \le ab \le 11$

    (B) $6 \le ab \le 11$

    (C) $6 \le ab \le 30$

    (D) $5 \le a + b \le 30$

    (E) $6 \le a + b \le 30$

9. The three vertices of $\triangle ABC$ are $A(0,4)$, $B(5,4)$, and $C(3,0)$ on the coordinates plane. Which of the following statement correctly describes $\triangle ABC$?

    (A) $\triangle ABC$ is a right triangle.

    (B) $\triangle ABC$ is a scalene triangle.

    (C) $\triangle ABC$ is an obtuse triangle.

    (D) $\triangle ABC$ is an isosceles triangle.

    (E) $\triangle ABC$ is an equilateral triangle.

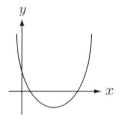

10. According to the graph of the quadratic function $y = ax^2 + bx + c$ shown above, which of the following statement must be true?

    (A) $a < 0$

    (B) $b > 0$

    (C) $c < 0$

    (D) $ac > 0$

    (E) $bc > 0$

11. A is a set of positive integers less than 100 that are divisible by 2. B is a set of positive integers less than 100 that are divisible by 3. How many positive integers belong to set A or set B ?

    (A) 64

    (B) 65

    (C) 66

    (D) 67

    (E) 68

12. It takes one minute to fill $\frac{3}{4}$ of a gas tank. How many more minutes will it take to fill the remaining gas tank?

    (A) $\frac{4}{3}$ minutes

    (B) $\frac{3}{2}$ minutes

    (C) $\frac{2}{3}$ minute

    (D) $\frac{1}{2}$ minute

    (E) $\frac{1}{3}$ minute

13. Two standard dice are rolled. What is the probability that the sum of the two numbers on top of each die is 7?

    (A) $\frac{1}{6}$

    (B) $\frac{1}{4}$

    (C) $\frac{1}{3}$

    (D) $\frac{5}{12}$

    (E) $\frac{1}{2}$

14. The length of cube A is 4 inches. If the length of cube A is increased by 75% to form cube B, how much greater, in square inches, is the surface area of cube B than the surface area of cube A ?

    (A) 33 square inches

    (B) 96 square inches

    (C) 132 square inches

    (D) 198 square inches

    (E) 279 square inches

15. What is the equation of the perpendicular bisector of a segment whose endpoints are $(-2, 0)$ and $(0, 4)$?

    (A) $x - 2y = 3$

    (B) $x + 2y = -3$

    (C) $x + 2y = 3$

    (D) $2x - y = 4$

    (E) $2x - y = -4$

16. Three points $A(x, y)$, $B(0, 0)$, and $C(2, -1)$ are on the coordinates plane. Point $A(x, y)$ lies in the first quadrant. Two segments $\overline{AB}$ and $\overline{CB}$ are perpendicular to each other. If the length of $\overline{AB}$ is $5\sqrt{5}$, what is the value of $x + y$?

    (A)   20

    (B)   15

    (C)   10

    (D)   7

    (E)   3

STOP

SAT Math Scoring Worksheet

Directions: In order to calculate your score correctly, fill out the blank spaces from A through K on the table below. After calculating your raw score, round the raw score to the nearest whole number. The scaled score can be determined using the *"SAT Math Test Score Conversion Table"* on the next page.

SAT Math Score			
A. Section 1 Number Correct		**F.** Section 1 Number Incorrect	
B. Section 2 Questions 1-8 Number Correct		**G.** Section 2 Questions 1-8 Number Incorrect	
C. Section 2 Questions 9-18 Number Correct			
D. Section 3 Number Correct		**H.** Section 3 Number Incorrect	
E. Total Correct A+B+C+D		**I.** Total Incorrect (F+G+H)÷4	
J. Total Unrounded Raw Score **E − I**		**K. Total Rounded Raw Score** **Round to nearest whole number**	

SAT Math Scaled Score:

SAT Math Test Score Conversion Table			
Raw Score	**Scaled Score**	**Raw Score**	**Scaled Score**
54	800	24	480
53	780	23	470
52	760	22	460
51	740	21	450
50	720	20	440
49	710	19	430
48	700	18	430
47	690	17	420
46	680	16	420
45	670	15	410
44	660	14	400
43	650	13	400
42	640	12	390
41	640	11	380
40	630	10	380
39	620	9	370
38	610	8	360
37	600	7	350
36	590	6	340
35	580	5	330
34	570	4	320
33	560	3	310
32	560	2	300
31	550	1	280
30	540	0	270
29	530	−1	250
28	520	−2	230
27	510	−3	210
26	500	−4 and below	200
25	490		

Answers and Solutions
SAT Math Practice Test 1
Section 1

Answers

1. C	2. D	3. A	4. B	5. B
6. B	7. A	8. B	9. D	10. C
11. B	12. D	13. E	14. D	15. A
16. C	17. D	18. C	19. C	20. B

Solutions

1. (C)

   A is a set of all multiples of 2 and B is a set of all multiples of 3. It is possible to determine the answer by simply listing out both sets as shown below.

   $$A = \{2, 4, 6, 8, 10, 12, 14, \cdots\}$$
   $$B = \{3, 6, 9, 12, \cdots\}$$

   Thus, there are only two positive integers less than 15 that belong to both sets A and B: 6 and 12. Additionally, if a number is both a multiple of 2 and 3, it is a multiple of 6. Thus, the positive integers less than 15 that are multiples of 6 are 6 and 12. Therefore, (C) is the correct answer.

2. (D)

   Plug in any positive integer values into the variables that match the description: x, y, and z are positive integers and z is greater than y which is greater than x. For instance, let $x = 1$, $y = 3$, and $z = 5$.

   $$(A) \quad z - x = 5 - 1 = 4$$
   $$(B) \quad z - y = 5 - 3 = 2$$
   $$(C) \quad x + y = 1 + 3 = 4$$
   $$(D) \quad y + z = 3 + 5 = 8$$
   $$(E) \quad x + z = 1 + 5 = 6$$

   Thus, the sum of the two largest integers, $y + z$, is the greatest in value. Therefore, (D) is the correct answer.

3. (A)

Since the two triangles are similar triangles, set up a proportion to determine the height of triangle DEF. First, let's define x as the height of triangle DEF.

$$\frac{5}{x} = \frac{10}{20}$$
$$x = 10$$

Thus, the height of triangle DEF is 10.

$$\text{Area of } \triangle DEF = \frac{1}{2}bh$$
$$= \frac{1}{2}(20)(10)$$
$$= 100$$

Therefore, the area of $\triangle DEF$ is 100.

4. (B)

Triangle ABC is a 30°-60°-90° special right triangle whose sides are in the ratio $1 : \sqrt{3} : 2$. $\overline{AC}$ is the shorter leg of the 30°-60°-90° triangle and is opposite the angle 30°. Thus, the length of $\overline{AC}$ is half the length of the hypotenuse, 5. $\overline{BC}$ is the longer leg and is opposite the angle 60°. Thus, the length of $\overline{BC}$ is $\sqrt{3}$ times the length of the shorter leg, $5\sqrt{3}$.

$$\text{The perimeter of } \triangle ABC = 10 + 5 + 5\sqrt{3} = 15 + 5\sqrt{3}$$

Therefore, the perimeter of $\triangle ABC$ is $15 + 5\sqrt{3}$.

5. (B)

Break each part of the verbal expression down. Let's define x as the number. Four less than three times a number means $3x - 4$ and five more than twelve times the number means $12x + 5$. Set the two expressions equal to each other and solve for x.

$$12x + 5 = 3x - 4$$
$$9x = -9$$
$$x = -1$$

Therefore, the number is -1.

6. (B)

Since $l \parallel m$, $\angle DEF \cong \angle ABE$ because they are corresponding angles. Since $\angle ABE$ and $\angle ABC$ are supplementary angles, $\angle DEF$ and $\angle ABC$ are also supplementary angles. Thus, the sum of the measures of $\angle DEF$ and $\angle ABC$ equals 180°. Therefore,

$$2x + 1 + 2x - 1 = 180$$
$$4x = 180$$
$$x = 45$$

Therefore, the value of x is 45.

7. (A)

If you cross multiply each proportion shown below, they equal to $16y = 2x$.

$$\frac{16}{x} = \frac{2}{y} \Longleftrightarrow 16y = 2x \Longleftrightarrow \frac{y}{x} = \frac{2}{16}$$

This means that $\frac{16}{x} = \frac{2}{y}$ is equivalent to $\frac{y}{x} = \frac{2}{16}$. Therefore, $\frac{y}{x} = \frac{2}{16} = \frac{1}{8}$.

8. (B)

Joshua has taken four out of five tests and received the scores: 87, 88, 92, and 89. In order to get an A for the math class, which is an average of 90 or more, the sum of the five tests must be at least 450. Set up the inequality and solve for s which represents the score needed on the 5th test.

$$87 + 88 + 92 + 89 + s \geq 450$$
$$s \geq 94$$

Joshua must obtain a score that is greater than or equal to 94 in order to receive an A for the math class.

9. (D)

Let's define x as the total number of students. Since 28% of the total number of students are taking French, the number of students taking French is $0.28x$. Thus,

$$0.28x = 560$$
$$x = \frac{560}{0.28} = 2000$$

So, there are 2000 students. Since 38% of the total number of students are taking Spanish, the number of students taking Spanish is $0.38x = 0.38(2000) = 760$.

10. (C)

Since Jennifer's row is the 29th row from the front, there are 28 rows in front of Jennifer. Since Jennifer's row is the 21st row from the back, there are 20 rows behind Jennifer. Thus, there are $28 + 1 + 20 = 49$ rows in the Auditorium. Since each row is occupied by 2 students, there are 98 students who went to the Auditorium.

11. (B)

The venn diagram below shows the complete breakdown of the given information.

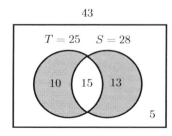

The shaded region in the venn diagram represents the sum of the number of students who play only Tennis or only Soccer, which is $10 + 13 = 23$.

12. (D)

The diagonals of all parallelograms are not necessarily perpendicular of each other. This is, however, a property of rhombus. I, III, and IV are correct statements: opposite angles are congruent, diagonals bisect each other, and consecutive angles are supplementary.

13. (E)

If it takes 4 people 6 days to paint half a house, 4 people will need 12 days to paint an entire house. In other words, the amount of work required to paint the entire house is equivalent to $4 _{\text{people}} \times 12 _{\text{days}} = 48 _{\text{people}\times\text{days}}$. Since half the house remains unpainted, the amount of work required is $\frac{1}{2} \times 48 _{\text{people}\times\text{days}} = 24 _{\text{people}\times\text{days}}$. Let x be the total number of people needed to paint half the house in 2 days. Then, the amount of work required in 2 days is $x _{\text{people}} \times 2 _{\text{days}} = 2x _{\text{people}\times\text{days}}$. Set up an equation in terms of the amount of work required and solve for x.

$$2x _{\text{people}\times\text{days}} = 24 _{\text{people}\times\text{days}}$$
$$x = 12$$

Thus, 12 people are needed to paint half the house in 2 days. Since there are already 4 people working on the house, the number of additional people needed is $12 - 4 = 8$ people.

14. (D)

Since the hexagonal shape is divided into six equilateral triangles with side length 6, the area of hexagonal shape is six times the area of the equilateral triangle. Thus,

$$\text{Area of the hexagonal shape} = 6 \times \text{Area of the equilateral triangle}$$
$$= 6 \times \frac{\sqrt{3}}{4} S^2$$
$$= 6 \times \frac{\sqrt{3}}{4} (6)^2$$
$$= 54\sqrt{3}$$

The hexagonal nut has a circle with radius of 3 at the center of the shape. Therefore,

$$\text{Area of the shaded region} = \text{Area of the hexagonal shape} - \text{Area of the circle}$$
$$= 54\sqrt{3} - \pi(3)^2$$
$$= 54\sqrt{3} - 9\pi$$

15. (A)

If the line is reflected over the x-axis, the x-intercept remains the same $(6,0)$ and the y-intercept changes to $(0,-3)$. Let's find the slope of the new line using the points, $(6,0)$ and $(0,-3)$.

$$\text{Slope of the new line} = \frac{-3-0}{0-6} = \frac{-3}{-6} = \frac{1}{2}$$

Thus, the slope of the new line is $\frac{1}{2}$ and the y-intercept is -3. Therefore, the equation of the new line is $y = \frac{1}{2}x - 3$.

16. (C)

From the first equation $xy = 1$, solve x in terms of y. Thus, $x = \frac{1}{y}$. Substitute x for $\frac{1}{y}$ in the second equation to solve for x.

$$x + \frac{1}{y} = 5 \qquad \text{Substitute } x \text{ for } \frac{1}{y}$$
$$x + x = 5$$
$$2x = 5$$
$$x = \frac{5}{2}$$

Since $x = \frac{5}{2}$ and $xy = 1$, $y = \frac{2}{5}$. Therefore, $y + \frac{1}{x} = \frac{2}{5} + \frac{2}{5} = \frac{4}{5}$.

17. (D)

In the morning, Jason headed to his office at an approximation of either 7:20 am or 7:55 am. Returning home, he looked at the clock at an approximation of either 5:10 pm or 5:40 pm.

$$\text{Greatest Time Away} = 5{:}40 \text{ pm} - 7{:}20 \text{ am}$$
$$= 17{:}40 - 7{:}20$$
$$= 10 \text{ hours and } 20 \text{ minutes}$$

18. (C)

The fastest way to solve this particular problem is to plug in numbers and observe which set of numbers satisfies the requirements in the problem. For instance, $k = 8$ and $n = 7$.

$$(A) \; kn + 2 = 58 \Longrightarrow \text{remainder of } 4$$
$$(B) \; kn + 3 = 59 \Longrightarrow \text{remainder of } 5$$
$$(C) \; kn + 4 = 60 \Longrightarrow \text{remainder of } 0$$
$$(D) \; kn + 5 = 61 \Longrightarrow \text{remainder of } 1$$
$$(E) \quad\; kn = 56 \Longrightarrow \text{remainder of } 2$$

19. (C)

Translate the distance from 2 to $|x - 2|$ and within 3 units to < 3. Therefore, a set of all real numbers within 3 units away from 2 is written as $|x - 2| < 3$.

20. (B)

Use the midpoint formula, $\left(\frac{x_1 + x_2}{2}, \frac{y_1 + y_2}{2}\right)$ to find the x and y coordinates of M, N, and P.

$$M = \left(\frac{3 + 7}{2}, \frac{1 + 9}{2}\right) = (5, 5)$$
$$N = \left(\frac{7 + 15}{2}, \frac{9 + 1}{2}\right) = (11, 5)$$
$$P = \left(\frac{3 + 15}{2}, \frac{1 + 1}{2}\right) = (9, 1)$$

In the figure below, the shaded region is a triangle whose vertices are M, N, and P.

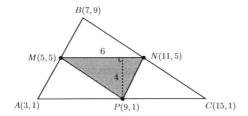

In triangle MNP, the length of the base $\overline{MN}$ is 6 and the length of the height is 4. Therefore,

$$\text{Area of } \triangle MNP = \frac{1}{2}(6)(4) = 12$$

Answers and Solutions
SAT Math Practice Test 1
Section 2

Answers

1. B	2. E	3. A	4. C
5. C	6. D	7. E	8. E
9. 81	10. 12	11. 100	12. 18
13. 66	14. 9	15. 33	16. $\frac{3}{7}$
17. 86	18. $\frac{7}{12}$		

Solutions

1. **(B)**

   Plug in the given values into the expression $b^2 - 4ac$.

   $$
   \begin{aligned}
   b^2 - 4ac &= (-3)^2 - 4(1)(-2) \\
   &= 9 + 8 \\
   &= 17
   \end{aligned}
   $$

2. **(E)**

   If the diameter is 4, then the radius is 2.

   $$\frac{\text{Circumference}}{\text{Area}} = \frac{2\pi(2)}{\pi(2)^2} = \frac{4\pi}{4\pi} = 1$$

   Therefore, the ratio of the circle's circumference to its area is $1:1$.

3. **(A)**

   Observe the graph to find out how much funds were raised. The amount of money raised from catalogs, candy bars, cookie dough, and discount cards are \$175, \$350, \$200, and \$75, respectively.

   $$
   \begin{aligned}
   \text{Total amount of money collected} &= 175 + 350 + 200 + 75 \\
   &= 800
   \end{aligned}
   $$

   Therefore,

   $$
   \begin{aligned}
   \text{Percent of cookie dough collected} &= \frac{200}{800} \times 100\% \\
   &= 25\%
   \end{aligned}
   $$

4. (C)

The measure of angle BCA is $70°$. Thus, the sum of the measures of angles A and B is $110°$. Define x as the measure of angle B. The measure of angle A is $\frac{5}{6}x$. Thus,

$$m\angle B + m\angle A = 110$$
$$x + \frac{5}{6}x = 110$$
$$\frac{11x}{6} = 110$$
$$x = 60$$

Therefore, the measure of angle B is $60°$.

5. (C)

Let x be the number of student tickets sold and y be the number of adult tickets sold. Since the sum of the student tickets and adult tickets sold is 385 tickets, $x + y = 385$. Additionally, since the number of student tickets sold is four more than twice the number of adult tickets sold, $x = 2y + 4$. Use the substitution method to solve for x.

$$x + y = 385 \qquad \text{Substitute } 2y + 4 \text{ for } x$$
$$2y + 4 + y = 385$$
$$3y + 4 = 385$$
$$y = 127$$

Thus, the number of adult tickets sold is 127. To find the number of student tickets sold, x,

$$x = 2y + 4 \qquad \text{Substitute 127 for } y$$
$$= 2(127) + 4$$
$$= 258$$

Therefore, the number of student tickets sold is 258.

6. (D)

In 2 years, you deposited \$1250 and in 9 years, you deposited \$3000. This can be written as ordered pairs, (x, y), where x represent years and y represents the amount deposited: $(2, 1250)$ and $(9, 3000)$. Find the slope of the line that passes through the points, $(2, 1250)$ and $(9, 3000)$, because it represents the amount of money deposited into the savings account every year.

$$\text{Slope} = \frac{y_2 - y_1}{x_2 - x_1}$$
$$= \frac{3000 - 1250}{9 - 2}$$
$$= \frac{1750}{7}$$
$$= \frac{\$250}{1 \text{ year}}$$

Therefore, the amount of money deposited into the savings account every year is \$250.

7. (E)

In the figure below, $\triangle ABC$ is an equilateral triangle because $AC = BC = AB = 12$. Thus,

$$\text{Area of } \triangle ABC = \frac{\sqrt{3}}{4}S^2 = \frac{\sqrt{3}}{4}(12)^2 = 36\sqrt{3}$$

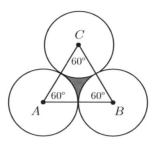

Additionally, there are three equal sectors whose central angle is 60° inside the equilateral triangle.

$$\text{Sum of areas of the three sectors} = 3 \times \pi(6)^2 \times \frac{60°}{360°}$$
$$= 3 \times 6\pi = 18\pi$$

The area of the shaded region equals to the area of the equilateral triangle ABC minus the sum of the areas of the three equal sectors. Therefore,

$$\text{Area of the shaded region} = 36\sqrt{3} - 18\pi$$

8. (E)

Define x as the speed of the airplane and y as the speed of the wind. Then, the speed of the airplane with the wind is $x + y$. The speed of the airplane against the wind is $x - y$. Use the Time $= \frac{\text{Distance}}{\text{Speed}}$ formula to set up two equations in terms of time. Let T_{AB} and T_{BA} be the time needed for the airplane to travel from city A to city B and from city B to city A, respectively.

With wind: $T_{AB} = \dfrac{d}{x + y} \Longrightarrow 2 = \dfrac{d}{x + y} \Longrightarrow x + y = \dfrac{d}{2}$

Against wind: $T_{BA} = \dfrac{d}{x - y} \Longrightarrow 3 = \dfrac{d}{x - y} \Longrightarrow x - y = \dfrac{d}{3}$

Use the linear combinations method to solve for y.

$$
\begin{aligned}
x + y &= \tfrac{d}{2} \\
\underline{x - y} &= \underline{\tfrac{d}{3}} \qquad\qquad \text{Subtract two equations}\\
2y &= \tfrac{d}{2} - \tfrac{d}{3} \\
2y &= \tfrac{d}{6} \\
y &= \tfrac{d}{12}
\end{aligned}
$$

Therefore, the speed of the wind is $\frac{d}{12}$.

9. (81)

$$\sqrt{3-x} = 9 \qquad \text{Square each side}$$
$$3 - x = 81 \qquad \text{Multiply each side by } -1$$
$$x - 3 = -81 \qquad \text{Take the absolute value of each side}$$
$$|x - 3| = 81$$

10. (12)

The blue team needs to move the ball a total of 20 yards within 4 plays in order to win the football game. In the first three plays, the blue team moves the ball 7 yards forward, 4 yards backward, and 5 yards forward. The total gain in yards is 8. Thus,

$$\text{Number of yards on the 4}^{\text{th}} \text{ play} = 20 - (7 - 4 + 5) = 12$$

Therefore, the blue team needs to move the ball 12 more yards forward in order to win the football game.

11. (100)

$$\text{Total number of points on a circle} = \frac{\text{Circumference of a circle}}{\text{Distance between each point}} = \frac{300}{3} = 100$$

Therefore, the number of posts for the circular garden is 100.

12. (18)

In the figure below, $AB = BC = DC = 12$ and $CE = 6$.

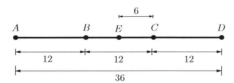

Therefore, $DE = DC + CE = 12 + 6 = 18$.

13. (66)

In the figure below, each side of the equilateral triangle in cut into a smaller equilateral triangle with side length of 3. So, the remaining figure is a hexagon.

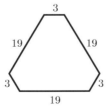

Therefore, the perimeter of the hexagon is $19 \times 3 + 3 \times 3 = 66$.

14. (9)

Write the 15th term and 4th term in terms of a_1 and d using the nth term, $a_n = a_1 + (n-1)d$ formula of the arithmetic sequence.

$$a_{15} = a_1 + 14d = 61$$
$$a_4 = a_1 + 3d = 17$$

Use the linear combinations method to solve for d and a_1.

$$a_1 + 14d = 61$$
$$\underline{a_1 + 3d = 17} \qquad \text{Subtract two equations}$$
$$11d = 44$$
$$d = 4$$

Substitute 4 for d in $a_4 = a_1 + 3d = 17$ and solve for a_1. Thus, $a_1 = 5$.

$$a_2 = a_1 + d = 5 + 4 = 9$$

Therefore, the second term in the arithmetic sequence is 9.

15. (33)

$$\begin{aligned}
ax^2 + bx + 11 &= 0 \qquad & \text{Substitute } -2 \text{ for } x \\
a(-2)^2 + b(-2) + 11 &= 0 & \text{Simplify} \\
4a - 2b + 11 &= 0 & \text{Subtract 11 from each side} \\
4a - 2b &= -11 & \text{Multiply each side by } -3 \\
-3(4a - 2b) &= -3(-11) \\
6b - 12a &= 33
\end{aligned}$$

Therefore, the value of $6b - 12a$ is 33.

16. $\left(\frac{3}{7}\right)$

Define y as the length of the two smaller rectangles, $BCFE$ and $EFDA$. The areas of the two smaller rectangles $BCFE$ and $AEFD$ are $y \times BE$ and $y \times AE$, respectively. Since the ratio of areas of the two smaller rectangles is $3 : 7$, set up a proportion and find the ratio of BE to AE.

$$\text{Area of BCFE : Area of AEFD} = 3 : 7$$
$$y \times BE : y \times AE = 3 : 7$$
$$\frac{y \times BE}{y \times AE} = \frac{3}{7} \qquad y \text{ cancels each other}$$
$$\frac{BE}{AE} = \frac{3}{7}$$

Therefore, the ratio of BE to AE is $\frac{3}{7}$.

17. (86)

Since 87 is the largest number and 4 is the smallest number of the set, it is possible to determine the largest integer of x so that the median of the six different integers is the greatest. The median of the six integers is the average of the 3rd and 4th number in the set. Let's consider two cases. The first case is when $x < 23$ and the second case is when $23 < x < 87$.

- Case 1 when $x < 23$: Arrange the six different numbers from smallest to largest.

$$4, 8, 14, x, 23, 87$$

Since the greatest possible value of x is 22, the median of the six integers is $\frac{14+22}{2} = 18$.

- Case 2 when $23 < x < 87$: Arrange the six different numbers from smallest to largest.

$$4, 8, 14, 23, x, 87$$

The median of the six integers is $\frac{14+23}{2} = 18.5$, which is the greatest. The median remains 18.5 no matter what value of x is.

The median, 18.5 is the greatest when $23 < x < 87$. Since $23 < x < 87$ and the six integers are different, the largest integer value of x is 86.

18. $\left(\frac{7}{12}\right)$

Substitute 5 for x and -7 for y into the function $y = a(x+1)(x-7)$ to solve for a.

$$
\begin{aligned}
y &= a(x+1)(x-7) \qquad \text{Substitute 5 for } x \text{ and } -7 \text{ for } y \\
-7 &= a(5+1)(5-7) \\
-12a &= -7 \\
a &= \frac{7}{12}
\end{aligned}
$$

Therefore, the value of a is $\frac{7}{12}$.

Answers and Solutions
SAT Math Practice Test 1
Section 3

Answers

1. D	2. D	3. A	4. A
5. D	6. B	7. C	8. B
9. D	10. C	11. A	12. C
13. C	14. B	15. E	16. A

Solutions

1. (D)

   In the figure below, $A = -3$, $B = -2$, $C = -1$ and $D = 1$.

   $$A \quad B \quad C \qquad D \quad E$$
   $$-3 \quad -2 \quad -1 \quad 0 \quad 1 \quad 2$$

   Plug-in the given values of A, B, and C into the expression $C(A - B)$.

   $$C(A - B) = -1(-3 - (-2)) = -1(-1) = 1$$

   Therefore, (D) is the correct answer.

2. (D)

   In the figure below, $BC = DC$ and $m\angle A = m\angle E = 90°$. Since C is the midpoint of $\overline{AE}$, $AC = EC$.

   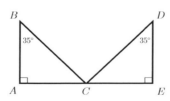

   Thus, triangles CBA and CDE are congruent. Since the corresponding parts of the congruent triangles are congruent, $\angle CBA \cong \angle CDE$. Therefore, $m\angle CBA = m\angle CDE = 35°$.

3. (A)

The graph below shows a line.

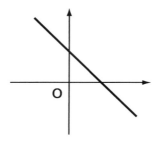

The line falls from left to right so the slope of the line is negative. Additionally, since the line crosses the y-axis above the origin, the y-intercept is positive. Write an equation of the line that has a negative slope and a positive y-intercept. For instance, $f(x) = -2x + 3$. Then, evaluate the function, $f(x)$, in each answer choice.

(A) $f(-5) = -2(-5) + 3 = 13$
(B) $f(-3) = -2(-3) + 3 = 9$
(C) $f(0) = -2(0) + 3 = 3$
(D) $f(3) = -2(3) + 3 = -3$
(E) $f(5) = -2(5) + 3 = -7$

Therefore, $f(-5)$ is the greatest in value.

4. (A)

In the figure below, the triangle is a 5-12-13 right triangle. Therefore, the length of the longest side, hypotenuse, is 13.

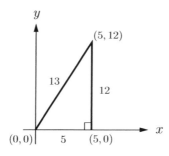

However, the answer can also be derived using the Pythagorean theorem. Define C as the length of the hypotenuse of the right triangle. Since C is the length, $C > 0$.

$$C^2 = 5^2 + 12^2$$
$$C = \sqrt{169}$$
$$C = 13$$

5. (D)

There are 60 seconds in 1 minute. Convert the time from minutes and seconds to just seconds.

$$1 \text{ minute and } 50 \text{ seconds} = 110 \text{ seconds}$$
$$2 \text{ minutes and } 5 \text{ seconds} = 125 \text{ seconds}$$
$$2 \text{ minutes and } 20 \text{ seconds} = 140 \text{ seconds}$$

Thus, the total lap time for the three runs is $110 + 125 + 140 = 375$ seconds.

$$\text{Average}_{\text{lap time}} = \frac{375 \text{ seconds}}{3 \text{ laps}}$$
$$= \frac{125 \text{ seconds}}{\text{lap}}$$

Therefore, the average lap time for the three runs is 125 seconds, which is 2 minutes and 5 seconds.

6. (B)

The fastest way to solve this type of problem is to plug-in the ordered pair into the system of linear equations. Substitute 2 for x and -3 for y into the system of linear equations in each answer choice to see if the equations hold true. In answer choice (B), both equations hold true:

$$2x + y = 1 \implies 2(2) + (-3) = 1 \quad \text{(True)}$$
$$3x - y = 9 \implies 3(2) - (-3) = 9 \quad \text{(True)}$$

Therefore, (B) is the correct answer.

7. (C)

In the figure below, $\triangle ABC$ is a 45°-45°-90° special right triangle whose sides are in the ratio $1 : 1 : \sqrt{2}$.

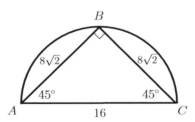

Since the radius of the semi-circle is 8, the diameter of the semi-circle and also the length of the hypotenuse is 16.

$$\text{Length of each leg} = \frac{\text{Length of Hypotenuse}}{\sqrt{2}} = \frac{16}{\sqrt{2}} = 8\sqrt{2}$$

The legs, $\overline{AB}$ and $\overline{BC}$, of the triangle ABC are the base and the height of triangle ABC.

$$\text{Area of } \triangle ABC = \frac{1}{2}bh = \frac{1}{2}(8\sqrt{2})(8\sqrt{2}) = 64$$

Therefore, the area of triangle ABC is 64.

8. (B)

Solve the equation for C.

$$\frac{9}{5}C + 32 = F \qquad \text{Subtract 32 from each side}$$

$$\frac{9}{5}C = F - 32 \qquad \text{Multiply each side by } \frac{5}{9}$$

$$C = \frac{5}{9}(F - 32)$$

9. (D)

The vertex is the minimum point when a parabola opens up. In the graph below, the vertex is located at $(-2, -4)$ before the graph is shifted.

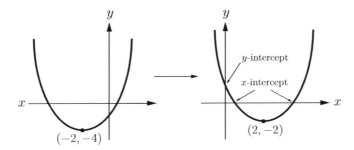

After the graph is shifted right 4 units and then up 2 units, the new x and y coordinates of the vertex is $(2, -2)$. Since the new graph never passes through the origin, there are two x-intercepts and one y-intercept. Therefore, the total number of the x-intercepts and the y-intercept is 3.

10. (C)

To solve a rational equation, cross multiply first and then solve the equation. Once you get the solutions, check the solutions by substituting the solutions in the original equation because some of them may be extraneous.

$$\frac{x-2}{x} = \frac{2}{x+3} \qquad \text{Cross multiply}$$

$$(x-2)(x+3) = 2x \qquad \text{Expand}$$

$$x^2 + x - 6 = 2x \qquad \text{Subtract } 2x \text{ from each side}$$

$$x^2 - x - 6 = 0 \qquad \text{Use the factoring method}$$

$$(x+2)(x-3) = 0 \qquad \text{Use the zero-product property}$$

$$x = -2 \quad \text{or} \quad x = 3$$

Substitute $x = -2$ and $x = 3$ in the original equation to check the solutions.

$$\frac{(-2)-2}{-2} = \frac{2}{-2+3} \qquad\qquad \frac{3-2}{3} = \frac{2}{3+3}$$

$$2 = 2 \quad \checkmark \text{ (Solution)} \qquad\qquad \frac{1}{3} = \frac{1}{3} \quad \checkmark \text{ (Solution)}$$

Therefore, $x = -2$ and $x = 3$ are the solutions.

11. (A)

In the figure below, define x as the width of the rectangular box. The length and the height are $3x$ and $2x$, respectively.

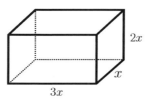

Additionally, the volume, V, of the box is $V = 3x \times x \times 2x = 6x^3$. Since the volume of the box is 162, substitute 162 for V and solve for x.

$$V = 6x^3 \qquad \text{Substitute 162 for } V$$
$$6x^3 = 162 \qquad \text{Divide each side by 6}$$
$$x^3 = 27$$
$$x = 3$$

Thus, the length, width, and height of the box are 9, 3, and 6, respectively. The surface area of the box consists of top and bottom sides, right and left sides, and front and back sides.

$$\text{Surface area} = \text{top+bottom+right+left+front+back}$$
$$= (9 \times 3) + (9 \times 3) + (3 \times 6) + (3 \times 6) + (9 \times 6) + (9 \times 6)$$
$$= 198$$

Therefore, the surface area of the rectangular box is 198.

12. (C)

Translate the verbal phrases into mathematical expressions.

$$\text{sum of } b \text{ and } c \quad \Longrightarrow \quad b + c$$
$$\text{product of } a \text{ and the sum of } b \text{ and } c \quad \Longrightarrow \quad a(b + c)$$
$$\text{quotient of } a \text{ and } c \quad \Longrightarrow \quad \frac{a}{c}$$

Thus, the verbal phrase, the product of a and the sum of b and c is divided by the quotient of a and c, can be translated to $\frac{a(b+c)}{\frac{a}{c}}$. Therefore,

$$\frac{a(b + c)}{\frac{a}{c}} = a(b + c) \div \frac{a}{c}$$
$$= a(b + c) \times \frac{c}{a}$$
$$= c(b + c)$$
$$= bc + c^2$$

13. (C)

To solve an exponential equation, both sides should have the same base. Note that $4^y = (2^2)^y = 2^{2y}$ and $8^z = (2^3)^z = 2^{3z}$. Simplify the expressions on the left side of the equation using the properties of the exponents.

$$\frac{2^x \cdot 4^y}{8^z} = 64$$

$$\frac{2^x \cdot 2^{2y}}{2^{3z}} = 2^6$$

$$2^{x+2y-3z} = 2^6$$

Since the expressions on both sides of the equation have the same base, the exponents on both sides are the same. Therefore, $x + 2y - 3z = 6$.

14. (B)

In the figure below, the radii of the two concentric circles are 1 and 2. Thus, the area of the shaded region is $\frac{1}{2} \times (\pi(2)^2 - \pi(1)^2) = \frac{3}{2}\pi$.

$$\text{Geometric probability} = \frac{\text{Area of the shaded region}}{\text{Area of larger circle}} = \frac{\frac{3}{2}\pi}{4\pi} = \frac{3}{8}$$

Therefore, the probability that the dart lands on the shaded area is $\frac{3}{8}$.

15. (E)

Use the definition of the arithmetic mean: the sum of all elements in a set divided by the number of elements in the set.

$$\frac{x + 2x - 3 + 3x - 5}{3} = y \implies \frac{6x - 8}{3} = y \implies 6x - 3y = 8$$

$$\frac{y - 1 + 2y - 2 + 3y - 4}{3} = x \implies \frac{6y - 7}{3} = x \implies 3x - 6y = -7$$

To find the value of $x + y$, it is not necessary to solve for x and y directly from the two equations shown above. Instead, subtract the second equation from the first equation. It will give you the value of $x + y$.

$$6x - 3y = 8$$
$$\underline{3x - 6y = -7} \qquad\qquad \text{Subtract two equations}$$
$$3x + 3y = 15 \qquad\qquad \text{Divide each side by 3}$$
$$x + y = 5$$

Therefore, the value of $x + y$ is 5.

16. (A)

The profit function, $P(x) = -\frac{1}{8}x^2 + 21x + 110$ where x represents the number of items, is the quadratic function with a negative leading coefficient, $-\frac{1}{8}$. It is displayed by the graph below.

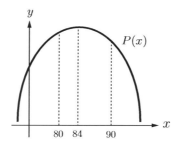

Thus, the graph of $P(x)$ opens down and its vertex is the maximum point. To find the x-coordinate of the vertex or axis of symmetry, use the $x = -\frac{b}{2a}$ formula.

$$x\text{-coordinate of vertex or axis of symmetry} = -\frac{b}{2a} = -\frac{21}{2(-\frac{1}{8})} = 84$$

If the factory would make 84 items, it would obtain the maximum profit. However, since the factory only makes the items in groups of 10, the possible answer choices are either 80 or 90. The graph above shows that the profit for 80 items is greater than the profit for 90 items. Therefore, the number of items that the factory should produce to obtain the maximum profit is 80.

Answers and Solutions
SAT Math Practice Test 2
Section 1

Answers

1. A	2. E	3. E	4. A	5. A
6. D	7. C	8. B	9. E	10. D
11. A	12. C	13. B	14. A	15. B
16. D	17. A	18. C	19. A	20. C

Solutions

1. (A)

A rhombus is a quadrilateral with four equal sides. Thus, set AD equal to CD and solve for x.

$$AD = CD$$
$$2x - 1 = x + 1$$
$$x = 2$$

Therefore, the value of x is 2.

2. (E)

Sue would have saved $0.20 per orange and $0.30 per mango if she went to the store today.

$$\text{Savings} = 2(1.19 - 0.99) + 2(1.89 - 1.59)$$
$$= 2(0.2) + 2(0.3)$$
$$= \$1.00$$

Therefore, Sue would have saved $1.00 if she went to the store today.

3. (E)

Translate the verbal phrase into a mathematical expression. The sum of $2x$ and $3x$ can be expressed as $2x + 3x$.

$$x(2x + 3x) = x(5x)$$
$$= 5x^2$$

Therefore, x multiplied by the sum of $2x$ and $3x$ is equal to $5x^2$.

4. (A)

In the figure below, $\triangle BAD$ is a 45°-45°-90° special right triangle whose sides are in the ratio $1 : 1 : \sqrt{2}$. Thus, $AD = BD = CD = 1$.

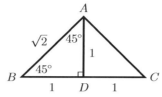

Therefore, the area of $\triangle BAC = \frac{1}{2}(BC)(AD) = \frac{1}{2}(2)(1) = 1$.

5. (A)

(A) $\dfrac{x}{3} \div \dfrac{x}{5} = \dfrac{x}{3} \times \dfrac{5}{x} = \dfrac{5}{3}$ (B) $\dfrac{x}{3} \div \dfrac{x}{4} = \dfrac{x}{3} \times \dfrac{4}{x} = \dfrac{4}{3}$

(C) $\dfrac{x}{4} \div \dfrac{x}{5} = \dfrac{x}{4} \times \dfrac{5}{x} = \dfrac{5}{4}$ (D) $\dfrac{x}{4} \div \dfrac{x}{6} = \dfrac{x}{4} \times \dfrac{6}{x} = \dfrac{3}{2}$

(E) $\dfrac{x}{5} \div \dfrac{x}{7} = \dfrac{x}{5} \times \dfrac{7}{x} = \dfrac{7}{5}$

Therefore, (A) is the correct answer.

6. (D)

Often, when solving problems regarding average, it is easier to solve the problems in terms of the sum. Define Sum_3 as the sum of the three numbers and Ave_3 as the average of the three numbers.

$$\text{Sum}_3 = 3 \times \text{Ave}_3$$
$$1 + 2 + x + 3 = 3k$$
$$x + 6 = 3k$$
$$x = 3k - 6$$

Therefore, the value of x in terms of k is $3k - 6$.

7. (C)

In the figure below, $\overline{AB} \parallel \overline{CD}$. $\angle BAC$ and $\angle DCE$ are corresponding angles so that $m\angle BAC = m\angle DCE = 70°$.

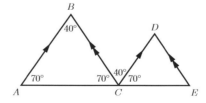

Since $m\angle ABC = 40°$, $m\angle BCA = 70°$ because the sum of the measures of interior angles of a triangle is 180°. The straight angle at C is 180°. Therefore, $m\angle BCD = 40°$.

8. (B)

   If 100 is divided by 3, the quotient is 33 and the remainder is 1. Thus, $q = 33$ and $r = 1$.

   $$100 = 3 \times 33 + 1$$
   $$100 = 3q + r$$

   Therefore, 100 can be expressed as $3q + r$.

9. (E)

   The solution to the inequality $0 \le x^2 \le 9$ is $-3 \le x \le 3$. Since the value of x are integers,

   $$-3 \le x \le 3 \quad \Longrightarrow \quad x = \{-3, -2, -1, 0, 1, 2, 3\}$$

   Therefore, there are seven elements in set S.

10. (D)

    $2x + 5$ and $x - 5$ are supplementary angles. Thus, the sum of their measures is $180°$.

    $$2x + 5 + x - 5 = 180$$
    $$3x = 180$$
    $$x = 60$$

    Additionally, $y + 5$ and $2y + 25$ are supplementary angles.

    $$y + 5 + 2y + 25 = 180$$
    $$3y + 30 = 180$$
    $$y = 50$$

    Therefore, $x + y = 60 + 50 = 110$.

11. (A)

    According to the table, the total amount of calories that Mr. Rhee lost in March is $15 \times 1400 = 21000$. Since 3500 calories is equal to 1 pound of body fat,

    $$\text{Total pounds of body fat lost} = \frac{21000}{3500} = 6$$

    Therefore, Mr. Rhee lost 6 pounds of body fat in March.

12. (C)

    Expand the numerator and split up the fraction into the sum of two fractions.

    $$\frac{x(y + z)}{yz} = \frac{xy + xz}{yz}$$
    $$= \frac{xy}{yz} + \frac{xz}{yz}$$
    $$= \frac{x}{z} + \frac{x}{y}$$

    Therefore, $\frac{x(y+z)}{yz} = \frac{x}{z} + \frac{x}{y}$.

13. (B)

Use the distance formula: distance = rate × time. Define t, in seconds, as how long Joshua and Jason have been running until they meet each other for the first time. Then, the distance that Joshua and Jason run for t seconds are $5t$ and $3t$, respectively. When Joshua and Jason meet each other, the sum of the distance that both run equals to the circumference of the circular track, 400 m. Thus,

$$5t + 3t = 400$$
$$8t = 400$$
$$t = 50$$

This means that Joshua runs for 50 seconds. Therefore, Joshua runs $50 \times 5 = 250$ meters.

14. (A)

This question is about finding the x-coordinate of the new quadratic function, $f(x + 10)$. To evaluate $f(x + 10)$, substitute $x + 10$ for x in $f(x)$.

$$f(x) = -2(x - 7)^2 + 16 \qquad \text{Substitute } x + 10 \text{ for } x$$
$$f(x + 10) = -2(x + 10 - 7)^2 + 16$$
$$= -2(x + 3)^2 + 16 \qquad \text{Vertex is } (-3, 16)$$

Since $f(x + 10)$ is expressed in the vertex form, the x-coordinate of the vertex of $f(x + 10)$ is -3. Therefore, $f(x + 10)$ has the maximum value at $x = -3$.

15. (B)

The surface area of the prism equals the sum of the areas of the five faces: top, bottom, front, right and left. In the figure below, the area of each right triangle on the top and bottom face is $\frac{1}{2}(8)(15) = 60$.

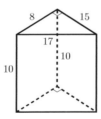

To find the surface area of the triangular prism, it is necessary to find the length of the missing side of the triangle on the top and bottom face of the prism. Use the Pythagorean theorem: $C^2 = 8^2 + 15^2$ or the Pythagorean triple: $8 - 15 - 17$. Thus, the length of the missing side of the triangle is 17. Thus,

$$\text{Surface area} = \text{top+bottom+front+right+left}$$
$$= 60 + 60 + (10 \times 17) + (10 \times 15) + (8 \times 10)$$
$$= 520$$

Therefore, the surface area of the triangular prism is 520.

16. (D)

Square both sides of the inequality.

$$\sqrt{x^2 + x} > \sqrt{419} \qquad \text{Square both sides}$$
$$x^2 + x > 419$$

So, you obtain $x^2 + x > 419$. Do not attempt to solve this inequality algebraically because it will take a long time to find the least positive integer value of x that satisfies the inequality. Instead, use the trial and error method. Substitute various positive integers to see which is the least integer. For instance, substitute $x = 10$ and $x = 15$ in the inequality $x^2 + x > 419$.

Substitute $x = 10$: $(10)^2 + 10 > 419$ Inequality is false

Substitute $x = 15$: $(15)^2 + 15 > 419$ Inequality is false

Keep substituting the positive integers until you find the least positive integer that satisfies the inequality.

Substitute $x = 20$: $(20)^2 + 20 > 419$ Inequality is true

Therefore, the least positive integer that satisfies the inequality is 20.

17. (A)

In the figure below, each of the two lines passes through the two vertices of the quadrilateral.

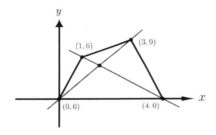

Write the equation of the line, $y = mx + b$, that passes through the points $(1, 6)$ and $(4, 0)$.

$$\text{Slope:} \quad m = \frac{0 - 6}{4 - 1} = \frac{-6}{3} = -2$$

So, $y = -2x + b$. Since $(4, 0)$ is on the line, substitute 4 for x and 0 for y to solve for b.

$$y = -2x + b \qquad \text{Substitute 4 for } x \text{ and 0 for } y$$
$$0 = -2(4) + b$$
$$b = 8$$

Thus, the equation of the line that passes through $(1, 6)$ and $(4, 0)$ is $y = -2x + 8$. Use the same procedures to write the equation of the line that passes through the points $(0, 0)$ and $(3, 9)$. You will obtain $y = 3x$.

Set up a system of linear equations: $y = -2x + 8$ and $y = 3x$. Use the substitution method to find the x and y coordinates of the intersection point of the two lines.

www.solomonacademy.net

$$y = -2x + 8 \qquad \text{Substitute } 3x \text{ for } y$$
$$3x = -2x + 8 \qquad \text{Solve for } x$$
$$x = \frac{8}{5}$$

Thus, the y-coordinate of the intersection point is $y = 3x = \frac{24}{5}$. Therefore, the x and y coordinates of the intersection point is $\left(\frac{8}{5}, \frac{24}{5}\right)$.

18. (C)

There are nine tick marks between $\sqrt{0.81} = 0.9$ and $\sqrt{6.25} = 2.5$ inclusive. Let's define interval as the length between any consecutive tick marks. There is one interval between two consecutive tick marks. There are two intervals between three consecutive tick marks, three intervals between four consecutive tick marks, and so on so forth. If the pattern continues, there are eight intervals between nine consecutive tick marks.

$$\text{Length of one interval} = \frac{\text{Distance between 0.9 and 2.5}}{8 \text{ intervals}} = \frac{1.6}{8} = 0.2$$

Therefore, the length between any consecutive tick marks is 0.2.

19. (A)

Find the sum of the numbers in any horizontal, vertical, or main diagonal. In table 1, there are four numbers on the diagonal so the sum is $13 + 11 + 6 + 4 = 34$.

1	x	y	4
		6	9
	11	10	
13			16

Table 1

1	x	y	4
		6	9
	11	10	5
13			16

Table 2

1	x	y	4
12	7	6	9
8	11	10	5
13			16

Table 3

Place 5 on the fourth column so that the sum is 34 as shown in table 2. Then, place 8 on the third row, 12 on the first column and 7 on the second row as shown in table 3. There are four numbers remaining: 2, 3, 14, and 15. Either 14 or 15 can not be on the fourth row because the sum exceeds 34. So, 14 and 15 must be on the first row and they are either x or y. Since $y > x$, x is 14.

20. (C)

Raise $x^{-\frac{1}{2}} = m^{\frac{1}{3}}$ to the power of -2, and raise $y^3 = n^2$ to the power of $\frac{1}{3}$ to find the value of x and y, respectively.

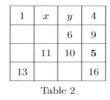

$$x^{-\frac{1}{2}} = m^{\frac{1}{3}}$$
$$(x^{-\frac{1}{2}})^{-2} = (m^{\frac{1}{3}})^{-2}$$
$$x = m^{-\frac{2}{3}}$$

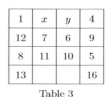

$$y^3 = n^2$$
$$(y^3)^{\frac{1}{3}} = (n^2)^{\frac{1}{3}}$$
$$y = n^{\frac{2}{3}}$$

Use the properties of exponents to simplify the product of x and y.

$$xy = m^{-\frac{2}{3}} \times n^{\frac{2}{3}} = (m^{-1} \times n)^{\frac{2}{3}} = \left(\frac{n}{m}\right)^{\frac{2}{3}}$$

Answers and Solutions
SAT Math Practice Test 2
Section 2

Answers

1. D	2. B	3. C	4. D
5. C	6. A	7. B	8. A
9. 1 or 9	10. 67	11. 10	12. 40
13. 4	14. 39	15. 5	16. $\frac{3}{5}$
17. $\frac{4}{5}$	18. $\frac{3}{4}$		

Solutions

1. (D)

   The first ounce costs $1.45 and each additional ounce costs $0.69. If a package weighs 10 ounces, the first ounce will cost $1.45 and the additional 9 ounces will cost $0.69 × 9. Therefore, the total cost of the package, in dollars, is $1.45 + 0.69(9)$.

2. (B)

   Use the area $A = \frac{1}{2}bh$ formula to find the height of $\triangle ABC$. Since the area of $\triangle ABC$ is 21 and $AC = AD + DC = 6$, the height, BC, is 7.

   $$\text{Area of the shaded region} = \text{Area of } \triangle ABD$$
   $$= \frac{1}{2}(AD)(BC)$$
   $$= \frac{1}{2}(4)(7)$$
   $$= 14$$

   Therefore, the area of the shaded region is 14.

3. (C)

   Let's start with the ordered pair $(0,0)$. Substitute 0 for x in each answer choice. Eliminate all the answer choices that give you nonzero value for y. Thus, eliminate answer choices (A) and (D). Additionally, use the ordered pair $(2,8)$. Substitute 2 for x in each of the remaining answer choices: (B), (C), and (E). Only answer choice (C) gives you 8 for y. Therefore, (C) is the correct answer.

4. (D)

$$
\begin{array}{lll}
(A) & 25 \div (2 + 5) & \implies & \text{remainder of } 4 \\
(B) & 32 \div (3 + 2) & \implies & \text{remainder of } 2 \\
(C) & 41 \div (4 + 1) & \implies & \text{remainder of } 1 \\
(D) & 47 \div (4 + 7) & \implies & \text{remainder of } 3 \\
(E) & 49 \div (4 + 9) & \implies & \text{remainder of } 10
\end{array}
$$

5. (C)

Use the binomial expansion $(x + y)^2 = x^2 + 2xy + y^2$ formula to evaluate $(x + \frac{1}{x})^2$.

$$
\begin{aligned}
\left(x + \frac{1}{x}\right)^2 &= x^2 + 2(x)\left(\frac{1}{x}\right) + \left(\frac{1}{x}\right)^2 \\
&= x^2 + 2 + \frac{1}{x^2} \qquad\qquad \text{Substitute 2 for } x^2 \\
&= 2 + 2 + \frac{1}{2} \\
&= \frac{9}{2}
\end{aligned}
$$

6. (A)

Both the axis of symmetry and the x-coordinate of the vertex are the mean of the x-intercepts of the quadratic function. Since the x-intercepts are -3 and 7, the axis of symmetry is $\frac{-3+7}{2} = 2$. Therefore, the equation of the axis of symmetry is $x = 2$.

7. (B)

In the graph below, the slope of the line is $-\frac{1}{3}$. Thus, the equation of the line is $y = -\frac{1}{3}x + b$, where b is the y-intercept.

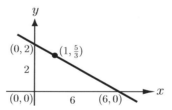

Since $(1, \frac{5}{3})$ is on the line, substitute 1 for x and $\frac{5}{3}$ for y in $y = -\frac{1}{3}x + b$ to find b.

$$
\begin{aligned}
y &= -\frac{1}{3}x + b \qquad\qquad \text{Substitute 1 for } x \text{ and } \frac{5}{3} \text{ for } y \\
\frac{5}{3} &= -\frac{1}{3}(1) + b \\
b &= 2
\end{aligned}
$$

Thus, the y-intercept, b, is 2 and the equation of the line that passes through $(1, \frac{5}{3})$ is $y = -\frac{1}{3}x + 2$. Let's find the x-intercept. Substitute 0 for y in the equation $y = -\frac{1}{3}x + 2$ and solve for x. Thus, the x-intercept is 6. The lengths of the base and the height of the triangular region are 6 and 2 as shown in the graph. Therefore, the area of the triangular region is $\frac{1}{2}(6)(2) = 6$.

8. (A)

In figure 1, car A is 80 miles west of a train station and car B is 35 miles south of the same train station at noon. Car B begins traveling 55 mph due north of the station at noon for two hours. Thus, car B is 75 miles north of the station at 2pm as shown in figure 2.

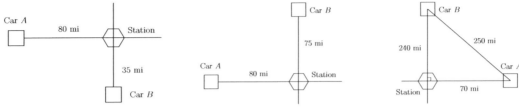

Figure 1: At noon   Figure 2: At 2pm   Figure 3: At 5pm

Additionally, car A begins traveling 50 mph due east of the station at 2pm for three hours. Thus, car A is 70 miles east of the station and car B is 240 miles north of the station at 5pm as shown in figure 3. To find the distance between car A and car B, use the Pythagorean theorem: $C^2 = 70^2 + 240^2$, or use a multiple of the Pythagorean triple: $(7 - 24 - 25) \times 10 = 70 - 240 - 250$. Therefore, car A and car B are 250 miles apart at 5pm.

9. (1 or 9)

$$|x - 5| = 4$$
$$x - 5 = \pm 4$$

$$x - 5 = 4 \qquad \text{or} \qquad x - 5 = -4$$
$$x = 9 \qquad \text{or} \qquad x = 1$$

Therefore, the possible values of x for which $|x - 5| = 4$ are 1 or 9.

10. (67)

Place point A in the middle on the number line as shown in figure 1. Since points A, B and C lie on the same number line, not necessarily in that order, place point B 50 units left of point A or 50 units right of point A.

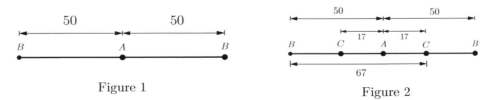

Figure 1   Figure 2

Point C and point A are 17 units apart. So, place point C 17 units left of point A or 17 units right of point A as shown in figure 2. Therefore, the maximum distance that point C and point B are apart is 67 units.

11. (10)

In the figure below, the circle whose center is $(0, 6)$ touches the x-axis. This means that the radius of the circle is 6. Since $\overline{AO}$ is the radius, $AO = 6$.

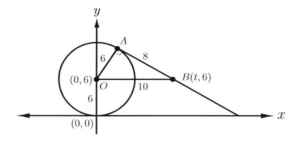

$\overline{BA}$ is tangent to the circle at A. Since a tangent line is perpendicular to the radius drawn to the point of tangency, $\overline{BA} \perp \overline{AO}$. Thus, $\triangle BAO$ is a right triangle with $AO = 6$ and $AB = 8$. To find the length of the hypotenuse of the right triangle, BO, use the Pythagorean theorem: $C^2 = 6^2 + 8^2$ or a multiple of the Pythagorean triple: $(3 - 4 - 5) \times 2 = 6 - 8 - 10$. Thus, $BO = 10$. Point B is 10 units from the point O horizontally. Therefore, the x-coordinate of point B, or t is 10.

12. (40)

In the figure below, the top and bottom faces of the cylinder are circles. The sum of the areas of the top and bottom faces is 32π. This means that the area of each face is 16π and its radius is 4.

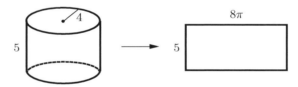

Unfold the cylinder as shown in the figure above. Then, it becomes a rectangle whose length equals the circumference of the top and bottom faces, $2\pi \times 4 = 8\pi$, and whose width equals the height of the cylinder, 5. Since the surface area excludes the area of the top and bottom faces, the surface area equals the area of the rectangle, which is $8\pi \times 5 = 40\pi$. Therefore, the value of a is 40.

13. (4)

$$\sqrt{6x - 8} = 2\sqrt{x} \qquad \text{Square both sides}$$
$$6x - 8 = 4x$$
$$2x = 8$$
$$x = 4$$

Substitute $x = 4$ in the original equation to check the solution.

$$\sqrt{6x - 8} = 2\sqrt{x} \qquad \text{Substitute 4 for } x$$
$$\sqrt{6(4) - 8} = 2\sqrt{4}$$
$$4 = 4 \qquad \checkmark \text{(Solution)}$$

14. (39)

The positive integers from 1 to 99 are under consideration. Let's define A as a set of integers divisible by 4, B as a set of integers divisible by 5, $A \cup B$ as a set of integers divisible by 4 or 5, and $A \cap B$ as a set of integers divisible by 4 and 5. Additionally, define $n(A)$, $n(B)$, $n(A \cup B)$, and $n(A \cap B)$ as the number of elements in set A, set B, set $A \cup B$, and set $A \cap B$, respectively.

$$A = \{4, 8, 12, \cdots, 92, 96\}, \qquad n(A) = 24$$
$$B = \{5, 10, 15, \cdots, 90, 95\}, \qquad n(B) = 19$$
$$A \cap B = \{20, 40, 60, 80\}, \qquad n(A \cap B) = 4$$

Note that $A \cap B = \{20, 40, 60, 80\}$ are multiples of 4 and 5. They are counted twice so they must be excluded in counting.

$$\begin{aligned} n(A \cup B) &= n(A) + n(B) - n(A \cap B) \\ &= 24 + 19 - 4 \\ &= 39 \end{aligned}$$

Therefore, the number of positive integers less than 100 that are divisible by 4 or 5 is 39.

15. (5)

Since -6 is a solution to the quadratic equation, substitute -6 for x in the equation and solve for b.

$$\begin{aligned} x^2 + bx - 30 &= 0 && \text{Substitute } -6 \text{ for } x \\ (-6)^2 + b(-6) - 30 &= 0 \\ -6b &= -6 \\ b &= 1 \end{aligned}$$

$x^2 + bx - 30 = 0$ becomes $x^2 + x - 30 = 0$. Use the factoring method to solve for other solution.

$$\begin{aligned} x^2 + x - 30 &= 0 && \text{Use the factoring method} \\ (x - 5)(x + 6) &= 0 && \text{Use the zero product property} \\ x = 5 \quad &\text{or} \quad x = -6 \end{aligned}$$

Therefore, the other solution to the quadratic equation is 5.

16. $\left(\frac{3}{5}\right)$

To solve an exponential equation, both expressions must have the same base. Change 8^{2x} to $(2^3)^{2x} = 2^{6x}$ and solve the equation.

$$\begin{aligned} 8^{2x} &= 2^{x+3} \\ (2^3)^{2x} &= 2^{x+3} \\ 2^{6x} &= 2^{x+3} \\ 6x &= x + 3 \\ x &= \frac{3}{5} \end{aligned}$$

·

17. $\left(\frac{4}{5}\right)$

In the figure below, $\overline{AB} \parallel \overline{DE}$ and $\overline{BC} \parallel \overline{EF}$. This implies that $\angle A \cong \angle D$ and $\angle C \cong \angle F$ because they are corresponding angles. Since the two interior angles of $\triangle ABC$ and $\triangle DEF$ are congruent, $\angle B \cong \angle E$. Thus, $\triangle ABC$ and $\triangle DEF$ are similar triangles.

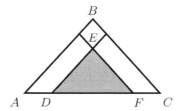

Since the ratio of DF to AC is 2 to 3, the ratio of areas of the similar triangles can be determined: the ratio of their areas is equal to the square of the ratio of of any pair of corresponding sides.

$$\frac{\text{Area of } \triangle DEF}{\text{Area of } \triangle ABC} = \left(\frac{DF}{AC}\right)^2 = \left(\frac{2}{3}\right)^2 = \frac{4}{9}$$

Since the ratio of their areas is 4 to 9, define $4x$ as the area of $\triangle DEF$ and $9x$ as the area of $\triangle ABC$. Then, the area of the unshaded region equals the area of $\triangle ABC$ minus the area of $\triangle DEF$, which can be expressed as $5x$.

$$\frac{\text{Area of shaded region}}{\text{Area of unshaded region}} = \frac{4x}{5x} = \frac{4}{5}$$

Therefore, the ratio of the area of the shaded region to that of the unshaded region is $\frac{4}{5}$.

18. $\left(\frac{3}{4}\right)$

Use the fundamental counting principle. Define event 1 and event 2 as selecting a number from the first and second die, respectively. There are six outcomes from each event. Thus, the total number of outcomes for event 1 and event 2 is $6 \times 6 = 36$. Instead of counting the number of outcomes whose product of the two numbers is even, let's count the number of outcomes whose product is odd because it is easier to count. Define event 3 and event 4 as selecting an odd number from the first and second die, respectively. There are three outcomes from each event: 1, 3, and 5. Thus, the total number of outcomes for event 3 and event 4 is $3 \times 3 = 9$. Thus,

$$\text{Probability that the product is even} = 1 - \text{Probability that the product is odd}$$
$$= 1 - \frac{9}{36}$$
$$= \frac{27}{36}$$
$$= \frac{3}{4}$$

Therefore, the probability that the product of the two numbers is even is $\frac{3}{4}$.

Answers and Solutions
SAT Math Practice Test 2
Section 3

Answers

1. D	2. E	3. E	4. B
5. B	6. A	7. C	8. C
9. D	10. C	11. B	12. E
13. E	14. D	15. B	16. B

Solutions

1. (D)

   Since $z = 3$, $y = 2z - 1 = 5$. Therefore, $x = 3y = 15$.

2. (E)

   The table shows that as the value of x is increased by 1, the value of y is increased by 4. Therefore, the value of y when $x = 5$ is $19 + 4 = 23$.

3. (E)

   Joshua and Alex ate half the pizza. So, the remaining part of the pizza is half of the pizza. One hour later, they ate $\frac{2}{3}$ of the remaining pizza. This means that they ate $\frac{2}{3} \times \frac{1}{2} = \frac{1}{3}$ the pizza one hour later. Therefore, the fractional part of the pizza they have eaten is $\frac{1}{2} + \frac{1}{3} = \frac{5}{6}$ pizza.

4. (B)

   In the figure below, $m\angle b = 55°$ because it is a vertical angle.

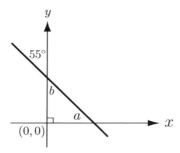

   $\angle a$ and $\angle b$ are complementary angles whose sum of their measures is 90°. Therefore, the measure of $\angle a$ is 35°.

5. (B)

The shaded region consists of two semicircles tangent to each other. Thus, the area of the shaded region equals the area of one circle with a radius of 4. Therefore, the area of the shaded region is $\pi(4)^2 = 16\pi$.

6. (A)

The sum of x and y is 12. This can be expressed as $x + y = 12$. Since $y = 2x - 3$, substitute $2x - 3$ for y in the equation $x + y = 12$ and solve for x.

$$
\begin{aligned}
x + y &= 12 & \text{Substitute } 2x - 3 \text{ for } y \\
x + 2x - 3 &= 12 \\
3x &= 15 \\
x &= 5
\end{aligned}
$$

Therefore, the value of $y = 2x - 3 = 7$.

7. (C)

Jason spent $16 on a calculator. Thus, he has a remaining balance of $133 - $16 = $117 in his savings account. Each book costs $15. Jason can not buy eight books because the cost for eight books is $120, which exceeds $117. Therefore, the maximum number of books Jason can buy is 7.

8. (C)

Since the radius of the circle is 3, the diameter of the circle is 6 which is also the height of the parallelogram. $\overline{AD}$ is the base of the parallelogram and $AD = 5$. Therefore, the area of the parallelogram is $bh = 5 \times 6 = 30$.

9. (D)

The list below shows the possible arrangements for the two math books and the history book (M and H are used for the math book and the history book, respectively).

$$
\begin{array}{ccc}
M & M & H \\
M & H & M \\
H & M & M
\end{array}
$$

Therefore, there are three possible arrangements for the two math books and the history book.

10. (C)

The first eight nonnegative even integers are 0, 2, 4, 6, 8, 10, 12, and 14.

$$
\text{Arithmetic mean} = \frac{0 + 2 + 4 + 6 + 8 + 10 + 12 + 14}{8} = \frac{56}{8} = 7
$$

Therefore, the arithmetic mean of the first eight nonnegative even integers is 7.

11. (B)

It is worth noting that an inequality symbol is reversed when multiplying or dividing each side of the inequality by a negative number.

$$-4 \le -2x + 2 \le 6 \qquad \text{Subtract } -2 \text{ from each side}$$
$$-6 \le -2x \le 4 \qquad \text{Divide each side by } -2$$
$$-2 \le x \le 3 \qquad \text{Reverse the inequality symbol}$$

12. (E)

Determine the number of factors in each answer choice.

$$(A) \quad 4 = \{1, 2, 4\}$$
$$(B) \quad 9 = \{1, 3, 9\}$$
$$(C) \quad 25 = \{1, 5, 25\}$$
$$(D) \quad 49 = \{1, 7, 49\}$$
$$(E) \quad 51 = \{1, 3, 17, 51\}$$

All of the answer choices have three factors except answer choice (E). Therefore, (E) is the correct answer.

13. (E)

For simplicity, let's choose two points, A and B, in the first quadrant: $A(1, 1)$ and $B(3, 4)$. Thus, the slope of the line that passes through point A and point B is $\frac{3}{2}$. If points A and B are reflected about the y-axis, they become A' and B' and their x and y coordinates are $A'(-1, 1)$ and $B'(-3, 4)$, respectively.

$$\text{Slope of new line} = \frac{4 - 1}{-3 - (-1)} = \frac{3}{-2} = -\frac{3}{2}$$

Therefore, the slope of the new line that passes through points A' and B' is $-\frac{3}{2}$.

14. (D)

There are 12 months in 1 year. Convert z years to $12z$ months. Define p as the number of cars that the car factory produce in $12z$ months. Set up a proportion in terms of cars and months.

$$x \text{ cars} : y \text{ months} = p \text{ cars} : 12z \text{ months}$$
$$\frac{x}{y} = \frac{p}{12z} \qquad \text{Use cross product property}$$
$$py = 12xz$$
$$p = \frac{12xz}{y}$$

Therefore, the number of cars that the car factory produce in z years is $\frac{12xz}{y}$.

15. (B)

Table 1 below shows the first couple of times swimming sessions and mandatory breaks begin.

9:00am-9:45am	Swim
9:45am-9:55am	Break
9:55am-10:40am	Swim
10:40am-10:50am	Break
10:50am-11:35am	Swim
11:35am-11:45am	Break

Table 1

12:30pm	Break begins
1:25pm	Break begins
2:20pm	Break begins
3:15pm	Break begins
4:10pm	Break begins
5:05pm	Break begins

Table 2

Since this question asks about what time the last break time begins, pay close attention to times at which breaks begin in table 1. The first break begins at 9:45am, second break at 10:40am, third break at 11:35am and so forth. These three break times suggest a pattern such that as the value of hours is increased by one: from 9_{am} to 10_{am} to 11_{am}, the value of minutes is decreased by five: from 45_{min} to 40_{min} to 35_{min}. Thus, the following breaks after 11:35am are 12:30pm, 1:25pm, 2:20 pm, and so on so forth as shown in table 2. Therefore, the last break time begins at 5:05pm.

16. (B)

In the figure below, $\overline{AC}$ is a tangent line to the circle at A. Thus, $\overline{AC}$ and $\overline{AO}$ are perpendicular to each other. Since $\overline{OD} \parallel \overline{AC}$, $\overline{OD}$ and $\overline{AO}$ are also perpendicular each other.

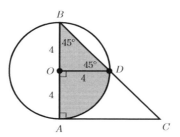

The circumference of the circle is 8π. Thus, the radius of the circle is 4. The shaded region consists of a sector whose central angle is $90°$ and triangle OBD. The sector is a quarter circle with a radius of 4 and triangle OBD is a $45°$-$45°$-$90°$ special triangle with $OD = 4$ and $OB = 4$.

$$\text{Area of shaded region} = \text{Area of sector} + \text{Area of triangle } OBD$$
$$= \frac{1}{4}\pi(4)^2 + \frac{1}{2}(4)(4)$$
$$= 4\pi + 8$$

Therefore, the area of the shaded region is $4\pi + 8$.

Answers and Solutions
SAT Math Practice Test 3
Section 1

Answers

1. E	2. B	3. C	4. D	5. A
6. E	7. B	8. D	9. D	10. E
11. B	12. C	13. D	14. E	15. C
16. C	17. D	18. D	19. D	20. D

Solutions

1. (E)

   Sue has two suitcases that weigh 43 pounds each and three backpacks that weigh 12 pounds each. Therefore, the total weight of her luggage in pounds is $2(43) + 3(12) = 122$.

2. (B)

   Use the distance formula, distance = rate × time. Therefore, the total distance that car A travels in three hours is 60 miles per hour × 3 hours = 180 miles.

3. (C)

   Each face of the cube is a square. Since the area of each face is 9, the length of the cube is 3. Therefore, the volume of the cube is $3 \times 3 \times 3 = 27$.

4. (D)

   There are 12 inches in one foot. Define x as the number of weeks that the tulip needs to grow 12 inches. Set up a proportion in terms of inches and weeks.

   $$\frac{1}{2} \text{ inch} : 1 \text{ week} = 12 \text{ inches} : x \text{ weeks}$$

   $$\frac{\frac{1}{2}}{1} = \frac{12}{x} \qquad \text{Use cross product property}$$

   $$\frac{1}{2}x = 12$$

   $$x = 24$$

   Therefore, it will take 24 weeks for the tulip to grow one foot.

5. (A)

   $\overline{OC}$ and $\overline{OD}$ are the lines with a positive slope. Since $\overline{OC}$ is steeper (closer to y-axis) than $\overline{OD}$, $\overline{OC}$ has the larger value of slope. Therefore, $\overline{OC}$ has the largest value of slope.

6. (E)

Answer choice (A) and (E) satisfy the Pythagorean theorem: $c^2 = a^2 + b^2$. However, $\sqrt{2}$ in answer choice (A) is not a positive integer. Thus, eliminate answer choice (A). Therefore, (E) is the correct answer.

7. (B)

$\overline{OB}$ is the longest line segment because it is the longest diagonal of the rectangular box. Therefore, (B) is the correct answer.

8. (D)

If two lines have the same slope, the two lines are parallel and do not intersect. The line $3y - 2x = 3$ is expressed in the standard form. Change it to the slope-intercept form: $y = \frac{2}{3}x + 1$. Thus, the slope of the line is $\frac{2}{3}$.

$$\text{(A)} \quad y = \frac{3}{2}x + 6 \quad \Longrightarrow \quad \text{slope} = \frac{3}{2}$$

$$\text{(B)} \quad y = -\frac{3}{2}x + 6 \quad \Longrightarrow \quad \text{slope} = -\frac{3}{2}$$

$$\text{(C)} \quad y = -\frac{2}{3}x - 2 \quad \Longrightarrow \quad \text{slope} = -\frac{2}{3}$$

$$\text{(D)} \quad y = \frac{2}{3}x + 2 \quad \Longrightarrow \quad \text{slope} = \frac{2}{3}$$

$$\text{(E)} \quad y = -\frac{2}{3}x + 2 \quad \Longrightarrow \quad \text{slope} = -\frac{2}{3}$$

Since $-2x + 3y = 6$ in answer choice (D) has a slope of $\frac{2}{3}$, it never intersect the line $3y - 2x = 3$. Therefore, (D) is the correct answer.

9. (D)

Use the properties of exponents: $(ab)^n = a^n b^n$

$$\begin{aligned} 6^x &= (2 \times 3)^x \\ &= 2^x \times 3^x \qquad\qquad \text{Substitute } a \text{ for } 2^x \text{ and } b \text{ for } 3^x \\ &= ab \end{aligned}$$

Therefore, 6^x in terms of a and b is ab.

10. (E)

$AB = 2\sqrt{2}$. Thus, the area of the square is $(2\sqrt{2})^2 = 8$. Since square $ABCD$ and triangle EFG have the same areas, the area of triangle EFG is 8. The base of triangle EFG is $\overline{EG}$ and $EG = 4\sqrt{2}$.

$$\begin{aligned} \text{Area of triangle } EFG &= \frac{1}{2} \times 4\sqrt{2} \times h \\ 8 &= 2\sqrt{2} \times h \\ h &= 2\sqrt{2} \end{aligned}$$

Therefore, the height of triangle EFG is $2\sqrt{2}$.

11. (B)

The graph $y = 2|x + 3| - 1$ crosses the y-axis at b. Thus, b is the y-intercept. To find the y-intercept, substitute 0 for x in the equation $y = 2|x + 3| - 1$ and solve for y.

$$\begin{aligned} y &= 2|x + 3| - 1 \qquad \text{Substitute 0 for } x \\ &= 2|0 + 3| - 1 \\ &= 5 \end{aligned}$$

Therefore, the y-coordinate of b is 5.

12. (C)

In the figure below, two quadrilaterals $ABCD$ and $DEFG$ are parallelograms. A straight line passes through the points B, D, and F. This means that $\overline{BC} \parallel \overline{DE}$.

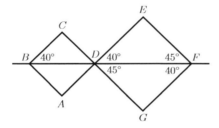

$\angle CBD \cong \angle EDF$ because they are corresponding angles. Thus, $m\angle CBD = m\angle EDF = 40°$. Use one of the properties of a parallelogram: opposite angles are congruent. In parallelogram $DEFG$, $\angle EDG$ and $\angle EFG$ are opposite angles. Since $m\angle EDG = 40° + 45° = 85°$, the measure of $\angle EFG$ is 85°.

13. (D)

From the table, notice that as the x value increases, the y value decreases. Among the answer choices, a rational function, $y = \frac{10}{x}$ best represents the table. Therefore, (D) is the correct answer.

14. (E)

In the geometric sequence, the first term is 9 and the second term is 27. This means that the common ratio (a number that you multiply or divide one term by to get the next term), $r = 3$. Use the nth term formula, $a_n = a_1 \times r^{n-1}$ where r is the common ratio, to find the ratio of the 19th term to the 17th term.

$$\begin{aligned} \frac{a_{19}}{a_{17}} &= \frac{a_1 \times r^{18}}{a_1 \times r^{16}} \\ &= r^2 \qquad \text{Since } r = 3 \\ &= 9 \end{aligned}$$

Therefore, the ratio of the 19th term to the 17th term is 9.

15. (C)

Expand $(x+b)^2$ using the binomial expansion formula: $(x+y)^2 = x^2 + 2xy + y^2$. Thus, $(x+b)^2 = x^2 + 2bx + b^2$.

$$x^2 - 6x + a = (x+b)^2$$
$$x^2 - 6x + a = x^2 + 2bx + b^2 \qquad \text{Subtract } x^2 \text{ from each side}$$
$$-6x + a = 2bx + b^2$$

The expression on the left side is equal to the expression on the right side. This means that the coefficients of x and constants on both expressions are the same: $-6 = 2b$ and $a = b^2$. Thus, $b = -3$ and $a = b^2 = (-3)^2 = 9$. Therefore, the value of $a + b = 9 - 3 = 6$.

16. (C)

In the figure below, $\overline{AO}$, $\overline{BO}$, and $\overline{CO}$ are radii of the circle. Thus, $AO = BO = CO = 10$. $\triangle AOC$ is an isosceles triangle so the base angles $\angle OAC$ and $\angle OCA$ are congruent. In other words, $m\angle OAC = m\angle OCA = 30°$. Since the sum of measures of the interior angles of $\triangle AOC$ is $180°$, $m\angle AOC = 120°$.

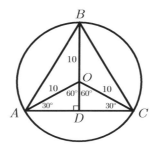

$\overline{OD}$, the height of $\triangle AOC$, is drawn from vertex O to $\overline{AC}$, the base of $\triangle AOC$. Thus, $\overline{OD} \perp \overline{AC}$. $\triangle AOD$ is a $30°$-$60°$-$90°$ special right triangle with $AO = 10$. Since $\overline{OD}$ is the shorter leg of $\triangle AOD$, OD is half AO, which is 5. The height of $\triangle ABC$ is BD and $BD = BO + OD = 15$. Therefore, the height of $\triangle ABC$ is 15.

17. (D)

In the figure below, Joshua is only allowed to walk either right or up, neither left nor down.

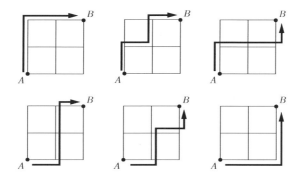

Therefore, there are six distinct 4-unit paths from point A to point B.

18. (D)

Use the difference of two squares pattern: $x^2 - y^2 = (x + y)(x - y)$.

$$x^2 - y^2 = 27 \qquad \text{Factor}$$
$$(x + y)(x - y) = 27 \qquad \text{Substitute 3 for } x - y$$
$$3(x + y) = 27$$
$$x + y = 9$$

Set up a system of equations: $x + y = 9$ and $x - y = 3$. Use the linear combinations method to solve for x and y.

$$x + y = 9$$
$$\underline{x - y = 3} \qquad \text{Add two equations}$$
$$2x \quad = 12$$
$$x = 6$$

Substitute 6 for x in $x + y = 9$ to solve for y.

$$x + y = 9$$
$$y + 6 = 9$$
$$y = 3$$

Therefore, $x^2 + y^2 = (6)^2 + (3)^2 = 45$.

19. (D)

In the figure below, the linear function $f(x)$ represents a line.

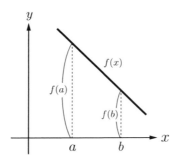

Thus, $f(a)$ and $f(b)$ represent the function's values at $x = a$ and $x = b$, respectively. Since $a < b$ and $f(a) > f(b)$, the linear function $f(x)$ must have a negative slope. Therefore, (D) is the correct answer.

www.solomonacademy.net

20. (D)

Define z as the distance between Joshua's home and Alex's house. Additionally, define T_{JA} and T_{AJ} as the times Joshua needed to travel from his home to Alex's house and Alex's house to his home, respectively. Use the time formula, time $= \frac{\text{distance}}{\text{rate}}$. Since Joshua averages x miles per hour on the way to Alex's house and averages y miles per hour on the way home, $T_{JA} = \frac{z}{x}$ and $T_{AJ} = \frac{z}{y}$.

$$\text{Average speed of entire trip} = \frac{\text{total distance}}{\text{total time}} = \frac{z + z}{T_{JA} + T_{AJ}}$$

$$= \frac{2z}{\frac{z}{x} + \frac{z}{y}} \qquad \text{Simplify the denominator}$$

$$= \frac{2z}{\frac{xz+yz}{xy}} \qquad \text{Factor } xz + yz$$

$$= \frac{2z}{\frac{z(x+y)}{xy}} \qquad \text{Simplify}$$

$$= \frac{2xyz}{z(x+y)} \qquad z \text{ cancels each other}$$

$$= \frac{2xy}{x+y}$$

Therefore, the average speed of the entire trip in terms of x and y is $\frac{2xy}{x+y}$.

Answers and Solutions

SAT Math Practice Test 3
Section 2

Answers

1. E	2. D	3. C	4. E
5. D	6. B	7. C	8. E
9. 5	10. 15	11. 50	12. 57
13. 23	14. 9	15. 0	16. 11
17. $\frac{1}{4}$	18. 6 or 10		

Solutions

1. (E)

$$
\begin{aligned}
AB + BC + CD &= AD \qquad \text{Substitute 15 for } AD \text{ and 14 for } BC \\
AB + CD + 14 &= 15 \\
AB + CD &= 1
\end{aligned}
$$

2. (D)

The perimeter of an equilateral triangle is the same as the perimeter of a square. Since the perimeter of the square with side length of 6 is 24, the perimeter of the equilateral triangle is also 24. Therefore, the length of the side of the equilateral triangle is $\frac{24}{3} = 8$.

3. (C)

To find the x and y coordinates of the midpoint between point $A(-2, -3)$ and point $B(4, 5)$, use the midpoint formula: $\left(\frac{x_1 + x_2}{2}, \frac{y_1 + y_2}{2} \right)$

$$
\begin{aligned}
\text{Midpoint} &= \left(\frac{x_1 + x_2}{2}, \frac{y_1 + y_2}{2} \right) \\
&= \left(\frac{-2 + 4}{2}, \frac{-3 + 5}{2} \right) \\
&= (1, 1)
\end{aligned}
$$

Therefore, the x and y coordinates of the midpoint between point A and point B is $(1, 1)$.

4. (E)

The clock indicates the first correct time at 12:12pm. Afterwards, it indicates correctly at 12:24pm, 12:36pm, 12:48pm and 1:00pm. This means that the clock only indicates 5 correct times every hour. Since there are five hours between 12:10pm to 5:10pm, the clock indicates time correctly $5 \times 5 = 25$ times. There are two additional times that the clock indicates correctly after 5pm: 5:12pm and 5:24pm. Therefore, the clock indicates time correctly 27 times from 12:10pm to 5:35pm.

5. (D)

Before finding $f(1)$, it is necessary to find the constant k by using the given information $f(-2) = 1$.

$$\begin{aligned}
f(x) &= \sqrt{x + k} & &\text{Substitute } -2 \text{ of } x \\
f(-2) &= \sqrt{-2 + k} & &\text{Substitute } f(-2) = 1 \\
1 &= \sqrt{-2 + k} & &\text{Square both sides and solve for } k \\
k &= 3
\end{aligned}$$

Thus, $f(x) = \sqrt{x + 3}$. Therefore, the value of $f(1) = \sqrt{1 + 3} = 2$.

6. (B)

I is true: Both 9^2 and $(-9)^2$ equal 81.

II is false: The value of $\sqrt{4}$ is 2, not -2.

III is true: Any number divided by 0 is undefined.

IV is false: If $x < 0$, $|x| = -x$.

Thus, statements I and III are correct. Therefore, (B) is the correct answer.

7. (C)

In the figure below, a rectangle is inscribed in the semicircle with center O. Since the length of the rectangle is twice the width of the rectangle, $\overline{OC}$ divides the rectangle into two smaller squares. Since $\overline{OA}$ and $\overline{OB}$ are the radii of the semicircle, $OA = OB = 6$. Additionally, $\overline{OA}$ and $\overline{OB}$ are diagonals of the two smaller squares. Thus, $\triangle OAC$ are $\triangle OBC$ are 45°-45°-90° special right triangles whose sides are in the ratio $1 : 1 : \sqrt{2}$ and are congruent. In $\triangle OBC$, $\overline{CB}$ is the leg and has a length of $\frac{6}{\sqrt{2}} = 3\sqrt{2}$. Thus, $AB = AC + CB = 6\sqrt{2}$.

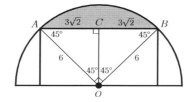

$m\angle AOB = 90°$. Thus, the length of arc AB is $\frac{1}{4}$ of the circumference of the circle with a radius of 6: $\frac{1}{4} \times 2\pi(6) = 3\pi$. The perimeter of the shaded region is the sum of the length of arc AB and the length of $\overline{AB}$. Therefore, the perimeter of the shaded region is $3\pi + 6\sqrt{2}$.

8. (E)

Mr. Rhee, Sue, Joshua, and Jason are taking a family photo. To count the total possible seating arrangements for Mr. Rhee's family, use permutation: $_4P_4 = 4! = 4 \times 3 \times 2 \times 1 = 24$, or use the fundamental counting principle: Mr. Rhee has 4 ways to choose his seat out of four seats. After his seat is taken, Sue has 3 ways to choose her seat out of the three remaining seats. Joshua has 2 ways and Jason has 1 way. Thus, there are $4 \times 3 \times 2 \times 1 = 24$ possible seating arrangements for Mr.Rhee's family. Define R, S, A, and B as Mr. Rhee, Sue, Joshua, and Jason, respectively. To count the number of seating arrangements in which Mr. Rhee and Sue sit next to each other, let's consider two cases:

Case 1: Mr. Rhee sits left side of Sue. There are six possible arrangements as shown below.

$$R \quad S \quad A \quad B \qquad A \quad R \quad S \quad B \qquad A \quad B \quad R \quad S$$
$$R \quad S \quad B \quad A \qquad B \quad R \quad S \quad A \qquad B \quad A \quad R \quad S$$

Case 2: Mr. Rhee sits right side of Sue. There are six possible arrangements.

$$S \quad R \quad A \quad B \qquad A \quad S \quad R \quad B \qquad A \quad B \quad S \quad R$$
$$S \quad R \quad B \quad A \qquad B \quad S \quad R \quad A \qquad B \quad A \quad S \quad R$$

Thus, there are 12 possible seating arrangements in which Mr. Rhee sits next to Sue. Therefore, the probability that Mr. Rhee and Sue sit next to each other is $\frac{12}{24} = \frac{1}{2}$.

9. (5)

Prime numbers are numbers that have only two factors: 1 and itself. There are five positive integers less than twelve that are prime numbers: 2, 3, 5, 7, and 11.

10. (15)

$$
\begin{aligned}
x &= y - 15 & \text{Switch sides} \\
y - 15 &= x & \text{Subtract } x \text{ from each side} \\
y - x - 15 &= 0 & \text{Add 15 to each side} \\
y - x &= 15
\end{aligned}
$$

11. (50)

In the figure below, the trapezoid consists of two congruent 45°-45°-90° special right triangles, $\triangle ABC$ and $\triangle FED$, whose sides are in the ratio $1 : 1 : \sqrt{2}$. Since $AB = FE = 5\sqrt{2}$, $AC = BC = DE = DF = 5$.

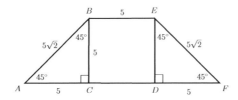

Triangles ABC and FED can be combined to create a square whose area is equal to the area of the square in the middle. The area of each square is 25; therefore, the area of the trapezoid is 50.

    www.solomonacademy.net

12. (57)

According to the survey, the most popular sport is the 100 meter sprint and the least popular sport is swimming.

$$100 \text{ meter sprint} = 300 \times 0.36 = 108$$
$$\text{Swimming} = 300 \times 0.17 = 51$$

Therefore, $108 - 51 = 57$ million more people are going to watch the 100 meter sprint compared to swimming.

13. (23)

There are 12 inches in one foot. Convert Mr. Rhee's height to inches. Mr. Rhee is $5 \times 12 + 9 = 69$ inches tall. Joshua is $\frac{2}{3} \times 69 = 46$ inches tall. Therefore, the difference in their heights in inches is $69 - 46 = 23$.

14. (9)

$y = |x|$ intersects $y = 9$ at $x = a$ and $x = b$. To find the value of a and b, substitute 9 for y and solve for x.

$$y = |x| \qquad\qquad \text{Substitute 9 for } y$$
$$9 = |x| \qquad\qquad \text{Solve for } x$$
$$x = 9 \quad \text{or} \quad x = -9$$

Since $a < b$, $a = -9$ and $b = 9$. Therefore, the value of b is 9.

15. (0)

In order to make the equation true, the only possible value for x is zero when $y > 0$.

16. (11)

Define x as the price of one book and y as the price of one DVD. Set up a system of linear equations in terms of x and y. The cost of one book and two DVDs is \$39. This can be expressed as $x + 2y = 39$. Additionally, the cost of two books and one DVD is \$27. This can be expressed as $2x + y = 27$.

$$x + 2y = 39$$
$$\underline{2x + y = 27} \qquad \text{Add two equations}$$
$$3x + 3y = 66 \qquad \text{Divide each side by 3}$$
$$x + y = 22$$

Thus, $x + y = 22$. This means that the price of one book and one DVD is \$22. Therefore, the average price of the book and the DVD is $\frac{x+y}{2} = \frac{22}{2} = 11$.

www.solomonacademy.net

17. $\left(\frac{1}{4}\right)$

On Tuesday, students drank $\frac{1}{4}$ of the water. Thus, $\frac{3}{4}$ of the water would be remaining on Tuesday. Students drank $\frac{1}{3}$ of the remaining water on Wednesday. Thus, $\frac{2}{3}$ of the remaining water would be remaining on Wednesday. This means that $\frac{2}{3} \times \frac{3}{4} = \frac{1}{2}$ of the water would be remaining on Wednesday. Students drank $\frac{1}{2}$ of the remaining water on Thursday. Thus, $\frac{1}{2}$ of the remaining water would be remaining. Therefore, $\frac{1}{2} \times \frac{1}{2} = \frac{1}{4}$ of the water would be remaining on Thursday.

18. (6 or 10)

Factor $xy + x + y + 1$.

$$xy + x + y + 1 = 77 \qquad \text{Factor}$$
$$x(y + 1) + (y + 1) = 77$$
$$(x + 1)(y + 1) = 77$$

Since x and y are positive integers and $77 = 7 \times 11$,

$$(x + 1)(y + 1) = 7 \times 11 \qquad \text{or} \qquad (x + 1)(y + 1) = 11 \times 7$$
$$x + 1 = 7 \quad \text{and} \quad y + 1 = 11 \qquad \text{or} \qquad x + 1 = 11 \quad \text{and} \quad y + 1 = 7$$

From the equations above, the values of $x + 1$ can be either 7 or 11. Therefore, the possible values of x are either 6 or 10.

Answers and Solutions
SAT Math Practice Test 3
Section 3

Answers

1. D	2. B	3. A	4. D
5. B	6. C	7. E	8. E
9. C	10. A	11. C	12. D
13. B	14. E	15. D	16. D

Solutions

1. (D)

   At store A, three pens cost \$2.04. However, at store B, three pen cost \$2.25. Thus, the difference in the cost of three pens is \$2.25 − \$2.04 = \$0.21. Therefore, the amount you save per pen is $\frac{21}{3} = 7$ cents.

2. (B)

   In a 30°-60°-90° special right triangle whose sides are in the ratio $1 : \sqrt{3} : 2$, the length of the side opposite the angle 30° is half the length of the hypotenuse. Since the length of the hypotenuse is 8, the length of the side opposite the angle 30° is 4.

3. (A)

   In the figure below, point X lies inside the square with side length of 10.

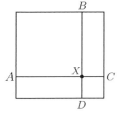

   Since $\overline{AC}$ and $\overline{BD}$ are parallel to the sides of the square, both $XA + XC$ and $XB + XD$ equal the side length of the square, 10. Thus, $XA + XC = 10$ and $XB + XD = 10$. Therefore, $XA + XB + XC + XD = 20$.

4. (D)

Define x as the number. Set up an equation and solve for x.

$$x^2 = x$$ Subtract x from each side
$$x^2 - x = 0$$ Factor
$$x(x-1) = 0$$ Use the zero product property
$$x = 0 \quad \text{or} \quad x = 1$$

5. (B)

Take the cube root of each side of the equation.

$$(x+2)^3 = 64$$
$$\sqrt[3]{(x+2)^3} = \sqrt[3]{64}$$
$$x + 2 = 4$$
$$x = 2$$

Therefore, the value of $\frac{1}{(x+2)} = \frac{1}{(2)+2} = \frac{1}{4}$.

6. (C)

In the figure below, the area of each sector is the area of a quarter circle with a radius of 2 because its central angle is $90°$.

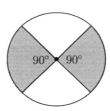

Thus, the sum of the area of the two sectors equals the area of half of the circle. Therefore, the area of the shaded region is $\frac{1}{2}\pi(2)^2 = 2\pi$.

7. (E)

Consecutive even integers are even numbers that have a difference of 2. Let x be the middle number. Then, the five consecutive even integers can be expressed as follows: $x - 4$, $x - 2$, x, $x + 2$ and $x + 4$. Since the sum of the five consecutive even integers is 120,

$$x - 4 + x - 2 + x + x + 2 + x + 4 = 120$$
$$5x = 120$$
$$x = 24$$

Thus, the value of the middle number, x, is 24. Since the largest consecutive even integer is $x + 4$, the value of the largest integer is $x + 4 = 24 + 4 = 28$.

8. (E)

The units digit also means ones digit. The first seven positive squares are 1, 4, 9, 16, 25, 36, and 49. Thus, the units digit of the first seven positive squares are 1, 4, 9, 6, 5, 6, and 9, respectively.

$$\text{Sum of units digits} = 1 + 4 + 9 + 6 + 5 + 6 + 9 = 40$$

Therefore, the sum of the units digits of the first seven positive squares is 40.

9. (C)

The base and height of $\triangle ABC$ are $2x - 2$ and x, respectively.

$$\begin{aligned} \text{Area of } \triangle ABC &= \frac{1}{2}bh = \frac{1}{2}(2x - 2)x \\ &= x(x - 1) = x^2 - x \end{aligned}$$

10. (A)

Distinct means different. There are five different positive integers in the set. It is necessary to solve this problem in terms of the sum: the sum is the average of the elements in the set times the number of the elements in the set. The average of the two smallest integers in the set is 2. This means that the sum of the two smallest integers is 4. Since the five integers in the set are positive and different, the two smallest positive integers in the set must be 1 and 3, neither 2 and 2, nor 0 and 4. Additionally, the averages of the three smallest integers, four smallest integers, and five integers in the set are 3, 4, and 5, respectively. Thus, the sums of the three smallest integers, four smallest integers and five integers in the set are 9, 16, and 25, respectively. Below shows how to obtain the five positive integers in the set.

$$\text{Sum of two smallest integers} = 1 + 3 = 4$$
$$\text{Sum of three smallest integers} = 1 + 3 + 5 = 9$$
$$\text{Sum of four smallest integers} = 1 + 3 + 5 + 7 = 16$$
$$\text{Sum of five integers in the set} = 1 + 3 + 5 + 7 + 9 = 25$$

Thus, there are 1, 3, 5, 7, and 9 in the set. Therefore, the largest integer in the set is 9.

11. (C)

To find the x-intercepts of $y = (x - p)(x + q)$, substitute 0 for y and solve for x.

$$(x - p)(x + q) = 0 \qquad \text{Use the zero product property}$$
$$x = p \quad \text{or} \quad x = -q \qquad \text{x-intercepts are p and $-q$}$$

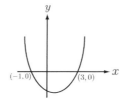

The graph above shows that $y = (x - p)(x + q)$ crosses the x-axis at $x = -1$ and $x = 3$. Thus, the x-intercepts of the quadratic function are 3 and -1. Since $|p| > |q|$, $p = 3$ and $-q = -1 \implies q = 1$. Therefore, the value of $p + q = 3 + 1 = 4$.

12. (D)

In the figure below, let x be the length of the shorter side of the rectangle. The rectangle is divided into two congruent smaller squares. Thus, the length of each square is x.

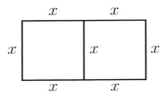

The total length of the fence can be expressed as $7x$ as shown above. Since the total length of the fence is 350 feet, $7x = 350 \implies x = 50$. Therefore, the length of the shorter side of the rectangular field is 50.

13. (B)

According to the definition of a function $x \, \Phi \, n = \frac{20-x}{\sqrt{n}}$,

$$(A) \quad 15 \, \Phi \, 20 = \frac{20-15}{\sqrt{20}} = \frac{5}{2\sqrt{5}}$$

$$(B) \quad 10 \, \Phi \, 20 = \frac{20-10}{\sqrt{20}} = \frac{10}{2\sqrt{5}}$$

$$(C) \quad 15 \, \Phi \, 40 = \frac{20-15}{\sqrt{40}} = \frac{5}{2\sqrt{10}}$$

$$(D) \quad 10 \, \Phi \, 40 = \frac{20-10}{\sqrt{40}} = \frac{10}{2\sqrt{10}}$$

$$(E) \quad 5 \, \Phi \, 80 = \frac{20-5}{\sqrt{80}} = \frac{15}{4\sqrt{5}} = \frac{7.5}{2\sqrt{5}}$$

Compare answer choices (A), (B), and (E) because they have the same denominator. Since (B) has the largest value in the numerator, (B) has the largest value among three answer choices. Thus, eliminate answer choices (A) and (E). Additionally, compare answer choices (C) and (D) because they have the same denominator. For the same reason, (D) has the larger value. Thus, eliminate answer choice (C). Now, answer choices (B) and (D) are remaining. Both (B) and (D) have the same numerator. Since (B) has the smaller denominator, (B) is larger. Thus, eliminate answer choice (D). Therefore, (B) has the largest value.

14. (E)

The sequence $19, 23, 27, \cdots, 131, 135$ is an arithmetic sequence with the common difference of 4. Use the nth term formula: $a_n = a_1 + (n-1)d$, where a_1 is the first term and d is the common difference.

$$a_n = a_1 + (n-1)d \qquad \text{Substitute 19 for } a_1, \text{ 4 for } d, \text{ and 135 for } a_n$$
$$135 = 19 + (n-1)4 \qquad \text{Subtract 19 from each side}$$
$$4(n-1) = 116 \qquad \text{Solve for } n$$
$$n = 30$$

Therefore, there are 30 terms between 19 and 135 inclusive.

15. (D)

In the figure below, $\triangle ABC$ is a right triangle with $AB = 10$ and $AC = 8$. To find BC, use the Pythagorean theorem: $10^2 = 8^2 + BC^2$ or use a multiple of Pythagorean triple: $(3 - 4 - 5) \times 2 = 6 - 8 - 10$. Thus, $BC = 6$.

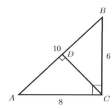

$\overline{AC} \perp \overline{BC}$. Consider $\overline{AC}$ and $\overline{BC}$ as the base and the height of $\triangle ABC$. Thus, the area of $\triangle ABC = \frac{1}{2} \times AC \times BC = \frac{1}{2}(8)(6) = 24$. Additionally, $\overline{CD} \perp \overline{AB}$. If you consider $\overline{AB}$ and $\overline{CD}$ as the base and the height of $\triangle ABC$, the area of $\triangle ABC = \frac{1}{2} \times AB \times CD$.

$$\text{Area of } \triangle ABC = \frac{1}{2} \times AB \times CD = 24 \qquad \text{Substitute 10 for } AB$$

$$\frac{1}{2}(10)\, CD = 24 \qquad \text{Solve for } CD$$

$$CD = 4.8$$

16. (D)

In the figure below, the tangent line is perpendicular to the radius drawn from the center $(1, 0)$ to the point of tangency $(4, 4)$. Since the slope of the radius is $\frac{4-0}{4-1} = \frac{4}{3}$, the slope of the tangent line is the negative reciprocal, or $-\frac{3}{4}$.

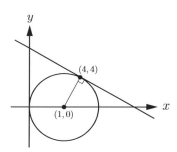

The equation of the tangent line is $y = -\frac{3}{4}x + b$, where b is the y-intercept. Since the tangent line passes through the point $(4, 4)$, substitute 4 for x and 4 for y to find the y-intercept.

$$y = -\frac{3}{4}x + b \qquad \text{Substitute 4 for } x \text{ and 4 for } y$$

$$4 = -\frac{3}{4}(4) + b \qquad \text{Solve for } b$$

$$b = 7$$

Thus, the equation of the tangent line is $y = -\frac{3}{4}x + 7$. Multiply each side of the equation of the tangent line by 4 to write the equation in standard form. Therefore, the equation of the tangent line is $3x + 4y = 28$.

Answers and Solutions
SAT Math Practice Test 4
Section 1

Answers

1. E	2. D	3. D	4. B	5. B
6. D	7. B	8. C	9. E	10. E
11. A	12. C	13. C	14. A	15. C
16. E	17. A	18. A	19. B	20. E

Solutions

1. (E)

   When multiplying or dividing an inequality by a negative number, reverse the inequality symbol.

   $$-3x > 6 \qquad \text{Divide each side by } -3$$
   $$x < -2 \qquad \text{Reverse the inequality symbol}$$

   Therefore, the solution to $-3x > 6$ is $x < -2$.

2. (D)

   There are six intervals between 6 and 7 so each interval is $\frac{1}{6}$. A is $6\frac{1}{6}$, B is $6\frac{2}{6}$, C is $6\frac{3}{6}$, and so forth. Since D is $6\frac{4}{6} \approx 6.67$, it is closest to 6.6.

3. (D)

   This is a geometric sequence with the common ratio of $\frac{1}{2}$.

   $$1, \frac{1}{2}, \frac{1}{4}, \frac{1}{8}, \frac{1}{16}, \frac{1}{32}, \cdots$$

   In other words, multiply each term by $\frac{1}{2}$ to obtain the next term. Therefore, the value of the fifth term is $\frac{1}{16}$.

4. (B)

   There are three feet in one yard. Jason is 300 feet ahead of Joshua. If Joshua is running 3 feet per second, he can run 300 feet in 100 seconds, which is equal to one minutes and 40 seconds. Therefore, it will take one minute and 40 seconds for Joshua to catch up to Jason.

5. (B)

The ratio of the area of the larger rectangle to that of the smaller rectangles is $3:1$. Define x as the area of the smaller rectangle. Then, the area of the larger rectangle is $3x$. The sum of the areas of the two smaller rectangles, $x + 3x$, is 16.

$$\text{Sum of areas of two smaller rectangles} = 16$$
$$x + 3x = 16$$
$$x = 4$$

Therefore, the area of the smaller rectangle is 4.

6. (D)

The perimeter of the square is 36. Thus, the length of the square is 9. Since a circle is inscribed in a square, the diameter of the circle equals the length of the square. Therefore, the diameter of the circle is 9.

7. (B)

Since $y = 8$ and $x < y$, the positive difference of x and y can be expressed as $y - x$. Since $y - x = 5$, the value of x is 3.

8. (C)

Take the square root of each side of the equation and solve for x.

$$(x - 1)^2 = 4$$
$$x - 1 = \pm 2$$
$$x - 1 = 2 \quad \text{or} \quad x - 1 = -2$$
$$x = 3 \quad \text{or} \quad x = -1$$

Since $x < 0$, the only possible value of x is -1.

9. (E)

Perpendicular lines have negative reciprocal slopes. The two linear equations in answer choice (E) show such characteristics.

$$\text{(E)} \quad y = \frac{1}{3}x + 4 \quad \Longrightarrow \quad \text{slope} = \frac{1}{3}$$
$$3x + y = 6 \quad \Longrightarrow \quad y = -3x + 6 \quad \Longrightarrow \quad \text{slope} = -3$$

Therefore, (E) is the correct answer.

10. (E)

Use the definition of the slope: slope $= \frac{y_2 - y_1}{x_2 - x_1}$. Since the slope of the line is -2, choose two points $(0, 3)$ and $(5, k)$ to set up an equation in term of the slope.

$$\text{Slope} = \frac{k - 3}{5 - 0} = -2$$
$$k - 3 = -10$$
$$k = -7$$

11. (A)

If all twelve dogs that have spots also have short hair as shown in the diagram below,

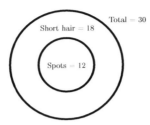

the largest number of dogs that can have short hair and spots is 12.

12. (C)

To find the expression that is equal to 2^{3-2x}, use the properties of exponents.

$$2^{3-2x} = 2^3 \times 2^{-2x}$$
$$= 2^3 \times \frac{1}{2^{2x}}$$
$$= \frac{8}{2^{2x}}$$
$$= \frac{8}{(2^2)^x}$$
$$= \frac{8}{4^x}$$

13. (C)

In the figure below, the diagonals of the rhombus are perpendicular and bisect each other. When the rhombus is divided into four congruent right triangles, the lengths of the legs of the triangles are half the lengths of the diagonals: 6 and 8.

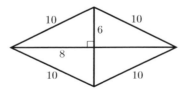

To find the length of the hypotenuse, use the Pythagorean theorem: $c^2 = 6^2 + 8^2$ or use a multiple of the Pythagorean triple: $(3 - 4 - 5) \times 2 = 6 - 8 - 10$. Thus, the length of the hypotenuse, the length of the rhombus, is 10. Therefore, the perimeter of the rhombus is $10 \times 4 = 40$.

14. (A)

The price of the pen is increased by 100%, which means that the price of the pen is doubled. Therefore, the price of the pen in May is $2 \times \$4.50 = \$9.00$.

15. (C)

In the graph below, the x-intercepts of the quadratic function are p and q. If the quadratic function is reflected about the y-axis, the x-intercepts, p and q, are also reflected about the y-axis so that they become $-p$ and $-q$.

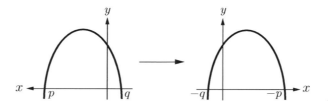

Therefore, the sum of the new x-intercepts in terms of p and q is $-p + (-q) = -p - q$.

16. (E)

Consider the first condition, $A + C < B$. B is greater than the sum of A and C. This implies that $A < B$ and $C < B$. To determine which one is greater among A and C, consider the fourth condition, $D - C > D - A$. Both A and C are subtracted from D. As a result, $D - C$ is greater than $D - A$. This implies that $C < A$. Up to now, it is determined that $C < A < B$. Additionally, the second condition, $B - D > 0$ implies that $B > D$. The Third condition, $A - D < 0$ implies that $A < D$. Therefore, the inequality that is true about A, B, C, and D is $C < A < D < B$.

17. (A)

In the figure below, the area of the shaded region equals the area of the triangle. Since the y-intercept of $y = x + 6$ is 6, the length of the base of the triangle is 6.

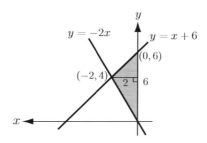

Two lines $y = x + 6$ and $y = -2x$ intersect. Set each equation equal to each other. Solve for x, the x-coordinate of the intersection point, which determines the height of the triangle.

$$x + 6 = -2x$$
$$3x = -6$$
$$x = -2$$

Since the x-coordinate of the intersection point is -2, the height of the triangle is 2. Therefore, the area of the shaded region is $\frac{1}{2}(6)(2) = 6$.

18. (A)

In the figure below, define x as the length of $\overline{AD}$. Then, the length of $\overline{CD}$ is $x - 4$.

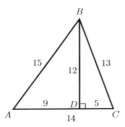

Since $AC = AD + CD$ and $AC = 14$,

$$AD + CD = AC \qquad \text{Substitute 14 for } AC$$
$$x + x - 4 = 14 \qquad \text{Solve for } x$$
$$x = 9$$

Thus, $CD = x - 4 = 5$. $\triangle BCD$ is a right triangle. To find the length of $\overline{BD}$, use the Pythagorean theorem: $13^2 = BD^2 + 5^2$ or use the Pythagorean triple: $5 - 12 - 13$. Thus, $BD = 12$. Therefore, the area of $\triangle BCD$ is $\frac{1}{2}(5)(12) = 30$.

19. (B)

In order to solve this problem, it is not necessary to determine the other terms. In a set of five terms of an arithmetic sequence, the third term is both the mean and the median. For instance, 13, 16, 19, 22, and 25 is an arithmetic sequence in which the third term, 19, is both the mean and the median. Thus, if 4 is added to each element in the set S, the mean and the median of the new set S is $19 + 4 = 23$. Therefore, the sum of the mean and median of the new set S is $23 + 23 = 46$.

20. (E)

In the figure below, each length, width, and height of the rectangular box is divided by 3, 4, and 5, respectively so that there are $3 \times 4 \times 5 = 60$ smaller cubes with sides of 1 foot.

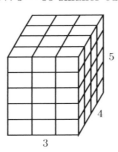

Each smaller cube has six faces. Thus, each has a surface area of 6 square feet. The total surface area of the 60 smaller cubes is $60 \times 6 = 360$ square feet. Since one can of paint is needed to paint 12 square feet, the total number of cans of paint is needed to paint the surface area of the 60 smaller cubes is $\frac{360 \text{ square feet}}{12 \text{ square feet/can}} = 30$ cans.

Answers and Solutions
SAT Math Practice Test 4
Section 2

Answers

1. C	2. E	3. B	4. C
5. B	6. D	7. B	8. A
9. $\frac{1}{4}$	10. 99	11. 10	12. 49
13. 360	14. $\frac{2}{7}$	15. 64	16. 5
17. 864	18. 33		

Solutions

1. (C)

   Use the midsegment theorem: the midsegment connecting the midpoints of two sides of a triangle is parallel to the third side and half as long.

   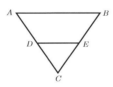

   $\overline{DE}$ is the midsegment. Since $AB = 10$, $DE = 5$.

2. (E)

   As the value of x changes, the value of y remains the same. Thus, the function that contains the four ordered pairs is $y = -3$. Therefore, (E) is the correct answer.

3. (B)

   The three segments, $\overline{AC}$, $\overline{CB}$, and $\overline{BD}$, are put together so that points A, C, B, and D are arranged on the number line in that order as shown in the figure below.

   Therefore, the length of the segment $\overline{AD}$ is 9.

4. (C)

Angle A and angle B are complementary angles. Thus, the sum of their measures is $90°$. Define x as the measure of $\angle B$. Since the measure of $\angle A$ is 30 less than twice the measure of $\angle B$, the measure of $\angle A$ can be expressed as $2x - 30$.

$$m\angle A + m\angle B = 90$$
$$2x - 30 + x = 90$$
$$x = 40$$

Therefore, the measure of $\angle A$ is $2x - 30 = 50°$.

5. (B)

The two vertices of the rectangle are on the x-axis at $x = -2$ and $x = 2$ as shown below. This means that the length of the rectangle is 4.

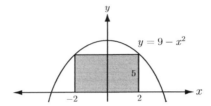

Additionally, the width of the rectangle is determined by the function's value at $x = 2$, or $f(2)$. To evaluate $f(2)$, substitute 2 for x in $f(x) = 9 - x^2$. Thus, $f(2) = 9 - 2^2 = 5$, which means that the width of the rectangle is 5. Therefore, the area of the rectangle is $4 \times 5 = 20$.

6. (D)

There are five intervals of twelve seconds in one minute. Thus, Mr. Rhee burns $3 \times 5 = 15$ calories per minute when he is running on the treadmill. Since $\frac{2}{3}$ of an hour is $\frac{2}{3} \times 60 = 40$ minutes, Mr. Rhee will burn $40 \times 15 = 600$ calories if he runs on the treadmill.

7. (B)

The amount of money in Sue's savings account increases at a constant rate throughout the years. This suggests that a linear function best describes the information in the table. Create two ordered pairs, $(9, 2580)$ and $(11, 2820)$ from the table and find the slope of the linear function, which determines the rate at which the amount of money increases per year.

$$\text{Slope} = \frac{y_2 - y_1}{x_2 - x_1} = \frac{2820 - 2580}{11 - 9} = 120$$

Thus, the linear function can be written as $y = 120x + b$, where x represents the number of years, b represents the initial amount of money that Sue deposited in the beginning, and y represents the total amount of money in the savings account in x years. To find b, substitute 9 for x and 2580 for y.

$$y = 120x + b \qquad \text{Substitute 9 for } x \text{ and 2580 for } y.$$
$$2580 = 120(9) + b \qquad \text{Solve for } b$$
$$b = 1500$$

Therefore, Sue deposited $1500 in her savings account in the beginning.

8. (A)

Joshua arranges the numbers 1 through 10 clockwise in order around a circle shown below. Joshua removes one number among the ten numbers and starts removing every third number clockwise. He removes 4 last.

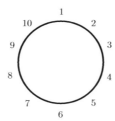

To find out the first number that Joshua removes, work backwards: Joshua removes 4 first. He keeps removing every third number counter-clockwise until the last number is left. For instance, Joshua removes 4 first. Next number he removes is 1, 8, 5, and so on. Below shows the complete steps in which Joshua removes the numbers 1 through 10.

$$4 - 1 - 8 - 5 - 10 - 6 - 9 - 2 - 7 - 3$$

Therefore, Joshua removes 3 first.

9. $\left(\frac{1}{4}\right)$

To evaluate the expression, substitute -2 for x.

$$\frac{x-1}{3(x-2)} = \frac{(-2)-1}{3((-2)-2)} \qquad \text{Substitute } -2 \text{ for } x$$
$$= \frac{-3}{-12}$$
$$= \frac{1}{4}$$

10. (99)

Take the reciprocal of each side of the inequality. It's worth noting that the inequality symbol is reversed when taking the reciprocal of each side of the inequality.

$$0.01 < \frac{1}{k} < 0.1 \qquad \text{Take the reciprocal of each side}$$
$$\frac{1}{0.01} > k > \frac{1}{0.1} \qquad \text{Inequality symbol is reversed}$$
$$10 < k < 100$$

Since k is an integer, the possible values of k for which $10 < k < 100$ is $k = 11, 12, \cdots, 98, 99$. Therefore, the largest possible value of k is 99.

11. (10)

Define x as the length of the longer side of the rectangle and $x - 1$ as the length of the shorter side of the rectangle. Then, the area of the rectangle can be expressed as $x(x - 1)$. Since the area of the rectangle is 110,

$$x(x - 1) = 110 \qquad \text{Expand } x(x - 1)$$
$$x^2 - x - 110 = 0 \qquad \text{Use the factoring method}$$
$$(x + 10)(x - 11) = 0 \qquad \text{Use the zero-product property}$$
$$x = -10 \quad \text{or} \quad x = 11$$

Since x represent the length, x must be positive. Thus, $x = 11$. Therefore, the length of the shorter side of the rectangle is $x - 1 = 10$.

12. (49)

Move the shaded region of the quarter circle that lies on the left square to the square on the right side as shown below.

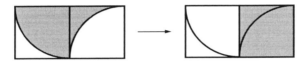

The area of the shaded region equals the area of the smaller square on the right side. Therefore, the area of the smaller square is half the area of the rectangle, or $\frac{1}{2}(98) = 49$.

13. (360)

Angles x, y, and z are the exterior angles of the triangle. The sum of the exterior angles of any polygon is always $360°$. Therefore, $m\angle x + m\angle y + m\angle z = 360°$.

14. $\left(\frac{2}{7}\right)$

The x-intercept of the line is -7 and the y-intercept of the line is 2. Convert the x and y intercepts to ordered pairs, $(-7, 0)$ and $(0, 2)$, respectively. Find the slope by using the slope formula and the given ordered pairs.

$$\text{Slope} = \frac{y_2 - y_1}{x_2 - x_1} = \frac{0 - 2}{-7 - 0} = \frac{2}{7}$$

Therefore, the slope of the line is $\frac{2}{7}$.

15. (64)

x is a positive integer greater than 1 for which $\sqrt{x}$ and $\sqrt[3]{x}$ are both integers. To obtain integer values for $\sqrt{x} = x^{\frac{1}{2}}$ and $\sqrt[3]{x} = x^{\frac{1}{3}}$, x must be expressed as $x = n^6$, where n is a positive integer. Otherwise, $\sqrt{x}$ and $\sqrt[3]{x}$ cannot be both integers. Since we are looking for the smallest possible value greater than 1 for x, choose $n = 2$. Thus, $x = 2^6 = 64$. Check the answer by substituting 64 for x in both $\sqrt{x}$ and $\sqrt[3]{x}$.

$$\sqrt{64} = 8 \quad \checkmark \text{(Integer)}, \qquad \sqrt[3]{64} = 4 \quad \checkmark \text{(Integer)}$$

Therefore, the smallest possible value of x for which $\sqrt{x}$ and $\sqrt[3]{x}$ that are both integers is $2^6 = 64$.

16. (5)

Since $g(x) = f(-2x)$, $p(x) = f(x) + f(-2x)$. To evaluate $p(-1)$, substitute -1 for x in $p(x)$.

$$p(x) = f(x) + f(-2x) \qquad \text{Substitute } -1 \text{ for } x$$
$$p(-1) = f(-1) + f(2) \qquad f(-1) = 7 \text{ and } f(2) = -2$$
$$= 7 - 2 = 5$$

Therefore, the value of $p(-1) = 5$.

17. (864)

The diameter of the ferris wheel is unnecessary information for this problem. Be sure not to get confused with extra information. There are 60 seconds in one minute. Convert 1 minute and 24 seconds to 84 seconds. Define x as the angle, in degrees, that the ferris wheel rotates for 84 seconds. Since the ferris wheel rotates $360°$ every 35 seconds, set up a proportion in terms of degrees (°) and seconds.

$$35\,_{\text{seconds}} : 360\,_{\text{degrees}} = 84\,_{\text{seconds}} : x\,_{\text{degrees}}$$
$$\frac{35}{360} = \frac{84}{x} \qquad \text{Use cross product property}$$
$$35x = 84(360) \qquad \text{Solve for } x$$
$$x = 864$$

Thus, the ferris wheel rotates $864°$ in one minute and 24 seconds, so does Jason. Therefore, Jason rotates $864°$ in one minute and 24 seconds.

18. (33)

A clock indicates 4:10 pm as shown below. The clock turns $360°$ in 12 hours so each hour is $\frac{360°}{12} = 30°$ apart. The minute hand of the clock is pointing at the 2 o'clock. It makes $30°$ with the 3 o'clock position.

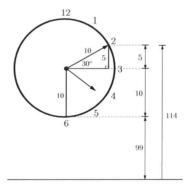

The diameter of the clock is 20 so the radius is 10. At the center of the circle, draw a right triangle in which the hypotenuse is the radius. It is a $30°$-$60°$-$90°$ special triangle whose sides are in the ratio $1 : \sqrt{3} : 2$. The length of the shorter leg, the side opposite the angle $30°$, is half the length of the hypotenuse, or $\frac{1}{2}(10) = 5$ feet. It means that the tip of the minute hand is 5 feet above the center of the circle and is also 15 feet above the bottom of the clock. Since the tip of the minute hand of the clock is 114 feet directly above the ground, the bottom of the clock is $114 - 15 = 99$ feet or 33 yards above the ground.

Answers and Solutions
SAT Math Practice Test 4
Section 3

Answers

1. C	2. E	3. C	4. B
5. B	6. E	7. C	8. E
9. B	10. C	11. A	12. E
13. A	14. C	15. D	16. A

Solutions

1. (C)

    Since $x = 24$, $y = 12$. $y = 3z = 12$. Thus, $z = 4$. Therefore, the value of z is 4.

2. (E)

    The ratio of the radius of the larger circle to that of the smaller circle is 2 to 1. Define x and $2x$ as the radii of the smaller circle and the larger circle, respectively.

    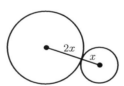

    The length of the segment connecting the center of each circle can be expressed as $2x + x = 3x$ and equals 15. Thus, $3x = 15 \implies x = 5$. Therefore, the radius of the larger circle is $2x = 10$.

3. (C)

    There are 12 inches in one foot and 3 feet in one yard. Thus, there are 36 inches in one yard. Since the length of the shorter piece is 8 inches, the length of the longer piece is $36 - 8 = 28$ inches.

4. (B)

    Define r as the common ratio, a number that you multiply or divide one term by to obtain the next term. Then, the fifth term, a_5, is $a_5 = a_4 \times r$, the sixth term, a_6, is $a_6 = a_5 \times r = a_4 \times r^2$.

    $$a_6 = a_4 \times r^2 \qquad \text{Substitute 11 for } a_4 \text{ and 99 for } a_6$$
    $$99 = 11 \times r^2 \qquad \text{Solve for } r$$
    $$r = 3 \quad \text{or} \quad r = -3.$$

    When $r = 3$, $a_5 = a_4 \times r = 11 \times 3 = 33$. When $r = -3$, $a_5 = a_4 \times r = 11 \times -3 = -33$. Therefore, (B) is the correct answer.

5. (B)

The price of the item is x. Store A gives 9% discount and store B gives 16% discount on the same item. The difference of the discounts that store A and store B gives equals the amount of money you would save. Therefore, the amount of money that you would save in terms of x is $16\% - 9\% = 7\%$ of x or $0.07x$.

6. (E)

Plug in the given values into the equation $y - 3 = |2 - x|$ to see which is a solution.

$$\text{(E)} \quad (5,6) \qquad y - 3 = |2 - x| \qquad \text{Substitute 5 for } x \text{ and 6 for } y$$
$$6 - 3 = |2 - 5|$$
$$3 = 3 \qquad \checkmark \text{(Equation holds true)}$$

Therefore, (E) is the correct answer.

7. (C)

Use the product property of the square roots: $\sqrt{ab} = \sqrt{a} \times \sqrt{b}$

$$\sqrt{8} = \sqrt{4} \times \sqrt{2} = 2\sqrt{2}$$
$$\sqrt{32} = \sqrt{16} \times \sqrt{2} = 4\sqrt{2}$$

Thus, $\sqrt{2} + \sqrt{8} + \sqrt{32} = \sqrt{2} + 2\sqrt{2} + 4\sqrt{2} = 7\sqrt{2}$. Therefore, the value of n is 7.

8. (E)

In the figure below, $\overline{AB} \parallel \overline{DE}$. Angles B and E, and angles A and D are alternate interior angles and are congruent. Thus, $\triangle ABC$ and $\triangle DEC$ are similar. To find the height of $\triangle DEC$, use the theorem regarding similar polygons: If two triangles are similar, the ratio of heights is equal to the ratio of any pair of corresponding sides.

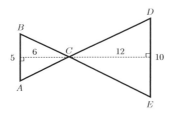

The length of the base of $\triangle ABC$, AB, is 5 and the area of $\triangle ABC = 15$. Thus, the height of $\triangle ABC$ is 6. The ratio of corresponding sides of the triangles is $AB : DE = 5 : 10 = 1 : 2$. This means that the ratio of the heights of the triangles is also $1 : 2$. Since the height of $\triangle ABC$ is 6, the height of $\triangle DEC$ is 12.

9. (B)

List the factors of 96.

$$\text{Factors of } 96 = \{1, 2, 3, 4, 6, 8, 12, 16, 24, 32, 48, 96\}$$

The odd factors of 96 are 1 and 3. Therefore, there are only two odd factors of 96.

10. (C)

The possible integer values of x for which $0 < x < 5$ are 1, 2, 3, and 4. As shown in the table below, substitute 1, 2, 3, and 4 for x in $y = 5 - x$ to see if the value of y is an integer. If the value of y is an integer, a point (x, y) is on the graph $y = 5 - x$ and has integer value of x and y.

x	$y = 5 - x$	Point (x, y)
1	$y = 5 - 1 = 4$	$(1, 4)$
2	$y = 5 - 2 = 3$	$(2, 3)$
3	$y = 5 - 3 = 2$	$(3, 2)$
4	$y = 5 - 4 = 1$	$(4, 1)$

Therefore, there are four points $(1, 4), (2, 3), (3, 2)$, and $(4, 1)$ on the graph that have integer values of x and y.

11. (A)

The length of the ladder is 10 feet. Although the top and bottom of the ladder are sliding down and sliding away, the length of the ladder remains the same. When the bottom of the ladder is 6 feet away from the wall, the top of the ladder is 8 feet above the ground as shown in the diagram below. Use the Pythagorean theorem: $10^2 = a^2 + 6^2$, where a is the height of the wall at which the top of the ladder leans against. It is also possible to use a multiple of the Pythagorean triple: $(3 - 4 - 5) \times 2 = 6 - 8 - 10$.

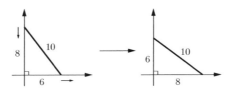

The top of the ladder is sliding down for 2 seconds at a rate of 1 foot per second so it is $8 - 2 = 6$ feet above the ground. To determine how far the bottom of the ladder is from the wall, use the same multiple of the Pythagorean triple: $6 - 8 - 10$. Therefore, the bottom of the ladder is 8 feet away from the wall after 2 seconds.

12. (E)

The quadratic function $y = (x - 1)(x - 3)$ is written in factored form. The graph of the function is shown below. Substitute 0 for y in the function and solve for x. Thus, the x-intercepts of the function are 1 and 3.

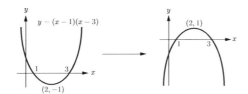

Since the x-coordinate of the vertex is the midpoint between 1 and 3, the x-coordinate of the vertex is $\frac{1+3}{2} = 2$. To find the y-coordinate of the vertex, substitute 2 for x in the function. $y = (2 - 1)(2 - 3) = -1$. The y-coordinate of the vertex is -1. Thus, the x and y coordinates of the vertex is $(2, -1)$. Therefore, when the graph is reflected about the x-axis, the new x and y coordinate of the vertex is $(2, 1)$.

13. (A)

The cone is put inside the cylinder as shown below. The volume of the cylinder is $\pi r^2 h$ and the volume of the cone is $\frac{1}{3}\pi r^2 h$. This means that the volume of the cone is $\frac{1}{3}$ of the volume of the cylinder.

Since the volume of the cylinder is given as V, the volume of the cone is $\frac{1}{3}V$. The unshaded region in the figure above represents the volume outside the cone but inside the cylinder. Therefore, the volume outside the cone but inside the cylinder is $V - \frac{1}{3}V = \frac{2}{3}V$.

14. (C)

C and D want to sit next to each other. Thus, the possible seating arrangements are either $C - D$ or $D - C$. Additionally, A and B do not want to sit next to each other. Thus, there are four possible seating arrangements shown below.

$$A - C - D - B \qquad B - C - D - A \qquad A - D - C - B \qquad B - D - C - A$$

A wants to sit left of C. There are two seating arrangements that satisfy it: $A - C - D - B$ or $A - D - C - B$. Since B wants to sit closer to D than to C, there is only one seating arrangement that satisfies it: $A - C - D - B$. Therefore, the seating arrangement that satisfies four students A, B, C, and D is $A - C - D - B$.

15. (D)

In the figure below, define x as the number of students who play both tennis and baseball. Then, the number of students who play baseball is $2x + 3$. Since the number of students who play tennis is three times the number of students who play baseball, it can be expressed as $3(2x + 3) = 6x + 9$.

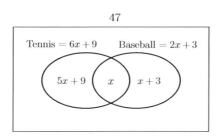

The total number of students in the class is 47. This can be expressed as the sum of $5x + 9$, x, and $x + 3$. Thus,

$$\text{Total number of students} = 5x + 9 + x + x + 3$$
$$7x + 12 = 47 \qquad \text{Solve for } x$$
$$x = 5$$

Therefore, the number of students who play only tennis is $5x + 9 = 5(5) + 9 = 34$.

16. **(A)**

Define x as the age of Jason at present. Then, the age of Joshua is $3x$. In six years, Jason will be $x + 6$ years old and Joshua will be $3x + 6$ years old. Below is the summary of the defined variables.

	Jason	Joshua
Age at present	x	$3x$
Age in 6 years	$x + 6$	$3x + 6$

Since Joshua will be twice as old as Jason in 6 years, set up an equation in terms of age in six years and solve for x.

$$3x + 6 = 2(x + 6)$$
$$3x + 6 = 2x + 12$$
$$x = 6$$

Thus, Jason is 6 years old and Joshua is $3x = 18$ years old at present. Define y as the number of years from present at which Jason will be $\frac{2}{3}$ as old as Joshua.

	Jason	Joshua
Age at present	6	18
Age in y years	$6 + y$	$18 + y$

Since Jason will be $\frac{2}{3}$ as old as Joshua in y years, set up an equation in terms of age in y years and solve for y.

$$6 + y = \frac{2}{3}(18 + y) \qquad \text{Multiply each side by 3}$$
$$3(6 + y) = 2(18 + y) \qquad \text{Expand each side}$$
$$3y + 18 = 2y + 36 \qquad \text{Solve for } y$$
$$y = 18$$

Therefore, Jason will be $\frac{2}{3}$ as old as Joshua in 18 years.

    www.solomonacademy.net

Answers and Solutions
SAT Math Practice Test 5
Section 1

Answers

1. A	2. E	3. C	4. B	5. E
6. B	7. C	8. E	9. D	10. C
11. A	12. E	13. E	14. C	15. A
16. D	17. D	18. B	19. E	20. B

Solutions

1. (A)

   The area of the square is 4. This means that the length of the side of the square is 2. Therefore, the perimeter of the square is $4 \times 2 = 8$.

2. (E)

   According to the definition of $\begin{vmatrix} a & b \\ c & d \end{vmatrix} = ad - bc$, $\begin{vmatrix} 5 & 6 \\ 5 & 7 \end{vmatrix} = (5 \times 7) - (6 \times 5) = 5$

3. (C)

   $AECF$ is a rectangle so $m\angle E = m\angle F = 90°$ and $\overline{EA} \cong \overline{FC}$. $ABCD$ is a rhombus. Since $\overline{AB}$ and $\overline{CD}$ are congruent sides of the rhombus, $\overline{AB} \cong \overline{CD}$. Thus, triangles AEB and CFD are congruent. Since the corresponding parts of the congruent triangles are congruent, $\overline{EB} \cong \overline{FD}$. Therefore, $FD = EB = 6$.

4. (B)

   Two numbers x and y are on a number line. The midpoint between x and y is 5. Thus,

   $$\frac{x + y}{2} = 5 \qquad \text{Multiply each side by 2}$$
   $$x + y = 10 \qquad \text{Subtract } y \text{ from each side}$$
   $$x = 10 - y$$

   Therefore, x in terms of y is $10 - y$.

5. (E)

Joshua walks due south 4 feet per second and Jason walks due west 3 feet per second. After 10 seconds, Joshua walks 40 feet and Jason walks 30 feet from the same location. The distance between Joshua and Jason can be determined by using the Pythagorean theorem: $c^2 = 40^2 + 30^2$, where c is the distance between Joshua and Jason, or use a multiple of the Pythagorean triple: $(3-4-5) \times 10 = 30-40-50$. Therefore, the distance between Joshua and Jason after 10 seconds is 50 feet.

6. (B)

To find the value of x for which $f(x) = 4$, substitute 4 for $f(x)$ and solve for x.

$$f(x) = \frac{2}{x} \qquad \text{Substitute 4 for } f(x)$$
$$\frac{2}{x} = 4 \qquad \text{Solve for } x$$
$$x = \frac{1}{2}$$

Therefore, the value of x for which $f(x) = 4$ is $\frac{1}{2}$.

7. (C)

Segment BE is drawn from vertex B to $\overline{DC}$ such that $\overline{BE} \parallel \overline{AD}$ as shown in the figure below. This means that $\overline{BE} \perp \overline{EC}$.

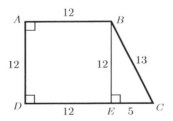

$ABED$ is a square with side length of 12. Thus, $AB = BE = DE = 12$. Since $CD = 17$, $CE = 5$. $\triangle CBE$ is a right triangle with $BE = 12$ and $CE = 5$. To find the length of $\overline{BC}$, use the Pythagorean theorem: $c^2 = 5^2 + 12^2$, where c is the length of $\overline{BC}$ or use the Pythagorean triple: $5 - 12 - 13$. Therefore, the length of $\overline{BC}$ is 13.

8. (E)

Mr. Rhee starts running. For the first second, he is running 7 meters away from the starting position. For the next second, he is running 3 meters toward the starting position. This means that Mr. Rhee is 4 meters farther away from the starting position every 2 seconds. After 10 seconds, Mr. Rhee is $5 \times 4 = 20$ meters away from the starting position. At the 11th second, Mr. Rhee is running another 7 meters away from the starting position. Therefore, after 11 seconds, Mr. Rhee is 27 meters away from the starting position.

9. (D)

To find the x-intercepts of the quadratic function $y = (2x - 3)(2x + 1)$, substitute 0 for y and solve for x.

$$y = (2x - 3)(2x + 1)$$ Substitute 0 for y

$$(2x - 3)(2x + 1) = 0$$ Use the zero product property

$$x = \frac{3}{2} \quad \text{or} \quad x = -\frac{1}{2}$$

Therefore, the sum of the x-intercepts of the quadratic function is $\frac{3}{2} + (-\frac{1}{2}) = 1$.

10. (C)

In the figure below, the diameter of the semicircle is 8. This means that the length of the side of the equilateral triangle is 8 and the radius of the semicircle is 4.

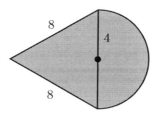

The perimeter is the distance around the figure. Since the diameter of the semicircle is inside the shaded region, it should be excluded from the perimeter of the shaded region. Thus, the perimeter of the shaded region equals the sum of the lengths of two sides of the equilateral triangle and half the circumference of the circle with a radius of 4. Therefore, the perimeter of the shaded region is $8 + 8 + \frac{1}{2}(2\pi(4)) = 16 + 4\pi$.

11. (A)

Define x as the total number of marbles in the bag. There are two red marbles and the probability of selecting a red marble is $\frac{1}{6}$.

$$\text{Probability of selecting a red marble} = \frac{\text{Number of red marbles}}{\text{Total number of marbles}}$$

$$\frac{1}{6} = \frac{2}{x} \qquad \text{Cross multiply}$$

$$x = 12$$

Thus, the total number of marbles in the bag is 12. Therefore, there are $12 - 2 = 10$ non-red marbles in the bag.

12. (E)

Define x as the number. Then, four more than twice a number can be expressed as $2x + 4$. At least is the same as greater than or equal to. At most is the same as less than or equal to. Set up an inequality accordingly and solve for x.

$$12 \le 2x + 4 \le 16 \qquad \text{Subtract 4 from each side}$$

$$8 \le 2x \le 12 \qquad \text{Divide each side by 2}$$

$$4 \le x \le 6$$

Therefore, the range of the number is $4 \le x \le 6$.

www.solomonacademy.net

13. (E)

Use the distance formula: distance = speed × time. Below shows the distance that Mr. Rhee traveled during the different time intervals.

Time	Average Speed	Distance traveled
9 am to 10 am	50 miles per hour	50 mph × 1 hour = 50 miles
10 am to 11:30 am	60 miles per hour	60 mph × 1.5 hour = 90 miles
11:30 am to 12:00pm	Break	0 mile
12:00 pm to 4:00 pm	55 miles per hour	55 mph × 4 hour = 220 miles

Therefore, the total distance that Mr. Rhee traveled between 9 am to 4 pm is $50 + 90 + 220 = 360$ miles.

14. (C)

$n\Psi$ is defined as the product of all positive consecutive odd integers less than or equal to n.

$$\frac{15\Psi}{12\Psi} = \frac{15 \times 13 \times 11 \times 9 \times 7 \times 5 \times 3 \times 1}{11 \times 9 \times 7 \times 5 \times 3 \times 1}$$
$$= 15 \times 13$$
$$= 195$$

Therefore, the value of $\frac{15\Psi}{12\Psi}$ is 195.

15. (A)

The minute hand rotates 360° in 60 minutes. This means that the minute hand rotates 6° per minute. There are 9 minutes from 9:33 pm to 9:42 pm. Therefore, the measure of the angle that the minute hand rotates from 9:33 pm to 9:42 pm is $9 \times 6° = 54°$.

16. (D)

Any triangle inscribed in a semicircle is a right triangle. In the figure below, $\triangle ABC$ is inscribed in the semicircle. Thus, it is a right triangle where $m\angle B = 90°$. Define x and $2x$ as the measure of angle C and the measure of angle A, respectively. Since $\angle A$ and $\angle C$ are complementary angles whose sum of their measures is 90°, $x + 2x = 90 \implies x = 30$. Thus, $m\angle C = 30°$ and $m\angle A = 60°$.

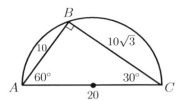

$\triangle ABC$ is a 30°-60°-90° special right triangle whose sides are in the ratio $1 : \sqrt{3} : 2$. $\overline{BC}$ is the longer leg, the side opposite the angle 60°, and $BC = 10\sqrt{3}$ is given. $\overline{AB}$ is the shorter leg, the side opposite the angle 30°, and $AB = \frac{10\sqrt{3}}{\sqrt{3}} = 10$. The length of the hypotenuse, AC, is twice the length of the shorter leg, AB. Thus, $AC = 2 \times AB = 2 \times 10 = 20$. Therefore, $AB + AC = 10 + 20 = 30$.

17. (D)

The quadratic function $y = -2(x + 1)^2 + 7$ is written in vertex form. Thus, the vertex of the quadratic function is $(-1, 7)$. Since the graph of the function opens down, the vertex is the maximum point. The maximum value of the function equals the y-coordinate of the vertex. Therefore, the maximum value of the function is 7.

18. (B)

There are two different type of questions on the math exam. One is worth 4 points and another is worth 3 points. Define x as the number of questions worth 4 points. Since there are 29 questions on the math exam, $29 - x$ is the number of questions worth 3 points. Below shows how to obtain the sum of points for each type of questions.

	A question worth 4 points	A question worth 3 points	Total
Number of questions	x	$29 - x$	29
Sum of points	$4x$	$3(29 - x)$	100

Since the math exam is worth a total of 100 points, set up an equation in terms of the sum of points shown on the table above.

$$4x + 3(29 - x) = 100 \qquad \text{Expand } 3(29 - x)$$
$$4x - 3x + 87 = 100 \qquad \text{Solve for } x$$
$$x = 13$$

Therefore, the number of questions that are worth 4 points is 13.

19. (E)

In the figure below, two lines $x = 9$ and $y = 6$ pass through the right upper corner of the rectangle located at $(9, 6)$. The line $y = -\frac{3}{4}x + 14$ intersects $y = 6$ at point A and also intersects $x = 9$ at point B.

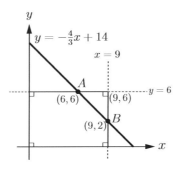

To find the x-coordinate of point A, substitute 6 for y in $y = -\frac{3}{4}x + 14$ and solve for x.

$$y = -\frac{4}{3}x + 14 \qquad \text{Substitute 6 for } y$$
$$6 = -\frac{4}{3}x + 14 \qquad \text{Solve for } x$$
$$x = 6$$

Since point A lies on the line $y = 6$, the x and y coordinates of point A is $(6, 6)$. Additionally, to find the y-coordinate of point B, substitute 9 for x in $y = -\frac{3}{4}x + 14$ and solve for y.

$$y = -\frac{4}{3}x + 14 \qquad \text{Substitute 9 for } x$$

$$y = -\frac{4}{3}(9) + 14 \qquad \text{Solve for } x$$

$$y = 2$$

Since point B lies on the line $x = 9$, the x and y coordinates of point B is $(9, 2)$. Finally, use the distance formula to find out the length of $\overline{AB}$.

$$\begin{aligned} AB &= \sqrt{(x_2 - x_1)^2 + (y_2 - y_1)^2} \qquad \text{Since } A(6,6) \text{ and } B(9,2) \\ &= \sqrt{(9-6)^2 + (2-6)^2} \\ &= \sqrt{(3)^2 + (-4)^2} \\ &= 5 \end{aligned}$$

Therefore, the length of $\overline{AB}$ is 5.

20. **(B)**

The digits 1 through 4 are randomly arranged to make a four-digit number. To count the total number of possible four-digit numbers, use permutation: $_4P_4 = 4! = 4 \times 3 \times 2 \times 1 = 24$, or use the fundamental counting principle. Define event 1, event 2, event 3, and event 4 as selecting a digit for the thousands' place, hundreds' place, tens' place, and ones' place, respectively. Event 1 has 4 ways to select a digit out of 4 digits. After one digit is taken, event 2 has 3 ways to select a digit out of the three remaining digits. Event 3 has 2 ways and event 4 has 1 way. Thus, there are $4 \times 3 \times 2 \times 1 = 24$ possible four-digit numbers using 1, 2, 3, and 4.

In order for a number to be divisible by 4, the last two digits of the number must be divisible by 4. Thus, the last two digits of the numbers should be either 12, 24, and 32. Let's consider three cases:

Case 1: The last two digits of the number is 12. There are two possible four-digit numbers as shown below.

$$3 \quad 4 \quad 1 \quad 2 \qquad\qquad 4 \quad 3 \quad 1 \quad 2$$

Case 2: The last two digits of the number is 24. There are two possible four-digit numbers as shown below.

$$1 \quad 3 \quad 2 \quad 4 \qquad\qquad 3 \quad 1 \quad 2 \quad 4$$

Case 3: The last two digits of the number is 32. There are two possible four-digit numbers as shown below.

$$1 \quad 4 \quad 3 \quad 2 \qquad\qquad 4 \quad 1 \quad 3 \quad 2$$

Thus, there are 6 four-digit numbers that are divisible by 4. Therefore, the probability that the four-digit number that is divisible by 4 is $\frac{6}{24} = \frac{1}{4}$.

Answers and Solutions
SAT Math Practice Test 5
Section 2

Answers

1. B	2. C	3. E	4. E
5. C	6. C	7. D	8. B
9. 120	10. 12	11. 7	12. 135
13. 72	14. 12	15. 19	16. 4
17. 120	18. 6		

Solutions

1. **(B)**

   The pattern consists of five different colors: red, blue, white, green, and yellow and it is repeated. This means that every fifth shirt is yellow. Thus, the 10th and 15th shirts are yellow, the 16th shirt is red, and the 17th shirt is blue.

2. **(C)**

   If the square is divided diagonally as shown below, it forms two 45°-45°-90° special right triangles whose sides are in the ratio $1 : 1 : \sqrt{2}$.

   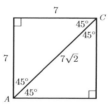

   The length of the diagonal of the square is the same as the length of the hypotenuse of the two right triangles, AC. Since the length of the hypotenuse is $\sqrt{2}$ times the length of each leg, $AC = 7\sqrt{2}$. Therefore, the length of the diagonal of the square is $7\sqrt{2}$.

3. **(E)**

   $$\sqrt{3-x} = 3 \qquad \text{Square each side}$$
   $$3 - x = 9 \qquad \text{Solve for } x$$
   $$x = -6$$

   Therefore, the value of x is -6.

4. (E)

Any ordered pair that satisfies the inequality $|x| + |y| \leq 5$ lies inside or on the shaded region shown below. This implies that any ordered pair that does not satisfy the inequality lies outside the shaded region.

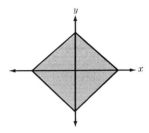

The ordered pair $(-4, -2)$ in answer choice (E) does not satisfy the inequality.

$$|x| + |y| \leq 5 \qquad \text{Substitute } -4 \text{ for } x \text{ and } -2 \text{ for } y$$
$$|-4| + |-2| \nleq 5$$
$$6 \nleq 5$$

Thus, $(-4, -2)$ lies outside the shaded region. Therefore, (E) is the correct answer.

5. (C)

Based on the properties of exponents: $a^m \times a^n = a^{m+n}$, $2^{n+2} = 2^n \times 2^2$.

$$2^{n+2} = 2^n \times 2^2 \qquad \text{Since } 2^n = 3$$
$$= 3 \times 2^2$$
$$= 12$$

Therefore, the value of 2^{n+2} is 12.

6. (C)

When a coin is tossed, there are two possible outcomes: head or tail. If you toss a coin three times, according to the fundamental counting principle, the total number of the possible outcomes is $2 \times 2 \times 2 = 8$. The table below shows the 8 possible outcomes.

H	H	H	
H	H	T	✓
H	T	H	✓
H	T	T	
T	H	H	✓
T	H	T	
T	T	H	
T	T	T	

Out of 8 possible outcomes, there are 3 outcomes that have two heads: $H\,H\,T$, $H\,T\,H$, and $T\,H\,H$. Therefore, the probability that two heads will be shown is $\frac{3}{8}$.

7. (D)

The graph of $y = 5x + 6$ is shown below. The slope of the line is 5 and the x and y coordinates of the y-intercept of the line is $(0, 6)$. When the line is shifted right 2 units and down 1 unit, the slope of the line remains the same. However, the y-intercept of the line, $(0, 6)$, is shifted to $(2, 5)$.

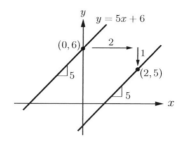

To write the equation of the new line, let's start with $y = mx + b$, where m is the slope and b is the y-intercept. The slope of the new line is 5 because the slope of the line remains the same after the shift. Thus, $m = 5$. Since the new line passes through $(2, 5)$, substitute 2 for x and 5 for y to solve for b.

$$y = 5x + b \qquad \text{Substitute 2 for } x \text{ and 5 for } y$$
$$5 = 5(2) + b \qquad \text{Solve for } b$$
$$b = -5$$

Therefore, the equation of the new line is $y = 5x - 5$.

8. (B)

In the figure below, the cube has a side length of 2 and point A is the midpoint of one side of the cube. Point C is directly below point A so that it is also the midpoint of another side of the cube. Thus, $CD = 1$. Draw a segment from point C to point B to form a triangle CBD. $\triangle CBD$ is a right triangle with $CD = 1$ and $DB = 2$. To find CB, use the Pythagorean theorem: $CB^2 = 1^2 + 2^2$. Thus, $CB = \sqrt{5}$.

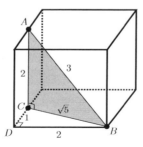

Draw a segments from point A to point C and draw another segment from point A to B to form triangle ABC. $\triangle ABC$ is a right triangle with $AC = 2$ and $CB = \sqrt{5}$. To find AB, use the Pythagorean theorem: $AB^2 = 2^2 + (\sqrt{5})^2$. Thus, $AB = 3$. Therefore, the length of $\overline{AB}$ is 3.

9. (120)

In quadrilateral $ABCD$ shown below, $m\angle D = 90°$. Since the ratio of the other three interior angles of the quadrilateral is $2 : 3 : 4$, let $2x$, $3x$, and $4x$ be the measure of angle A, B, and C, respectively.

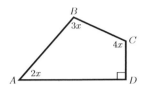

The sum of the measures of the interior angles of a quadrilateral is $360°$. Thus,

$$2x + 3x + 4x + 90 = 360$$
$$9x + 90 = 360$$
$$x = 30$$

Therefore, the measure of the largest interior angle of the quadrilateral is $4x = 4(30) = 120°$.

10. (12)

Substitute -1 for x in the equation $x^2 - 11x - C = 0$ and solve for C.

$$x^2 - 11x - C = 0 \qquad \text{Substitute } -1 \text{ for } x$$
$$(-1)^2 - 11(-1) - C = 0$$
$$1 + 11 - C = 0$$
$$C = 12$$

Therefore, the value of C is 12.

11. (7)

The graph below shows the two lines $y = -3x + 7$ and $y = 3x + 7$.

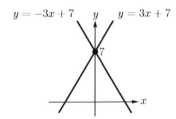

Both lines have the same y-intercept and intersect at $(0, 7)$. Therefore, the sum a and b is $a + b = 0 + 7 = 7$.

12. (135)

In the figure below, the line $y = x$ makes an angle of $45°$ with the positive x-axis.

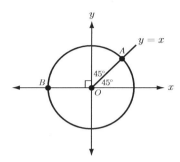

Therefore, the measure of $\angle AOB$ in degrees is $45° + 90° = 135°$.

13. (72)

In the figure below, $\triangle ABC$ is an equilateral triangle. The height, $\overline{BD}$, is drawn from vertex B to side AC so that $\triangle ABC$ is divided into two $30°$-$60°$-$90°$ special right triangles whose sides are in the ratio $1 : \sqrt{3} : 2$.

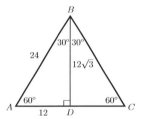

In $\triangle ABD$, $\overline{BD}$ is the longer leg and also the height of $\triangle ABC$. Thus, $BD = 12\sqrt{3}$. $\overline{AD}$ is the shorter leg and its length is $\frac{12\sqrt{3}}{\sqrt{3}} = 12$. Since the length of the hypotenuse is twice the length of the shorter leg, $AB = 2AD = 24$. Therefore, the perimeter of the equilateral triangle is $24 \times 3 = 72$.

14. (12)

Since $z > 0$, divide each side of the equation $xz + yz - 12z = 0$ by z and solve for $x + y$.

$$\frac{xz + yz - 12z}{z} = \frac{0}{z} \qquad \text{Divide each side by } z$$

$$\frac{xz}{z} + \frac{yz}{z} - \frac{12z}{z} = 0 \qquad \text{Simplify}$$

$$x + y - 12 = 0 \qquad \text{Add 12 to each side}$$

$$x + y = 12$$

Therefore, the value of $x + y$ is 12.

15. (19)

Define x as the smaller consecutive odd integer. Then, the larger consecutive odd integer can be expressed as $x+2$ and the sum of the two integers can be expressed as $x+x+2$. Since the average of the two integers is 18, the sum of the integers is $2 \times 18 = 36$. Thus,

$$x + x + 2 = 36 \qquad \text{Solve for } x$$
$$x = 17$$

Therefore, the value of the larger integer is $x + 2 = 19$.

16. (4)

A square with side length of 4 is cut into only smaller squares so that there is no wasted area. The side lengths of the smaller squares are integer values less than four. This means that the possible lengths of the smaller squares are either 1, 2 or 3. The three figures below show how the square is divided into the smaller squares with the different integer values of the side lengths.

Fig. 1: 16 smaller squares   Fig. 2: 8 smaller squares   Fig. 3: 4 smaller squares

In figure 1, the square is divided into smaller squares with side length of 1. There are 16 smaller squares. In figure 2, the square is divided into two types of smaller squares: one with side length of 3 and another with side length of 1. There are 8 smaller squares in total. In figure 3, the square is divided into smaller squares with side length of 2. There are 4 smaller squares. Therefore, the smallest number of smaller squares that can be cut is 4.

17. (120)

In the figure below, $ABCD$ is an isosceles trapezoid. Draw a segment from vertex B to $\overline{AD}$ and draw another segment from C to $\overline{AD}$ such that $\overline{BE} \perp \overline{AD}$ and $\overline{CF} \perp \overline{AD}$. Since $BC = 12$, $EF = 12$ and $AE = FD = \frac{18-12}{2} = 3$.

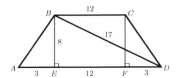

$\triangle BED$ is a right triangle with $BD = 17$ and $ED = 15$. To find the length of $\overline{BE}$, use the Pythagorean theorem: $17^2 = BE^2 + 15^2$ or use the Pythagorean triple: $8 - 15 - 17$. Thus, $BE = 8$. Therefore,

$$\text{Area of trapezoid } ABCD = \frac{1}{2}(b_1 + b_2)h \qquad b_1 = BC,\ b_2 = AD,\ h = BE$$
$$= \frac{1}{2}(12 + 18)8$$
$$= 120$$

www.solomonacademy.net

18. (6)

In the figure below, the diameter of a sphere is the same as the length of a cube since the sphere is inscribed in the cube. Define $2x$ as the length of the cube. Then, the diameter of the sphere is $2x$ and the radius is x.

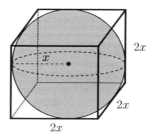

The volume of the cube can be expressed as $(2x)^3 = 8x^3$ and the volume of the sphere can be expressed as $\frac{4}{3}\pi x^3$. Thus,

$$\frac{\text{Volume of sphere}}{\text{Volume of cube}} = \frac{\frac{4}{3}\pi x^3}{8x^3} = \frac{\pi}{6}$$

Since the ratio of the volume of the sphere to that of the cube is $\frac{\pi}{6}$, the value of n is 6.

Answers and Solutions

SAT Math Practice Test 5
Section 3

Answers

1. D	2. A	3. E	4. B
5. C	6. B	7. D	8. A
9. C	10. E	11. C	12. E
13. B	14. D	15. A	16. B

Solutions

1. (D)

Substitute 2 for y in the equation $x + xy = y + 4$ and solve for x.

$$x + xy = y + 4 \qquad \text{Substitute 2 for } y$$
$$x + 2x = 2 + 4 \qquad \text{Solve for } x$$
$$x = 2$$

Therefore, the value of x is 2.

2. (A)

Two lines are parallel as shown below.

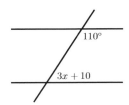

Since the two lines are parallel, angles $3x + 10$ and $110°$ are consecutive angles and supplementary angles whose sum of their measures is $180°$. Thus,

$$3x + 10 + 110 = 180$$
$$3x = 60$$
$$x = 20$$

Therefore, the value of $2x = 2(20) = 40$.

3. (E)

There are 60 minutes in one hour. Set up a proportion in terms of pages and minutes.

$$6 \text{ pages} : 10 \text{ minutes} = x \text{ pages} : 60 \text{ minutes}$$

$$\frac{6}{10} = \frac{x}{60} \qquad \text{Use cross product property}$$

$$10x = 360$$

$$x = 36$$

Therefore, Sue will read 36 pages in 1 hour.

4. (B)

The length of a square is $x + 3$. The area of the square is $(x + 3)^2$. To expand $(x + 3)^2$, use the binomial expansion formula: $(x + y)^2 = x^2 + 2xy + y^2$.

$$(x + 3)^2 = x^2 + 2(x)(3) + 3^2 = x^2 + 6x + 9$$

Therefore, the area of the square in terms of x is $x^2 + 6x + 9$.

5. (C)

The days of the week repeat every 7 days. If May 5th falls on a Thursday, the 12th and 19th are both Thursdays. Since May 18th is the day before May 19th, it is a Wednesday.

6. (B)

The lengths of the three sides of a triangle is 4, 5, and n. To find the largest possible integer value of n, use the triangle inequality theorem: The length of a side of a triangle is always less than the sum of the lengths of the other two sides, but always greater than the difference of the lengths of the other two sides.

$$5 - 4 < n < 5 + 4 \qquad \text{Use the triangle inequality theorem}$$

$$1 < n < 9 \qquad n \text{ is a positive integer}$$

$$n = 2, 3, \cdots, 8$$

Therefore, the largest possible value of n is 8.

7. (D)

$$|2 - x| = 5$$

$$2 - x = \pm 5$$

$$2 - x = 5 \qquad \text{or} \qquad 2 - x = -5$$

$$-x = 3 \qquad \text{or} \qquad -x = -7$$

$$x = -3 \qquad \text{or} \qquad x = 7$$

Therefore, the sum of the solutions is $-3 + 7 = 4$.

8. (A)

In the figure below, $\triangle OAB$ is an isosceles right triangle. This means that $AB = OA = 4$ and $m\angle AOB = m\angle OBA = 45°$. Thus, the radius of the circle, $\overline{OA}$, is 4.

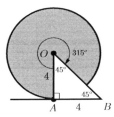

The area of the shaded region equals the area of a sector whose central angle is $315°$. Therefore,

$$\text{Area of shaded region} = \pi(4)^2 \times \frac{315°}{360°} = 16\pi \times \frac{7}{8} = 14\pi$$

9. (C)

$$5^{y+1} = \left(\frac{1}{5}\right)^{2y-2}$$
$$5^{y+1} = (5^{-1})^{2y-2}$$
$$5^{y+1} = 5^{-2y+2}$$

Since the expressions on both sides of the equation have the same base, the exponents on both sides must be the same. Thus,

$$y + 1 = -2y + 2 \quad \implies \quad y = \frac{1}{3}$$

Therefore, the value of y is $\frac{1}{3}$.

10. (E)

In the figure below, a function $f(x)$ crosses the x-axis at $A(-1, 0)$ and $B(3, 0)$. This means that the x-intercepts of the function are -1 and 3. Thus, $f(-1) = 0$ and $f(3) = 0$.

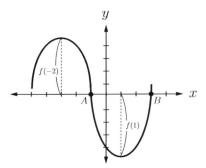

Since $f(0)$ represents the y-intercept of the function, $f(0) = -4$. Additionally, $f(1)$ and $f(-2)$ represent the function's values at $x = 1$ and $x = -2$, respectively. $f(1) \approx -4.5$ and $f(-2) \approx 4.5$. Therefore, $f(-2)$ in answer choice (E) has the largest value.

11. (C)

The first train left the station at 7 am and the last train left the station at 10 am. The table below shows the time at which the train left the station between 7 am and 10 am.

Time	Departure Time	Time at which train left the station
7:00 am-8:00 am	Every 10 minutes	7:00, 7:10, 7:20, 7:30, 7:40, 7:50
8:00 am-9:00 am	Every 15 minutes	8:00, 8:15, 8:30, 8:45
9:00 am-10:00 am	Every 20 minutes	9:00, 9:20, 9:40, 10:00

Do not count the following time twice: 8:00 am and 9:00 am because only one train left the station at that time. Between 7:00 am to 7:50 am, 6 trains left the station. Between 8:00 am to 8:45 am, 4 trains left the station. Between 9:00 am to 10:00 am 4 trains left the station. Therefore, a total of 14 trains left the station between 7:00 am to 10:00 am.

12. (E)

In the figure below, points D, E, and F are the midpoints of the three sides of an equilateral triangle whose area is $16\sqrt{3}$.

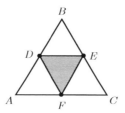

According to the midsegment theorem, a segment connecting the midpoints of the two sides of a triangle is parallel to the third side and is half as long, $DE = \frac{1}{2}AC$, $FE = \frac{1}{2}AB$ and $DF = \frac{1}{2}BC$. This implies that equilateral triangle ABC can be divided equally into four smaller equilateral triangles. Thus, the area of $\triangle DEF$ equals $\frac{1}{4}$ of the area of equilateral triangle ABC. Therefore, the area of $\triangle DEF$ is $\frac{1}{4}(16\sqrt{3}) = 4\sqrt{3}$.

13. (B)

Set S consists of 5 positive integers: x, y, 7, 12, and 14. The mean of the five integers in set S is 10, which means that the sum of the five integers is $5 \times 10 = 50$. Set up an equation in terms of the sum and find the value of $x + y$.

$$x + y + 7 + 12 + 14 = 50 \qquad \text{Subtract 33 from each side}$$
$$x + y = 17$$

Thus, $x + y = 17$. Since the mode of set S is 7, let's consider two cases:

Case 1: x and y are both 7.
If $x = 7$ and $y = 7$, $x + y = 14$. It does not satisfy $x + y = 17$. Thus, x and y can not be both 7.

Case 2: either x or y is 7.
If $x = 7$, $y = 10$ so that $x + y = 17$. For the same reason, if $y = 7$, $x = 10$.

Therefore, the product of xy is $xy = 7(10) = 70$.

14. (D)

A line $y = 3x + 4$ intersects a parabola $y = x^2$ as shown below.

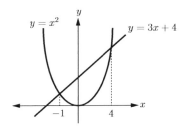

Set the two equations equal to each other and solve for x.

$$x^2 = 3x + 4 \qquad \text{Subtract } 3x + 4 \text{ from each side}$$
$$x^2 - 3x - 4 = 0 \qquad \text{Use the Factoring method}$$
$$(x + 1)(x - 4) = 0 \qquad \text{Use the zero-product property}$$
$$x = -1 \quad \text{or} \quad x = 4$$

Therefore, the x-coordinates of the two intersection points are -1 or 4.

15. (A)

There are six non-prime numbers from 1 to 10: 1, 4, 6, 8, 9, and 10. There are four prime numbers: 2, 3, 5, and 7. If all six non-prime numbers are selected, the next number will be a prime number. Therefore, seven cards must be selected to guarantee that at least one prime number is selected.

16. (B)

A penny, a nickel, a dime, and a quarter are in a bag. Two coins are selected at random. The table below shows different possible total values if two coins are selected. Define P, N, D, and Q as a penny, a nickel, a dime, and a quarter, respectively.

$P + N$	6 cents
$P + D$	11 cents
$P + Q$	26 cents
$N + D$	15 cents
$N + Q$	30 cents
$D + Q$	35 cents

Therefore, there are six different possible total values.

Answers and Solutions
SAT Math Practice Test 6
Section 1

Answers

1. C	2. B	3. D	4. B	5. A
6. B	7. D	8. C	9. C	10. E
11. B	12. C	13. B	14. C	15. D
16. D	17. D	18. B	19. A	20. C

Solutions

1. (C)

   Since the length of the cube is 3, the volume of the cube is $s^3 = 3^3 = 27$.

2. (B)

   The sum of x and y is 18 can be expressed as $x + y = 18$. The difference of y and x is 4. Since $x < y$, it can be expressed as $y - x = 4$. Therefore, the system of linear equations in answer choice (B) is the correct answer.

3. (D)

   There are 100 integers between 1 and 100 inclusive. Since half the 100 integers are odd integers, there are 50 odd integers between 1 and 100.

4. (B)

   Start with the equation $y = kx$. First, find the value of k using the given information.

   $$y = kx \qquad \text{Substitute 3 for } x \text{ and 6 for } y$$
   $$6 = 3k \qquad \text{Solve for } k$$
   $$k = 2$$

   So, the direct variation is $y = 2x$. To find x when $y = 4$, substitute 4 for y in the equation $y = 2x$.

   $$y = 2x \qquad \text{Substitute 4 for } y$$
   $$4 = 2x \qquad \text{Solve for } x$$
   $$x = 2$$

   Therefore, the value of x when $y = 4$ is 2.

5. (A)

Triangle ABC is a right triangle with $CB = \sqrt{2}$ and $AC = \sqrt{3}$. To find the length of the hypotenuse, AB, use the Pythagorean theorem: $AB^2 = (\sqrt{2})^2 + (\sqrt{3})^2$. Therefore, the length of $\overline{AB}$ is $\sqrt{5}$.

6. (B)

To find the median of set B, arrange the numbers from least to greatest. Thus,

$$B = \{5, 6, 9, 11, 12, 15\}$$

Since there are six numbers in set B, the median is the average of the 3rd number and 4th number, or $\frac{9+11}{2} = 10$. Therefore, the median of set B is 10.

7. (D)

$$6(p - q) = 36 \qquad \text{Divide each side by 6}$$
$$p - q = 6 \qquad \text{Multiply each side by 4}$$
$$4(p - q) = 24 \qquad \text{Expand}$$
$$4p - 4q = 24$$

8. (C)

In the figure below, $\triangle ABC$ is an isosceles right triangle with $AB = BC = 4$. The area of $\triangle ABC$ is $\frac{1}{2}bh$ or 8. Since $AB = DE = 4$, $\triangle ABC$ and $\triangle DEF$ are congruent. Thus, the area of $\triangle DEF$ is also 8.

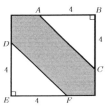

The area of the shaded region equals the area of the square minus the sum of the areas of $\triangle ABC$ and $\triangle DEF$. Therefore,

$$\text{Area of shaded region} = \text{Area of square} - (\text{Area of } \triangle ABC + \text{Area of } \triangle DEF)$$
$$= 6^2 - (8 + 8)$$
$$= 20$$

9. (C)

There are three numbers that are divisible by 3: 3, 6, and 9. Also, there are two numbers that are divisible by 4: 4, and 8. Thus, there are five numbers that are divisible by three or four. Since there are 10 numbers in the hat, five numbers are neither divisibly by 3 nor 4. Therefore, the probability that the number is neither divisible by 3 nor 4 is $\frac{5}{10}$ or $\frac{1}{2}$.

10. (E)

For simplicity, let's choose $\frac{1}{4}$ for the value of x. Plug in $\frac{1}{4}$ into the value of x for each answer choice to find out which of the following expression has the largest value.

(A) $x = \dfrac{1}{4}$

(B) $x^2 = \dfrac{1}{16}$

(C) $x^3 = \dfrac{1}{64}$

(D) $\dfrac{1}{x} = \dfrac{1}{\frac{1}{4}} = 4$

(E) $\dfrac{1}{x^2} = \dfrac{1}{\frac{1}{16}} = 16$

Therefore, (E) is the correct answer.

11. (B)

$$x^2 - 3x < 0 \qquad \text{Factor}$$
$$x(x - 3) < 0 \qquad \text{Solve inequality}$$
$$0 < x < 3 \qquad x \text{ is a positive integer}$$
$$x = 1,\ 2$$

Therefore, there are two positive integer values of x for which $x^2 - 3x < 0$.

12. (C)

In the figure below, $\triangle ABC$ and $\triangle DEC$ are isosceles right triangles. So, they are $45°$-$45°$-$90°$ special right triangles whose sides are in the ratio $1 : 1 : \sqrt{2}$.

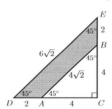

In $\triangle ABC$, $AC = 4$. Thus, $BC = 4$ and $AB = 4\sqrt{2}$. In $\triangle DEC$, $DC = 6$. Thus, $EC = 6$ and $DE = 6\sqrt{2}$. Therefore,

$$\text{Perimeter of shaded region} = DE + EB + AB + DA$$
$$= 6\sqrt{2} + 2 + 4\sqrt{2} + 2$$
$$= 10\sqrt{2} + 4$$

13. (B)

Add the two equations to eliminate the variables y and z. Then, solve for x.

$$x + y = 10 - z$$
$$\underline{x - y = 16 + z} \qquad \text{Add two equations}$$
$$2x = 26$$
$$x = 13$$

Therefore, the value of x is 13.

14. (C)

Joshua plans to spend 29% of his time studying English, 20% on science, 12% on history, and 6% on others. Thus, the percentage of his time studying math can be determined by $100\% - (29 + 20 + 12 + 6)\%$ or 33%. Since the total study hours is 10 hours, the total number of hours that Joshua plans to study math is $10 \times 0.33 = 3.3$ hours. Since 0.3 hour is equal to 0.3×60 minutes $= 18$ minutes, Joshua will spend 3 hours and 18 minutes on math.

15. (D)

In the figure below, $y = 1$ intersects $y = -|x| + 7$ at points A and B.

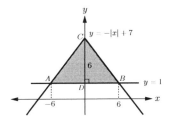

To find the x-coordinates of points A and B, substitute 1 for y in $y = -|x| + 7$ and solve for x.

$$-|x| + 7 = 1 \qquad \text{Subtract 1 from each side}$$
$$-|x| = -6 \qquad \text{Multiply each side by } -1$$
$$|x| = 6 \qquad \text{Solve for } x$$
$$x = -6 \quad \text{or} \quad x = 6$$

Since the values of x are 6 or -6, $AB = 12$. The y-intercept of $y = -|x| + 7$ is 7. Thus, the x and y coordinates of point C is $(0, 7)$. Since point D is on the line $y = 1$, the x and y coordinates of point D is $(0, 1)$. Thus, $CD = 6$. The area of the shaded region equals the area of $\triangle ACB$. Therefore, the area of the shaded region is $\frac{1}{2} \times AB \times CD = \frac{1}{2} \times 12 \times 6 = 36$.

16. (D)

In order to solve time problems, use the time $= \frac{\text{distance}}{\text{speed}}$ formula. Since $\frac{220 \text{ miles}}{55 \text{ miles per hour}} = 4$ hours, it took Sue 4 hours to travel 220 miles. On the return trip, if she travels at 50 miles per hour, it will take her $\frac{220 \text{ miles}}{50 \text{ miles per hour}} = 4.4$ hours. This means that it will take her 0.4 hour longer on the return trip. Since 0.4 hour is equal to 0.4×60 minutes $= 24$ minutes, it will take Sue 24 minutes longer on the return trip.

17. (D)

There are 3 feet in 1 yard. Thus, there are 24 feet in 8 yards. A ball is dropped from a height of 24 feet. Each time the ball strikes the ground, it bounces up to half its previous height. The table below summarizes the height of the ball when it strikes the ground.

Strike	Height of ball
1st strike	12 feet
2nd strike	6 feet
3rd strike	3 feet
4th strike	1.5 feet

Therefore, the ball needs to strike the ground four times before its height is less than 3 feet.

18. (B)

x, y, and z are positive integers. To write z in terms of y, substitute $3y$ for x in the equation $z = x^2 + y^2$.

$$z = x^2 + y^2 = (3y)^2 + y^2 = 10y^2$$

Since y is a positive integer, $z = 10y^2$ implies that z must be a positive integer that is a multiple of 10. Answer choice (B) cannot be equal to z because 36 is not a multiple of 10. Therefore, (B) is the correct answer.

19. (A)

It will take too much time to calculate the distance between Mr. Rhee and the starting position in each move as shown below. Instead, calculate the overall distances for the north and south direction, and the east and west direction. It is easier and faster to calculate the distance between Mr. Rhee and the starting position after the 8th move.

Move	Direction	Distance
1st	South	1 foot
2nd	West	2 feet
3rd	North	3 feet
4th	East	4 feet
5th	South	5 feet
6th	West	6 feet
7th	North	7 feet
8th	East	8 feet

To calculate the overall distances for the north and south direction, assign $+$ to the north direction and $-$ to the south direction. For instance, walk 3 feet due north can be written as $+3$ and walk 1 foot due south as -1. Thus,

Overall distances for north and south $= -1 + 3 - 5 + 7 = +4$

$+4$ indicates that Mr. Rhee has moved 4 feet north overall. Next, calculate the overall distances for the east and west direction. Assign $+$ to the east direction and $-$ to the west direction.

Overall distances for east and west $= -2 + 4 - 6 + 8 = +4$

$+4$ indicates that Mr. Rhee has moved 4 feet east overall. Thus, Mr. Rhee has moved 4 feet north and 4 feet east after the 8th move. In the figure below, O represent the starting position and P represents where Mr. Rhee is after the 8th move.

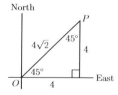

To find the distance between Mr. Rhee and the starting postion, OP, use the 45°-45°-90° special right triangle ratio: $1 : 1 : \sqrt{2}$, or use the Pythagorean theorem: $OP^2 = 4^2 + 4^2$. Thus, $OP = 4\sqrt{2}$. Therefore, Mr. Rhee is $4\sqrt{2}$ feet away from the staring position after the 8th move.

20. (C)

In the figure below, the central angle $AOB = x°$. Let the radius of the circle be r.

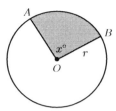

The area of the shaded region equals the area of a sector whose central angle is $x°$ and can be expressed as $\pi r^2 \times \frac{x°}{360°}$. The length of minor arc AB whose central angle is $x°$ can be expressed as $2\pi r \times \frac{x°}{360°}$. Since the area of the shaded region is three times the length of the minor arc AB,

Area of shaded region $= 3 \times$ Length of minor arc AB

$$\pi r^2 \times \frac{x°}{360°} = 3 \times 2\pi r \times \frac{x°}{360°} \qquad \frac{x°}{360°} \text{ cancels each other}$$

$$\pi r^2 = 6\pi r \qquad\qquad\qquad \text{Divide each side by } \pi r$$

$$r = 6$$

Therefore, the radius of the circle is 6.

Answers and Solutions
SAT Math Practice Test 6
Section 2

Answers

1. A	2. E	3. B	4. D
5. D	6. C	7. D	8. E
9. 7	10. 50	11. 20	12. $\frac{5}{12}$
13. $\frac{30}{11}$	14. 5	15. 165	16. $\frac{1}{2}$
17. $\frac{3}{4}$	18. $\frac{8}{5}$		

Solutions

1. (A)

Since $y - 1 = 1$, $y = 2$. Substitute 2 for y in the equation $2x + 3y = 12$ and solve for x.

$$2x + 3y = 12 \qquad \text{Substitute 2 for } y$$
$$2x + 6 = 12 \qquad \text{Solve for } x$$
$$x = 3$$

Therefore, the value of x is 3.

2. (E)

Two points $(-1, 2)$ and $(1, 8)$ are given. Use the definition of the slope.

$$\text{Slope} = \frac{y_2 - y_1}{x_2 - x_1} = \frac{8 - 2}{1 - (-1)} = 3$$

Therefore, the slope of the line that passes through the points $(-1, 2)$ and $(1, 8)$ is 3.

3. (B)

x years ago from now, Jason was y years old, which implies that he is $y + x$ years old now. Therefore, in x years from now, Jason will be $y + x + x$ or $y + 2x$ years old.

4. (D)

To find the value of k, select any of the listed ordered pairs in the table and substitute the x and y coordinate values into the given equation $y = (x - k)^2$. Let's select the ordered pair $(3, 1)$.

$$y = (x - k)^2 \qquad \text{Substitute 3 for } x \text{ and 1 for } y$$
$$1 = (3 - k)^2 \qquad \text{Take the square root on each side}$$
$$3 - k = 1 \quad \text{or} \quad 3 - k = -1 \qquad \text{Solve for } k$$
$$k = 2 \quad \text{or} \quad k = 4$$

Thus, the possible values for k are 2 or 4. Therefore, (D) is the correct answer.

5. (D)

There are 60 seconds in one minute. Thus, there are $60 \times z$ or $60z$ seconds in z minutes. Define n as the number of feet that Joshua will walk in z minutes. Set up a proportion in terms of feet and seconds and solve for n.

$$x_{\text{feet}} : y_{\text{seconds}} = n_{\text{feet}} : 60z_{\text{seconds}}$$
$$\frac{x}{y} = \frac{n}{60z} \qquad \text{Use cross product property}$$
$$ny = 60xz \qquad \text{Solve for } n$$
$$n = \frac{60xz}{y}$$

Therefore, Joshua will walk $\frac{60xz}{y}$ feet in z minutes.

6. (C)

In the venn diagram below, let's define A as a set of rectangles, B as a set of rhombuses, $A \cup B$ as a set of parallelograms, and $A \cap B$ as a set of squares since they are both rectangles and rhombuses. Additionally, define $n(A)$, $n(B)$, $n(A \cup B)$, and $n(A \cap B)$ as the number of elements in set A, set B, set $A \cup B$, and set $A \cap B$, respectively.

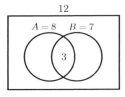

Since there are 12 parallelograms, 8 rectangles, and 7 rhombuses, $n(A \cup B) = 12$, $n(A) = 8$, and $n(B) = 7$. Thus,

$$n(A \cup B) = n(A) + n(B) - n(A \cap B)$$
$$12 = 8 + 7 - n(A \cap B)$$
$$n(A \cap B) = 3$$

Therefore, three of the parallelograms are squares.

www.solomonacademy.net

7. (D)

Use the answer choices to determine which number satisfies the given conditions. ABC represents a three-digit number greater than 200. Eliminate answer choice (A) because 136 is less than 200. Digits B and C are multiples of digit A. Thus, eliminate both answer choices (C) and (E) because they do not satisfy it. The remaining answer choices are (B) and (D). Since digit C is three more than digit B, eliminate answer choice (B) because 8 is not three more than 4. Therefore, (D) is the correct answer.

8. (E)

To evaluate the value of $x^2 - y^2$, use the special factoring pattern: $x^2 - y^2 = (x+y)(x-y)$. First, find the value of $x + y$ by squaring each side in the first equation $(x+y)^{\frac{1}{2}} = 4$. Thus, $x + y = 16$. Next, find the value of $x - y$ from the second equation $(x-y)^{\frac{3}{2}} = 8$.

$$(x-y)^{\frac{3}{2}} = 8 \qquad \text{Square each side}$$
$$(x-y)^3 = 64 \qquad \text{Take the cube root of each side}$$
$$x - y = (4^3)^{\frac{1}{3}} \qquad \text{Use the properties of exponents}$$
$$x - y = 4$$

Since $x + y = 16$ and $x - y = 4$,

$$x^2 - y^2 = (x+y)(x-y) = 16(4) = 64$$

Therefore, the value of $x^2 - y^2$ is 64.

9. (7)

Since $x - 2 = -7$, $x = -5$. Substitute -5 for x in the expression.

$$\frac{8 - 4x}{4} = \frac{8 - 4(-5)}{4} \qquad \text{Substitute } -5 \text{ for } x$$
$$= \frac{28}{4}$$
$$= 7$$

Therefore, the value of $\frac{8-4x}{4}$ is 7.

10. (50)

A square is a rhombus. To find the area of the square when the length of the diagonal is given, use the area of a rhombus formula: $A = \frac{1}{2}d^2$, where d is the length of the diagonal. Since the length of the diagonal of the square is 10,

$$\text{Area of square} = \frac{1}{2}d^2 = \frac{1}{2}(10)^2 = 50$$

Therefore, the area of the square is 50.

www.solomonacademy.net

11. (20)

In figure 1 below, there are 8 lines that connect three points. In figure 2, there are 4 lines that connect two points. In figure 3, there are 8 additional lines that connect other two points.

Figure 1

Figure 2

Figure 3

Therefore, there are $8 + 4 + 8 = 20$ different lines that connect at least two points.

12. ($\frac{5}{12}$)

Two numbers are selected at random without replacement from the set $\{1, 2, 3, 4\}$ to form a two-digit number. To find the total number of two-digit numbers, use the fundamental counting principle. Define event 1 and event 2 as selecting a digit for the tens' place, and ones' place, respectively. Event 1 has 4 ways to select a digit out of 4 digits. After one digit is taken, event 2 has 3 ways to select a digit out of the three remaining digits. Thus, there are $4 \times 3 = 12$ possible two-digit numbers using 1, 2, 3, and 4, which are shown below.

12 possible two-digit numbers: 12, 13, 14, 21, 23, 24, 31, 32, 34, 41, 42, and 43

Out of 12 possible two-digit numbers, there are 5 prime numbers: 13, 23, 31, 41, and 43. Therefore, the probability that the two-digit number selected is a prime number is $\frac{5}{12}$.

13. ($\frac{30}{11}$)

The largest value of $\frac{xy}{x+y}$ can be determined by using the smallest and largest values for both x and y. Use 2 and 5 for x, and 3 and 6 for y. When $x = 2$ and $y = 3$, the value of $\frac{xy}{x+y}$ is $\frac{2 \times 3}{2+3} = \frac{6}{5}$ shown in the table below. The table summarizes the possible values of $\frac{xy}{x+y}$.

		\multicolumn{2}{c}{x}	
		2	5
y	3	$\frac{2 \times 3}{2+3} = \frac{6}{5}$	$\frac{5 \times 3}{5+3} = \frac{15}{8}$
	6	$\frac{2 \times 6}{2+6} = \frac{12}{8}$	$\frac{5 \times 6}{5+6} = \frac{30}{11}$

There are four possible values of $\frac{xy}{x+y}$. Out of the four possible values, $\frac{30}{11}$ is the largest value.

14. (5)

When 100 is divided by 3, the quotient is 33 and the remainder is 1. Thus, 100 can be expressed as $100 = 3 \times 33 + 1$. Likewise, when n is divided by k, the quotient is q and the remainder is 5. Thus, n can be expressed as $n = kq + 5$. To find the remainder when $n - k$ is divided by k,

$$n = kq + 5 \qquad \text{Subtract } k \text{ from each side}$$
$$n - k = kq - k + 5 \qquad \text{Factor } kq - k$$
$$n - k = k(q - 1) + 5$$

$n - k = k(q - 1) + 5$ implies that the remainder is 5 when $n - k$ is divided by k.

15. (165)

The sequence $4, 11, 18, 25, \cdots$ is an arithmetic sequence, where the first term, $a_1 = 4$ and the common difference, $d = 11 - 4 = 7$. Use the nth term formula to find the 24th term.

$$a_n = a_1 + (n-1)d \qquad \text{Substitute 24 for } n$$
$$a_{24} = 4 + (24-1)7 = 165$$

Therefore, the value of the 24th term is 165.

16. $\left(\frac{1}{2}\right)$

In the figure below, points A, C, and D are on the same line. Since $AC : CD = 1 : 2$, let x be the length of $\overline{AC}$ and $2x$ be the length of $\overline{CD}$.

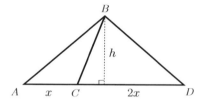

$\triangle ABC$ and $\triangle CBD$ have the same height, h. Thus,

$$\frac{\text{Area of } \triangle ABC}{\text{Area of } \triangle CBD} = \frac{\frac{1}{2} \times AC \times h}{\frac{1}{2} \times CD \times h} \qquad \text{Since } AC = x \text{ and } CD = 2x$$

$$= \frac{\frac{1}{2}xh}{\frac{1}{2}(2x)h} \qquad \frac{1}{2}xh \text{ cancels out}$$

$$= \frac{1}{2}$$

Therefore, the ratio of the area of $\triangle ABC$ to that of $\triangle CBD$ is $\frac{1}{2}$.

17. $\left(\frac{3}{4}\right)$

If it takes 6 people 4 days to paint a house, the total amount of work required to paint the entire house is equivalent to $6_{\text{ people}} \times 4_{\text{ days}} = 24_{\text{ people}\times\text{days}}$. Since the amount of work provided by 3 people in 6 days is $3_{\text{ people}} \times 6_{\text{ days}} = 18_{\text{ people}\times\text{days}}$, the fractional part of the house painted can be determined by the ratio of the amount of work provided by 3 people in 6 days to the total amount of work required. Thus,

$$\text{What fractional part of the house is painted} = \frac{18_{\text{ people}\times\text{days}}}{24_{\text{ people}\times\text{days}}} = \frac{3}{4}$$

Therefore, 3 people can paint $\frac{3}{4}$ of the house in 6 days.

18. $\left(\frac{8}{5}\right)$

The two lines $y = ax + 2$ and $y = -2x + 8$ intersect at $(t, t + 3)$, which means that the line $y = -2x + 8$ passes through the point $(t, t + 3)$. Substitute t for x and $t + 3$ for y in the equation $y = -2x + 8$ and solve for t.

$$y = -2x + 8 \qquad \text{Substitute } t \text{ for } x \text{ and } t + 3 \text{ for } y$$
$$t + 3 = -2t + 8 \qquad \text{Solve for } t$$
$$t = \frac{5}{3}$$

Since $t = \frac{5}{3}$, $t + 3 = \frac{5}{3} + 3 = \frac{14}{3}$. The x and y coordinates of the point $(t, t + 3)$ is $\left(\frac{5}{3}, \frac{14}{3}\right)$.

Additionally, $\left(\frac{5}{3}, \frac{14}{3}\right)$ is the intersection point between the lines $y = ax + 2$ and $y = -2x + 8$, which means that the line $y = ax + 2$ also passes through the point $\left(\frac{5}{3}, \frac{14}{3}\right)$. Substitute $\frac{5}{3}$ for x and $\frac{14}{3}$ for y in the equation $y = ax + 2$ and solve for a.

$$y = ax + 2 \qquad \text{Substitute } \frac{5}{3} \text{ for } x \text{ and } \frac{14}{3} \text{ for } y$$
$$\frac{14}{3} = \frac{5}{3}a + 2 \qquad \text{Subtract 2 from each side}$$
$$\frac{8}{3} = \frac{5}{3}a \qquad \text{Solve for } a$$
$$a = \frac{8}{5}$$

Therefore, the value of a is $\frac{8}{5}$.

Answers and Solutions
SAT Math Practice Test 6
Section 3

1. C	2. B	3. B	4. B
5. D	6. E	7. A	8. A
9. D	10. A	11. C	12. E
13. C	14. B	15. D	16. D

Solutions

1. **(C)**

   Use the distance formula to find the distance between points $A(0,6)$ and $B(8,0)$.

   $$d = \sqrt{(x_2 - x_1)^2 + (y_2 - y_1)^2} = \sqrt{(8-0)^2 + (0-6)^2} = 10$$

   Therefore, the distance between points A and B is 10.

2. **(B)**

   In $\triangle ABC$ shown below, $m\angle C = 90°$ and $m\angle B = 60°$. Thus, $\triangle ABC$ is a 30°-60°-90° special right triangle whose sides are in the ratio $1 : \sqrt{3} : 2$.

   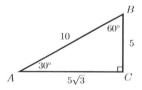

   $\overline{AC}$, the side opposite the angle 60°, is the longer leg of $\triangle ABC$ and its length is $5\sqrt{3}$. $\overline{BC}$, the side opposite the angle 30°, is the shorter leg and its length is $\frac{5\sqrt{3}}{\sqrt{3}} = 5$. Since the length of the hypotenuse of $\triangle ABC$ is twice the length of the shorter leg, $AB = 2BC$ or 10. Therefore, the length of $\overline{AB}$ is 10.

3. **(B)**

   To find P(profit), plug in the given values of R(revenue) and E(expenses) into the equation $P = R - 2E$. Since $R = \$3250$ and $E = \$1250$,

   $$P = R - 2E = 3250 - 2(1250) = 750$$

   Therefore, when the expenses is $1250 and the revenue is $3250, the profit of the company is $750.

4. (B)

1% means 1 out of 100. Thus, 75% is equal to $\frac{75}{100} = \frac{3}{4}$ and 20% is equal to $\frac{20}{100} = \frac{1}{5}$. Let x be the number. 75% of a number is 20% of 30 can be written as $\frac{3}{4}x = \frac{1}{5} \times 30$.

$$\frac{3}{4}x = \frac{1}{5} \times 30 \qquad \text{Solve for } x$$
$$x = 8$$

Therefore, the number is 8.

5. (D)

In the figure below, $\triangle ABC$ is an isosceles triangle such that $CA = CB$. Draw a segment from vertex C to point D such that $\overline{CD} \perp \overline{AB}$. Then, point D is the midpoint between two points $A(2, 3)$ and $B(6, 3)$.

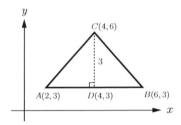

To find the x and y coordinates of the midpoint, D, use the midpoint formula: $\left(\frac{x_1 + x_2}{2}, \frac{y_1 + y_2}{2}\right)$. Thus, the midpoint, D, is $\left(\frac{2+6}{2}, \frac{3+3}{2}\right)$ or $(4, 3)$. The area of $\triangle ABC$ is 6 and the length of the base, AB, is 4. Thus, the height of $\triangle ABC$, CD, must be 3, which implies that point C is 3 units directly above point $D(4, 3)$. Therefore, the x and y coordinates of point C is $(4, 6)$.

6. (E)

Approach this problem in terms of the sum rather than the average. Use the definition of the sum shown below.

$$\text{Sum of a set} = \text{Average of a set} \times \text{Number of elements in a set}$$

Set S has three numbers and the average of the set is x. Thus, the sum of the three numbers in set S is $3x$. Additionally, Set T has four numbers and the average of the set is y. Thus, the sum of the four numbers in set T is $4y$. The total sum of the numbers in sets S and T is $3x + 4y$. There are seven numbers in total in sets S and T. To find the average of sets S and T, divide the total sum of numbers in sets S and T by 7.

$$\text{Average of sets } S \text{ and } T = \frac{\text{Total sum}}{7}$$
$$= \frac{3x + 4y}{7}$$

Therefore, the average of the two sets, S and T, is $\frac{3x+4y}{7}$.

7. (A)

To evaluate $f(k)$ and $f(0)$, substitute k and 0 for x in the function $f(x) = -x^2 + 4x + 5$.

$$f(k) = -(k)^2 + 4(k) + 5 = -k^2 + 4k + 5$$
$$f(0) = -(0)^2 + 4(0) + 5 = 5$$

Since $f(k) = f(0)$, set the two expressions shown above equal to each other and solve for k.

$-k^2 + 4k + 5 = 5$	Subtract 5 from each side
$-k^2 + 4k = 0$	Multiply each side by -1
$k^2 - 4k = 0$	Use the factoring method
$k(k - 4) = 0$	Use the zero product property
$k = 0$ or $k = 4$	

Therefore, (A) is the correct answer.

8. (A)

$S(x)$ is the sum of all positive integers less than or equal to x. Thus,

$$S(20) = 1 + 2 + \cdots + 9 + \cdots + 20$$
$$S(9) = 1 + 2 + \cdots + 9 \qquad \text{Subtract } S(9) \text{ from } S(20)$$
$$S(20) - S(9) = 10 + 11 + \cdots + 20 = 165$$

Therefore, the value of $S(20) - S(9)$ is 165.

9. (D)

Use the answer choices to determine which number satisfies all of the given conditions. Eliminate answer choice (C) because 18 is divisible by 9. Eliminate answer choices (A) and (B) because both 30 and 24 have 8 factors. Additionally, eliminate answer choice (E) because 6 has only 4 factors. Therefore, (D) is the correct answer.

10. (A)

Since a parallelogram has two pairs of parallel sides, it can not be a trapezoid which only has one pair of parallel sides. Thus, statement III is false. Not all rectangles have four congruent sides. Thus, statement IV is false. Only statement I and II are true. Therefore, (A) is the correct answer.

11. (C)

Two numbers are selected at random without replacement from the set $\{2, 3, 5, 7\}$ to form a fraction: one number for the numerator and another number for the denominator. If the numerator of the fraction is 2, there are three possible numbers for the denominator: 3, 5, and 7. Thus, there are three fractions that can be formed using these numbers: $\frac{2}{3}, \frac{2}{5}, \frac{2}{7}$. All of the fractions are proper fractions. The table below shows a list of all possible fractions that can be formed when the numerator of fractions are 2, 3, 5, or 7.

www.solomonacademy.net

Numerator	Denominator	Fraction	Proper fraction
2	3	$\frac{2}{3}$	✓
2	5	$\frac{2}{5}$	✓
2	7	$\frac{2}{7}$	✓
3	2	$\frac{3}{2}$	
3	5	$\frac{3}{5}$	✓
3	7	$\frac{3}{7}$	✓
5	2	$\frac{5}{2}$	
5	3	$\frac{5}{3}$	
5	7	$\frac{5}{7}$	✓
7	2	$\frac{7}{2}$	
7	3	$\frac{7}{3}$	
7	5	$\frac{7}{5}$	

Out of 12 fractions, there are 6 proper fractions. Therefore, the probability that the fraction formed is a proper fraction is $\frac{6}{12}$ or $\frac{1}{2}$.

12. (E)

Use the phrase **Less-And Great-Or** to solve compound inequalities. Solving an absolute value inequality with a less than inequality symbol creates an And compound inequality.

$$|2x + 4| < 6 \qquad \text{Create And compound inequality}$$
$$-6 < 2x + 4 < 6 \qquad \text{Subtract 4 from each side}$$
$$-10 < 2x < 2 \qquad \text{Divide each side by 2}$$
$$-5 < x < 1$$

13. (C)

x is a positive integer. List positive integers starting from 1 and find out the units digits of the square of the positive integers as shown in the table below. For instance, if a positive integer is 4, the square of 4 is 16. Thus, the units digit of 16 is 6.

x	1	2	3	4	5	6	7	8	9	10	11	12	13	$\cdots$
x^2	1	4	9	16	25	36	49	64	81	100	121	144	169	$\cdots$
Units digit	1	4	9	6	5	6	9	4	1	0	1	4	9	$\cdots$

The table above shows a pattern of the units digits: $1, 4, 9, 6, 5, 6, 9, 4, 1, 0$ and is repeated. From the pattern, digits 0, 1, 4, 5, 6, and 9 are used for the units digits. Therefore, there are four digits that can not be the units digits of the square of x: 2, 3, 7, and 8.

14. (B)

The diagonals of square $ABCD$, $\overline{AC}$ and $\overline{BD}$, are perpendicular to each other. This means that $\overline{AC}$ and $\overline{BD}$ have negative reciprocal slopes. Thus, the product of the slopes equals -1. For instance, if the slope of $\overline{AC}$ is 1, the slope of $\overline{BD}$ is -1, and the product of the slopes is $1 \times -1 = -1$. Therefore, the product of the slopes of the two diagonals, $\overline{AC}$ and $\overline{BD}$, is -1.

15. (D)

In $\triangle ABC$ shown below, $AB = 6$, $BC = 8$, and $AC = 10$. There are three semicircles on each side of the triangle. Thus, the radii of the three semicircles are 3, 4, and 5.

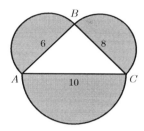

To find the total area of the shaded regions which equals the sum of the areas of the three semicircles, use the area of a semicircle formula: $\frac{1}{2}\pi r^2$.

$$\text{Total area of shaded regions} = \text{Sum of the areas of three semicircles}$$
$$= \frac{1}{2}\pi(3)^2 + \frac{1}{2}\pi(4)^2 + \frac{1}{2}\pi(5)^2$$
$$= 25\pi$$

Therefore, the total area of the shaded regions is 25π.

16. (D)

Define x, y, and z as the age of Mr. Rhee, Joshua, and Sue, respectively. Then, the sum of all ages of Mr. Rhee, Joshua, and Sue can be expressed as $x + y + z$, and the sum of the ages of Mr. Rhee and Joshua is 47 can be expressed as $x + y = 47$. Additionally, the sum of the ages of Joshua and Sue is 46 can be expressed as $y + z = 46$, and the sum of the ages of Sue and Mr. Rhee is 79 can be expressed as $z + x = 79$. To find the sum of all ages of Mr. Rhee, Joshua, and Sue, add the three equations shown below.

$$x + y = 47$$
$$y + z = 46$$
$$\underline{z + x = 79} \qquad \text{Add three equations}$$
$$2x + 2y + 2z = 172 \qquad \text{Divide each side by 2}$$
$$x + y + z = 86$$

Therefore, the sum of all ages of Mr. Rhee, Joshua and Sue, $x + y + z$, is 86.

     www.solomonacademy.net

Answers and Solutions
SAT Math Practice Test 7
Section 1

Answers

1. E	2. A	3. D	4. A	5. E
6. A	7. B	8. A	9. C	10. C
11. D	12. D	13. E	14. B	15. C
16. C	17. C	18. B	19. B	20. A

Solutions

1. (E)

   A cube has 12 edges.

2. (A)

   x is a positive integer and y is a negative integer. Since $x > 0$ and $y < 0$, $x - y > 0$. For instance, if $x = 3$ and $y = -2$, $x - y = 3 - (-2) = 5$. Therefore, (A) is the correct answer.

3. (D)

   The sequence $-1, 1, -1, 1, \cdots$ suggests a pattern such that odd numbered terms are -1 and even numbered terms are 1. For instance, the third term, a_3, is -1 and the fourth term, a_4, is 1. Since the 28th term is an even numbered term, the value of the 28th term is 1.

4. (A)

   Select an ordered pair $(1, -2)$ that the graph $y = ax^2$ passes through. Substitute 1 for x and -2 for y in $y = ax^2$ to solve for a.

   $$y = ax^2 \qquad \text{Substitute 1 for } x \text{ and } -2 \text{ for } y$$
   $$-2 = a(-1)^2 \qquad \text{Solve for } a$$
   $$a = -2$$

   Therefore, the value of a is -2.

www.solomonacademy.net

5. (E)

A circular pizza with a radius of 8 is cut into 8 equal slices. In order to find the sum of the area of 5 slices, multiply the area of the entire pizza by $\frac{5}{8}$.

$$\text{Area of 5 slices} = \frac{5}{8} \times \pi(8)^2 = 40\pi$$

Therefore, the sum of the area of the 5 slices is 40π.

6. (A)

For simplicity, let's consider a part of the graph shown below, where $x > 0$.

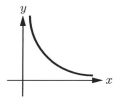

The graph suggest that the value of y decreases as the value of x increases. The only function that has this kind of characteristic is a rational function, $y = \frac{1}{x}$. Therefore, (A) is the correct answer.

7. (B)

Instead of setting up an equation mathematically, use the given answer choices. 11 is the only number that satisfies the given conditions. If 11 is divided by 2, 3, 4, 5, and 6, the remainders are 1, 2, 3, 1, and 5, respectively.

8. (A)

Since x, y, and z represent the measures of the interior angles of a triangle, the sum of the measures of the interior angles expressed as $x + y + z$ is $180°$. Thus,

$$\frac{x+2}{4} + \frac{y+1}{4} + \frac{z-3}{4} = \frac{x+y+z}{4} = \frac{180}{4} = 45$$

Therefore, the value of the expression is $45°$.

9. (C)

In the figure below, $ABDC$ is a trapezoid whose sides $\overline{BD} \parallel \overline{AC}$. Since $\overline{DC} \perp \overline{AC}$, $\overline{DC} \perp \overline{BD}$. Thus, $m\angle C = m\angle D = 90°$. $\triangle ABC$ is an equilateral triangle. Thus, $m\angle ABC = m\angle BCA = 60°$.

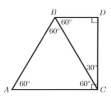

Since $m\angle C = 90°$ and $m\angle BCA = 60°$, $m\angle BCD = 30°$. $\angle DBC$ and $\angle BCD$ are complementary angles whose sum of their measures is $90°$. Thus, $m\angle DBC = 60°$. Since the measure of $\angle ABD$ equals the sum of the measures of $\angle ABC$ and $\angle DBC$, the measure of $\angle ABD$ is $60° + 60° = 120°$.

10. (C)

$$2x^2 - 5x + 2 = 0 \qquad \text{Use the factoring method}$$
$$(x - 2)(2x - 1) = 0 \qquad \text{Use the zero product property}$$
$$x = 2 \quad \text{or} \quad x = \frac{1}{2}$$

The solutions to the equation $2x^2 - 5x + 2$ are 2 and $\frac{1}{2}$. Therefore, the product of the solutions is $2 \times \frac{1}{2} = 1$.

11. (D)

Use the midpoint formula, $(\frac{x_1+x_2}{2}, \frac{y_1+y_2}{2})$, to find the midpoints M and N.

$$\text{Using two points } A(-1, 2) \text{ and } B(3, 2): \qquad M = \left(\frac{-1+3}{2}, \frac{2+2}{2} \right) = (1, 2)$$

$$\text{Using two points } C(2, 3) \text{ and } B(2, -1): \qquad N = \left(\frac{2+2}{2}, \frac{3+(-1)}{2} \right) = (2, 1)$$

Finally, use the distance formula to find the distance between $M(1, 2)$ and $N(2, 1)$.

$$MN = \sqrt{(x_2 - x_1)^2 + (y_2 - y_1)^2} = \sqrt{(2 - 1)^2 + (1 - 2)^2} = \sqrt{2}$$

Therefore, the distance between M and N is $\sqrt{2}$.

12. (D)

Use the properties of exponents.

$$\left(\frac{1}{4} \right)^x = (2^{-2})^x = 2^{-2x}$$
$$= (2^x)^{-2} = \left(\frac{1}{3} \right)^{-2} \qquad \text{Since } 2^x = \frac{1}{3}$$
$$= (3^{-1})^{-2} = 3^2$$
$$= 9$$

13. (E)

This problem is about a direct variation. Since y is proportional to $x - 2$, let's start with the equation $y = k(x - 2)$, where k is the constant of variation. To find the value of k, substitute 5 for x and 15 for y in the equation.

$$y = k(x - 2) \qquad \text{Substitute 5 for } x \text{ and 15 for } y$$
$$15 = k(5 - 2) \qquad \text{Solve for } k$$
$$k = 5$$

Thus, the equation that relates y and $x - 2$ is $y = 5(x - 2)$. Substitute -10 for y in $y = 5(x - 2)$ and solve for x as shown below.

$$-10 = 5(x - 2) \quad \Longrightarrow \quad x = 0$$

Therefore, the value of x when $y = -10$ is 0.

14. (B)

In order for a number to be divisible by 3, the sum of its digits must be divisible by 3. Three-digit numbers are formed by using only the three digits, 1, 2, and 3. Since the sum of the three digits, $1 + 2 + 3 = 6$, is divisible by 3, all the three-digit numbers are divisible by 3. There are six three-digit numbers that are divisible by 3: 123, 132, 213, 231, 312, and 321.

15. (C)

Mr. Rhee traveled 120 miles at 60 miles per hour to visit his friend. It took him $\frac{120\,\text{miles}}{60\text{mph}}$ or 2 hours to drive to his friend's house. The total distance for the entire trip is 2×120 miles or 240 miles. Since the average speed for the entire trip is 40 miles per hour, the total time for the entire trip is $\frac{240\,\text{miles}}{40\text{mph}}$ or 6 hours. This implies that it took Mr. Rhee $6 - 2 = 4$ hours to drive back to his home. Therefore, the rate at which Mr. Rhee traveled on the way home is $\frac{120\,\text{miles}}{4\,\text{hours}}$ or 30 miles per hour.

16. (C)

Let x be the amount of money in Jason's savings account in the beginning. Jason spent half of his money, $\frac{x}{2}$, on books. The remaining money in his account is $x - \frac{x}{2}$ or $\frac{x}{2}$. A few days later, Jason spent $\frac{2}{3}$ of the remaining money, $\frac{2}{3} \times \frac{x}{2}$ or $\frac{x}{3}$ on clothes. Thus, the remaining balance in his account after spending money on books and clothes is $x - \frac{x}{2} - \frac{x}{3}$ or $\frac{x}{6}$. The table below summarizes how much money Jason spent on books and clothes and the remaining balance in terms of x.

Initial amount	Books	Clothes	Remaining balance
x	$\frac{x}{2}$	$\frac{2}{3} \times \frac{x}{2} = \frac{x}{3}$	$\frac{x}{6} = \$100$

Since the remaining balance, $\frac{x}{6}$, is \$100, solve the equation $\frac{x}{6} = 100$. Thus, $x = 600$. Therefore, Jason had \$600 in his savings account in the beginning.

17. (C)

In the figure below, $\triangle ACB$ and $\triangle AEB$ have the same base, $\overline{AB}$, and the same height, h. Thus, statement I is true.

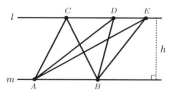

Since point C is closest to point A, and point E is farthest to point A, statement II is true. From the figure above, it is easily determined that $m\angle EAB < m\angle DAB < m\angle CAB$. Since lines l and m are parallel, $\angle CDA$ and $\angle DAB$ are alternate interior angles and congruent. Thus, $m\angle EAB < m\angle CDA < m\angle CAB$ is true, which means that statement III is false. Therefore, (C) is the correct answer.

18. (B)

The highest point on the graph of $y = -3(x + 1)^2 + 2$ is the vertex. Since the quadratic function $y = -3(x+1)^2 + 2$ is written in the vertex form, the coordinates of the vertex is $(-1, 2)$. Therefore, (B) is the correct answer.

   www.solomonacademy.net

19. (B)

Since the ratio of chocolate chip cookies to oatmeal cookies is $1:2$, let x and $2x$ be the number of chocolate chip cookies and oatmeal cookies, respectively. Joshua ate four chocolate chip cookies and half of the oatmeal cookies. Thus, the remaining chocolate chip cookies and oatmeal cookies are $x - 4$ and x, respectively. The table below summarizes the number of the chocolate and oatmeal cookies in terms of x.

	Chocolate chip	Oatmeal
Number of cookies in the beginning	x	$2x$
How many Joshua ate	4	$\frac{1}{2}(2x) = x$
How many cookies are left	$x - 4$	x

The new ratio of chocolate chip cookies to oatmeal is $3:4$. Set up an equation and solve for x as shown below.

$$\frac{x-4}{x} = \frac{3}{4} \qquad \text{Cross multiply}$$
$$4(x-4) = 3x \qquad \text{Use the distribute property to expand}$$
$$4x - 16 = 3x \qquad \text{Solve for } x$$
$$x = 16$$

Therefore, the number of chocolate chip cookies that are left in the jar is $x - 4 = 12$.

20. (A)

Define a and d as the first term and the common difference of the arithmetic sequence, respectively. Then, the first five terms of the arithmetic sequence can be expressed as a, $a + d$, $a + 2d$, $a + 3d$ and $a + 4d$. Since the sum of the first two terms is 7 and the sum of the next three terms is 33,

Sum of first two terms: $a + a + d = 7 \implies 2a + d = 7$

Sum of next three terms: $a + 2d + a + 3d + a + 4d = 33$
$$3a + 9d = 33 \implies a + 3d = 11$$

To find the first term in the sequence, use the linear combinations method.

$$2a + d = 7 \xrightarrow{\text{Multiply by 3}} 6a + 3d = 21$$
$$a + 3d = 11 \xrightarrow{\text{Multiply by } -1} -a - 3d = -11$$

Add the two equations to eliminate d variables.

$$\begin{array}{r} 6a + 3d = 21 \\ -a - 3d = -11 \\ \hline 5a \quad\quad = 10 \\ a = 2 \end{array} \qquad \text{Add two equations}$$

Therefore, the first term, a, in the sequence is 2.

Answers and Solutions
SAT Math Practice Test 7
Section 2

Answers

1. B	2. D	3. D	4. A
5. C	6. B	7. A	8. E
9. 5	10. 49	11. 75	12. 96
13. $\frac{2}{3}$	14. 36	15. 96	16. 59
17. 6	18. 200		

Solutions

1. **(B)**

   Every two pens you purchase, you get the third pen for free of charge. The cost of one pen is k. The cost of three pens is $2k$ since the third pen is free. In other words, you pay $2k$ for every three pens you purchase. Therefore, the total costs for 15 pens is $5 \times \$2k = \$10k$.

2. **(D)**

   Two angles are supplementary if the sum of the measures of the two angles is $180°$. Let x be the measure of angle A. Then, $2x + 30$ represents the measure of angle B. Set the sum of the two measures equal to $180°$ and solve for x.

   $$x + 2x + 30 = 180$$
   $$x = 50$$

   Therefore, the measure of angle B is $2x + 30 = 2(50) + 30 = 130°$.

3. **(D)**

   Use the properties of exponents: $(x^2)^3 = x^6$.

   (A) $x^2 \cdot x^3 = x^{2+3} = x^5$

   (B) $x^3 \cdot x^3 \cdot x^3 = x^{3+3+3} = x^9$

   (C) $\dfrac{x^{12}}{x^2} = x^{12-2} = x^{10}$

   (D) $\left(x^3\right)^2 = x^6$

   (E) $\left(x^{-1}\right)^7 = x^{-7}$

   Therefore, (D) is the correct answer.

4. (A)

Mr. Rhee was originally 180 pounds but lost 30 pounds.

$$\% \text{ loss} = \frac{30}{180} \times 100\% = \frac{1}{6} \times 100\% = 16\frac{2}{3}\%$$

Therefore, Mr. Rhee lost $16\frac{2}{3}\%$ of his weight.

5. (C)

For simplicity, let the volumes of the smaller cube and the larger cube be 8 and 27, respectively. Thus, the ratio of the volume of the smaller cube to that of the larger cube remains the same: $8 : 27$. The volume of a cube is s^3, where s is the side length of the cube. Thus, the side lengths of the smaller cube and the larger cube are 2 and 3, respectively. Since the surface area of a cube is $6s^2$, the ratio of the surface area of the smaller cube to that of the larger cube is $\frac{6(2)^2}{6(3)^2} = \frac{4}{9}$.

6. (B)

When $x = -2$, $\sqrt{2x+4}$ is equal to $\sqrt{2(-2)+4} = \sqrt{0} = 0$. Since 0 is not positive, statement I is false. When $2x + 4 \geq 0$, the expression inside the square root is greater than or equal to 0 and $\sqrt{2x+4}$ is defined. The domain of $\sqrt{2x+4}$ is a set of values of x for which $2x + 4 \geq 0$. Thus, the domain is $x \geq -2$ so statement III is false. As the value of x increases, the value of $\sqrt{2x+4}$ also increases. Thus, statement II is true. Therefore, (B) is the correct answer.

7. (A)

In the figure below, points D, E, and F are the midpoints of $\overline{AB}$, $\overline{BC}$, and $\overline{AC}$, respectively. Since the vertices $A(x, -2)$ and $B(y, 6)$ are given and the x-coordinate of midpoint D is 1, the x-coordinate of D can be expressed as $\frac{x+y}{2} = 1$ according to the midpoint formula $\left(\frac{x_1+x_2}{2}, \frac{y_1+y_2}{2}\right)$. Multiply each side of the equation, $\frac{x+y}{2} = 1$, by 2 to obtain $x + y = 2$.

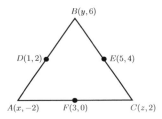

Likewise, the x-coordinate of E can be expressed as $\frac{y+z}{2} = 5$ which is equivalent to $y + z = 10$. The x-coordinate of F can be expressed as $\frac{z+x}{2} = 3$ which is equivalent to $z + x = 6$. Thus,

$$x + y = 2$$
$$y + z = 10$$
$$\underline{z + x = 6} \qquad \text{Add three equations}$$
$$2x + 2y + 2z = 18 \qquad \text{Divide each side by 2}$$
$$x + y + z = 9$$

Therefore, the sum of x, y, and z is 9.

8. (E)

For integers p and q, $p \blacktriangle q = p^2 + q^2$ and $p \blacktriangledown q = p^2 - q^2$. Thus, $x \blacktriangle y = x^2 + y^2 = 61$ and $x \blacktriangledown y = x^2 - y^2 = 11$.

$$x^2 + y^2 = 61$$
$$\underline{x^2 - y^2 = 11} \qquad \text{Add two equations}$$
$$2x^2 \quad\;\; = 72 \qquad \text{Divide each side by 2}$$
$$x^2 = 36$$

Since $x^2 = 36$ and $x^2 - y^2 = 11$, $y^2 = 25$. The solutions to $x^2 = 36$ and $y^2 = 25$ are $x = \pm 6$ and $y = \pm 5$, respectively. Therefore, the smallest value of $x + y$ is $-6 - 5 = -11$.

9. (5)

A number is an odd integer. If the number is multiplied by 2, the new number becomes an even integer. Therefore, there are 5 possible units digits for the new number: 2, 4, 6, 8, and 0.

10. (49)

The area of a circle is πr^2, where r is the radius. Since the radius of the circle is $\frac{7}{\sqrt{\pi}}$,

$$\text{Area of circle} = \pi \left(\frac{7}{\sqrt{\pi}}\right)^2 = \pi \times \frac{49}{\pi} = 49$$

Therefore, the area of the circle is 49.

11. (75)

The ratio of the interior angles of a triangle is $3 : 4 : 5$. Let $3x$, $4x$, and $5x$ be the measures of the interior angles of the triangle. Then, the sum of the measures of the interior angles can be expressed as $3x + 4x + 5x$ or $12x$. Since the sum of the measures of interior angles of any triangle is $180°$, $12x = 180°$. Thus, $x = 15°$. Therefore, the degree measure of the largest angle, $5x$, is $5 \times 15° = 75°$.

12. (96)

In the figure below, two identical squares with side length of 8 are overlapped such that one vertex of each square is at the center of the other square. The unshaded region represents the common area where the two squares overlap and is a square with side length of 4. Thus, the area of the unshaded region is 16.

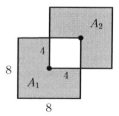

The area of the shaded region is the sum of the areas of A_1 and A_2. The area of each shaded region A_1 and A_2 is equal to the area of the square minus the area of the unshaded region, which is $64 - 16 = 48$. Therefore, the area of the shaded region is $A_1 + A_2 = 48 + 48 = 96$.

13. $\left(\frac{2}{3}\right)$

The line $y = ax - 1$ passes through point $(6, 3)$ which means that point $(6, 3)$ is on the line. Since point $(6, 3)$ in on the line, $(6, 3)$ is a solution to the equation $y = ax - 1$. Substitute 6 for x and 3 for y in the equation and solve for a.

$$y = ax - 1 \qquad \text{Substitute 6 for } x \text{ and 3 for } y$$
$$3 = 6a - 1 \qquad \text{Solve for } a$$
$$a = \frac{4}{6} \qquad \text{Simplify}$$
$$a = \frac{2}{3}$$

Therefore, the value of a is $\frac{2}{3}$.

14. (36)

This problem is about the geometric mean in a geometric sequence. In the geometric sequence $a, b, c, \cdots$, b is the geometric mean of a and c such that $b = \sqrt{ac}$. For instance, in the geometric sequence $2, 4, 8, \cdots$, 4 is the geometric mean of 2 and 8 because $4 = \sqrt{2 \times 8}$. Likewise, in the geometric sequence $4, x, 36, y, 324, \cdots$, 36 is the geometric mean of x and y. Thus, $36 = \sqrt{xy}$. Therefore, the value of $\sqrt{xy}$ is 36.

15. (96)

It's easier to calculate the profit if the number of oranges that Joshua buys and sells is the same. Since Joshua buys a package of 4 oranges and sells a package of 3 oranges, the least common multiple (LCM) of 3 and 4 is 12. This means that if Joshua buys 12 oranges for $3 \times \$0.75 = \$2.25$ and sells 12 oranges for $4 \times \$1 = \$4$, he makes $\$4 - \$2.25 = \$1.75$ profit for every 12 oranges that he sells. Since $\dfrac{\$14}{\$1.75} = 8$, the number of oranges that Joshua needs to sell to make profit of \$14 is 8×12 or 96.

16. (59)

Let x be the fixed daily fee and y be the total hourly charge on the first day. Sue paid \$99 which includes the fixed daily fee and the total hourly charge on the first day. This can be expressed as $x + y = 99$. On the second day, she drove the car three times as much as she did on the first day and paid \$179, which can be expressed as $x + 3y = 179$. Use the linear combinations method to solve for y.

$$
\begin{aligned}
x + 3y &= 179 \\
\underline{x + y} &= \underline{99} \qquad && \text{Subtract two equations} \\
2y &= 80 \qquad && \text{Divide each side by 2} \\
y &= 40
\end{aligned}
$$

Since $y = 40$ and $x + y = 99$, $x = 59$. Therefore, the fixed daily fee, x, is \$59.

17. (6)

Both the mean and the mode of the set $\{7, 11, 11, 15\}$ are 11. After adding four positive integers to the set, the mean of the new set is 10 which means that the sum of the eight integers in the new set is $8 \times 10 = 80$. Since the sum of the four positive integers in the set, $7 + 11 + 11 + 15$, is 44, the sum of four positive integers that are added to the set is $80 - 44 = 36$. The mode of the new set is 10. This implies that three of the four positive integers that are added to the set are 10. Since the sum of four positive integers that are added to the set is 36, the four positive integers that are added to the set are 10, 10, 10, and 6. Therefore, the smallest integer for the new set $\{6, 7, 10, 10, 10, 11, 11, 15\}$ is 6.

18. (200)

In the figure below, the radius of each of the two identical circles is 20. Since $\overline{AB}, \overline{BC}, \overline{CD}, \overline{AD}$, and $\overline{AC}$ are radii, $AB = BC = CD = AD = AC = 10$. Thus, $\triangle ABC$ and $\triangle ADC$ are both equilateral triangles with side length 20.

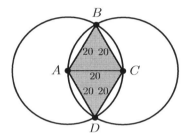

The area of an equilateral triangle is $\frac{\sqrt{3}}{4}s^2$, where s is side length. Thus, the area of each $\triangle ABC$ and $\triangle ADC$ is $\frac{\sqrt{3}}{4}(20)^2 = 100\sqrt{3}$. Since the area of the shaded region equals the sum of the areas of $\triangle ABC$ and $\triangle ADC$, the area of the shaded region is $100\sqrt{3} + 100\sqrt{3} = 200\sqrt{3}$. Therefore, the value of n is 200.

Answers and Solutions
SAT Math Practice Test 7
Section 3

Answers

1. C	2. C	3. D	4. B
5. E	6. A	7. D	8. E
9. C	10. B	11. B	12. A
13. D	14. D	15. D	16. B

Solutions

1. (C)

$$4(x + 2) = 16 \qquad \text{Divide each side by 4}$$
$$x + 2 = 4 \qquad \text{Subtract 2 from each side}$$
$$x = 2$$

Therefore, the value of $\frac{x+4}{2}$ is $\frac{2+4}{2} = 3$.

2. (C)

Since C is located at 1 and $A - C = 2$, $A = 3$. Furthermore, since C is located at 1 and $B - C = -2$, $B = -1$. Therefore, the distance between points A and B is $3 - (-1)$ or 4.

3. (D)

There are three time periods at which the price of gasoline decreases: from May to June, from July to August, and from August to September as shown on the table below.

Month	Regular gas price
May	$3.71
June	$3.57
July	$3.64
August	$3.61
September	$3.37
October	$3.49

From May to June, the price of gasoline is decreased by $0.14. From July to August, the price of gasoline is decreased by $0.03. Furthermore, From August to September, the price is decreased by $0.24. Therefore, (D) is the correct answer.

4. (B)

Cross multiply and solve for x.

$$\frac{4}{x+3} = \frac{6}{x+4}$$ Cross multiply

$$6(x+3) = 4(x+4)$$ Use the distributive property

$$6x + 18 = 4x + 16$$ Solve for x

$$2x = -2$$

$$x = -1$$

Therefore, the value of x is -1.

5. (E)

Each face of a cube is a square. In the figure below, the three segments $\overline{AC}$, $\overline{CD}$, and $\overline{AD}$ are the diagonals of the square faces and are same in length. Thus, $\triangle ACD$ is an equilateral triangle.

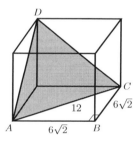

$\overline{AC}$ is the diagonal of the square face and is the hypotenuse of the $\triangle ABC$, which is a 45°-45°-90° special right triangle whose sides are in ratio $1 : 1 : \sqrt{2}$. Since the length of the hypotenuse, AC, is $\sqrt{2}$ times the length of one leg, AB, $AC = AB \times \sqrt{2} = 6\sqrt{2} \times \sqrt{2} = 12$. Therefore, the perimeter of the triangle is $3 \times AC = 3 \times 12 = 36$.

6. (A)

In the Venn diagram below, C represents students who take chess club, S represents students who take swimming club, and $C \cap S$ represents students who take both chess club and swimming club.

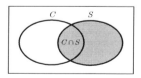

All the students taking swimming club are juniors, which is represented by the shaded region in the diagram above. Thus, any students who belong to the shaded region are also juniors. Since $C \cap S$, the common area where C and S overlap, belongs to the shaded region, students taking both chess club and swimming club must be juniors. Therefore, (A) is the correct answer.

7. (D)

1% means 1 out of 100. Thus, 75% means 75 out of 100, which is equivalent to $\frac{75}{100} = \frac{3}{4}$. Likewise, 120% is equivalent to $\frac{120}{100} = \frac{6}{5}$. x is 25% less than y. In other words, x is 75% of y which can be expressed as $x = \frac{3}{4}y$. Since z is 20% more than y, z is 120% of y which can be expressed as $z = \frac{6}{5}y$.

$$\text{Ratio of } z \text{ to } x = \frac{z}{x} = \frac{\frac{6}{5}y}{\frac{3}{4}y} = \frac{\frac{6}{5}}{\frac{3}{4}} = \frac{8}{5}$$

Therefore, the ratio of z to x is $8 : 5$.

8. (E)

In the figure below, both $\triangle ACB$ and $\triangle ADB$ are isosceles triangles. The sum of the measures of interior angles of a triangle is $180°$. Since $m\angle C = 84°$, $m\angle CAB = m\angle CBA = \frac{180-84}{2} = 48°$.

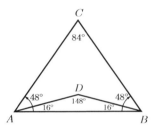

Since $m\angle DAB = \frac{1}{3}m\angle CAB$, $m\angle DAB = m\angle DBA = \frac{1}{3}(48°) = 16°$. Therefore, the degree measure of $\angle D$ is $180° - m\angle DAB - m\angle DBA$ or $180° - 16° - 16° = 148°$.

9. (C)

Two quadratic functions $y = x^2 - 4$ and $y = x^2 - 5x$ intersect as shown below.

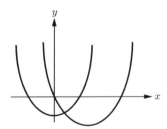

In order to find the x-coordinate of the intersection point, set both equations equal to each other and solve for x.

$$x^2 - 5x = x^2 - 4 \qquad \text{Subtract } x^2 \text{ from each side}$$
$$-5x = -4 \qquad \text{Divide each side by } -5$$
$$x = \frac{4}{5}$$

Therefore, the x-coordinate of the intersection point is $\frac{4}{5}$.

10. (B)

Convert 2000 and 5000 to scientific notation as 2×10^3 and 5×10^3, respectively.

$$2000 \times 5000 = 2 \times 10^3 \times 5 \times 10^3$$
$$= 10 \times 10^6$$
$$= 1 \times 10^7$$

Since the product of 2000 and 5000 can be written as $1 \times 10^{n-1}$, $n - 1$ must be equal to 7. Therefore, the value of n is 8.

11. (B)

In the figure below, a horizontal line $y = k$ intersects a function $f(x)$ shown below.

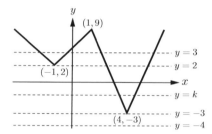

Depending on the value of k, the number of times that the horizontal line $y = k$ intersects the function $f(x)$ varies. If $2 < k < 9$, $y = k$ intersects the function $f(x)$ four times. For instance, when $k = 3$, the horizontal line $y = 3$ intersects the function four times. If $-3 < k < 2$, the horizontal line $y = k$ intersects the function $f(x)$ twice. Therefore, the value of k is $-3 < k < 2$.

12. (A)

Jason filled a cup with equal amounts of orange juice, apple juice, and grape juice. Thus, the amount of each fruit juice was equal to $\frac{1}{3}$ of the cup as shown in figure 1.

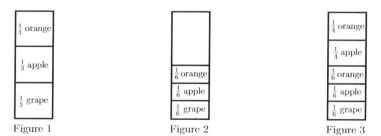

After Jason drank half of the cup, the remaining fractional part of each fruit juice was $\frac{1}{6}$ of the cup as shown in figure 2. Afterwards, Jason filled the remaining cup with equal amounts of orange and apple juice. Since only half of the cup was available to fill, Jason added $\frac{1}{4}$ cup of orange juice and $\frac{1}{4}$ cup of apple juice as shown in figure 3. Therefore, the fractional part of the cup was filled with the apple juice is $\frac{1}{6} + \frac{1}{4} = \frac{5}{12}$.

     www.solomonacademy.net

13. (D)

Group 2 numbers to make a pair as shown below.

$$\begin{aligned}
S &= -1 + 2 - 3 + 4 + \cdots - 97 + 98 - 99 + 100 \\
&= (-1 + 2) + (-3 + 4) + \cdots + (-97 + 98) + (-99 + 100) \\
&= 1 + 1 + \cdots + 1 + 1 \\
&= 50
\end{aligned}$$

The sum of each pair is 1. Since there are 50 pairs, the sum of the 50 pairs is 50. Therefore, the value of S is 50.

14. (D)

Use the linear combinations method. Multiply the first equation by 3 and the second equation by -2.

$$2x + 3y = 26 \quad \xrightarrow{\text{Multiply by 3}} \quad 6x + 9y = 78$$

$$3x - 2y = 13 \quad \xrightarrow{\text{Multiply by } -2} \quad -6x + 4y = -26$$

Add equations to eliminate x variables.

$$\begin{aligned}
6x + 9y &= 78 \\
\underline{-6x + 4y} &= \underline{-26} \qquad \text{Add two equations} \\
13y &= 52 \\
y &= 4
\end{aligned}$$

Substitute 4 for y in the second equation and solve for x.

$$\begin{aligned}
3x - 2y &= 13 && \text{Substitute 4 for } y \\
3x - 2(4) &= 13 && \text{Add 8 to each side and then solve for } x \\
x &= 7
\end{aligned}$$

Therefore, the value of $x + y = 7 + 4 = 11$.

15. (D)

If you cross multiply a proportion $\dfrac{a}{b} = \dfrac{c}{d}$, you will get $ad = bc$. Cross multiply proportions in the answer choices to determine which proportion is not equivalent to $ad = bc$. The proportions in answer choices (A), (B), and (C) are equivalent to $ad = bc$. To determine if the proportion in answer choice (E), $\frac{a+b}{b} = \frac{c+d}{d}$, is equivalent to $ad = bc$, cross multiply and simplify it.

$$\begin{aligned}
\frac{a+b}{b} &= \frac{c+d}{d} && \text{Cross multiply} \\
d(a+b) &= b(c+d) && \text{Use the distributive property} \\
ad + bd &= bc + bd && \text{Subtract } bd \text{ from each side} \\
ad &= bc
\end{aligned}$$

Thus, the proportion in answer choice (E) is equivalent to $ad = bc$. Therefore, (D) is the correct answer.

16. (B)

In the figure below, O is the center of the larger semicircle with a radius of 10 and C is the center of the smaller semicircle which is inscribed in the larger semicircle. Since $\overline{OA}$ and $\overline{OB}$ are the radii of the larger semicircle, $OA = OB = 10$. Since any triangle inscribed in the semicircle is a right triangle, $\triangle OAB$ is a 45°-45°-90° special right triangle whose sides are in the ratio $1 : 1 : \sqrt{2}$. The length of the hypotenuse, AB, is $\sqrt{2}$ times the length of each leg. Thus, $AB = \sqrt{2} \times OA = 10\sqrt{2}$. Since AB is the diameter of the smaller semicircle, the radius of the smaller semicircle, AC, is $5\sqrt{2}$.

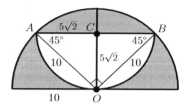

The area of the shaded region is equal to the area of the larger semicircle minus the area of the smaller semicircle. Thus,

$$\text{Area of shaded region} = \text{Area of larger semicircle} - \text{Area of smaller semicircle}$$
$$= \frac{1}{2}\pi(10)^2 - \frac{1}{2}\pi(5\sqrt{2})^2$$
$$= 50\pi - 25\pi$$
$$= 25\pi$$

Therefore, the area of the shaded region is 25π.

Answers and Solutions
SAT Math Practice Test 8
Section 1

Answers

1. B	2. D	3. A	4. B	5. B
6. D	7. A	8. C	9. C	10. A
11. B	12. E	13. C	14. B	15. E
16. D	17. C	18. A	19. B	20. E

Solutions

1. (B)

   The area and height of a triangle is $10\sqrt{3}$ and 5, respectively. Use the area of a triangle formula, $A = \frac{1}{2}bh$, to find the base of the triangle.

   $$A = \frac{1}{2}bh \qquad \text{Substitute } 10\sqrt{3} \text{ for } A \text{ and } 5 \text{ for } h$$
   $$10\sqrt{3} = \frac{1}{2}(5)b \qquad \text{Divide each side by 5}$$
   $$2\sqrt{3} = \frac{1}{2}b \qquad \text{Multiply each side by 2}$$
   $$b = 4\sqrt{3}$$

   Therefore, the base of the triangle is $4\sqrt{3}$.

2. (D)

   In the figure below, 4 congruent squares are placed side by side to form a rectangle. Define x as the length of each square. Then, the perimeter of the rectangle can be expressed as $10x$. Since the perimeter of the rectangle is 50, $10x = 50$. Thus, $x = 5$.

   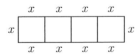

   The area of each square is $x^2 = 5^2 = 25$. Therefore, the area of two squares is $2 \times 25 = 50$.

3. (A)

   The mean of three numbers is 5 which means that the sum of these three numbers is $5 \times 3 = 15$. Since 13 is added to the sum of the three numbers, the sum of the four numbers is $15 + 13 = 28$. Therefore, the mean of the four numbers is $\frac{28}{4} = 7$.

4. (B)

There are 60 minutes in one hour. To find out how fast Sue traveled in miles per hour, set up a proportion in terms of miles and minutes.

$$42 \text{ miles} : 45 \text{ minutes} = x \text{ miles} : 60 \text{ minutes}$$

$$\frac{42}{45} = \frac{x}{60} \qquad \text{Use cross product property}$$

$$45x = 42 \times 60 \qquad \text{Divide each side by 45}$$

$$x = \frac{42 \times 60}{45} \qquad \text{Simplify}$$

$$x = 56$$

$x = 56$ means that Sue traveled 56 miles in one hour. Therefore, she traveled at 56 miles per hour.

5. (B)

Since $f(x) = x^2 + 3x - 4$, multiply each side of the equation by -1 to find $-f(x)$.

$$f(x) = x^2 + 3x - 4 \qquad \text{Multiply each side of the equation by } -1$$

$$-f(x) = -x^2 - 3x + 4$$

To find the y-intercept of $-f(x)$, substitute 0 for x in the equation $-f(x) = -x^2 - 3x + 4$.

$$-f(x) = -x^2 - 3x + 4 \qquad \text{Substitute 0 for } x$$

$$-f(0) = -(0)^2 - 3(0) + 4 = 4$$

Therefore, the y-intercept of $-f(x)$ is 4.

6. (D)

Convert $1,000,000$ to scientific notation as 1×10^6. According to the table below, when the energy, $E = 1 \times 10^6$, the energy conversion, $C = 6$.

E(Energy)	C(Energy Conversion)
$1 \times 10^4 \leq E < 1 \times 10^5$	4
$1 \times 10^5 \leq E < 1 \times 10^6$	5
$1 \times 10^6 \leq E < 1 \times 10^7$	6
$1 \times 10^7 \leq E < 1 \times 10^8$	7

To find the Richter scale, R, substitute 6 for C in the equation $R = \frac{2}{3}C + 1.5$.

$$R = \frac{2}{3}C + 1.5 \qquad \text{Substitute 6 for } C$$

$$= \frac{2}{3}(6) + 1.5$$

$$= 5.5$$

Therefore, the value of the Richter scale, R, when $E = 1,000,000$ is 5.5

7. (A)

The vertex of a quadratic function written in vertex form $y = (x - h)^2 + k$ is (h, k). For instance, the vertex of a quadratic function $y = (x - 4)^2$ is $(4, 0)$. The graphs below show the quadratic functions given in the answer choices.

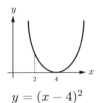
$y = (x - 4)^2$

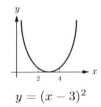
$y = (x - 3)^2$

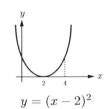
$y = (x - 2)^2$

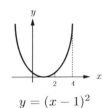
$y = (x - 1)^2$

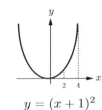
$y = (x + 1)^2$

Only $y = (x - 4)^2$ is the quadratic function that is decreasing over the entire interval $2 < x < 4$. Therefore, (A) is the correct answer.

8. (C)

The degree measure of the arc in a circle is $360°$. If all six angles in the figure below were congruent, the measure of each angle would be $\frac{360}{6} = 60°$.

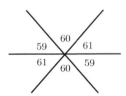

However, the measures of the six angles are integer values and not all congruent. Thus, the measure of some of the six angles are not $60°$. To determine the smallest possible degree measure of the largest angle, add the smallest positive integer value of the measure of an angle, $1°$, to $60°$. Therefore, the smallest possible degree measure of the largest angle is $61°$.

9. (C)

The tens' and ones' place can be either 1, 2, or 3 with replacement. Therefore, there are $3 \times 3 = 9$ possible two-digit numbers: 11, 12, 13, 21, 22, 23, 31, 32, and 33.

10. (A)

The area of a trapezoid is $\frac{1}{2}(b_1 + b_2)h$, where b_1 and b_2 are the lengths of the top side and bottom side, respectively, and h is the height of the trapezoid. In the figure below, $b_1 = 4$, $b_2 = 8$, and $h = 5$.

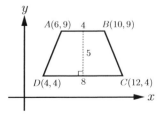

Therefore, the area of the trapezoid is $\frac{1}{2}(4 + 8)(5)$ or 30.

11. (B)

List prime numbers: $2, 3, 5, 7, 11, \cdots$. It is worth noting that 2 is the smallest and the first prime number, and the only even prime number. Other than 2, all the prime numbers are odd numbers. If $n = 2$ and $k = 3$, $n + k = 5$ and $nk = 6$. Thus, eliminate answer choices (A) and (C). If $n = 5$ and $k = 3$, $n + k = 8$, which is not a prime number. Eliminate answer choice (D). Finally, If $k = 7$ and $n = 5$, $k - n = 2$, which is not divisible by 3. Eliminate answer choice (E). If $n > 2$ and $k > 2$, n and k are odd numbers. Thus, $n + k$ is an even number. Therefore, (B) is the correct answer.

12. (E)

Use the properties of exponents.

$$9(9)^3 = 9^{1+3} = (3^2)^4 = 3^8$$

13. (C)

The table below shows the assigned values for each alphabet letter.

Alphabet	A	B	C	$\cdots$	L	M	N	O	$\cdots$	S	$\cdots$	Z
Assigned value	1	2	3	$\cdots$	12	13	14	15	$\cdots$	19	$\cdots$	26

The letter L, M, N, O, and S have assigned values of 12, 13, 14, 15, and 19, respectively. Therefore,

$$\text{Sum of assigned values of SOLOMON} = 19 + 15 + 12 + 15 + 13 + 15 + 14 = 103$$

14. (B)

Factor out ab from $a^2b + ab^2$. Thus, $a^2b + ab^2 = ab(a + b)$. Since $a + b = 1$ and $ab = -12$, the value of $a^2b + ab^2 = ab(a + b) = -12$.

15. (E)

In the figure below, $\triangle AED$, $\triangle EBC$, and $\triangle DEC$ have the same height of 6. Since the area of a triangle is $\frac{1}{2}bh$, the areas of $\triangle AED$, $\triangle EBC$, and $\triangle DEC$ can be written as $\frac{1}{2}AE(6)$, $\frac{1}{2}BE(6)$, and $\frac{1}{2}DC(6)$, respectively.

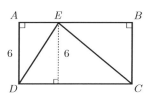

The ratio of the areas of $\triangle AED$, $\triangle EBC$, and $\triangle DEC$ is $1 : 2 : 3$. Thus,

$$\frac{1}{2}AE(6) : \frac{1}{2}BE(6) : \frac{1}{2}DC(6) = 1 : 2 : 3 \qquad \text{Multiply left side by 2}$$
$$6AE : 6BE : 6DC = 1 : 2 : 3 \qquad \text{Divide left side by 6}$$
$$AE : BE : DC = 1 : 2 : 3$$

Therefore, $AE : BE : DC = 1 : 2 : 3$. In general, if triangles have the same height but have different bases, the ratio of their areas is the same as the ratio of their bases.

16. (D)

Translate the verbal phrases into mathematical expressions. Define x as the original number. A number is increased by 8 and then the result is doubled can be expressed as $2(x + 8)$. One less than three times the original number can be expressed as $3x - 1$. Set the two expressions equal to each other and solve for x.

$$2(x + 8) = 3x - 1$$
$$2x + 16 = 3x - 1$$
$$x = 17$$

Therefore, the value of the original number, x, is 17.

17. (C)

Define x as the acceptable tire pressure for a certain car model. Since the acceptable tire pressure is between 28 PSI and 32 PSI, inclusive, it can be written as $28 \leq x \leq 32$. Instead of solving each inequality in the answer choices to find out which inequality has the solution $28 \leq x \leq 32$, directly set up an absolute value inequality from the solution. The mean of 28 and 32 is $\frac{28+32}{2} = 30$. 28 is far left from the mean, and 32 is far right from mean. Both 28 and 32 are 2 units from the mean. Since we try to find all the numbers within 2 units from the mean, the inequality can be expressed as $|x - \text{Mean}| \leq \text{Distance}$. Thus, the inequality that has the solution $28 \leq x \leq 32$ is $|x - 30| \leq 2$. Therefore, (C) is the correct answer.

18. (A)

Points $A(x, -2)$, $B(-1, 2)$, and $C(3, 5)$ are on the same coordinates plane. Use the distance formula, $d = \sqrt{(x_2 - x_1)^2 + (y_2 - y_1)^2}$, to determine BC.

$$BC = \sqrt{(x_2 - x_1)^2 + (y_2 - y_1)^2}$$
$$= \sqrt{(3 - (-1))^2 + (5 - 2)^2}$$
$$= 5$$

Since $AB = BC$, $AB = 5$. Set up an expression for AB by using the distance formula and solve for x.

$$AB = \sqrt{(x - (-1))^2 + (-2 - 2)^2} \qquad \text{Substitute 5 for } AB$$
$$\sqrt{(x - (-1))^2 + (-2 - 2)^2} = 5 \qquad \text{Square each side}$$
$$(x + 1)^2 + 4^2 = 25 \qquad \text{Subtract 16 from each side}$$
$$(x + 1)^2 = 9 \qquad \text{Take the square root of each side}$$
$$x + 1 = \pm 3 \qquad \text{Solve for } x$$
$$x + 1 = 3 \quad \text{or} \quad x + 1 = -3$$
$$x = 2 \quad \text{or} \quad x = -4$$

The possible values for x are 2 and -4. Therefore, (A) is the correct answer.

19. (B)

A circular track whose circumference is 120 meters has 6 different labeled positions: A, B, C, D, E, and F. There are $\frac{120}{6} = 20$ meters in between each different labeled position. Joshua and Jason run in opposite directions from position A at a rate of 4 meters per second clockwise and 2 meters per second counterclockwise, respectively. Let t be the time when Joshua and Jason meet for the first time. Then, the distances that Joshua and Jason run for time t are $4t$ and $2t$, respectively. When Joshua and Jason meet for the first time, the sum of the distances they run is equal to the circumference of the circular track, 120 meters. Set up an equation in terms of the sum of distances and solve for t.

$$4t + 2t = 120 \quad \Longrightarrow \quad t = 20$$

$t = 20$ implies that Joshua and Jason meet each other every 20 seconds. Joshua and Jason meet for the first time at $t = 20$ and second time at $t = 40$. At $t = 40$, Joshua runs $4 \times 40 = 160$ meters and Jason runs $2 \times 40 = 80$ meters. Therefore, Joshua and Jason meet each other for the second time at position C.

20. (E)

Three numbers are selected at random without replacement from the set $\{1, 2, 3, 4\}$ to form a three-digit number. To find the total number of three-digit numbers, use the fundamental counting principle. Define event 1, event 2, and event 3 as selecting a digit for the hundreds' place, tens' place, and ones' place, respectively. Event 1 has 4 ways to select a digit out of 4 digits. After one digit is taken, event 2 has 3 ways, and event 3 has 2 ways to select a digit. Thus, there are $4 \times 3 \times 2 = 24$ possible three-digit numbers using 1, 2, 3, and 4. Out of 24 possible three-digit numbers, there are four three-digit numbers that satisfy $A < B < C$: 123, 124, 134, and 234. Therefore, the probability that the three-digit number formed is an increasing number is $\frac{4}{24}$ or $\frac{1}{6}$.

Answers and Solutions
SAT Math Practice Test 8
Section 2

Answers

1. C	2. A	3. E	4. C
5. D	6. E	7. E	8. D
9. 9	10. 10	11. 360	12. 125
13. 7	14. 259	15. 20	16. 17
17. 16	18. 9		

Solutions

1. (C)

In order to multiply two binomials, use the distributive property.

$$(x-1)(x+2) = x^2 + 2x - x - 2 \qquad \text{Use the distributive property}$$
$$= x^2 + x - 2$$

2. (A)

Three fifths of students in a class are boys. One third of the boys in the class wear glasses. This means that the fractional part of the students in the class who are boys that wear glasses is $\frac{1}{3} \times \frac{3}{5}$ or $\frac{1}{5}$.

3. (E)

In the figure below, $BA = 7$ and $CD = 8$. The two segments $\overline{BA}$ and $\overline{CD}$ are overlapped so that the four points A, C, B, and D are arranged in that order and are on the same line.

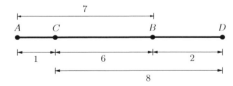

Since $BA = 7$ and $BC = 6$, $AC = 1$. Additionally, since $CD = 8$ and $BC = 6$, $BD = 2$. Therefore, the length of $\overline{AD}$ is $AC + BC + BD = 1 + 6 + 2$ or 9.

4. (C)

The graph of a quadratic function $y = x^2 - 5x + 6$ is shown below. Change standard form $y = x^2 - 5x + 6$ to factored form as $y = (x - 2)(x - 3)$.

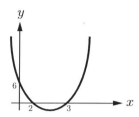

To find the x-intercepts of the quadratic function $y = (x - 2)(x - 3)$, substitute 0 for y and solve for x. The x-intercepts of the quadratic functions are 2 and 3. To find the y-intercept of the quadratic function, substitute 0 for x. Thus, the y-intercept of the quadratic function is $y = (0 - 2)(0 - 3) = 6$. Therefore, the total number of the y-intercept(s) and x-intercept(s) is 3.

5. (D)

In the venn diagram below, define M, C, $M \cup C$, and $M \cap C$ as the number of students who are taking math, chemistry, either math or chemistry, and both math and chemistry, respectively.

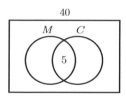

There are 40 students who are taking either math or chemistry and 5 students who are taking both math and chemistry. Thus, $M \cup C = 40$ and $M \cap C = 5$. Since the number of students taking math is twice as many as the number of students taking chemistry, $M = 2C$.

$$M \cup C = M + C - M \cap C \qquad \text{Substitute } 2C \text{ for } M$$
$$40 = 2C + C - 5$$
$$3C = 45$$
$$C = 15$$

Since $M = 2C$, $M = 2 \times 15 = 30$. Therefore, the number of students taking math is 30.

6. (E)

A line $ax + by = 5$ can be written in slope-intercept form as $y = -\frac{a}{b}x + \frac{5}{b}$. Since the two lines $ax + by = 5$ and $y = \frac{3}{4}x$ are parallel, their slopes must be the same. The slopes of the two lines are $-\frac{a}{b}$ and $\frac{3}{4}$. Thus,

$$-\frac{a}{b} = \frac{3}{4} \quad \Longrightarrow \quad \frac{a}{b} = -\frac{3}{4}$$

Therefore, the value of $\frac{a}{b}$ is $-\frac{3}{4}$.

7. (E)

$$\frac{1}{\sqrt{x-2}} = \sqrt{x-2}$$ Multiply each side by $\sqrt{x-2}$

$$\sqrt{x-2} \cdot \frac{1}{\sqrt{x-2}} = \sqrt{x-2} \cdot \sqrt{x-2}$$ Simplify

$$x - 2 = 1$$

$$x = 3$$

Therefore, the solution to the equation is $x = 3$.

8. (D)

In the figure below, the radius of the circle is 6. Segments $\overline{AB}$ and $\overline{AC}$ are tangent to the circle at points B and C and are perpendicular to the radii drawn to points B and C. Thus, $m\angle OBA = m\angle OCA = 90°$.

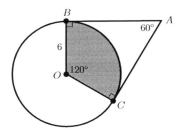

The area of the shaded region equals the area of the sector. To find the area of the sector, it is necessary to find the measure of the central angle of the sector. Points A, B, O, and C form a quadrilateral whose sum of the measures of interior angles is 360°. Since $m\angle A = 60°$, the measure of the central angle, $m\angle BOC$, can be determined by $360° - 90° - 90° - 60°$ or 120°. Thus,

$$\text{Area of sector} = \pi r^2 \times \frac{\theta}{360°}, \text{ where } \theta \text{ is the central angle}$$

$$= \pi (6)^2 \times \frac{120°}{360°}$$

$$= 12\pi$$

Therefore, the area of the shaded region is 12π.

9. (9)

$$x(y + z) = 24$$ Substitute 2 for x and 3 for z

$$2(y + 3) = 24$$ Divide each side by 2

$$y + 3 = 12$$ Subtract 3 from each side

$$y = 9$$

Therefore, the value of y is 9.

10. (10)

A chord is a line segment that connects two points on the circle. There are five points on the circle as shown below: A, B, C, D, and E. Choose any two points to draw a chord. Note that $\overline{AB}$ and $\overline{BA}$ are the same chord so do not draw it twice. There are 10 different chords can be drawn: $\overline{AB}$, $\overline{AC}$, $\overline{AD}$, $\overline{AE}$, $\overline{BC}$, $\overline{BD}$, $\overline{BE}$, $\overline{CD}$, $\overline{CE}$, and $\overline{DE}$.

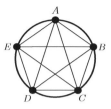

Additionally, the total number of chords can be easily determined by the combination formula, $_nC_r = \frac{n!}{(n-r)! \times r!}$. Out of 5 points, choose 2 points to draw a chord. Thus, the total number of chords is $_5C_2 = \frac{5!}{3! \times 2!} = 10$. Therefore, the total number of chords that can be drawn is 10.

11. (360)

The figure below can be broken up into two different triangles whose sum of the measures of interior angles is 180° each.

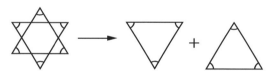

Therefore, the sum of the measures of all the marked angles is $180° + 180° = 360°$.

12. (125)

The table below shows a pattern such that $y = x^3$. For instance, when $x = 4$, $y = 4^3 = 64$.

x	2	3	4	5
y	8	27	64	k

Therefore, the value of k when $x = 5$ is $k = 5^3 = 125$.

13. (7)

Square both sides to eliminate the square root in the equation $\sqrt{x^2 + 15} = 8$.

$$\sqrt{x^2 + 15} = 8 \qquad \text{Square both sides}$$
$$x^2 + 15 = 64 \qquad \text{Subtract 15 from each side}$$
$$x^2 = 49 \qquad \text{Take the square root of each side}$$
$$x = \pm 7 \qquad \text{Since } x > 0$$
$$x = 7$$

Therefore, the solution to the equation $\sqrt{x^2 + 15} = 8$ is 7.

14. (259)

Machine A can print 30 posters in 20 minutes or 90 posters in an hour. Machine B can print 62 posters in 30 minutes or 124 posters in an hour. In the first half hour, only machine A prints the posters. Thus, it prints $90 \times \frac{1}{2} = 45$ posters alone. In the next hour, both machine A and B print together. Thus, they print $90 + 124 = 214$ posters together. Therefore, the total number of posters that machine A and machine B print is $45 + 214 = 259$.

15. (20)

In the figure below, M, C, and B represent McLean, Centreville, and Brambleton, respectively. Centreville is 16 miles due south of McLean and 12 miles due east of Brambleton.

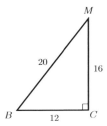

To find the distance between McLean and Brambleton, MB, use the Pythagorean theorem: $MB^2 = 12^2 + 16^2$ or use a multiple of the Pythagorean Triple: $(3 - 4 - 5) \times 4 = 12 - 16 - 20$. Thus, $MB = 20$. Therefore, McLean and Brambleton are 20 miles apart.

16. (17)

It is worth noting that an inequality symbol is reversed when each side of the inequality is divided by a negative number.

$$-49 \leq -3x + 2 < 11 \qquad \text{Subtract 2 from each side}$$
$$-51 \leq -3x < 9 \qquad \text{Divide each side by } -3$$
$$-3 < x \leq 17 \qquad \text{Reverse the inequality symbol}$$
$$x = -2, -1, 0, 1, \cdots, 16, 17 \qquad \text{Since } x \text{ is an integer}$$

Although there are 20 possible integer values of x: $-2, -1, 0, \cdots, 16, 17$, exclude the 3 non-positive integers: $-2, -1$, and 0. Therefore, there are $20 - 3 = 17$ positive integer values of x that satisfy $-49 \leq -3x + 2 < 11$.

17. (16)

The mean of a set of five positive integers is 10, which means that the sum of the five integers is 50. Since the mode and the median of the set are 5 and 9, respectively, the set has the following five integers, which are arranged from least to greatest: $5, 5, 9, x$ and y, where x and y are unknown integers and $x < y$. Since the sum of the five integers is 50,

$$\text{Sum} = 5 + 5 + 9 + x + y = 50 \implies x + y = 31$$

To find the greatest possible range of the set, $y - 5$, x must be the smallest possible integer value and y must be largest possible integer value given that $x + y = 31$. Since $x > 9$, $x = 10$ because the smallest possible integer greater than 9 is 10. Since $x + y = 31$ and $x = 10$, $y = 21$. Therefore, the greatest possible range, $y - 5$, of the set of five integers is $21 - 5 = 16$.

18. (9)

In the figure below, there are three circles with a radius of 3. Draw three segments, $\overline{AB}$, $\overline{BC}$, and $\overline{AC}$, that connect the centers of each circle. The three segments form an equilateral triangle ABC with side length of 6. The height, $\overline{BD}$, is drawn from vertex B to side AC so that $\triangle ABC$ is divided into two 30°-60°-90° special right triangles whose sides are in the ratio $1 : \sqrt{3} : 2$.

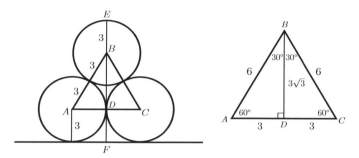

In $\triangle ABD$, $\overline{BD}$ is the longer leg and also the height of $\triangle ABC$. Thus, $BD = 3\sqrt{3}$. The distance between the top of the third orange to the ground, EF, is equal to the sum of the height of $\triangle ABC$, BD, and two radii. Thus, $EF = EB + BD + DF = 6 + 3\sqrt{3}$. Therefore, the value of $a + b = 6 + 3 = 9$.

Answers and Solutions
SAT Math Practice Test 8
Section 3

Answers

1. E	2. A	3. C	4. B
5. C	6. B	7. A	8. C
9. D	10. D	11. C	12. E
13. A	14. D	15. C	16. B

Solutions

1. (E)

   Use the property of exponent: $a^m \cdot a^n = a^{m+n}$.

   $$2^n = 2^3 \times 2^5 = 2^{3+5} = 2^8$$

   Thus, $2^n = 2^8$. Therefore, $n = 8$.

2. (A)

   $$\text{Volume of a cylinder} = \text{Base area} \times \text{Height}$$
   $$= 36\pi \times 6$$
   $$= 216\pi$$

3. (C)

   The table below shows the grams of protein for each type of food that Joshua ate for his breakfast.

Per serving	Protein	Food that Joshua ate	Protein that Joshua ate
1 scrambled egg	7g	2 scrambled eggs	14g
1 strip of bacon	2.5g	2 strips of bacon	5g
1 cup of hash brown	2.8g	$\frac{1}{2}$ cup of hash brown	1.4g
1 slice of bread	4g	2 slices of bread	8g

   According to the table above, the total grams of protein that Joshua ate in his breakfast is $14 + 5 + 1.4 + 8 = 28.4$.

4. (B)

$$4(2x + 4y) = 4 \times 2(x + 2y)$$ Factor out a 2 from inside the parenthesis
$$= 4k$$ Since $2(x + 2y) = k$

Therefore, the value of $4(2x + 4y)$ in terms of k is $4k$.

5. (C)

Translate verbal phrases into mathematical expressions according to the guidelines shown below.

	Verbal phrase					
	what	percent	of	20	is	15
Math expression	x	$\frac{1}{100}$	$\times$	20	$=$	15

For instance, **what** can be translated into x, and **percent** can be translated into $\frac{1}{100}$. Furthermore, **of** can be translated into $\times$(multiplication), and **is** can be translated into $=$(equal sign). Thus, what percent of 20 is 15 can be translated to $x \times \frac{1}{100} \times 20 = 15$. Once the equation is set up, solve for x.

$$x \times \frac{1}{100} \times 20 = 15$$
$$\frac{20}{100}x = 15$$
$$\frac{1}{5}x = 15$$
$$x = 75$$

Therefore, (C) is the correct answer.

6. (B)

In the figure below, the sum of the degree measures of x and y is three times the degree measure of z, or $x + y = 3z$.

Since the straight angle has the degree measure of $180°$, the sum of the degree measures of x, y, and z is $180°$.

$$x + y + z = 180$$ Since $x + y = 3z$
$$3z + z = 180$$ Solve for z
$$z = 45$$

Therefore, the degree measure of z is $45°$.

7. (A)

The table below shows the three ordered pairs on a line: $(0, 6), (1, 9),$ and $(2, 12)$.

x	0	1	2
y	6	9	12

Using two ordered pairs, $(1, 9)$ and $(2, 12)$, find the slope of the line.

$$\text{Slope} = \frac{y_2 - y_1}{x_2 - x_1} = \frac{12 - 9}{2 - 1} = 3$$

Since the line passes through $(0, 6)$ which is on the y-axis, the y-intercept of the line is 6. Thus, the slope-intercept form of the line is $y = 3x + 6$. To find the x-intercept of the line, substitute 0 for y and solve for x.

$$y = 3x + 6 \qquad \text{Substitute 0 for } y$$
$$0 = 3x + 6 \qquad \text{Solve for } x$$
$$x = -2$$

Therefore, the x-intercept of the line is -2.

8. (C)

Add or multiply the two given inequalities as shown below.

$2 \le a \le 5$ $\qquad\qquad\qquad$ $2 \le a \le 5$

$\underline{3 \le b \le 6}$ $\quad$ Add two Inequalities $\qquad$ $\underline{3 \le b \le 6}$ $\quad$ Multiply two Inequalities

$5 \le a + b \le 11$ $\qquad\qquad\qquad$ $6 \le ab \le 30$

Therefore, (C) is the correct answer.

9. (D)

In the figure below, the three vertices of $\triangle ABC$ are $A(0, 4)$, $B(5, 4)$, and $C(3, 0)$.

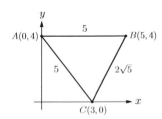

Use the distance formula, $d = \sqrt{(x_2 - x_1)^2 + (y_2 - y_1)^2}$, to find the lengths of $\overline{AB}$, $\overline{AC}$, and $\overline{BC}$.

Distance between $A(0, 4)$ and $B(5, 4)$: $\quad AB = \sqrt{(5 - 0)^2 + (4 - 4)^2} = \sqrt{25} = 5$

Distance between $A(0, 4)$ and $C(3, 0)$: $\quad AC = \sqrt{(3 - 0)^2 + (0 - 4)^2} = \sqrt{25} = 5$

Distance between $B(5, 4)$ and $C(3, 0)$: $\quad BC = \sqrt{(3 - 5)^2 + (0 - 4)^2} = \sqrt{20} = 2\sqrt{5}$

Since $AB = AC$, $\triangle ABC$ is an isosceles triangle.

10. (D)

The graphs below shows a quadratic function $y = ax^2 + bx + c$. Since the quadratic function opens up, $a > 0$.

To find the y-intercept of the quadratic function $y = ax^2 + bx + c$, substitute 0 for x. Thus, $y = c$ which means that the y-intercept is c. Since the quadratic function crosses the y-axis above the x-axis, the y-intercept is positive. In other words, $c > 0$. Since $a > 0$ and $c > 0$, $ac > 0$. Therefore, (D) is the correct answer.

11. (C)

The positive integers from 1 to 99 are under consideration. Define A as a set of integers that are divisible by 2, B as a set of integers that are divisible by 3, $A \cup B$ as a set of integers that are divisible by 2 or 3, and $A \cap B$ as a set of integers that are divisible by 2 and 3. Additionally, define $n(A)$, $n(B)$, $n(A \cup B)$, and $n(A \cap B)$ as a number of elements in set A, set B, set $A \cup B$, and set $A \cap B$, respectively.

$$A = \{2, 4, 6, \cdots, 96, 98\}, \qquad n(A) = 49$$
$$B = \{3, 6, 9, \cdots, 96, 99\}, \qquad n(B) = 33$$
$$A \cap B = \{6, 12, 18, \cdots, 96\}, \qquad n(A \cap B) = 16$$

Note that $A \cap B = \{6, 12, 18, \cdots, 96\}$ are multiples of 2 and 3, which are multiples of 6. They are counted twice so they must be excluded in counting.

$$n(A \cup B) = n(A) + n(B) - n(A \cap B)$$
$$= 49 + 33 - 16$$
$$= 66$$

Therefore, the number of positive integers less than 100 that are divisible by 2 or 3 is 66.

12. (E)

$\frac{3}{4}$ of the gas tank is filled which means that $\frac{1}{4}$ of the gas tank is empty. Set up a proportion as shown below.

$$1_{\text{minute}} : \frac{3}{4}_{\text{tank}} = x_{\text{minutes}} : \frac{1}{4}_{\text{tank}}$$
$$\frac{1}{\frac{3}{4}} = \frac{x}{\frac{1}{4}} \qquad \text{Use cross product property}$$
$$\frac{3}{4}x = \frac{1}{4}$$
$$x = \frac{1}{3}$$

Therefore, it will take $\frac{1}{3}$ minute longer to fill the gas tank.

13. (A)

The first and the second die have 6 possible outcomes each: 1, 2, 3, 4, 5, and 6, which are shown in the second row and the second column of the table below. There are total number of $6 \times 6 = 36$ possible outcomes. Each of the 36 outcomes represents the sum of the two numbers on the top of the first and the second die. For instance, when 2 is on the first die and 5 is on the second die, expressed as $(2, 5)$, the sum of the two numbers is 7.

		\multicolumn{6}{c}{1st die}
		1	2	3	4	5	6
2nd die	1						7
	2					7	
	3				7		
	4			7			
	5		7				
	6	7					

There are 6 outcomes for which the sum of the two numbers is 7: $(1, 6)$, $(2, 5)$, $(3, 4)$, $(4, 3)$, $(5, 2)$, and $(6, 1)$. Therefore, the probability that the sum of the two numbers on the top of each die is 7 is $\frac{6}{36}$ or $\frac{1}{6}$.

14. (D)

The length of cube A is increased by 75%, which means that it becomes 1.75 times longer than the original length. Since the length of cube A is 4, the length of cube B is $4 \times 1.75 = 7$. Use the surface area of a cube formula: $A = 6s^2$, where s is the length of a cube.

$$\text{Difference of surface areas} = \text{Surface area of cube } B - \text{Surface area of cube } A$$
$$= 6(7)^2 - 6(4)^2$$
$$= 198$$

Therefore, the surface area of cube B is 198 square inches greater than that of cube A.

15. (C)

The slope of the line segment connected by $(-2, 0)$ and $(0, 4)$ is $\frac{4-0}{0-(-2)} = 2$. The midpoint between $(-2, 0)$ and $(0, 4)$ is $\left(\frac{-2+0}{2}, \frac{0+4}{2}\right) = (-1, 2)$. The slope of the perpendicular bisector is the negative reciprocal of 2 or $-\frac{1}{2}$. Thus, the equation of the perpendicular bisector in slope-intercept form is $y = -\frac{1}{2}x + b$. The perpendicular bisector passes through the midpoint of the line segment which means that $(-1, 2)$ is on the perpendicular bisector. In other words, $(-1, 2)$ is the solution to the equation $y = -\frac{1}{2}x + b$.

$$y = -\frac{1}{2}x + b \qquad \text{Substitute } -1 \text{ for } x \text{ and } 2 \text{ for } y$$
$$2 = -\frac{1}{2}(-1) + b \qquad \text{Solve for } b$$
$$b = \frac{3}{2}$$

Thus, the equation of the perpendicular bisector is $y = -\frac{1}{2}x + \frac{3}{2}$, which is equivalent to $x + 2y = 3$ in standard form. Therefore, the equation of the perpendicular bisector of a segment whose endpoints are $(-2, 0)$ and $(0, 4)$ is $x + 2y = 3$.

16. (B)

Three points $A(x, y)$, $B(0, 0)$, and $C(2, -1)$ are on the coordinates plane as shown below. Point $A(x, y)$ lies in the first quadrant.

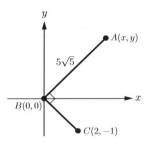

The slope of $\overline{CB}$ is $\frac{-1-0}{2-0} = -\frac{1}{2}$. Since $\overline{AB}$ and $\overline{CB}$ are perpendicular to each other, the slope of $\overline{AB}$ is the negative reciprocal of $-\frac{1}{2}$ or 2. $\overline{AB}$ passes through the origin, which means that the y-intercept of $\overline{AB}$ is 0. Thus, the equation of $\overline{AB}$ is $y = 2x$. The length $\overline{AB}$ is $5\sqrt{5}$. Use the distance formula, $d = \sqrt{(x_1 - x_2)^2 + (y_1 - y_2)^2}$, to write AB in terms of x and y.

$$AB = \sqrt{(x - 0)^2 + (y - 0)^2}$$ Substitute $5\sqrt{5}$ for AB and $2x$ for y
$$5\sqrt{5} = \sqrt{(x)^2 + (2x)^2}$$ Square both sides
$$5x^2 = 125$$ Divide each side by 5
$$x^2 = 25$$ Solve for x
$$x = 5 \quad \text{or} \quad x = -5$$

Since point $A(x, y)$ lies in the first quadrant, $x > 0$ and $y > 0$. Thus, $x = 5$ and $y = 2x = 10$. Therefore, the value of $x + y$ is 15.

Made in the USA
Lexington, KY
05 February 2014